FRIEDRICH SCHLEIERMACHER: BETWEEN ENLIGHTENMENT AND ROMANTICISM

Friedrich Schleiermacher's groundbreaking work in theology and philosophy was forged in the cultural ferment of Berlin at the convergence of the Enlightenment and Romanticism. The three sections of this book include illuminating sketches of Schleiermacher's relationship to his contemporaries (Mendelssohn, Hegel, and Kierkegaard), his work as a public theologian (dialog on Jewish emancipation, founding the University of Berlin), as well as the formation and impact of his two most famous books, *On Religion: Speeches to its Cultured Despisers* and *The Christian Faith*. Richard Crouter examines Schleiermacher's stance regarding the status of doctrine, church, and political authority, and the place of theology among the academic disciplines. Dedicated to the Protestant Church in the line of Calvin, Schleiermacher was equally a man of the university who brought the highest standards of rationality, linguistic sensitivity, and a sense of history to bear upon religion.

RICHARD CROUTER is Emeritus Professor of Religious Studies, Carleton College, Minnesota. He is best known for his work on Friedrich Schleiermacher, especially the highly acclaimed *Schleiermacher: On Religion: Speeches to its Cultured Despisers* (1996).

D1557471

FRIEDRICH SCHLEIERMACHER

Between enlightenment and romanticism

RICHARD CROUTER

CAMBRIDGE
UNIVERSITY PRESS

CAMBRIDGE UNIVERSITY PRESS
Cambridge, New York, Melbourne, Madrid, Cape Town, Singapore, São Paulo

Cambridge University Press
The Edinburgh Building, Cambridge CB2 8RU, UK

Published in the United States of America by Cambridge University Press, New York

www.cambridge.org
Information on this title: www.cambridge.org/9780521805902

First published 2005
This digitally printed version 2008

A catalogue record for this publication is available from the British Library

ISBN 978-0-521-80590-2 hardback
ISBN 978-0-521-01201-0 paperback

Contents

Acknowledgments

While working on the present book I have incurred numerous debts to other Schleiermacher scholars and specialists in his theological and cultural milieu. In recent years, the Schleiermacher essays by B. A. Gerrish in *The Old Protestantism and the New: Essays on the Reformation Heritage* (Chicago: University of Chicago Press, 1982) and *Continuing the Reformation: Essays on Modern Religious Thought* (Chicago: University of Chicago Press, 1993) have set the standard for English-language Schleiermacher interpretation. Gerrish's delightful portrait, *A Prince of the Church: Schleiermacher and the Beginnings of Modern Theology* (Philadelphia: Fortress Press, 1984) situates Schleiermacher theologically but does not address the cultural sources of the theologian's productivity. In fact, English-language historical studies of Schleiermacher in the full round are few and far between. In Germany Schleiermacher's name resonates with his illustrious contemporaries, Novalis, Goethe, Hegel, Fichte, Friedrich and A. W. Schlegel, Hörderlin, and Schelling. He also deserves to be in such company in the English-speaking world.

Although I once harbored the ambition to do a full-scale biography of Schleiermacher, I have been more drawn to the task of relating specific aspects of his legacy directly to their cultural and lived situation. Happily, the Schleiermacher biography of the late Leipzig scholar Kurt Nowak, *Schleiermacher: Leben, Werk und Wirkung* (Göttingen: Vandenhoeck and Ruprecht, 2001), is now available. For German readers Nowak's work supplants Martin Redeker, *Schleiermacher: Life and Thought* (Philadelphia: Fortress Press, 1973).

It is my hope that these essays will complement the work of others who have been my mentors and colleagues along the way. Foremost among these is my late teacher, Wilhelm Pauck, whose critical acumen in the craft of interpreting the past remains unsurpassed. I owe more debts to the work of B. A. Gerrish (University of Chicago, now Richmond, Virginia), as well as that of the late Kurt Nowak (Leipzig) than either can ever have known. Walter E. Wyman, Jr. (Whitman College) and Brent Sockness (Stanford) have been constant intellectual companions who help keep me honest, as has my Munich colleague, Friedrich Wilhelm Graf, during our editorship of the bilingual *Zeitschrift für Neuere Theologiegeschichte/Journal for the History of Modern Theology*. For more than two decades Julie Klassen (German, Carleton College) has been a conversation partner on matters related to Schleiermacher, as was the late John Clayton (Boston). The Nineteenth-Century Theology Group and the Schleiermacher Group of the American Academy of Religion provided initial venues for a number of the essays included in this book. Fulbright and DAAD grants enabled me to keep in touch with German scholarship. In AAR and other professional circles I have benefited from conversations about Schleiermacher with Günter Meckenstock (Kiel), Sarah Coakley (Harvard), Francis Fiorenza (Harvard), Garrett Green (Connecticut College), Julia Lamm (Georgetown), Ted Vial (Virginia Wesleyan), Wayne Proudfoot (Columbia), Joe Pickle (Colorado College), and David Klemm (Iowa). Among my oldest scholarly friends, Wolfgang Harnisch (Marburg), Michael Zuckert (Notre Dame), and the late Roger Poole (Nottingham) were and are faithful and ever stimulating colleagues. Each has a priceless ability to help me see how my interests relate to their respective fields of New Testament studies, Political Theory, and Literary Studies, especially the legacy of Kierkegaard.

I owe an immense debt to Carleton College, where colleagues in the Department of Religion as well as in other departments, plus vigorous classroom debates, have been a great source of intellectual vitality. My gratitude is extended to Dean of the College Shelby Boardman and to President Robert Oden, who continue to support my work as an emeritus professor. I wish to express appreciation of the willingness of publishers to allow chapters that first appeared in journal or book form to find a new home in this collection of essays. In chronological order, these are:

"Hegel and Schleiermacher at Berlin: A Many-Sided Debate," *Journal of the American Academy of Religion* 48/1 (March 1980): 19–43, reprinted, by permission, from Oxford University Press.

"Rhetoric and Substance in Schleiermacher's Revision of *The Christian Faith* (1821–1822)," *Journal of Religion* 60/3 (July 1980): 285–306, reprinted, by permission, copyright 1980 by the University of Chicago. All rights reserved.

"Schleiermacher and the Theology of Bourgeois Society: A Critique of the Critics," *Journal of Religion* 66/3 (July 1986): 302–23, reprinted, by permission, copyright 1986 by the University of Chicago. All rights reserved.

"The *Reden* and Schleiermacher's Theory of Language: The Ubiquity of a Romantic Text," in *Schleiermacher und die Wissenschaftliche Kultur des Christentums*, ed. Günter Meckenstock with Joachim Ringleben (Berlin: de Gruyter, 1991), 335–47, reprinted, by permission, from Walter de Gruyter and Co.

"Kierkegaard's not so Hidden Debt to Schleiermacher," *Zeitschrift für Neuere Theologiegeschichte/Journal for the History of Modern Theology* 1/2 (1994): 205–25, reprinted, by permission, from Walter de Gruyter and Co.

"Schleiermacher's *On Religion*: Hermeneutical Musings After Two Hundred Years," *Zeitschrift für Neuere Theologiegeschichte/Journal for the History of Modern Theology* 6/1 (1999): 1–22, reprinted, by permission, from Walter de Gruyter and Co.

"Schleiermacher's *Letters on the Occasion* and the Crisis of Berlin Jewry," in *Ethical Monotheism: Past and Present*, ed. Theodore M. Vial and Mark Hadley (Atlanta: Brown Judaic Studies [Society for Biblical Literature], 2001), 74–91, reprinted, by permission, from Brown Judaic Studies.

"Schleiermacher, Mendelssohn, and the Enlightenment: Comparing *On Religion* (1799) with *Jerusalem* (1783)," *Zeitschrift für Neuere Theologiegeschichte/Journal for the History of Modern Theology* 10/2 (2003): 165–95, reprinted, by permission, from Walter de Gruyter and Co.

Lastly, I am grateful to the editors at Cambridge University Press for encouraging this project as well as to the Press for permission to print chapter 9 here as well as in the *Cambridge Companion to Schleiermacher*, ed. Jacqueline Mariña (in press).

Abbreviations

SCHLEIERMACHER TEXTS

BO
: *Brief Outline on the Study of Theology.* Tr. Terrence N. Tice. Richmond: John Knox Press, 1966.

CF
: *The Christian Faith.* Tr. H. R. Mackintosh and J. S. Stewart. Edinburgh: T. and T. Clark, 1928.

Friedländer et al.
: David Friedländer, Friedrich Schleiermacher, and Wilhelm Abraham Teller. *A Debate on Jewish Emancipation and Christian Theology in Old Berlin.* Ed. and tr. Richard Crouter and Julie Klassen. Indianapolis: Hackett Publishing Company, 2004.

HC
: *Hermeneutics and Criticism and Other Writings.* Ed. Andrew Bowie. Cambridge: Cambridge University Press, 1998.

KGA
: *Friedrich Daniel Ernst Schleiermacher Kritischer Gesamtausgabe.* Ed. Hermann Fischer (general editor), Ulrich Barth, Konrad Cramer, Günter Meckenstock, and Kurt-Victor Selge. Berlin: Walter de Gruyter, 1980–.

LL
: *On the Glaubenslehre: Two Letters to Dr. Lücke.* Tr. James Duke and Francis Fiorenza. Oxford: Oxford University Press, 1981.

LS
: *The Life of Schleiermacher as unfolded in his Autobiography and Letters,* I–II. Ed. and tr. Frederica Rowan. London: Smith, Elder and Co., 1860.

OR (Crouter)
: *On Religion: Speeches to its Cultured Despisers.* Ed. and tr. Richard Crouter. First edition, 1799. Cambridge: Cambridge University Press, 1996.

OR (Oman)	*On Religion: Speeches to its Cultured Despisers.* Tr. John Oman. Forward Jack Forstman. Fourth edition, 1831. Louisville: Westminster Press/John Knox Press, 1994.
OT	*Occasional Thoughts on Universities in the German Sense with an Appendix Regarding a University soon to be Established.* Tr. Terrence N. Tice and Edwina Lawler. Lewiston: Edwin Mellen Press, 1991.
Schl Briefe	*Aus Schleiermachers Leben. In Briefen*, I–IV. Ed. Ludwig Jonas and Wilhelm Dilthey. Berlin: Watter de Gruyter, 1974.
ThEnz	*Friedrich Schleiemacher Theologische Enzyklopaedie (1831–32): Nachschrift David Friedrich Strauß.* Ed. Walter Sachs. Berlin: Walter de Gruyter, 1987.

OTHER WORKS

JP	*Søren Kierkegaard's Journals and Papers*, I–VII. Ed. and tr. Howard V. Hong and Edna H. Hong. Bloomington: Indiana University Press, 1975.
Jerusalem	Moses Mendelssohn, *Jerusalem, or, On Religious Power and Judaism.* Tr. Allan Arkush. Introduction and commentary Alexander Altmann. Hanover: University Press of New England, 1983.
Hoffmeister	J. Hoffmeister, ed. *Briefe von und an Hegel*, I–IV. Hamburg: Meiner, 1952–60.
Nicolin	G. Nicolin, ed. *Hegel in Berichten seiner Zeitgenossen.* Hamburg: Meiner, 1970.

Introduction

People frequently ask why I am fascinated by the work of Friedrich Schleiermacher (1768–1834), German philosopher and Protestant theologian. When the question arises, I typically respond that my interest rests on the brilliance and versatility of his achievement in shaping a distinctively modern Protestant Christian thought. But that answer scarcely does justice to the details of his illustrious career or the relevance of his work for today. A founding member of the University of Berlin faculty, Schleiermacher taught philosophy and theology (1809–34) during the initial rise of that university to European prominence. At the time, Schleiermacher was the soul of the theology department. He lectured on every topic of the curriculum (with the exception of the Hebrew Bible), and preached regularly at the Trinity Church. His career mirrors a Berlin that was, in the words of Theodore Ziolkowski, a "rising cultural metropolis,"[1] the intellectual center of the German Enlightenment in Prussia.

The cultural life and political challenges of this city, which grew from 170,000 in 1800 to nearly 500,000 in 1850,[2] form the essential setting for the work of this illustrious scholar. Schleiermacher's Berlin overlaps with the pursuit of German Enlightenment ideals, and a radical questioning of these ideals by a circle of young romantic poets and writers. No passive observer, Schleiermacher played an active role in shaping these movements. Taken as a whole, these essays reflect Schleiermacher's cultural location between Enlightenment and Romanticism, the appellations we give to the intellectual movements that name his cultural worlds. In themselves the labels do not suggest the self-critical consciousness with

---

1 Theodore Ziolkowski, *Berlin: Aufstieg einer Kulturmetropole* (Stuttgart: Klett-Cotta, 2002).
2 Helga Schultz, *Berlin 1650–1800: Sozialgeschichte einer Residence* (Berlin: Akademie-Verlag, 1987), 296–7.

which Schleiermacher stood at the confluence of these movements. But that gets slightly ahead of our story.

Ever since Wilhelm Dilthey's classic, still untranslated, *Life of Schleiermacher* (1870), scholars have believed that Schleiermacher's thought cannot be understood apart from his cultural setting. Of course, some scholarship on Schleiermacher still ignores Dilthey's admonition and treats the father of modern Protestant liberalism's teaching as if it were timeless. Schleiermacher's teachings regarding the significance of religion and the viability of the Christian faith do make claims on persons today. But as one trained in history as well as theology my sympathies are with Dilthey. By insisting that we approach his teaching in its original setting, we are better able to capture the nuances of that teaching, including sets of anxious questions that are unresolved in our own era.

The essays in this book began to appear in 1980. To those originally published in journals, newer studies have been added, which further pursue different issues or convey a more comprehensive view of his legacy. The chapters seek to illuminate Schleiermacher's achievements as theologian, preacher, philosopher of religion, Plato translator, clergyman, and political activist. He was a thoroughly dedicated academic, wholly committed both to the university with its canons of truth and to the church with its historic legacy and socially embodied community. I admit to admiring his work and the mind behind it. But I am suspicious of the "great man" approach to studying the past, where scholars approach their subjects, as it were, on their knees. Schleiermacher's grappling with the basic issues of Christian thought (and related issues in public institutions and personal life) is worthy of our respect, even when we respond with puzzlement or a raised eyebrow.

The model maintained by Schleiermacher as a man of the church as well as the university has become increasingly rare. His practical religious leadership as a pastor and preacher in the Trinity Church (pictured on the book's cover in a Johann Rosenberg engraving) took place a few blocks from Unter den Linden, the main thoroughfare in old Berlin since the days of Friedrich the Great. In his artful hands the sermon was morally uplifting as well as personally illuminating. A gift of unusual powers of concentration enabled him to produce thoughtful addresses from a few words scribbled on a scrap of paper.[3] In his *Letters from Berlin* the Jewish

---

3 See Wolfgang Trillhaas, "Der Berliner Prediger," in *Friedrich Schleiermacher 1768–1834: Theologe – Philosoph – Pädagoge*, ed. Dietz Lange (Göttingen: Vandenhoeck and Ruprecht, 1985), 9–23.

poet Heinrich Heine records the impression the sermons made upon him: "I confess to having no special divinely blessed feelings aroused in me by his preaching; but I find myself in a better sense thereby edified, empowered and whipped up by his caustic language from the soft featherbed of flabby indifference. This man only needs to throw away the black churchly garb and he stands there as a priest of truth."[4] Though he was irenic by nature, Schleiermacher stood near the storm center of sharp theological disputes regarding the status of doctrine, church authority and rituals, church–state relations, relations between Christians and Jews, and the place of theology among the academic disciplines. Officially a Reformed theologian in the line of Calvin, Schleiermacher served a United Protestant church in Berlin that included the legacies of Luther and Calvin.

His commitment to affairs of the Academy was equally prominent. Not only was he an architect of the new University of Berlin (chapter 6), but also a lifelong contributor to the Berlin Academy of Sciences, and university lecturer from 1810 until his death in 1934. The range of those lectures becomes more apparent in the essays that follow.[5] The Academy served as a research institute; he held memberships in its divisions of history and philosophy. Here Schleiermacher contributed papers on Greek philosophy, theories of the state, and aesthetics, among other fields. His nearly complete German translation of Plato was a standard work of German cultural history and continues to be widely read. All these pursuits were held together by a genial intellectual versatility. By hindsight it may be tempting to see his lifework as flowing from a single river. Closer inspection suggests that his many-faceted pursuits were laced with ironic surprises and challenges that could never have been anticipated. Certain of his favorite projects, including his ethics, dialectics, and hermeneutics, had not achieved final form at the time of his death.

BETWEEN ENLIGHTENMENT AND ROMANTICISM

I have chosen to frame these essays for publication by positioning Schleiermacher's work between the Enlightenment and Romanticism.[6]

4 Heinrich Heine, *Sämmtliche Werke*, VI, ed. Jost Hermand (Hamburg: Hoffmann and Campe, 1973), 30 (from March 16, 1822).
5 Charts showing a complete list of Schleiermacher's works and lecture courses at the university (1788–1834) are given in Dieter Burdorf and Reinhold Schmücker, eds., *Dialogische Wissenschaft: Perspektiven der Philosophie Schleiermachers* (Paderborn: Ferdinand Schöningh, 1998), 267–89.
6 In what follows I use upper case (Romantic or Romanticism) for the cultural movement and lower case (romantic or romanticism) for the particular sensibility of the movement's participants.

The tension suggested by the book's subtitle is deliberate. The Enlighten-ment and Romanticism are hardly uniform categories with crisp edges, and readers deserve a word on how I view Schleiermacher with regard to each of these movements. Details within the essays that follow touch further on the ways that Schleiermacher's intellectual choices relate to these themes.

The received view of the Enlightenment names it as an "age of reason," and there is truth in the label. Kant's "Dare to know" is the intellectual counterpart of the political coming to maturity of the French and Ameri-can revolutions. Yet even the Enlightenment is far from uniform in its teaching. Since the work of Carl Becker, we have known that its radicality is held in check by an optimism regarding moral progress and education.[7] Kant's call for moral autonomy does not question the prerogatives of the state.[8] When the movement's precursor, Herbert of Cherbury, wrote his tract on deism (1624), he sought to establish belief in God, virtue, and immortality, not to undermine these tenets. Admittedly, theological rationalism was well represented in the previous generation; figures like Schleiermacher's Halle teacher Johann August Eberhard, the popular Berlin preacher Johann Joachim Spalding, and Provost of the Berlin Church, Wilhelm Abraham Teller, come to mind.[9] But even the Enlight-enment was not of one mind on its central concerns. We are now more aware than ever that the pietists' emphasis on individual experience is not antithetical to the self-discovering impulses of the Aufklärer. It is no accident that Halle, a modern university founded by pietists (1694), hosted the rationalist Christian Wolff in the early eighteenth century.[10] Closer to the end of the century, writers like J. G. Hamann and F. H.

---

7 Carl L. Becker, *The Heavenly City of the Eighteenth-Century Philosophers* (New Haven: Yale University Press, 1932).

8 Frederick C. Beiser, *Enlightenment, Revolution, and Romanticism: The Genesis of Modern German Political Thought, 1790–1800* (Cambridge, MA: Harvard University Press, 1992), writes about Kant's "restricted conception of political change," 53.

9 On Eberhard see Kurt Nowak, *Schleiermacher: Leben, Werk und Wirkung* (Göttingen: Vandenhoeck and Ruprecht, 2001), 35–9; on Spalding, Albrecht Beutel, "Aufklärer höherer Ordnung? Die Bestimmung der Religion bei Schleiermacher (1799) und Spalding (1797)," in *200 Jahre "Reden über die Religion": Akten des 1. Internationalen Kongresses der Schleiermacher-Gesellschaft Halle, 14.-17 März 1999*, ed. Ulrich Barth and Claus-Dieter Osthövener, 277–310, plus Wolfgang Virmond's response to Beutel, 259–61, and his edition of Spalding's "Religion, an Angelegenheit des Menschen," 939–87; on Teller, Martin Bollacher, "Wilhelm Abraham Teller: Ein Aufklärer der Theologie," in *Über den Prozess der Aufklärung in Deutschland im 18. Jahrhundert*, ed. Hans Erich Bödeker and Ulrich Hermann (Göttingen: Vandenhoeck and Ruprecht, 1987), 39–52.

10 Charles E. McClelland, *State, Society, and University in Germany, 1700–1914* (Cambridge: Cambridge University Press, 1980), 34–5.

Jacobi sharply questioned the assumptions of Kant by launching lines of criticism that remain current today.[11]

Having been born in 1768 and become settled in Berlin in the 1790s, Schleiermacher came to maturity in the late German Enlightenment. He was born into a world marked by the ascendency of Kant in philosophy and a tradition of rationalist preachers and thinkers in theology. In this setting it was necessary for him to carve out his own intellectual milieu. He did so through careful study of the moral philosophy of Kant and Aristotle, while steeping himself in the works of Plato. The process was aided through his reading of Jacobi on Kant and Spinoza. The challenge of developing a self-consistent philosophic life that bears on his work is likely to have been the motivation that unites Schleiermacher's endeavors. His penchant for restless criticism and reformulation reflects the original energy of an *Aufklärer* as reformer of traditions. An interest in fostering self-formation or *Bildung*, a consistent ethical existence, and an abiding sense of confidence also mark his roots in the Enlightenment. These elements remain throughout his life, even when he criticizes deism in the name of a turn to history, reflects on reason's acute limitations, and argues that a desire to understand the world and to bend it to utilitarian ends corrupts the human spirit. We have reason to doubt whether there is a typical Enlightenment thinker or uniform way of thinking in the period. Yet it is undeniable that its impulses run deep in his formative work.

If the Enlightenment lacks tidy definition, this is even more true with respect to German Romanticism. In a 1965 article "The Genesis of Romanticism," the distinguished German literary scholar Hans Eichner notes: "Romanticism is an unpleasantly vague term, whose meaning depends only too often on the preoccupations of the person who uses the word."[12] The task was not as difficult for Eichner, who approaches the topic as a thoroughly literary movement. But his words readily apply to much of the received scholarship on Schleiermacher. Theological and philosophical scholars, the usual academic tribes that are drawn to Schleiermacher, are generally not trained in German literature, where the themes and issues raised by early Romanticism had their origin.

---

11 See Garrett Green, "Modern Culture Comes of Age: Hamann versus Kant on the Root Metaphor of Enlightenment," in *What is Enlightenment? Eighteenth-Century Answers and Twentieth-Century Questions*, ed. James Schmidt (Berkeley: University of California Press, 1996), 291–305; Frederick C. Beiser, *The Fate of Reason: German Philosophy from Kant to Fichte* (Cambridge, MA: Harvard University Press, 1987), chs. 1–2; and Dale E. Snow, "Jacobi's Critique of the Enlightenment," in *What is Enlightenment?*, ed. Schmidt, 306–16.

12 *Queen's Quarterly* 72 (1965): 213.

Admittedly, Romanticism is diffuse as a movement; Frederick Beiser divides it into the phases of early Romanticism (1797–1802), high Romanticism (1802–15), and late Romanticism (1815–30), each with differing emphases.[13] The received view of romanticism as antirational, communal, and conservative, in opposition to the rationality, individualism, and liberalism of the Enlightenment, does not apply to the work of early German Romantics, from where Schleiermacher took his bearings on the movement.[14] It is little wonder that confusion reigns when we ponder the cultural provenance of Schleiermacher's actual views.

Today the tide has begun to shift towards more sweeping interpretations of Romanticism as especially formative for the rise of historical consciousness and the biological sciences. Theodore Ziolkowski's *Clio the Romantic Muse: Historicizing the Faculties in Germany* (2004) traces this impact through the fields of history, philosophy, theology, law, and medicine, while Darwin scholar Robert J. Richards' *The Romantic Conception of Life: Science and Philosophy in the Age of Goethe* (2002) sees a confluence between the aesthetic-intuitional impulses of early Romanticism and the tradition of *Naturphilosophie* that stands behind Darwin.[15] Both works associate Schleiermacher with the broad contours of this movement, while recognizing that his romanticism was initially displayed within a narrower compass range.

That Schleiermacher is seriously invested in the circle of early German Romantics in Berlin is not in doubt. His premier youthful work, *On Religion: Speeches to its Cultured Despisers* (1799) written while he shared in the production of A. W. Schlegel's and Friedrich Schlegel's *Athenaeum*, testifies to his sensibilities in the late 1790s. Schleiermacher interpretation is secure on that point. The picture becomes murky and arguments tend

---

13 See Frederick Beiser, "Early Romanticism and the *Aufklärung*," in *What is Enlightenment?*, ed. Schmidt, 318; Hans Dierkes views philosophical romanticism as extending from Fichte's *Wissenschaftslehre* 1794–95 to the death of Schelling in 1854; he distinguishes between early (1795–1800) and late romanticism (1806–54), which frame a transitional phase from 1800 to 1804 or 1806; see "Philosophie der Romantik," in *Romantik-Handbuch*, ed. Helmut Schanze (Stuttgart: Alfred Kröner Verlag, 1994), 433–4.

14 See Beiser, "Early Romanticism," 317, and especially the work of Manfred Frank, *The Philosophical Foundations of Early German Romanticism*, tr. Elizabeth Millán-Zaibert (Albany: State University of New York Press, 2004), a version of part 3 of *"Unendliche Annäherung": Die Anfänge der philosophischen Frühromantik* (Frankfurt-on-Main: Suhrkamp, 1998); here, as in his other German publications, Frank argues for the philosophic originality of the early Romantics' critique of Idealist philosophies.

15 See Theodore Ziolkowski, *Clio the Romantic Muse: Historicizing the Faculties in Germany* (Ithaca: Cornell University Press, 2004); and Robert J. Richards, *The Romantic Conception of Life: Science and Philosophy in the Age of Goethe* (Chicago: University of Chicago Press, 2002).

to divide on a series of related questions. Facing these problems some fifteen years ago when translating the original 1799 edition of *On Religion*, I decided that scholarly opinion on Schleiermacher and romanticism falls into three camps. (1) Those who think Schleiermacher is thoroughly infused with romanticism – most literary scholars since Paul Kluckhohn belong here, though philosophical rationalists like Hegel who object to Schleiermacher's views fit in here as well.[16] Among such philosophers, most typically deny that there is an ongoing philosophic impulse and integrity to his work. (2) Those who present romanticism as a passing phase of his thought – most theologians and some literary scholars belong here (e.g., Wilhelm Dilthey, Martin Redeker, and Rudolf Haym).[17] The unstated premise of this view is that his youthful poetic mind eventually outgrew its dalliance as he accepted the tasks of a serious theologian. (3) Those who recognize Schleiermacher's affinity with romanticism, but stress his distinctive contribution to a movement that, from its inception, was always heterogeneous (e.g., Jack Forstman, Hans Dierkes, and the late Kurt Nowak in Germany).[18] At the time I placed myself in this third camp as the most coherent way of viewing his work, a position I continue to hold. But I had not yet puzzled out whether or how the elements of Schleiermacher's Romanticism mingle with his roots in the Enlightenment as perennial features of his lifework.

I have subsequently come to see that for Schleiermacher the artistry of poetic insight, the desire to clarify categories, and dialectical turns of reason prominent in the early German Romantics combine to feed his Enlightenment rationality. Indeed, these tools of his reasoning were first hammered into shape in the company of Friedrich Schlegel and Novalis. In Schleiermacher's work rationality is radicalized, not diminished, by criticism; common moral assumptions are deepened, not eradicated, by individual subjectivity; and institutions are challenged, not overthrown, by a new sense of freedom. Frederick C. Beiser correctly states that "if the [early German] romantics were critics of the *Aufklärung*, they were also its

16 See Hans Dierkes, "Die problematische Poesie: Schleiermachers Beitrag zur Frühromantik," in *Internationaler Schleiermacher-Kongress Berlin 1984*, 1 (Berlin: Walter de Gruyter, 1985), 61–98.
17 See ibid., 66, 87 on Dilthey's "total opposition"; Martin Redeker, *Schleiermacher: Life and Thought* (Philadelphia: Fortress Press, 1973), 33; Rudolph Haym, *Die romantische Schule: Ein Beitrag zur Geschichte des deutschen Geistes* (Berlin: R. Gaertner, 1870).
18 See Jack Forstman, *A Romantic Triangle: Schleiermacher and Early German Romanticism* (Missoula: Scholars Press, 1977), 65–94, and Kurt Nowak, *Schleiermacher und die Frühromantik: Eine literaturgeschichtliche Studie zum romantischen Religionsverständnis und Menschenbild* (Göttingen: Vandenhoeck and Ruprecht, 1986), 11–16.

disciples."[19] The more I work on Schleiermacher, the more I am convinced that the lines between the Enlightenment and Romanticism in his thought are blurred. Not all card-carrying early Romantics took the implications of that upheaval in the same directions. Friedrich Schlegel's turn to conservative Catholicism in 1808 was not a harbinger of what must happen with all Romantics. We will not grasp the contours of Schleiermacher's distinctive appropriation of romanticism by fitting him into generalizations that draw from the choices made by other figures within the period.

Other features of Schleiermacher's work exude interests and concerns that are irrevocably linked with the Enlightenment. His advocacy of political rights for Berlin's Jews (chapter 5) and his sympathy with the original aims of the French revolution show how deeply he was in touch with the eighteenth-century ideals of liberty, fraternity, and equality. His admiration of the American model of separation of church and state – an ideal far from duplicated in the Enlightenment Prussia of his day – aligns him with the political theory of Thomas Jefferson.[20]

In Germany the Enlightenment stood for the boldness of individual discovery, the autonomy of self-expression, and the demand to produce strictly rational explanations of the human and scientific worlds. Without ceasing to honor these ideas, Schleiermacher became embued with the spirit of early German Romanticism. It provided the mental tools for a mode of rationalty that sought to acknowledge fully the dimensions of unknowability and contingency within human experience. In his world both poetic and scientific experience were highly valued. By hindsight we can see that Schleiermacher's work embraces what we see as a perennial tension between Enlightenment and Romanticist perspectives. By studying the underlying commitments and motivations that inform his thought and his relationship to near and far contemporaries, we can rethink his significance. Like Schleiermacher as writer, scholar, and theologian, Prussia, after Friedrich the Great the most modern state of Germany, was constantly evolving.

19 Beiser, "Early Romanticism," 318: "The young romantics never put themselves in self-conscious opposition against the *Aufklärung* as a whole. If they strongly criticized it in some respects, they also firmly identified themselves with it in others."

20 Commenting in 1821 on his early enthusiasm for the American model, Schleiermacher makes clear that it is not universally applicable; see *On Religion: Speeches to its Cultured Despisers*, tr. John Oman (Louisville: Westminster Press/John Knox Press, 1958) (hereafter *OR* (Oman)), 196–8.

SCOPE AND INTEREST

During the last two decades my interest in and approaches to Schleiermacher have shifted. Part of that shift lies in the configuration I have just sketched. But the aim of analyzing his religious, theological, and social teaching within the nooks and crannies of his career has remained constant. An interest in his romanticism culminated in the first English-language translation of the 1799 edition of his *On Religion: Speeches to its Cultured Despisers* (1988), which reflects his relationship to Friedrich Schlegel and the Berlin romantic circle. Even then, however, I was becoming aware of Schleiermacher as political actor and agent of Prussian reform. While revisiting the earlier essays in this collection, I have occasionally added a nuance to an argument, either on stylistic or on substantive grounds. But I have not attempted to intervene and recast the fundamental views that are represented in those earlier essays. That would be tantamount to altering the record and disallowing readers from forming their own conclusions about a body of work. Similarly with regard to the earlier essays: in addition to citing the new critical Schleiermacher edition, where it is now available, I have updated much of the secondary literature in English and in German sources. I hope neither to have ignored nor to have overemphasized the possibility that readers will see a degree of thematic coherence and overlapping interests in this set of Schleiermacher essays.

Two features of the book deserve a further word. First, the availability of texts in the new German critical edition of Schleiermacher (Walter de Gruyter) has gone hand in hand with a predilection for viewing the world historically that dates from my student days at Occidental College. My work owes much to the publication of the German critical edition (hereafter cited as *KGA*) and the painstaking philological and historical work of its editors.[21] The historian in me is committed to the task of locating religious debates and questions within the complex details of personal, social, and institutional history. At meetings of the Ernst-Troeltsch-Gesellschaft in Berlin in February 2004, a panel discussion was held on the significance of critical editions for the future of

---

21 Notes that follow use the German citation form, e.g., *KGA* 1/7, 1: 23–42 = volume 7, part 1, of the first division (Writings and Sketches), pages 23–42. Though most volumes in division 1 have appeared, and some in 11 (Lectures), volumes in 111 (Sermons) and 1v (Translations) have yet to be published. Division v (Correspondence) now extends to 1802 (in five volumes).

Protestantism.[22] American scholars present at that gathering tended to smile at the arcane-sounding topic. Jonathan Edwards is the only bona fide theologian for whom we have such an edition. Yet whatever one may think of the formulation, critical editions are crucial tools for the future of Protestant *scholarship*. Only when the complex stakes in a debate are made clear does the motivating power of history become alive in ways that illuminate Schleiermacher's choices, as well as point to equally complex parallels today.

Second, my predilection for viewing the world of religious and philosophical reflection through an historical lens has already been mentioned. In support of this orientation I can only paraphrase Cicero to the effect that not to know any history is to forever remain a child.[23] The lesson that historical understanding humanizes the enterprise and tasks of theology was learned years ago at the feet of Wilhelm Pauck, who had gained this insight directly from Troeltsch and Harnack. A number of these essays approach Schleiermacher in a comparativist manner. This is obvious in chapters that ask how Schleiermacher relates to Mendelssohn, to Hegel, or to Kierkegaard. The tendency is also evident in chapters that treat *On Religion*, the *Brief Outline on the Study of Theology*, and *The Christian Faith* in the light of Schleiermacher's own revisions. The comparative dimension of that task is ignored at our peril, even if the received wisdom that we should take a work in its most mature formulation still has merit. Such inquiries constitute an intertextual comparison of Schleiermacher's habits of mind within his own corpus. Even where his alterations of prior editions seem minor, they increase our understanding of how Schleiermacher's thinking adapted and expressed itself over time. Readers will note that certain of these essays draw less from historical settings and concentrate directly on textual analysis, abstracted from the lives and passions that produced them. When dealing with a body of complex teaching, such a systematic approach is often required. I harbor the old-fashioned idea that authors' intentions matter. These essays were written from the belief that we grasp authors best when we are able to retrace their thought through the questions, contexts, and contingencies that originally informed their work.

22 "Geschichte durch Geschichte überwinden," *Ernst Troeltsch in Berlin. 8. Internationaler Kongress der Ernst-Troeltsch Gesellschaft, 26. bis 29. Februar 2004*, with a podium discussion "Erinnerungsarbeit durch Klassikeredition: Die Bedeutung akademischer Selbsthistorisierung für die Zukunft des Protestantismus."

23 See Cicero, *Orator*, xxxiv.120 (London: Heinemann, 1962): "To be ignorant of what occurred before you were born is to remain always a child."

SECTIONS AND THEMES

Each of the book's three sections takes up a different dimension of Schleiermacher. Part 1, "Taking the Measure of Schleiermacher," begins with the insistence of Wilhelm Dilthey that we must study Schleiermacher historically, even biographically, in order to fathom his intellectual work. While debating that proposition, chapter 1 compares Schleiermacher's view of history with Dilthey's specific injunction. The issue of how the past bears on our understanding of religion and theology, here made explicit, is implied elsewhere in the approach of this book. Other chapters in part 1 treat Schleiermacher's relationships with philosophical or theological luminaries among contemporaries and near contemporaries. The first of these figures, the Jewish philosopher and fellow Berliner Moses Mendelssohn, died in 1786, and was not acquainted with the younger Protestant clergyman. Here the noted Enlightenment classic of German Jewry is set alongside its Protestant Christian counterpart within Romanticism. Despite the received view of their orientations, Mendelssohn's *Jerusalem, or on Religious Power and Judaism* has a great deal in common with Schleiermacher's *On Religion: Speeches to its Cultured Despisers.* Both authors invent strategies to defend Jewish or Christian religious commitments, while using the tools of rationality in this defense.

Among Christian philosophers of the period, Schleiermacher's relationship with Hegel is especially problematic. Their relationship is a specific case of how Schleiermacher relates to his contemporaries within German Idealism.[24] In this setting, Schleiermacher reaches into broader modes of inquiry and assumes a more pluralistic stance towards the intellectual tasks at hand. Although he upholds the value of reason, his romantic sensibility also points to its limits. In reaction Hegel seeks to overcome Schleiermacher's subjectivity and passion by a more thorough appeal to reason. When Schleiermacher used the phrase "feeling of absolute dependence" to describe religion, his colleague responded sarcastically by saying that, if true, "a dog would be the best Christian, for it possesses this in the highest degree and lives mainly in this feeling."[25] I continue to think that the work of Schleiermacher in the 1820s was more

---

24 Schleiermacher appears only marginally in most accounts of German Idealism. He is all but absent from *The Cambridge Companion to German Idealism*, ed. Karl Ameriks (Cambridge: Cambridge University Press, 2000), and modestly present in Terry Pinkard, *German Philosophy 1760–1860: The Legacy of Idealism* (Cambridge: Cambridge University Press, 2002), 148–58, and elsewhere.

25 See below, chapter 3.

shaped by reactions to Hegel (and vice versa) than I am able to show here.[26] Their overlapping Berlin careers in the departments of philosophy and theology (1818–31) constitute a two-person version of Kant's "Battle of the Faculties." Chapter 3, which charts their philosophical, personal, and institutional differences, can be best understood as being analogous to entrenched theoretical quarrels within our own universities.

If Hegel epitomizes Enlightenment rationalism in Schleiermacher's world, his Berlin room-mate, Friedrich Schlegel, is the key theorist of early German Romanticism. From 1796 to 1802 they developed a deep friendship, even though Schlegel could never fathom why Schleiermacher – who seemed reasonable in every other way – was intent on defending the claims of historic Christianity. In contrast to the theologian, Schlegel sought to substitute the sacredness of modern poetry and literature for the Bible. Eventually a falling out with his Romantic friend ensued. Like his beloved Plato ("a divine man"), Schleiermacher sought to develop an artistic as well as a dialogical approach to truth. He brought this criticism of the moral strictures of Enlightenment thought to bear on his contributions to the Schlegels' *Athenaeum*, the journal of the early German romantics. Chapter 4 examines this relationship by analyzing Schleiermacher's *Confidential Letters on Schlegel's "Lucinde,"* his controversial defense of Schlegel's effort to explore marriage and love with a candor that shocked contemporaries. Schleiermacher's use of a Socratic indirect method in this work attracted the attention of the Danish philosopher Søren Kierkegaard, who in the 1840s similarly adopted a pose of pseudonymity in his literary work. Kierkegaard's admiration for Schleiermacher rests on an awareness of an ability to invent fictional personae and to place them in dialog as a means of shedding light on life's complexities. Evidence suggests that Schleiermacher's literary playfulness contributed to Kierkegaard's famed method of indirect communication. In addition, the Danish philosopher followed Schleiermacher's Janus-like stance of

26 The publication of rival editions of Schleiermacher's unpublished lectures on dialectics (*Friedrich Schleiermacher Dialektik*, 1–11, ed. Manfred Frank [Frankfurt-on-Main: Suhrkamp, 2001] and *KGA* 11/10, 1–2, ed. Andreas Arndt [Berlin: de Gruyter, 2002]) has unleashed a vigorous discussion of Schleiermacher as philosopher that has yet to be addressed by English-speaking scholars. See the Manfred Frank review of *KGA* 11/10 in *Die Zeit* 39 (2003): 53; Andreas Arndt, "'Die Dialectik . . . will ein wahres Organon des realen Wissens sein.' Eine neu zugängliche Nachschrift zu Schleiermachers Dialektik-Vorlesung 1818/19," *Zeitschrift für Neuere Theologiegeschichte/Journal for the History of Modern Theology* (hereafter *ZNThG/JHMTh*) I(2002): 329–53, as well as essays in *Schleiermachers Dialektik: Die Liebe zum Wissen in Philosophie und Theologie*, ed. Christine Helmer, Christiane Kranich and Birgit Rehme-Iffert (Tübingen: Mohr Siebeck, 2003).

using a romantic sensibility to criticize narrow forms of Enlightenment rationalism without leaving the dictates of reason behind.[27] Kierkegaard and Schleiermacher never met, though Schleiermacher was highly feted during a week's visit to Copenhagen in September 1833, when the 20-year-old Kierkegaard was studying at the university.[28] The book's initial section locates Schleiermacher's work alongside these significant Judaic, philosophical, and literary contemporaries within European intellectual history.

Part II, "Signposts of a Public Theologian," traces Schleiermacher's engagement with the world of social and political life through examples from his life and work. The first essay analyzes his relationship to Berlin's Jews in the little-known tract *Letters on the Occasion,* written in the summer of 1799.[29] Published anonymously, the work consists of six fictive letters from a nameless Protestant clergyman to a nameless Prussian political leader. At the time, Jewish life in German cities was under strict government regulation. On balance, the debate between Schleiermacher, David Friedländer, and Wilhelm Abraham Teller is marked by civility; its participants issued a pladoyer on behalf of their interests and traditions. Friedländer's plea to use Christian baptism as the vehicle for civil and political rights was earmarked for failure; Prussian Jews did not obtain civil and political rights as a matter of law until the dawn of German unification after 1869.[30] Schleiermacher's youthful involvement in this debate reveals much about his knowledge of Berlin Judaism and its relationship to Berlin Protestantism. Having become acquainted with the aspirations of Berlin's Jewish elites through his friend and confidante Henriette Herz, the 31-year-old clergyman argues against making conversion to Christianity a religious test for Jewish citizenship. His argument for that view rests on the Enlightenment grounds of reason's universality. By doing so, Schleiermacher aligns himself with the principles of the contemporary French and American revolutions.

---

27 Emanuel Hirsch viewed Kierkegaard as the greatest disciple of Schleiermacher of his generation, *Geschichte der Neueren Protestantischen Theologie,* third edition (Gütersloh: Gerd Mohn, 1964), v, 454. For evidence of commonality in their theological teaching, see Richard Crouter, "More than Kindred Spirits: Kierkegaard and Schleiermacher on Repentance" in *Schleiermacher and Kierkegaard: Subjectivity and Truth,* ed. Niels Jørgen Cappelørn et al. (Berlin: Walter de Gruyter, 2006).

28 For relevant documents see Jon Stewart, "Schleiermacher's Visit to Copenhagen in 1833," in *ZNThG / JHMTh* 11 (2004): 279–302.

29 Texts that bear on this debate are found in Friedländer et al.

30 On July 3, 1869 the Reichstag of the Northern German Confederation granted Jews civil and political rights without a religious test.

Chapter 6 in this section turns directly to Schleiermacher's role in the founding of the University of Berlin. Few professors have contributed so profoundly to the origins of an institution where they practiced their lifework, as did Schleiermacher. Much has been written about his role as secretary of the founding commission, headed by Wilhelm von Humboldt. It can be argued that certain of his judgments about the institutional structures and procedures of higher learning (teaching as well as scholarship) were decisive for the subsequent flowering of the nineteenth-century German university.[31] This chapter seeks to plumb not just his contributions to the university as institution, but also to adumbrate the outlines of the anti-Fichtean educational philosophy that accompanied these efforts. In today's Germany, Schleiermacher is heralded as a pioneer in pedagogical theory as well as in theology. In his own fashion he fostered the Pestalozzian revolution and the values of classical humanism against more elitist and intellectualist models of education. His reflections on education show great respect for the variety in individual experience, an attitude that permeates his scholarship and public engagements.

Chapter 7 treats a pervasive aspect of Schleiermacher's public engagement as reflected in the early twentieth-century debate about his theological liberalism that was inaugurated by the neo-Orthodox revolution of Karl Barth. Here, the charge of being a cultural Christian, who measures Christian truth by its ability to accommodate modern culture, was heavily lodged against Schleiermacher. Portrayals of Schleiermacher as a cultural accommodator run deep in English-language secondary literature on his theology, despite the fact that they rest on misleading ideas about his actions and innocence regarding the theological options of his day. A close reading of his political activities during the Napoleonic wars and their aftermath, including affairs of church and state that affected his work, provides resounding reasons to question stereotypical views of this matter.

In Germany, even more than in the United States, the perception of Schleiermacher as having diminished the meaning of Christianity through cultural accommodation is significantly dated. Among scholars in the history of theology the anti-Schleiermacher revolution of Karl Barth's theology has run its course. Schleiermacher no longer has to be defended against the Swiss theologian's ahistorical criticism. Both figures properly belong to the *history* of theology and must be regarded in the cool light of

---

31 See Thomas Albert Howard, *Protestant Theology and the Making of the Modern German University* (Oxford: Oxford University Press, in press).

history, where judgments are backed up by evidence. When this essay defending Schleiermacher against charges of cultural accommodation first appeared in 1986, that situation was less obvious in the United States or in Germany.

In addressing Schleiermacher's stance as a civic-minded fomentor of public debate we do well to recall that in the Enlightenment Prussian clergy constituted a class of civil servants who were beholden to the reigning authorities. Schleiermacher's loyalties to Prussia as a state ran deep.[32] Even here, however, Schleiermacher stands out as a somewhat special case. Neither a blind patriot nor wholly subservient to authorities, his championing of the needs of the lower classes and nonconforming university students arose from an underlying sense of patriotism. One can surmise that a proclivity toward civic responsibility came naturally to the son of a military field chaplain. In early professional life Schleiermacher was lucky in having well-placed friends, as his connections with Wilhelm von Humboldt and Alexander von Dohna attest.[33] His gregarious nature freed Schleiermacher from being limited in his associations. The success of his career owed much to an ability to combine a convivial nature with single-minded devotion to work. Schleiermacher's death in February 1834 was met with a spontaneous outpouring of grief. His colleague, the historian Leopold von Ranke, estimated that some 20,000 people, including the Prussian King Friedrich Wilhelm III, lined the city streets to pay homage to the theologian, teacher, and public educator. Friedrich the Great may have brought the Enlightenment to Berlin, but it was the scholars at the newly founded university (Barthold Georg Niebuhr in history, August Boeckh in classical philology, Johann Gottlieb Fichte [succeeded by Hegel] in philosophy, Karl Friedrich Savigny in law, Christoph Wilhelm Hufeland in medicine, Schleiermacher in theology) who fostered the bold sorts of inquiry that put the university on the map and established the ground for its prominence within German educational history.[34]

The essays of part III, "Textual Readings and Milestones," move from the world of public life to look at the specific ways that Schleiermacher's work seeks to bring religion into accord with modern culture and sensibilities. In treating themes and topics related to *On Religion* and *The*

---

32 See Rudolf von Thadden, "Schleiermacher und Preussen," in *Internationaler Schleiermacher-Kongress Berlin 1984*, 2 (Berlin: Walter de Gruyter, 1985), 1099–106.
33 On the impact of these figures see passages cited in Nowak, *Schleiermacher*, 607, 613.
34 Ziolkowski, *Berlin*, 175–7.

Christian Faith, these essays examine further his efforts to defend a truly modern form of Christianity, while avoiding the excesses of rationalism or supernaturalism. The tasks examined constitute the intellectual underpinnings of Schleiermacher's public face. Sketches of Schleiermacher's work return us to the book's thematic subtitle. If the confidence in reason and relative optimism of his age that informs his politics and institutional commitments draws from Enlightenment sources, the restlessness of intellect and the sense of how mystery inheres in modernity has its roots in his romanticism. Characteristically, his intellectual work seeks to defend levels of insight that do not yield readily to reason. At its best, religion speaks to our private human needs through symbols and metaphors, a stance that calls for intellectual defense and justification.

Chapter 8, on religious language as conceived by Schleiermacher, arose from my awareness of the pervasiveness of literary tropes and rhetorical patterns in *On Religion.* That work was not merely the central event of his youth; its postures and thematic interrogations resonate throughout his subsequent corpus, including his mature dogmatics, *The Christian Faith.* Religious insight rests on immediate consciousness, a natural human capacity for cultivating a sense of the mystery and complexity in the universe. Thus defined, religion is reconcilable with modern science and intellectual thought. Today the depiction of religion as "natural to humans" more than the voluntary choice of a "belief system" is hardly novel. Something like this view is seen in the late biologist Stephen Jay Gould's *Rocks of Ages: Science and Religion in the Fullness of Life* (1999) as well as in Elaine Pagels' *Beyond Belief* (2003), both widely read in our own day. To become aware of how a heightened sense of mystery in the universe eludes full rational explanation, and to identify this dimension of life with religion, was Schleiermacher's pioneering insight. Even without naming him, contemporaries who adopt a similar stance are his heirs. Like human nature and human history, the universe that science studies is infinitely complex, full of restless striving towards newer forms of life. While drawing from his training and education in theology, philosophy, Greek culture and civilization, Schleiermacher sought to help Germany develop a sense of modern culture that would embrace these complexities.

One might debate whether chapter 9, which treats Schleiermacher's *Brief Outline on the Study of Theology,* might fit under the rubric "public intellectuality." Teaching at a public university was, after all, the act of a civil servant. Here I present it as a textual study. The chapter explores the weight of historical learning in the theology of Schleiermacher and provides a precis of his theological encyclopedia (as it was known) as publicly presented at the university. Like his contemporaries in other disciplines, including Hegel in philosophy, Schleiermacher felt it incumbent upon himself to publish an account of what he did and of how he represented the various disciplines of theology. Here a form of public accountability occurs through the printed word more than through the activities and societal interventions that mark chapters in the previous section. It seems appropriate to think of this material as being a public guide to the internal matrix of his theological imagination as it had matured during his years of service to university and church.

With his threefold discussion of theology as philosophical, historical, and practical, Schleiermacher consolidated a view of theological education that continues to influence the curricula of divinity schools. By today's standards the range of disciplines and subfields of mastery requisite for the preparation of pastoral ministers is staggering in its breadth and expectations. Chapter 9 draws from Schleiermacher's published lecture outline, as well as from a detailed transcript of these lectures from 1831–2 produced by his student and subsequent critic David Friedrich Strauß. I am struck by the vividness and passion that inform those classroom lectures, and see them as the theologian's way of giving the world a reckoning of his work.

Chapter 10, on *The Christian Faith*, joins chapter 9, on the *Brief Outline*, in speaking to Schleiermacher's concerns as a professional theologian. The chapter originated in 1977 as a guest lecture as a Fulbright professor at Marburg University in Hesse. Prior investigation of *On Religion* (published 1799, revised 1806, 1821, reprinted in 1831), showed Schleiermacher to be a relentless reviser of his works. His penchant for self-criticism and revision struck me as worthy of reflection. Does this habit of mind undermine, or does it enhance, the credibility of his teaching? At the time, the critical edition of *The Christian Faith* (1821–2, and 1830–1) had not yet appeared in the *KGA*. The chapter now includes annotations and additional cross-references that draw from relevant volumes of the new critical edition.

Chapter 11 stands alone in this book in tracing the impact of Schleiermacher, in this case his seminal book on religion, down to our own time. Originally published during the bicentenary of Schleiermacher's *On Religion*, the chapter treats that work's patterns of reception through a typology. I argue that when we are dealing with classical religious texts (and presumably also with other modes of thought), instability of interpretation goes hand in hand with indispensability. Schleiermacher could never have anticipated the permutations of his teachings that arose over the last two centuries. This essay returns to the theme of chapter 1, on

Dilthey, by asking whether the *history* of a text's reception can ever be an adequate guide to the meaning of a work. Against aspects of my inclination to affirm a historical understanding of the past, I end the essay, and thus the book, by arguing that a direct encounter with a text, the act of grasping its meaning, must also suspend time.

In presenting these essays, old and new, I hope to convey a rounded impression of Schleiermacher as scholar, teacher, preacher, and public intellectual. His dual posture as theorist and as practical reformer of institutions is all too rare in human history. Even where we may think certain of his views or approaches are passé, his stance as an engaged intellectual in the field of religion remains needed in today's world. The question of whether and how religion – in this case Protestant Christianity – can be reconciled with modernity remains highly pertinent. Schleiermacher's sense of the place of religion in modernity reflects an acute sense of contingency in human affairs. That degree of intellectual discomfort and instability regarding the human condition constitutes the spark that aligned him initially with his peers among the early German Romantics. But his lifelong effort to defend this insight (and its permutations) intellectually has its roots in Enlightenment rationality.

PART I

Taking the measure of Schleiermacher

CHAPTER I

Revisiting Dilthey on Schleiermacher and biography

In his monumental yet never completed (or translated) biography, *Life of Schleiermacher* (1870), Wilhelm Dilthey maintained that, unlike Kant, Schleiermacher's significance can only be grasped through his biography. In the foreword to the first edition of that famous book we read: "The philosophy of Kant can be wholly understood without a closer engagement with his person and his life; Schleiermacher's significance, his worldview and his works require a biographical portrayal for their thorough understanding."[1] With these words, which stand without further comment, Dilthey champions a distinctive approach to Schleiermacher. In contrast with Kant, knowledge of Schleiermacher's life is apparently needed for us to grasp what Dilthey sees as his significance, his worldview, and his works. It seems that study of works alone will not yield full significance or worldview in the case of Schleiermacher, though for reasons unstated by Dilthey, this does not hold for Kant.

Dilthey's claim about how Schleiermacher must be studied is eye-catching as well as methodologically puzzling. It raises a host of further questions. Dilthey appears to sponsor a historicist agenda[2] that tilts Schleiermacher studies strongly, if not overwhelming, towards the discipline of history. A turn away from theology and philosophy seems to be suggested, despite Schleiermacher's long pedigree in these fields as his major areas of achievement. To fulfill Dilthey's mandate would require a scholar to attain mastery of the social and cultural history of Prussia in

---

1 *LS*, 1, xxxiii. Unless otherwise noted, all translations from German sources are my own. When I mentioned this quotation to a colleague in history, he was astonished not by what is said of Schleiermacher, but by what is said of Kant.
2 Here I follow H. P. Rickman's depiction of historicism as arising from the effort of historians to claim "that everything human beings have done, thought, believed, and produced is accessible to historical treatment, and that the field of historical study is, therefore, the whole of human reality in time." Wilhelm Dilthey, *Pattern and Meaning in History: Thoughts on History and Society*, ed. and tr. H. P. Rickman (New York: Harper and Brothers, 1961), 52–3.

addition to Schleiermacher's texts. Perhaps that might be manageable, if we recognize that our knowledge is always incomplete. More controversial is Dilthey's claim that a biographical portrayal is needed for attaining a "thorough understanding" of Schleiermacher's works. The merits and implications of that proposition are not immediately obvious. It requires minimal hermeneutical sophistication to be aware that lives are elusive, often full of half-conscious truths and dark secrets. To propose to get at the significance of a thinker or his works through an analysis of his life raises issues that have substantive epistemological as well as practical consequences.

Before analyzing Dilthey's proposal further, a word on my own disciplinary predilections as an American scholar may be useful. Trained in history and theology, I have been preoccupied with historical studies of theology since graduate school in the 1960s. Because my work often walks a tightrope that stretches between history and theology, I favor giving Dilthey a careful hearing. Yet whether we initially favor Dilthey, or find his view suspect, we must recognize that the task of depicting the lives of famous people is complicated by assumptions within our own culture. Popular religious culture as well as lofty cultural criticism like nothing more than to probe the vagaries of private lives relentlessly. Kierkegaard, it seems, lost his battle to preserve the realm of privacy, at least in the United States. In the 1840s the Danish student of modernity predicted that a love of individual gossip and a process of indiscriminate leveling inevitably follow the demise of social and political authority.[3]

Today, interest in the life of Jesus and in sharing one's "spiritual journey" threatens to supplant the themes of classical theology.[4] If we follow this cultural trend we shall not stop by being interested in

---

3 In the case of the Danish thinker, the self-imposed strategy of pseudonymous writing makes it all but impossible to relate his uneventful but inwardly tormented life to his formal works. See, e.g., Henning Fenger, *Kierkegaard: The Myths and their Origins. Studies in the Kierkegaardian Papers and Letters,* tr. George C. Schoolfield (New Haven: Yale University Press, 1980), and the work of Roger Poole, *Kierkegaard: The Indirect Communication* (Charlottesville: University of Virginia press, 1993).

4 Such tendencies may mark the triumph of the "biography as theology" movement over the last quarter of a century; see James William McClendon, Jr., *Biography as Theology: How Life Stories can Remake Today's Theology* (Nashville: Abingdon Press, 1974). In Germany academic interest in biography (*Lebensgeschichte*) as a resource for practical theology is also evident; see Christian Albrecht, "Paradigmatische Rekonstruktion des ganzen Menschen: Autobiographische Integrität als Theoriebildungsmotiv bei Schleiermacher und Freud," in *Der "Ganze Mensch": Perspektiven Lebensgeschichtlicher Individualität* (Festschrift für Dietrich Rössler zum siebzigsten Geburtstag), ed. Volker Drehsen et al. (Berlin: Walter de Gruyter, 1997), 131–73.

Schleiermacher's theory of subjectivity.[5] We shall want to know more than it is useful to know or to recover the details of his relationships with Henriette Herz and Eleonore Grunow and the psychological reasons he took issue with Friedrich Schlegel, Fichte, or Hegel, among his intellectual rivals. Within the discourse of cultural studies and popular religious culture the line between public and private is obliterated in ways that Dilthey could not have imagined. Hence, even if one thinks Dilthey's proposal has merit, it raises many warning flags.

In what follows I first address these issues by examining Dilthey's proposal alongside examples drawn from recent writing about Friedrich Schleiermacher. I then take the debate back to Schleiermacher, to ask where he stands on the tension-filled relationship between life and thought. Dilthey's stress on life as relevant for thought resonates not just with Schleiermacher's theory but also with his practice. In the end, I argue that, properly understood, Schleiermacher would not find Dilthey's view unreasonable. The issue is misconstrued if we view a biographical approach as being inimicable to the normative claims of theology. At some level of generalization, historians, like theologians, claim truthfulness for their accounts, even if the metaphysical dimension of their claims remains hidden. A thorough understanding of Schleiermacher's significance, worldview, and work is difficult to envisage apart from our making judgments of his life. But the yield of this process is hardly automatic. To act wisely on Dilthey's claim requires us to avoid the twin perils of idolizing the theologian's life or of trivializing his considerable body of thought.

PRECURSORS AND HEIRS OF DILTHEY

A student of Schleiermacher would do well to realize that Wilhelm Dilthey does not stand alone in stressing the significance of Schleiermacher's life. Recognition of the centrality of his life occurs regularly in nineteenth- and twentieth-century scholarship. Linguist and historian Frederica Maclean Rowan expressed it poignantly in her 1858 English translation of the first two-volume German edition of Schleiermacher's

---

5 In Europe and North America the theme of Schleiermacher's theory of subjectivity continues to attract scholarly attention. A joint conference of the German Schleiermacher Society and the Danish Kierkegaard Society addressed the theme "Subjectivity and Truth" at a scholarly meeting in Copenhagen, October 9–13, 2003.

letters.[6] Rowan's Victorian prose voices the widespread longing for knowledge of Schleiermacher's biography.[7]

The translator undertook to introduce to the English reader the *man* Schleiermacher, not the theologian; and the man and his private life, at least, are portrayed in these letters with a minuteness of detail that leaves nothing to be desired, while as a necessary consequence of the sincerity and the harmonious constitution of his mind and character, much light is also shed by them on his religious and philosophical views.[8]

A similar, if less effusive, stance is also seen in American and German scholarship that appeared in 1911, the year of Dilthey's death. Writing from the Newton Theological Institution, George Cross introduced Americans to Schleiermacher's still untranslated *Glaubenslehre* (*The Christian Faith*) with the words, "The sketch of his life offered in the Introduction is drawn mainly from his published correspondence and directs attention to the experiential basis of his doctrine – indispensable to a clear grasp of it."[9] Cross takes it for granted that connections exist between the theologian's life and his experiential interpretation of Christian theology.

Emphasis upon Schleiermacher's life persists as a theme within twentieth-century German scholarship. The subtitle of Hans Westerburg's 1911 book *Schleiermacher as a Man of Science, as Christian and as Patriot* gets

---

6 *LS*, 1, ix–xx. On the history of this edition, see Hans-Joachim Birkner, "Introduction," in *Schl Briefe*, ix–xi. Letters in the first two volumes, published under anonymous editorship in 1858, had been selected by Schleiermacher's daughter, Hildegard Gräfin Schwerin, and his stepson, Ehrenfried von Willich. Dilthey came to the idea of doing a Schleiermacher biography by working on an expanded set of these letters, which he took over as a project from Ludwig Jonas.
7 *LS*, 1, xi–xii, "Five-and-twenty years elapsed, and though Schleiermacher's name and influence were kept alive by his theological and philosophical works and his numerous printed sermons, the admirers and disciples of the great theologian looked in vain for a biography of him, which should exhibit the inner harmony that had existed between the preacher, the scholar, and the man. Such a biography, it was thought, would be doubly interesting and important to those who had not known Schleiermacher personally, as by all who had enjoyed that privilege it was universally maintained, that great as he was as a writer, and wonderful as were the versatility and profundity which he evinced in treating the most diversified branches of human life and human knowledge, it was, nevertheless, through the living influence of his entire personality that he had effected most in the world. Under such circumstances the book, a translation of which is here presented to the English public, though neither a biography nor an autobiography in the strict sense of the word, but a record of thoughts and feelings fresh and warm as they flowed from his mind and heart, in confidential communion with friends and relatives, could not fail to meet with a hearty welcome in Germany, where it has, indeed, so to say, made Schleiermacher once more a living presence among his countrymen."
8 *LS*, 1, xiii.
9 *The Theology of Schleiermacher: A Condensed Presentation of his Chief Work, "The Christian Faith"* (Chicago: University of Chicago Press, 1911), viii.

directly to the point: *An Introduction into the Understanding of his Person-ality.*"[10] The director of the German literary archives in Berlin, Heinrich Meisner, published three volumes of letters in the early Weimar Republic. The first consists of letters to and from Schleiermacher's fiancée, Henri-ette von Willich, while two others consist of letters between family and friends, 1783–1834.[11] Meisner's editions seek to memorialize as well as to honor Schleiermacher. An adulatory reading of the first of these books is encouraged by the inclusion of a ribbon-type bookmark with an attached card ("Merkzettel beachtenswerter Textstellen") on which readers can record the pages of its most memorable passages. Closer to our own day, Martin Redeker's *Schleiermacher: Life and Thought*[12] also begins with biographical background for Schleiermacher's systematic treatises. As editor of Dilthey's unfinished *Life of Schleiermacher*, Redeker published that work along with Dilthey's unfinished papers on Schleiermacher's system as philosophy, theology, and hermeneutics (II/1–2).[13] Redeker's own biography speaks of an "intuitive-creative" and a "systematic period" of Schleiermacher's thought, and makes little effort to integrate life and thought.[14]

Today, fresh interest in Schleiermacher in Germany is as apt to occur in circles that study cultural theory, education, German Romanticism, or historical analyses of eighteenth-century *Bildung*, as it is within theology. In their 1998 edition of interdisciplinary essays, *Dialogische Wissenschaft: Perspektive der Philosophie Schleiermachers*, Dieter Burdorf and Reinhold Schmücker maintain that

---

10 Hans Westerburg, *Schleiermacher als Mann der Wissenschaft, als Christ und Patriot: Eine Einführung in das Verständnis seiner Persönlichkeit* (Göttingen: Vandenhoeck and Ruprecht, 1911).
11 Heinrich Meisner, ed., *Friedrich Schleiermachers Briefwechsel mit seiner Braut*, second edition. (Gotha: Friedrich Andreas Perthes, 1920); *Schleiermacher als Mensch: Sein Werden. Familien- und Freundesbriefe 1783–1804* (Gotha: Friedrich Andreas Perthes, 1922). Meisner's editions remain an invaluable resource pending completion of the correspondence in the *KGA*.
12 Martin Redeker, *Friedrich Schleiermacher: Leben und Werk* (Berlin: Walter de Gruyter, 1968); English tr., John Wallhausser, *Friedrich Schleiermacher: Life and Thought* (Philadelphia: Fortress Press, 1973).
13 See above note 1.
14 Redeker, *Schleiermacher: Life and Thought*, 64. Cf., in this regard, Horace L. Friess, ed., *The Soliloquies* (1926) (Chicago: Open Court Publishing Company, 1957), who writes, "In my Introduction I have tried to characterize the romantic spirituality of the *Soliloquies*, to show its origins in the growth of our culture and its relations to modern religious currents. This theme seems to me to be the most significant one in the first half of Schleiermacher's life, that is from 1768–1800. The second half of his life, from 1800 to 1834, is another story, and one that I have not attempted to tell on the same scale (vi).

like few other philosophers since Socrates Schleiermacher stands in greatest repute among his contemporaries not so much as the author of significant works, but above all on the basis of his personal impact – within society, his circle of friends, at the pulpit or lecture podium.[15]

The scholar's life seems central to his cultural impact. The first research symposium sponsored by the German Schleiermacher Gesellschaft, founded in 1996, took place in March 2001 on the topic of "Schleiermacher's Theory of Culture." Designed for graduate students in all disciplines, the conference featured plenary papers on cultural sociology, culture as a process of education, and the hermeneutics of culture.[16]

QUESTIONING BIOGRAPHY

How, then, apart from Dilthey, does biography as a genre relate to history in the eyes of historians of theology? A century ago Adolf von Harnack expressed skepticism, despite his interest in the personal impact of Jesus on world history, in *What is Christianity?*[17] The Berlin historian of doctrine held biography at arm's length. For him, the old Latin adage "Individuum est ineffabile" signaled a boundary of scholarly investigation that history cannot bridge. Addressing a student conference in 1920, Harnack maintained that one must

sharply distinguish between "history" and "biography." The goal of historical research is to completely exclude the subjective element and to erect a large edifice based on strictest objectivity. By contrast the biographer must be able to re-experience his hero in order to then have him rise anew . . . a biography can never be anything but a double-picture; it is always also a *self-biography* of the biographer.[18]

For Harnack, biography needs to be subordinated to broad historical perspectives that place individual lives within larger cultural forces. Insight regarding individual humans or institutions is only part of the larger

15 Dieter Burdorf and Reinhold Schmücker, eds., *Dialogische Wissenschaft: Perspektive der Philosophie Schleiermachers* (Paderborn: Ferdinand Schöningh, 1998).

16 See http://anu.theologie.uni-halle.de/ST/SF/SG/ST/SF/tagungen/symposion_2001.

17 Adolf von Harnack, *What is Christianity?*, tr. Thomas Bailey Saunders, introduction by Rudolf Bultmann (Philadelphia: Fortress Press, 1986); reissued in German as Adolf von Harnack, *Das Wesen des Christentum*, ed. Trutz Rendtorff (Berlin: Walter de Gruyter, 2001).

18 Adolf von Harnack, "Was hat die Historie an fester Erkenntnis zur Deutung des Weltgeschehens zu bieten?," *Ausgewählte Reden und Aufsätze*, ed. Agnes von Zahn-Harnack and Axel von Harnack (Berlin: Walter de Gruyter, 1951), 183.

canvas of world history. Such material must be woven into the fabric of the past in order to render history intelligible and useful for the present.[19]

As best I can determine, Dilthey lacks Harnack's caution with regard to the craft of biographical investigation. For Dilthey, the practice of history as an art is both empirical and imaginative. In his final essays on historical theory (*Gesammelte Schriften*, VII), Dilthey shows respect for autobiography, which enables us to reflect on our lives by placing events and deeds within larger patterns of meaning. Autobiography sheds light on the motivations and impulses behind our intellectual pursuits. In Dilthey's words, "Autobiography is the literary expression of the individual's reflection on his life. When this reflection is transferred to the understanding of another's existence it emerges in the form of biography."[20] As if referring to his own biography of Schleiermacher, Dilthey writes:

But the historical individual whose existence leaves a permanent mark is worthy, in a higher sense, to live on in a biography which is a work of art. Among these, those whose actions have arisen from the depths of human life which are not easy to understand will draw the particular attention of the biographer. They allow us a deeper insight into human life and its individual forms.[21]

Yet even for Dilthey, biography is not the final category of historical investigation. Without losing its point of contact with an individual's life, biography must be placed in the objective context of "a dynamic and meaningful system" of history. "No biography," he writes, "can perform this task with more than partial success."[22] On Dilthey's view, the insight of history contributes to self-knowledge; for him, knowledge of self is not, as he believed Nietzsche maintained, to be gained solely through introspection.[23] The difference between Harnack and Dilthey on the matter of biography stems from Dilthey's self-reflective hermeneutic, which recognizes how our psychophysical nature affects the past selves that we study as well as the self of a researcher. Dilthey's humanistic social science

---

19 Ibid., 187.
20 Dilthey, *Pattern and Meaning*, 89, drawing from *Gesammelte Schriften*, VII (Leipzig: B. G. Teubner, 1921).
21 Ibid., 90.
22 Ibid., 91.
23 Ibid., 92; see Rudolf A Makkreel, *Dilthey: Philosopher of the Human Studies* (Princeton: Princeton University Press, 1992), 54: "According to Dilthey, inner experience (*innere Erfahrung*) possesses an initial intelligibility. To suppress this would be to destroy the source from which we derive the meaning of socio-historical, as well as individual, experience. Admittedly, inner experience is limited in scope by personal dispositions and presuppositions. Such individual perspectives need not be denied, but through reflection their horizons of meaning can be shifted so as to be made more and more encompassing."

contrasts markedly with the rationalist tradition of social science. The late Ernest Gellner, a champion of the latter approach, views the contemporary turn to subjectivity as a "re-enchantment industry" and warns against our trying to fathom the unfathomable. Gellner ridicules the effort of academics to endorse this world of reenchantment: "Privacy is no longer abandoned to the Joyces and Prousts of this world, but can be formally taught and most scientifically authenticated."[24] If the self-depiction of autobiography invariably mixes *Dichtung* and *Wahrheit*, then biography, to the extent that it relies on first-person accounts, must face these same problems.

That biography can be useful for the study of theologians is not, however, wholly in doubt. Theological scholars of erudition and distinction practice the craft. In an 1891 essay entitled "What we should and should not learn from the Roman Church," Adolf von Harnack writes more favorably about the power of individuals within history. Here the liberal Protestant calls attention to the difference individuals can make within the dogmatic and hierarchical tendencies of Roman Catholicism. In his words, "One St. Francis has become more powerful than many princes of the church."[25] Reform rests more on individual persons, the great monks of Catholic history, than on constitutional changes. Wilhelm Pauck, a critical-minded student of Harnack and Troeltsch, appreciated the impact of great personalities within Christian history and depicted them in a wholly unsentimental manner. In the hands of Pauck, Luther's person and work are indelibly interwoven. The self-understanding of the theologian plays a vital part in revealing the underlying contours of thought.[26] Pauck's critical yet empathetic and personal memoir, *Harnack and Troeltsch: Two Historical Theologians*, pays tribute to both figures as models for the craft of studying theology historically.[27] Pauck's students are aware of how often he characterized certain theologians as

---

24 Ernest Gellner, *Spectacles and Predicaments: Essays in Social Theory* (Cambridge: Cambridge University Press, 1979), 55.

25 Harnack, *Ausgewählte Reden*, 68.

26 On the prophetic consciousness of Luther, see Wilhelm Pauck, "Luther's Faith," *Heritage of the Reformation* (Glencoe: Free Press, 1961), 19–28. In depicting "The Character of Protestantism in the Light of the Idea of Revelation" (*Heritage*, 184), Pauck writes: "In this case [the Protestant Reformation] the tension between character and concrete life situations which determines all human life is of a particular complexity."

27 Wilhelm Pauck, *Harnack and Troeltsch: Two Historical Theologians* (Oxford: Oxford University Press, 1968).

"autobiographical thinkers," most prominently, Paul Tillich.[28] Pauck was not claiming that Tillich substituted his life story for the difficult tasks of intellectual inquiry. He only meant that Tillich – in this sense an heir of Schleiermacher – was thoroughly enmeshed in the cultural world around him.

In view of the examples of Harnack and Pauck, it might even be the case that collectors of letters like Frederica Rowan and Henrich Meisner were on the right track in wanting to honor Schleiermacher's personal character. Schleiermacher's commitment to the social good and to deep friendships with contemporaries deserve to be recognized. If his was an exemplary character, and if this character is reflected in his scholarly work, why should we not wish to recognize this fact? Schleiermacher's Berlin colleague Leopold von Ranke, a pious Lutheran but hardly an advocate of sentimentality in history, upon hearing of the theologian's death interrupted his lecture on the social disruption of Europe during the Thirty Years' War to remark that Schleiermacher's "whole being, his striving, deeds and life were aimed at reconciliation . . . his life was like his thought: the picture of the most beautiful equanimity. His name is grounded in eternity; no one is apt to be born who is equal to him."[29] Of course, such a remark, conceived in grief, is invariably personal. But such expressions and testimonies can in principle be confirmed by the testimonies of others. It does not seem misguided or willful to suppose that the contingencies of life and personal character of those we study bear on their formal productions.

If Dilthey were only calling for a biography of Schleiermacher, his proposal would be uncontroversial. Unclarity arises when we try to puzzle out just how a "biographical portrayal" might relate in detail to Schleiermacher's theology. How does biography as knowledge of a life contribute to our understanding of a writer's carefully nuanced

---

28 Wilhelm Pauck, "To Be Or Not To Be: Tillich on the Meaning of Life," in *The Thought of Paul Tillich*, ed. James Luther Adams, Wilhelm Pauck, and Roger Lincoln Shinn (San Francisco: Harper and Row, 1985), 32, writes of Tillich: "He remembered clearly the lessons he had learned from his teachers and the circumstances in which he had learned them. He was acutely mindful of the insights his friends gave to him. He recalled exactly what impression the reading of books or visits to museums had made upon his mind, and he never forgot productive conversations and discussions. He was an autobiographical thinker. His books are full of references to persons whom he called his teachers." B. A. Gerrish, *A Prince of the Church: Schleiermacher and the Beginnings of Modern Theology* (Philadelphia: Fortress Press, 1984), 23, similarly refers to Luther and Schleiermacher as "autobiographical thinkers."

29 Cited in Karl Kupisch, "Die Wiederentdeckung der Religion," *Zeichen der Zeit: Evangelische Monatsschrift* 13 (1959): 50

arguments? Analyzing texts requires us to make logical distinctions and to criticize ideas in ways that move beyond narrative form. We still may not be sure why Dilthey was plagued by irresolution on the question of how to relate biography to theology. His narrative of the life of Schleiermacher breaks off in the early 1800s before the thinker had assumed his post at the University of Berlin.[30] Rudolf Makkreel attributes Dilthey's failure to complete his Schleiermacher book to the clash between his historicism and systematic inquiry: "Whereas a theoretical justification for his biographical volume of the *Leben Schleiermachers* could be found in historicism, Dilthey realized that it would be inadequate for the proposed systematic volume."[31] Makkreel may well be correct to hold that "this personal *Weltanschauung* [of the Romantic circle] . . . does not seem to provide any critical standard for a systematic evaluation of Schleiermacher's work."[32] It is as if the Schleiermacher volume were prematurely published before Dilthey had sufficiently wrestled with historicism. Yet Makkreel's view gives us a limited and specific case of where historical (read also "biographical") thought fails at the task of analyzing systematic texts. Dilthey's inability to complete his sections on Schleiermacher's thought appears to be more a tactical error of scholarly judgment than evidence for a wholesale claim of incompatibility between the relevant tasks.

SCHLEIERMACHER ON LIFE AND HISTORY

Given this moot state of affairs, we might well inquire into Schleiermacher's own view of how life is related to thought. When we do so, we see quite handily that Schleiermacher championed an approach that connects individual lives and judgments of individual persons with intellectual understanding. A hint of his position is seen in a March 1799 letter to Henriette Herz, written as he was composing *On Religion*. When Herz reported her enthusiasm for a portion of that text she had read, Schleiermacher asks, "Are you sure that you pumped out your affection for me sufficiently before you put in your judgment?"[33] He appreciates her enthusiasm but raises the possibility that her prior acquaintance with him

30 *LS*, 1/1–2.
31 Makkreel, *Dilthey*, 52–3. Since his other major work, the *Einleitung in die Geisteswissenschaften*, was also left unfinished, Dilthey is reported to have been known in Berlin circles as a "Mann der ersten Bände" – a man of first volumes; Makkreel, *Dilthey*, 51, citing Max Dessoir in Frithjof Rodi, *Morphologie und Hermeneutik: Zur Methode von Diltheys Ästhetik.* (Stuttgart: Kohlhammer, 1969), 11.
32 Makkreel, *Dilthey*, 53.
33 *LS*, 1/1, 194.

may distort her judgment. "This is the very question," Schleiermacher writes to Herz, "which we are unable to resolve, because our experiments are so much wanting in the *akribeia* [Greek for "exactness"or "precision"]."[34] Schleiermacher's remark is obscure, and he says nothing more about it in this letter. But the random comment shows him wrestling with a version of Dilthey's question.

Schleiermacher's early studies of Greek philosophy relate to our topic. Michael Welker convincingly shows that Schleiermacher's belief that "we live deeper than we think" arose in his 1788 commentary on Aristotle's *Nichomachean Ethics*, 8–9, the earliest Schleiermacher text to come down to us, and states: "We owe the genius of his ethical proposal to the fact that his thought is profoundly anchored in the depth of life."[35] That philosophy is not just a way of thinking but also a way of life was encountered in Schleiermacher's studies of Plato's dialogs. Julia Lamm writes that for Schleiermacher, "The essential unity of Plato's thought was, rather, to be found not in a particular doctrine, but in Plato himself – in his artistic genius."[36] On Lamm's reading, Schleiermacher appears to view Plato in much the same way as Dilthey views Schleiermacher.

But if there is a general connection between life and thought, as these examples claim, in what ways are biographical (or autobiographical) details crucial for the understanding of texts? While in his twenties Schleiermacher recorded an account of his earliest years, reaching back to the death of his father in 1794.[37] But this material, produced as a resumé, fails to shed light on the issue at hand. More pertinent are the self-reflections of the *Soliloquies* from 1800. This work is widely viewed as Schleiermacher's most dreamy romantic work, a self-obsessive philosophical meditation that responds to Fichte's idealism with a vision of embodied love.[38] Yet the *Soliloquies*, like *On Religion*, was printed three times during his lifetime and never renounced. Read closely, its text provides an understanding of how its author's life – autobiography, inner experience, and aspiration – sustains his projects in the larger world. Commenting on the intimate relationship between "self-development" and "outward expression," he writes:

---

34 Ibid.
35 See Michael Welker, "'We Live Deeper Than We Think': The Genius of Schleiermacher's Earliest Ethics," *Theology Today* 56 (July 1999): 179.
36 Julia A. Lamm, "Schleiermacher as Plato Scholar," *Journal of Religion* 80/2 (April 2000), 223.
37 *LS*, 1/1, 1–18; *Aus Schleiermacher's Leben. In Briefen*, 1, 1–15.
38 It is likely that the *Soliloquies* are the least studied text among today's Schleiermacher scholars.

Whatever the active community of humanity can produce shall pass before me, shall stir and affect me in order to be affected by me in turn, and in the manner I receive and treat it, I intend always to find my freedom and to develop my distinctiveness through its outward expression.[39]

The passage confirms Schleiermacher's view that life is played out as a set of polarities between spontaneity and receptivity, where freely unfolding subjectivity interacts with multiple historical givens.[40] In a new preface to the *Soliloquies,* reissued with *On Religion* when Schleiermacher was publishing his dogmatics in 1821, he observes:

The life of every individual, as it appears to others, suggests at one time his essential, ideal self [*seinem Urbild*], and at another his distorted self [*seinem Zerrbild*]. Now only when following out the first suggestion, that toward the ideal self can self-examination yield results fit for publication and communicable to others; introspection in the other direction, toward the distorted self, is soon lost too deep in those recesses of the private life which, as some sage has already said, a man had best conceal even from himself.[41]

I take Schleiermacher's point to be that, for all its inwardness, the written words of the *Soliloquies* only represent his ideal self and do not record his murky and distorted inner being. The unfathomable dimensions of our inner life cannot be lifted up to the bar of historical scrutiny. But the "ideal self" aspect of life comes to expression self-reflectively as personal history. This inner history of human lives may differ from the external history of the Protestant church as it competes with Roman Catholicism, or the Prussian state as it struggles to rebuild itself after Napoleon, but it remains a crucial form of history as the bedrock of human existence.[42]

Schleiermacher's point about the significance of human lives is reinforced in a passage of the *Brief Outline* that treats exegetical theology. In setting forth a hermeneutic of reading texts in connection with the drama of human lives, section 140 states:

No writing can be fully understood except in connection with the total range of ideas out of which it has come into being and through a knowledge of the various relations important to the writers' lives of those for whom they write.[43]

39 Friess, ed. and tr., *Soliloquies,* 72–3, tr. slightly altered.
40 In his 1926 introduction to the *Soliloquies,* Horace Friess comments, xxxii–xxxiii: "Schleiermacher's fundamental problem is to find a world view which does justice to human personality, on the one hand, and to the infinite universe that stands over against man, on the other. He wants the advantages of both Kantian and Spinozistic metaphysics, of freedom and determinism."
41 Friess, 5, tr. slightly altered; *KGA,* 1/12, 326.
42 See below, chapter 9, on the cognate problem of Schleiermacher's well-known construal of dogmatics as historical theology.
43 *BO,* 58 (§140).

The passage clearly puts emphasis on the individual lives of biblical authors. Summing up his remarks on historical theology, Schleiermacher speaks about individual lives with more nuance. In section 251 he writes:

In the Christian Church, a preeminent influence of individuals upon the mass is minimal on the whole. Yet it is still more appropriate for historical theology than for other areas of historical study to attach its picture of times which are epoch-making – even if only in a subordinate sense – and which can as such be apprehended as a unity, to the lives of prominently influential individuals.[44]

For Schleiermacher, the influence of individuals is said to be minimal in comparison with Christ as absolute. But individuals play a greater role in historical theology than in general history, because theology has to do with the lives of individuals. In the explanation of section 251, we read: "It must also be added that particular deviations in doctrine which are noteworthy as indications and anticipations of various kinds are often *best understood by reference to the lives of their authors*" (emphasis added).[45] Here Schleiermacher holds that historical thinking in the form of biography is useful in reaching a judgment about the meaning of a doctrine. In fact the more elaborate 1830 formulation of section 251 draws from a single phrase from 1811 (§5): "The elements of every historical-theological presentation are far more biographical than in certain other fields of history."[46]

Corroboration of these points is found in the 23-year-old D. F. Strauß' student transcript of the lectures on the 1831–2 version of the *Encyclopedia*. There Strauß records Schleiermacher saying that "§251 has as its subject the relation of biographical to historical theology."[47] There follows a passage that explicates the role of "personality" in Christian history, beginning with the founder, Christ. Despite the fluctuating impact of individuals in various epochs, the great number of biographies that have appeared in the last twenty-five years "speak for sound progress in the treatment of church history."[48] The same page of Strauß' transcription shows Schleiermacher acknowledging that in strict science thought is everything, and that the thinker breaks free from personality so that the association of ideas presents itself in a purely objective manner. The text immediately continues: "But in the field of religion thought is only a means of bringing forth the inner stirring of life, and this is always essential in the individual, so the individual must necessarily grasp thought in the context of his inner movement of life in order to be at work

44 *BO*, 87 (§251).   45 *BO*, 87.   46 *KGA*, 1/6, 1998, 413.
47 *Th Enz*, 244.   48 *Th Enz*, 245.

religiously."[49] The thrust of the argument is that, though pure science exists, it is not what historical theology is about, with its paramount interest in religion, church leadership, and individual persons.

A similar position is famously articulated in section 10 of *The Christian Faith* (1830–1) : "Each particular form of communal piety has both an outward unity, as a fixed fact of history with a definite commencement, and an inward unity, as a peculiar modification of that general character which is common to all developed faiths of the same kind and level; and it is from both of these taken together that the peculiar essence of any particular form is to be discerned."[50] Behind these words is Schleiermacher's conviction that the particularities of history are foundational for religion. Christian life and consciousness arise as individuals freely develop in the historic Christian community. The teaching occurs in *On Religion*, in the christological convictions of his dogmatics, and in the lectures on the historical Jesus which Schleiermacher began to give in 1819. Despite the challenges involved, his *Life of Jesus* reflects positively on a need to grasp the lives of individuals.

What is the actual task of a biography which is to correspond wholly to the idea of a description of a life? We have to reply: The task is to grasp what is inward in the man with such certainty that it can be said: I can say with a measure of assurance how what is outward with respect to the man would have been if what affected him and also what he affected had been different than was actually the case, for only then do I have an actual knowledge of what is inward in him, because I can also construe it as the constant factor to different results. But we shall be able to achieve only a certain approximation of this; there is a maximum, and even he who possesses the greatest talent for comprehending an inner distinctiveness will only believe he has worked out a solution of the task within certain limits.[51]

Throughout his career Schleiermacher's intellectual as well as social-political choices mirror a sense of the historical nature of human existence. His formal teachings arise from personal situations, which in turn inform these teachings. Dilthey's point is that Schleiermacher's significance cannot be realized if we analyze his works in abstraction from his life. Dilthey stated the position with conviction, even if he was unable to bring it fully to bear on his full-scale interpretation of the theologian.

49 *Th Enz*, 245–6.   50 *CF*, 44.
51 Jack C. Verheyden, ed., *The Life of Jesus* (Philadelphia: Fortress Press, 1975), 8; on the reconstruction of the "inner unity" as a task for biography, see Hermann Fischer, *Friedrich Daniel Ernst Schleiermacher* (Munich: C. H. Beck, 2001), 130.

CONCLUSIONS

A biographical dimension, including the lives of subjects and the lives of their investigators, appears to be present within the general task of historical thinking. To be aware of human lives and biographies is to be aware of an author's choices, motivations, and intentions and of how these interact over time. Knowledge of persons is indispensable for the process of coming to judgment about the intent of textual arguments. On this point Michel Foucault writes vigorously:

> The work of an author is not only in the books that he publishes; in the end, his chief work is he himself, who writes his books. The life of persons and their work are connected, not because the work "translates" the life, but because it is comprised of life just as much as text. The work is more than the work: the subject, who writes, is part of the work.[52]

Foucault seems correct in arguing that the totality of what a thinker stands for must in principle be fair game for consideration, since it is implicitly present in a writer's productions. The entire field of authorial experience interacts with the influences of the cultural and political settings where we formulate our interpretations.

The line between life and thought is thus more thin and porous than we may suspect. This is the case even if we do not have a tidy genre that reflects this reality. Reviewing Stephen Greenblatt's biography of Shakespeare (2004) in *The New Yorker*, Adam Gopnik notes:

> Whatever our official pieties, deep down we all believe in lives. The sternest formalists are the loudest gossips, and if you ask a cultural-studies maven who believes in nothing but collective forces and class determinisms how she came to believe this doctrine, she will begin to tell you, eagerly, the story of her life.[53]

A more formal position on this matter was framed in the work of Heidegger, which saw phenomenology and history as an integral part of philosophy. Kurt Flasch reminds us that Heidegger was not interested in professional philology or detailed discussions of historical methodology.[54] Instead, he called attention to the factual experience of life from which we all take our bearings. That orientation includes the stance of an academic

---

52 Cited Ibid., 15, from Michel Foucault *Dits et Écrits* (1954–1988) (Paris: Gallimard, 1994), IV, 606f.
53 Stephen Greenblatt, *Will in the World* (New York: W.W. Norton, 2004), reviewed by Adam Gopnik, "Will Power," in *The New Yorker* (September 13, 2004): 90.
54 Kurt Flasch, "Was heißt es: einen philosophischen Text historisch lesen?," in *Bochumer philosophisches Jahrbuch für Antike und Mittelalter*, ed. Burkhard Mojsisch, Olaf Pluta, and Rudolf Rehn, 1 (1996): 21.

discipline, the accessibility or inaccessibility of certain data, and the interpretative schemes that are on hand at a given time. As an historian of medieval philosophy, Flasch maintains that "We read philosophical texts historically, because we have given up the illusion that we can simply keep away from or forget prior schemes of ordering or images of the past."[55] Such historical thinking about individuals is exactly what Dilthey recommends as necessary if we are to grasp Schleiermacher's significance, worldview, and work. Among the patterns and types of historical investigation, biography is neither special nor unique. It simply focuses upon individuals and attends as carefully as possible to their thoughts, aims, and influences as these relate to their productions.

It may still be natural for us to question how biographical insight can be decisive for our understanding of systematic questions. Biography is about other people's lives, and, similarly to Heideggerian philosophy, it is our own lives that cry out for answers, in Schleiermacher's case theological answers. To see no relationship at all between biographical insight and the systematic analysis of texts misconstrues the subtle processes by which we come to judgments. I understand Dilthey to have in mind that biography, that is, attention to life, provides a way of coming to grips with thought. He holds that such an approach is necessary, even if not sufficient. Biographical insight into lives is indispensable as a hermeneutical tool through which we test our readings and confirm our judgments about texts.

What follows from Dilthey's admonition for the future of Schleiermacher scholarship? As best I can see, Dilthey's recommendation of a biographical approach to Schleiermacher encourages greater attention to intertextual readings of his works. This is happening today with the help of the new critical edition (*KGA*). Attention to life is necessary in order to grasp changes over time and assist with problems of periodization. It is to our peril if we are so blinded by Schleiermacher's debt to the early Romantics that we do not see that he never forsook the ideals of the French revolution. In the words of *On Religion*, reprinted in 1831, that revolution was "the most sublime event of history,"[56] even if the terror and excesses of the aftermath, plus the assault of Napoleon on Prussian territories, were another matter. Schleiermacher's dedication to the ideal of

55 Ibid. See also Kurt Flasch, *Philosophie hat Geschichte*, vol. 1, *Historische Philosophie: Beschreibung einer Denkart* (Frankfurt-on-Main: Vittorio Klostermann, 2003).
56 *Über die Religion: Reden an die Gebildeten unter ihren Verächtern*, seventh edition (Berlin: G. Reimer, 1878), 8.

free public expression had a dimension that is unwavering. It constitutes a worldview that stands near the center of his hermeneutics, educational theory, political philosophy, as well as his theology, ethics, and dialectics. In Schleiermacher the Kantian admonition "Dare to Know" combines with "Dare to Act." The public sphere is wedded to, and sustained by, a sense of the private. When we probe this public dimension we do well to bear in mind that he was born to a proud military chaplain in the service of Friedrich the Great, for whom the son was named. The public spiritedness of Enlightenment aspirations is a constant ingredient in the romantic soul of Schleiermacher.

In defending Dilthey's approach it is not necessary to contend that all historical knowledge of the life of Schleiermacher is equally relevant for our grasp of his significance. Much in Schleiermacher's letters may contribute little to our understanding of his theology; some passages only reveal that the writers and thinkers we honor were engaged in the humdrum problems of daily living.[57] Even his theological texts are not all equally relevant for deepening our grasp of his theology. One must constantly weigh the various editions of such texts, while ferreting out and arguing for the most representative of his views. Without the work of historians and philology-astute editors, theologians are unable to estimate the relative importance of texts, expecially those left unfinished in their author's lifetime. Interpreters must weigh arguments in original, historically conditioned languages that are never devoid of cultural contexts. Of course, at some levels the normativity of theology puts it at odds with the craft of historical inquiry. Truth claims about God exceed the capacity of the historian. That may go without saying. But I am equally struck by how frequently formal theological thought argues in a way that draws from historical judgments.

By the time we get the yield of historical thinking the processes of coming to judgment have already been resolved. Meanwhile, the historian's desire to write truthfully parallels the theologian's effort to set forth proper claims about God's nature and existence. Both give arguments in support of their contentions that never exhaust all the issues. Granted, a greater sense of ultimacy seems to be involved in the craft of dogmatic

---

57 His personal letters sometimes show Schleiermacher complaining repeatedly about stomach aches (and seeking a magnetic treatment for them from his physician), worrying about the health of his wife and children, grousing about cold, damp weather, regretting that his favorite quill pen is broken, or just sitting at 10 p.m. drinking tea and reading a song from the *Odyssey* to his half-sister Nanny.

theology. That also constitutes a problem in the reception of Schleiermacher's theology.[58] But historical and theological thought, though distinctive intellectual pursuits, were not mutually exclusive in the work of Schleiermacher. Nor should they be in our own work today. Whatever Dilthey may ultimately have had in mind by his own radical historicism and quest for a "life philosophy," his passion for historical insight into the life of the mind was learned from the study of Schleiermacher.

58 See below, chapter 9.

CHAPTER 2

Schleiermacher, Mendelssohn, and the Enlightenment: comparing On Religion (1799) with Jerusalem (1783)

At first glance, Friedrich Schleiermacher as Protestant theologian among the early German Romantics seems to have little in common with Moses Mendelssohn (1729–86), Enlightenment philosopher of modern Judaism.[1] On the surface, a comparison of their famous controversial books *On Religion* (1799) and *Jerusalem* (1783) seems an unlikely, even improbable, project.[2] Schleiermacher's extravagant first book launched an approach to religion that unleashed a controversy that reaches to this day. Mendelssohn's book is that of an older man, entwined in numerous controversies, who seeks to vindicate his entire career. The prominence of these classic apologetic works, *Jerusalem: or on Religious Power and Judaism* and *On Religion: Speeches to its Cultured Despisers*, has assured their lively reception. Each is a paradigm of modern religious thought. Their authors belong to two different generations; Schleiermacher was attending Moravian boarding school when Mendelssohn published *Jerusalem*. Yet the culture of 1790s Berlin, and certainly the salon of Henriette Herz frequented by Schleiermacher, was vividly in touch with the signs of Mendelssohn's legacy.[3]

Although each work constitutes its author's considered efforts to reconcile his religious tradition with an understanding of modernity,

---

1 It may seem a leap for a Schleiermacher scholar to trespass into Jewish studies to tangle with the legacy of Moses Mendelssohn. Yet the prominence of Mendelssohn within Schleiermacher's Berlin warrants the effort. For years I have been struck by a "family resemblance" between Mendelssohn and Schleiermacher in their determination to struggle with modernity and marvel at the range of opinion among their interpreters, especially how each figure is viewed as a *bête noire* by defenders of Jewish or Christian religious orthodoxy.

2 It is taken for granted that both books have near canonical status in modern western religious thought. An account of either writer's contribution must inevitably consider the positions espoused in these works.

3 Schleiermacher's relation to Mendelssohn's follower within Berlin's Jewish community, David Friedländer, is taken up in chapter 5. Numerous ties link the two figures in Berlin. Henriette Herz was a good friend of Mendelssohn's daughter, Brendel, while her husband, the physician

comparison is burdened by incongruities of time, audience, and the specific location of their authors within the Berlin of a dominant Christian majority or a Jewish minority. Each figure has strong advocates. But their reception is also marked by sharply critical voices. Mendelssohn's position in *Jerusalem* is seen as an "ephemeral solution" (Michael A. Meyer, 1967) and "his Judaism is questionable" (Allan Arkush, 1999), while Schleiermacher's *On Religion* is viewed an example of "cultural accommodation" (H. R. Niebuhr, 1951) and defends an "incoherent thesis" (Wayne Proudfoot, 1985).[4] Neither figure is easily explained solely within conventional views of the German Enlightenment or early German Romanticism. Reflecting on them together provides an occasion for seeing how their arguments relate to one another as well as to Enlightenment and romanticist interpretations of religion. We are helped by the fact that differentiated, more nuanced views of the labels "Enlightenment" and "Romanticism" have emerged in recent years. James Schmidt's introduction to the anthology *What is Enlightenment?* eloquently makes this case for the Enlightenment.[5] A similar reinterpretation of Romanticism is also under way, even if the term *Romanticism* has a predominantly pejorative connotation within the fields (theology, philosophy, Jewish studies, and religious studies) that bear most directly on this chapter. Above all, this chapter is written on the premise that the Enlightenment and Romanticism are handy categories for cultural periodization but misleading if we suppose they signify a sharp divide that utterly separates two distinct eras.[6]

Marcus Herz (b. 1747), knew Mendelssohn directly; Mendelssohn's oldest daughter, Dorothea, left her husband, Simon Veit, for Schleiermacher's friend, Friedrich Schlegel; Mendelssohn's grandson, Felix Mendelssohn (Bartholdy), achieved fame as a musical prodigy during Schleiermacher's later years in Berlin. Lastly, the popular philosopher of faith, F. H. Jacobi, who vigorously engaged Mendelssohn in debates about pantheism and Spinoza, was much admired by Schleiermacher, who once planned to dedicate his dogmatics (1821–22) to him.

4 Michael A. Meyer, *The Origins of the Modern Jew: Jewish Identity and European Culture in Germany, 1769–1824* (Detroit: Wayne State University Press, 1967); Allan Arkush, "The Questionable Judaism of Moses Mendelssohn," *New German Critique* 77 (spring–summer): 29–44; H. Richard Niebuhr, *Christ and Culture* (New York: Harper and Row, 1951), 94; Wayne Proudfoot, *Religious Experience* (Berkeley: University of California Press, 1985), 18.

5 See James Schmidt, "What is Enlightenment? A Question, its Context, and Some Consequences," in James Schmidt, ed., *What is Enlightenment?: Eighteenth-Century Answers and Twentieth-Century Questions* (Berkeley: University of California Press, 1996), 1–44.

6 See Albrecht Beutel, "Aufklärer höhere Ordnung? Die Bestimmung der Religion bei Schleiermacher (1799) and Spalding (1797)," in *200 Jahre "Reden über die Religion,"* ed. Ulrich Barth and Claus-Dieter Osthövener (Berlin: Walter de Gruyter, 2000), 277–310, on the striking parallels between Schleiermacher's *On Religion* (1799) and the work of the older Enlightenment

A successful comparison of these two texts requires an analytic framework. At the outset, I must make it clear that I am most struck, if not occasionally astounded, by certain overriding similarities between Schleiermacher and Mendelssohn. These are, to be sure, found more in their aims and argumentative strategies than in the details of their content or their ultimate goals. As we shall see, the similarities extend to the patterns of the works' reception histories. By examining these texts as personally engaged, political works that wrestle deeply with the issue of particularity of confession versus universality of religion, we seek a path that will examine some surprisingly common elements in a way that does not deny each work's distinctiveness. The age-old dissonance and clash of Judaic and Protestant Christian religious cultures cannot obscure the fact that the authors of *Jerusalem* and *On Religion* belonged to the same social-political world and shared the challenge of writing about religion within that world. Of course, a mass of scholarship surrounds both figures, and especially these two texts. But the advantage of a succinct comparison is that it may enable light to be shed on each text as it is contrasted with its unlikely Other.

TEXTS OF PERSONAL ENGAGEMENT

Of course, *On Religion* seems to most readers to display more overt passion and subjectivity than *Jerusalem*. One can scarcely imagine the sedate Moses Mendelssohn writing, "I am so permeated by religion that I must finally speak and bear witness to it."[7] Yet the difference of tone ought not to obscure the fact that Mendelssohn's lifework was at stake in the arguments of his book. Each work constitutes an *apologia* (in the classic Greek sense of "defense") that champions what its author holds most dear in religion. Each boldly challenges its original readers' assumptions, while seeking to correct misunderstandings of religion in a way that promotes the interest of Judaism or Protestant Christianity. If Schleiermacher's book is addressed to poets and young romantics as "cultured despisers of religion," Mendelssohn's is addressed to state officials and Enlightenment theologians as "cultured despisers of Judaism."

---

theologian Johann Joachim Spalding, which he owned, entitled, *Religion, a Concern of Man* (1797). For the latter text, see "Johann Joachim Spalding, Religion, eine Angelegenheit des Menschen, Erste Auflage, Leipzig 1797," ed. Wolfgang Virmond, in *200 Jahre "Reden über die Religion,"* 941–987.

7 *OR* (Crouter), 9.

By looking more closely into these matters we can attain further insight into elements that are unique to each writer and his aims.

The story of Moses Mendelssohn's illustrious career in Berlin is well documented.[8] Long before writing *Jerusalem* he was heralded as a popular teacher within the Haskalah (movement of Jewish Enlightenment) and as undisputed leader of the Berlin Jewish community.[9] Although Mendelssohn might have written something like *Jerusalem* even without provocation, the book was occasioned by immediate circumstances. In his 1782 preface to a German edition of *Vindiciae Judaeorum*, a seventeenth-century work by the Amsterdam rabbi, Menasseh ben Israel,[10] Mendelssohn called for an end to the ban of excommunication within the synagogue and argued that when freedom of conscience (noncoerciveness) is practiced within the Jewish community, it will foster toleration and the granting of civil rights to Jews by the wider gentile world. Mendelssohn's impassioned plea in the preface was intended to complement the work of his friend, Christian von Dohm, *On the Civil Improvement of the Jews*.[11] In an anonymous tract published by August Friedrich Cranz, *The Searching for Light and Right*,[12] Cranz endorsed Mendelssohn's universal morality but called for Mendelssohn to clarify the degree of his allegiance to his Jewishness. Mendelssohn's commitment to Judaism certainly seemed implied by the spirited words of the preface. A direct espousal of his faith had been expressed only circumspectly in the 1760s when the Zurich preacher Johann Caspar Lavater actively called for his conversion.[13] In Cranz' words: "Perhaps you have now come closer to the faith of Christians."[14] As reasonable as Cranz found Mendelssohn's

8 Alexander Altmann, *Moses Mendelssohn: A Biographical Study* (Alabama: University of Alabama Press, 1973); Michael A. Meyer, *Origins of the Modern Jew*; Allan Arkush, *Moses Mendelssohn and the Enlightenment* (Albany: State University of New York Press, 1994); David Sorkin, *Moses Mendelssohn and the Religious Enlightenment* (Berkeley: University of California Press, 1996); Allan Arkush, reviewer [Sorkin], "Moses Mendelssohn and the Religious Enlightenment," *Modern Judaism* 17 (1997): 179–85.

9 David Sorkin, *The Berlin Haskalah and German Religious Thought: Orphans of Knowledge* (London: Vallentine Mitchell, 2000).

10 Meyer, *Origins of the Modern Jew*, 46; see Moses Mendelssohn, *Gesammelte Schriften: Schriften zum Judentum*, vol. VIII, ed. Alexander Altmann (Stuttgart–Bad Cannstatt: Friedrich Fromann Verlag, 1983), XIII–XXIII, 1–25.

11 Christian Wilhelm von Dohm, *Über die bürgerliche Verbesserung der Juden* (1781) (Hildesheim and New York: Olms, 1973).

12 The full title is *The Searching for Light and Right in a Letter to Mr. Moses Mendelssohn Occasioned by his Remarkable Preface to Menasseh ben Israel* (Berlin, 1782), printed in *Gesammelte Schriften*, VIII, 73–87

13 *Gesammelte Schriften*, VIII, 77.   14 Ibid., 81.

arguments to be, the same arguments seemed to undercut the authoritarian and theocratic faith of his fathers.[15] In a further, two-page appendix to Cranz' work, army chaplain Daniel Ernst Mörscher asked even more pointedly whether the author of the preface was not actually a deist who was indifferent to all revelation, Jewish as well as Christian.[16]

Jerusalem was written in direct response to these concerns about religious freedom and revelation. Mendelssohn had come a long way from what Michael A. Meyer has called his "judicious policy to avoid discussing religion with gentiles."[17] The high personal stakes behind the writing of *Jerusalem* may not be obvious on the surface of the work. Overall Mendelssohn's passion seems subdued; direct first-person appeals or intrusions ("my oppressed nation") are only sporadic. Such an instance occurs near the end of part 1, where he points out the latitude and apparent hypocrisy of the English when the state required its clergy to submit to the Thirty-Nine Articles: "Count them [those in high office in England who no longer assent to the Thirty-Nine Articles], and then still say that civil liberty cannot be granted to my oppressed nation because so many of its members think little of an oath!"[18] Part 1 on religious freedom is a relatively formal tract and shorter than the more specific (and impassioned) defense of Judaic teaching of part 2.

Mendelssohn clearly felt the urgency of reconciling his Judaism with Prussian political reality, which, in this instance, accorded Jews only circumscribed rights and a stratified social existence.[19] For all the emphasis on toleration at the enlightened court of the philosopher-king Friedrich the Great (1740–86), these values stood in stark contrast "with his mistrustful policy of strict supervision and control of the Jews, attested by his Revised General Code, the Jewry Reglement of 1750."[20] As we are now aware, the struggle of the late eighteenth century was fought not so much about Jewish rights as it was over the issue of Jewish national

---

15 Ibid., 79; Arkush, "Questionable Judaism," 35–7.
16 *Gesammelte Schriften*, VIII, 92.
17 Meyer, *Origins of the Modern Jew*, 29.
18 *Jerusalem*, 68; see *Gesammelte Schriften* VIII, LXXXVIII–LXXXIX, on the subsequent controversy over the 39 Articles of the Church of England, in which Johan David Michaelis contended (mistakenly) against Mendelssohn that the English clergy were not required to swear allegiance to the Articles.
19 A succinct account of six levels of Jewish social stratification in eighteenth-century Berlin is given in Jacob Allerhand, *Das Judentum in der Aufklärung* (Stuttgart–Bad Cannstatt: Fromann-Holzboog, 1980), 53–4.
20 Michael Graetz, *German-Jewish History in Modern Times*, vol. 1, Tradition and Enlightenment 1600–1780, ed. Michael A. Meyer (New York: Columbia University Press, 1996), 265.

character compared with German.[21] Despite his apparent affection for Mendelssohn, age-old prejudicial beliefs about Jews are seen even in a philosopher like Kant.[22] Awareness of the vicious qualities of these stereotypes were present among the Berlin neologists and enlightened leaders of the Berlin Protestant church, Johann Joachim Spalding (1714–1804) and Wilhelm Abraham Teller (1734–1804), each of whom served in high church office in the Berlin Protestant community.[23]

Mendelssohn's notoriety in Berlin was earned through his work in consolidating the early Haskalah reform of Jewish learning in a world of entrenched Christian institutions. As David Sorkin's *The Berlin Haskalah and German Religious Thought* shows, German Enlightenment Jewry offered more options than just the stark alternative of remaining orthodox, living in cultural isolation and speaking Yiddish, or of wholesale assimilation into German institutions. Degrees of assimilation and diverse strategies of indigenous Jewish intellectual renewal coexist in the first half of the eighteenth century. By the 1780s the move to politicize the Haskalah led to calls for civil rights and emancipation, the themes that lie behind *Jerusalem*.[24] Sorkin views the mythopoetic Germanizing legend of Mendelssohn, which treats him solely on the basis of his German works, as badly in need of correction by an account of him as continuing the internal work of Jewish reform of the early Haskalah.[25]

21 See Paul Lawrence Rose, *Revolutionary Antisemitism in Germany from Kant to Wagner* (Princeton: Princceton Univeersity Press, 1990) especially chapter 5, "The Jewish Question: Conceptions and Misconceptions," 61–9.

22 Consider Kant's notorious passage on the Jews from *Anthropology from a Practical Point of View*, ed. and tr. Mary J. Gregor (The Hague: Martinus Nijhoff, 1974), 77, "The Palestinians living among us have, for the most part, earned a not unfounded reputation for being cheaters, because of their spirit of usury since their exile. Certainly, it seems strange to conceive of a nation of cheaters; but it is just as odd to think of a nation of merchants, the great majority of whom, bound by an ancient superstition that is recognized by the State they live in, seek no civil dignity and try to make up for this loss by the advantage of duping the people among whom they find refuge, and even one another. The situation could not be otherwise, given a whole nation of merchants, as non-productive members of society (for example, the Jews in Poland)."

23 Albrecht Beutel, "Aufklärer höherer Ordnung?," and Martin Bollacher, "Wilhelm Abraham Teller: Ein Aufklärer der Theologie," in *Über den Prozess der Aufklärung in Deutschland im 18. Jahrhundert*, ed. Hans Erich Bödeker and Ulrich Herrmann (Göttingen: Vandenhoeck and Ruprecht, 1987), 39–52.

24 Sorkin, *Berlin Haskalah*, 111–24. "Mendelssohn had grave reservations about the shape of the emancipation debate: he endorsed emancipation on the basis of natural right but refused to accept any exchange of religious practice or regeneration for rights" (126).

25 David Sorkin, "The Mendelssohn Myth and its Method," *New German Critique* 77 (spring–summer 1999): 7–28, argues that Mendelssohn's Hebrew works have been largely neglected in mainstream Mendelssohn interpretation, and seeks to make good on that omission in his own scholarship. Yet such a view should also not be allowed to beg the question of whether *Jerusalem* is fundamentally a Judaic or a German book by viewing it largely (or predominantly) as a work of accommodation to gentile readers.

Although it arose at the outset of his career in a less encumbered setting, Schleiermacher's *On Religion* was also written in response to the curiosity of contemporaries. A young Protestant preacher and hospital chaplain, Schleiermacher was surrounded by Enlightenment theologians and neologists whose Christianity exuded elements of a rationalist moralism, a view that tended to translate religion into categories of morality. Of course, Schleiermacher exaggerated the intellectual shortcomings of such persons; his account is doubtless headstrong, the rhetoric of a young man in a hurry to make his mark. The stimulus to write *On Religion* arose not only from an effort to protest against the official theology of clerical circles, but also to satisfy his immediate circle of romanticist friends, including Henriette Herz and Friedrich Schlegel, who longed to have a greater sense of Schleiermacher's religious views.[26] These friends wanted to discover how *one of their own* – a sensitive, romantic soul, who wrote for A. W. Wilhelm and Friedrich Schlegel's *Athenaeum* – could defend his radical sense of religion while clinging to an institutional form of Protestantism.

If Mendelssohn's Christian admirers sought to attract him to their ranks, Schleiermacher's poetic friends, the "cultured despisers of religion" of his subtitle, had the same ambition. Like Mendelssohn, Schleiermacher was aware that his public audience, beyond these close friends, consisted of established Protestant authorities. He feared that charges of atheism and pantheism would be forthcoming from his ecclesiastical superior, F. S. G. Sack, and was not proved wrong. Sack also protested against the young male theologian's socializing in the Jewish salon of Henriette Herz and counting such persons among his friends.[27] Like *Jerusalem* in this respect, *On Religion* seeks to meet as well as to undercut the expectations of its audience. In this case, those free poetic spirits who think they are not religious (the cultured despisers) live and breathe a level of poetic insight into reality that lies close to the core of religion, while the established leaders of Enlightenment Protestantism in Prussia hold moralistic and legalistic views that are ultimately damaging to religion.[28] Behind Schleiermacher's entire argument an appeal is made that draws from the Reformation rallying cry of "grace alone." If some of the tough issues

26 Schlegel aimed at developing a new canon of poetry that would supplant the Bible in its canonical authority.
27 Albert L. Blackwell, "The Antagonistic Correspondence of 1801 between Chaplain Sack and his Protégé Schleiermacher," *Harvard Theological Review* 74 (1981): 131.
28 Sorkin, *Berlin Haskalah* questions this conventional stereotype. Yet considerable evidence of the equation of morality with religion was nonetheless present in the era.

related to Mendelssohn's Jewishness, that is, just how he differs from or relates to the official rabbinate, were suppressed in his book owing to his audience and literary strategy, the same is true of Schleiermacher's concealed status as clergyman. On this matter he states in the first address, "My speech would not have betrayed me, and the eulogies of my fellow guild members would not either."[29] Yet Schleiermacher's text freely alludes to the experiences of hymnody, preaching, liturgy, and pastoral care that stem from his work with clergymen.[30] Similarly, Mendelssohn's work embodies a rhetoric that vigorously conveys his arguments, while not shying away from interpreting rabbinic teachings.[31] He avoids partisan or anti-Christian pleading in presenting his views on religion, and even endorses the saying of Jesus of Nazareth "Render unto Caesar that which is Caesar's and unto God what is God's."[32] Sensitivity to audience and social circumstances in Berlin marks the careers of both Mendelssohn and Schleiermacher, and nowhere is this clearer than in the high stakes arguments of these two books.

POLITICS AS THE "SINE QUA NON" OF RELIGIOUS COMMUNITY

Since few readers of *On Religion* think of this highly rhetorical work as a political document, its crucial social-political argument is easily missed. This is partly due to the habit of lifting up the second and fifth speeches for comparison as a "set topic" in university and divinity school courses on modern religion and theology. This practice short-circuits the challenge of grasping the work in its entirety as its author intended it to unfold in the mind of a reader. Like *Jerusalem*, *On Religion* cries out to be read as a whole, in light of its aims and underlying assumptions. When that approach is taken, a rich analysis of political life of its third and fourth speeches presents a theory of modernity as inimicable to the book's claims about religion.

The third of these speeches ("On Self-Formation for Religion") sets the stage for political analysis. For Christian, as for Jew, coercion of any kind is alien to religion, which "knows no other means to that final goal than

29 *OR* (Crouter), 4. The mixed motivations that lie behind *On Religion* are taken up below, in chapter 11.
30 For example, *OR* (Crouter), 55–6: "How often have I struck up the music of my religion in order to move those present, beginning with soft individual tones and longingly progressing with youthful impetuosity to the fullest harmony of religious feelings?"
31 *Jerusalem*, 39, 60, 123, 130.
32 Matthew 22:21; *Jerusalem*, 132, and the commentary on rabbinic parallels by Altmann, 234–5.

that it expresses and imparts itself freely."[33] Ever since the Constantinian turn, Christian interpreters have noted the ambiguous, if not dire, consequences of politics for religion in Europe.[34] For Schleiermacher, the heavy hand of the state's utilitarian interests stifles the mystery of the universe. The otherwise unfettered imagination of youth becomes chained in adulthood. Commenting on the "longing of young minds for the miraculous and supernatural," Schleiermacher notes that "this proclivity is now forcibly suppressed from the beginning. Everything supernatural and miraculous is proscribed and the imagination is not to be filled with empty images."[35] His third and fourth speeches anticipate Max Weber's thesis about the institutionalization of religion with its "routinization [*Veralltäglichung*] of charisma."[36] Peter L. Berger describes this dimension of the book as "a precocious treatise in the sociology of religion."[37] When religion turns to the state for support it performs an act of looking at Medusa's head and is turned to stone.[38] Without the heavy hand of the state, the naturally flowing images and habits of youth would enliven religion and preserve its vitality. Natural human religiosity becomes imperilled when it is too heavily overlaid by institutional demands.

In Schleiermacher's view, "Once there is religion, it must necessarily also be social. That not only lies in human nature but also is preeminently in the nature of religion."[39] Apart from alluding to the Aristotelian dictum about our being political-social animals by nature, Schleiermacher scarcely mentions a single political philosopher in *On Religion*.[40] In this he differs from Mendelssohn, whose pages are replete with references to the great social contract theories of the seventeenth and eighteenth centuries. Yet Schleiermacher's insistence that religious liberty requires freedom from state control echoes Mendelssohn's chief concern of part 2,

---

33 *OR* (Crouter), 55.
34 The classic work on the ambiguity of post-Constantinian politics and religion in the West is, of course, St. Augustine's *City of God*.
35 *OR* (Crouter), 59, 60.
36 *OR* (Crouter), 84. Of course, for all his dire warnings about utilitarian and rationalist assaults on the human spirit, it is well beyond Schleiermacher to have entertained the metaphor of a Weberian "iron cage" as the dominant image of modernity.
37 Peter L. Berger, *The Heretical Imperative: Contemporary Possibilities of Religious Affirmation* (Garden City, NY: Anchor-Doubleday, 1979), 131.
38 *OR* (Crouter), 86: "Such constitutional charter of political existence affects the religious society like the terrible head of Medusa. Everything turns to stone as soon as it appears." Cf. 90: "Away, therefore, with every such union of church and state! That remains my Cato's counsel to the end, or until I experience seeing every such union actually destroyed."
39 *OR* (Crouter), 73.
40 Spinoza is mentioned once in *OR* (Crouter), 52, though not in the context of politics.

including the refusal of either thinker to recommend an ideal political regime. Schleiermacher greatly admired the church and state polity of Jefferson's United States.[41] Ideal religious community can, he holds, consist of mutual truth-seekers who find themselves drawn to one another as leaders and followers. The idea of an *ecclesiola in ecclesia* (little church within a big church) reflects Schleiermacher's eighteenth-century pietist family background. For all of his emphasis on the personal and subjective dimensions of religion, a utopian ideal of universal human community also looms large in Schleiermacher's thought. Repeatedly, the argument of *On Religion* appeals to the progressive betterment of humanity, which typifies Enlightenment teaching from Rousseau through Lessing and Kant. In his words:

One thing we can hope for from the perfection of the sciences and arts is that they will make these dead forces subject to us, that they might turn the corporeal world and everything of the spiritual world that can be regulated into a fairy palace where the god of the earth needs only to utter a magic word or to press a button to have his commands done.[42]

Far from being uniquely romantic, the theme depicts Germany moving beyond Catholic and Protestant religious wars toward an ever brighter future. Schleiermacher arrives at this relative optimism more through his sense of the times as filtered through historical experience, interpreted through biblical allusion, than through contractarian political theory. Written within a dominant Protestant culture, its optimism and progressive cast of mind marks *On Religion* as still within the broad strata of Enlightenment thought and sensibility.

Of course, there had been developments in Berlin's life. But the basic culture of the Prussian capital, shaped by Mendelssohn's contemporary Friedrich the Great, remained fully intact when Schleiermacher began to write at the end of the century. Since the sixteenth century the Protestant Reformation had sought a balance in church–state relations that would break with Catholic hegemony. What emerged in the 1555 Peace of Augsburg as *cuius regio eius religio* ("whose region, his religion"), and was restated by the 1648 Peace of Westphalia, yielded a territorialism that was more practical compromise than product of political theory. As heir of Luther and Calvin as well as of Augsburg and Westphalia,

---

41 Admiration of religious freedom in the new world is expressed directly in the set of "explanations" to his fourth speech that Schleiermacher added in the work's third edition (1821); see *OR* (Oman), 181–209.

42 *OR* (Crouter), 93.

Schleiermacher shared Mendelssohn's view that Europe lacked a permanent teaching or a settled polity on church and state.[43] To paint in broad
strokes: Mendelssohn had the problematic task of having to be a Luther
and a Kant at the same time. It was necessary to reinterpret Jewish
teaching and practices; but it was also necessary to defend Judaism's
ancient ways while drawing from dominant Wolffian canons of rationality. Like Luther, Mendelssohn needed to carve out a new way of being
Jewish and to do so in a way that had public credibility; like Kant, his
intellectual world required him to pursue this task under the dictates of
strict rationality.

The point of part I of *Jerusalem*, is to establish the inviolability of
religious liberty. Mendelssohn and his compatriots were not able to live
in Prussia's capital unless they conformed to sets of elaborate burea-
cratic regulations where one's religious practices and allegiances were suspect. Of course, the political nature of his book is ambiguously reflected
in the term "power" of its subtitle, "Religious Power and Judaism."[44]
Mendelssohn had inspired his friend, the military councilor Christian
Wilhelm von Dohm, whose treatise *On the Civil Improvement of the Jews*
(1781) set out an extensive and detailed juridical and moral argument for
Jewish emancipation.[45] Mendelssohn's preface to Manasseh ben Israel's
work credited Dohm with making the case for Jewish emancipation along
strictly rational lines.[46] Hence it is entirely appropriate that *Jerusalem* sets
forth a view of politics and the state that could serve as a specifically Judaic
counterpart to Dohm's plea for rights and emancipation.[47]

43 Of course, the greatest modern social experiment of the French Revolution was the political
watershed that distinguished Mendelssohn's era from that of Schleiermacher. The fact that the
Christian theologian could find no gain for religion in the politics of the revolution tends to
reinforce Mendelssohn's point about the range of political thought in the period.
44 In the subtitle, "religious power" (*religiöse Macht*) captures the tension between structures of
(political and economic) power and the inherently subjective, personal (and noncoercive) claims
of religion, which must work through persuasion and never through domination.
45 See Alexander Altmann, "The Philosophical Roots of Mendelssohn's Plea for Emancipation,"
in *Essays in Jewish Intellectual History* (Hanover, NH: University Press of New England, 1981),
154–69.
46 See *Gesammelte Schriften*, VIII, 5: "Als philosophisch-politischer Schriftsteller, dünkt mich, hat
Herr Dohm die Materie fast erschöpft, und nur eine sehr geringe Nachlese zurück gelassen.
Seine Absicht ist, weder für das Judenthum, noch für die Juden eine Apologie zu schreiben."
The sentence makes it clear that *Jerusalem* became Mendelssohn's effort to write just that
apology for Jews and Judaism that had not been undertaken by Dohm as a Prussian statesman.
47 His extensive reading in political theory ranged from Grotius and Pufendorf down to the
modern theorists of the state, Thomas Hobbes and John Locke. The latter's work was known to
him especially through the work of Adam Ferguson, *Institutes of Moral Philosophy* (Edinburgh,
1769), which had been translated into German by Christian Garve as *Adam Fergusons
Grundsätze der Moralphilosophie* (Leipzig, 1772).

Clarity on politics was indispensable in order to obtain a proper view of religious liberty.

State and religion – civil and ecclesiastical constitution – secular and churchly authority – how to oppose these pillars of social life to one another so that they are to balance and do not, instead, become burdens on social life, or weigh down its foundations more than they help to uphold it – this is one of the most difficult tasks of politics.[48]

The passage reflects Mendelssohn's realism with respect to the social order.[49] For Mendelssohn, when secular and religious authority are sharply divided "mankind is the victim of their discord."[50] But when they are in "agreement, the noblest treasure of human felicity is lost; for they seldom agree but for the purpose of banishing from their realms a third moral entity, *liberty of conscience*, which knows how to derive some advantage from their disunity."[51] The Reformation did not permanently produce an effective and harmonious resolution between church and state any more than did earlier political theory. Referring to seventeenth-century juridical traditions, he writes that "one finds the writings of those times full of vague and wavering ideas whenever the definition of ecclesiastical power is discussed."[52] For all their justified critique of Catholic tyranny, the Protestant reformers did not develop a settled political teaching that would properly adjudicate and give justice to religious minorities in dominant cultures.

Mendelssohn's dominant quarrel is more with Hobbes and Locke than with Calvin or Luther, who were not wrestling with the aftermath of Reformation teaching and the Wars of Religion. Yet he rests comfortably with neither of the illustrious English political theorists. The teaching that "all *right* is grounded in *power*, and all *obligation* in *fear*"[53] permits Hobbes, in his desire for tranquillity during the English civil wars, to develop a state in which the monarch fears God. There is no free authority relegated for religion to practice and shape its own external (worshipping) practices; everything in religion, for Hobbes, is subject to the dictates, if not the whims, of the state. Mendelssohn argues that "this very fear of the

---

48 *Jerusalem*, 33.
49 Students of Christian political theory may see Mendelssohn as wrestling with a two-kingdoms teaching that resembles Augustine or a Luther. But the social contract and juridical theory of his era wove treatment of religion into the camps of territorialism, with its Hobbesian dominion of state authority, and collegialism, with its Lockean consent of the governed, which appears better to ensure religious liberty within believing communities.
50 *Jerusalem*, 33.
51 Ibid.   52 Ibid., 34.   53 Ibid., 35.

Omnipotent, which should bind kings and princes to certain duties toward their subjects, can also become a source of obligation for every individual in the state of nature."[54] His point is that if individuals are not bound by nature to any duty, they do not have a duty to keep their contracts. For Mendelssohn this law of nature is something "solemn" and something quite other than a "war of all against all."

By contrast, the teaching of John Locke's *Letters on Toleration* would seem to be more promising for Mendelssohn, especially in its basic definition of the state as "*a society of men who unite for the purpose of collectively promoting their temporal welfare.*"[55] Although Mendelssohn favors this view, Locke's religious toleration only works because of its fundamental indifference towards matters of religion. Locke's solution is good; but it only goes so far. What happens, for example, when the society of men decides not just to promote its temporal welfare, but has a scheme for taking public measures to promote man's eternal felicity as well? Mendelssohn's inclination to view Locke with favor is tempered by a realization that this moderate teaching could not suffice to quell the passions at work in Locke's native England, from which he was forced to flee into exile during the civil wars.[56]

Mendelssohn's view of Hobbes and Locke may be stated quite simply. Hobbes errs by sacrificing religious liberty to the interests of the state, while Locke errs by distancing and preserving religious liberty from state authority, thus allowing conceptual space for new forms of tyranny (though he does not name it as such) to spring forth from an authoritarian religion. Ever the diplomat, Mendelssohn uses a Catholic example of the latter abuse, for example, Catholic teaching under Cardinal Bellarmine, thus not risking giving further grounds for offence to the authorities of Protestant Prussia.[57] Mendelssohn brings the temporal and eternal realms into a relationship of efficacy and respect, while declining to debate the exact nature of the best regime. He rejects outright any effort to give the public realm exclusively to politics, while restricting religion to the inner

---

54 Mendelssohn adds, 37, "And so we would have a solemn law of nature, even though Hobbes does not want to admit it. In this fashion, in our day, every student of natural law can gain a triumph over Thomas Hobbes, to whom, at bottom, he nevertheless owes this triumph."

55 *Jerusalem*, 37. Locke's *Two Treatises* were not known by Moses Mendelssohn, who only consults the *Letter on Toleration*.

56 *Jerusalem*, 38.

57 Ibid., 39, "It is, in the strictest sense, neither in keeping with the truth nor advantageous to man's welfare to sever the temporal so neatly from the eternal." Mendelssohn was wrestling with the irreconcilable and necessarily competing interests of church and state that were held in permanent tension.

life. Religion can no more be synonymous with the state than it can be
free from a properly social dimension. This is what the rabbis taught
about "this life" as a "vestibule" for the future life; how we comport
ourselves in the one has consequences for our destiny in the other.[58] On
Mendelssohn's view, a common good that arises from the fulfillment of
our duties flows from "actions and convictions" that cut across earthly and
spiritual realms.[59] For him, religion and the state are both grounded in
public institutions that shape the formation (*Bildung*) of humankind.

As we have seen, Mendelssohn's account of politics draws from social
contract and earlier political theory. A section that treats "the origin of the
rights of coercion" and "the validity of contracts among men" appeals to
the medieval distinction between the state's perfect rights and the imperfect rights of religion.[60] He distinguishes compulsory (perfect) rights and
duties from freely undertaken (imperfect) rights and duties in the form of
claims of conscience (duty) or petitions, such as alms-seeking (a right).
Whereas compulsory rights may be enforced by state authority, claims of
conscience are imprecise in the degree of enactment they demand of us,
and petitions made to others may be legitimately denied. Mendelssohn's
exposition brings out the full social and political reciprocity of rights and
duties in these transactions. In the state of nature an individual's *positive*
duties towards others are imperfect, that is, they arise from acts of
judgment.

Mendelssohn plainly teaches that church (the term is used in the
juridical sense to cover churches, synagogues, or mosques) and state have
definite common interests: "Both must teach, instruct, encourage, motiv-
ate." At the same time, in the realm of beliefs and convictions, that is, in
the realm of religion, nothing can be coerced. "The right to our own
convictions is inalienable, and cannot pass from person to person; for it
neither gives nor takes away any claim to property, goods and liberty."[61]
Mendelssohn does not take a stand on the actual form of governance
within religion. Rather, he espouses something like a freely formed
religious community. In answer to the question, "What form of government is therefore advisable for the church?," he responds, "None."[62] Like
Schleiermacher, Mendelssohn's political reflections are essentially those of

58 Ibid.   59 Ibid., 40.
60 Ibid., 45–56. A perfect right is one in which "all the conditions under which the predicate
    belongs to the subject are invested in the holder of the right," whereas with an imperfect right "a
    part of the conditions under which the right applies is dependent on the knowledge and
    conscience of the person who bears the duty" (46).
61 Ibid., 61.   62 Ibid., 62.

a religious thinker whose view of the political order must ensure religious freedom.

UNIVERSALITY OF RELIGION VERSUS PARTICULARITY OF A CONFESSION

Part 1 of *Jerusalem* endorses universal reason and deism while aligning itself with pre-Kantian rationalist philosophy (Wolff) and certain strata of medieval Jewish teaching (Judah Ha-Levi, among others).[63] Mendelssohn makes no secret of his endorsement of Enlightenment religion in the form of a deistic natural religion that consists of God, virtue, and immortality.

Without God, providence, and a future life, love of our fellow man is but an innate weakness, and benevolence is little more than a foppery into which we seek to lure one another so that the simpleton will toil while the clever man enjoys himself and has a good laugh at the other's expense.[64]

In this passage, which follows his denunciation of atheism and Epicureanism, Mendelssohn confidently depicts the central tenets of natural religion as needed to support the moral order of society: "One of the state's principal efforts must be to govern men through morals and convictions."[65] Such aid should occur through education (*Bildung*) and persuasion, not law, and "it is here that religion should come to the aid of the state, and the church should become a pillar of civil felicity."[66] More so than Schleiermacher but without using the concept, Mendelssohn endorses the theme of civil religion launched by Rousseau's *Social Contract* (1762) and carried forth by Locke.

Among recent interpreters, Allan Arkush has depicted *Jerusalem* as Mendelssohn's thorough endorsement of deism, while the arguments of part 2 on behalf of the distinctive claims and practices of Judaism remain ambiguously stated at best, and are downright weak at worst, even to the

---

63 David Sorkin argues that Mendelssohn's *Jerusalem* is as much shaped by medieval sources as it is by an effort to echo Enlightenment philosophy of the dominant Christian society. See "Mendelssohn and Modernity: Was Mendelssohn the First Modern or the Last Medieval Jewish Thinker?" in *What is Modern about the Modern Jewish Experience?*, ed. Marc Lee Raphael (Williamsburg, VA: College of William and Mary Press, 1997), 64–77. "Throughout his work, Mendelssohn consistently reiterated the notion of 'heteronomy.' In so doing he drew on the tradition of medieval Jewish philosophy usually identified with Jehudah Ha-Levi. In fact, Mendelssohn's understanding of religious obligation was far closer to that medieval tradition than to any seventeenth- or eighteenth-century European thinker" (68).
64 *Jerusalem*, 63.
65 Ibid., 43.   66 Ibid.

point that their author did not believe in his own project.[67] For Arkush, the particularities of traditional Judaism, a Torah revealed by God on Mount Sinai that requires legal adherence to ritual and communal practices, can scarcely be inferred or deduced from the moral law of eighteenth-century philosophy. Indeed, the emphasis on natural law and natural religion is so pronounced in part 1 of *Jerusalem* as to undercut the defense of Judaism in part 2. We return to Arkush's position on Mendelssohn in a subsequent section. Here it suffices to observe that no writer on religion in Germany of the 1780s could get a hearing for his work without addressing the intellectual elites' widespread acceptance of deistic views.

Readers of Schleiermacher's *On Religion* are well aware that the work takes an entirely different approach to the topic of natural religion. Yet the book also betrays its setting amid late eighteenth-century proposals of deism and a religion of reason. The hold of that way of thinking on his contemporaries becomes the object of Schleiermacher's contempt. Unlike Mendelssohn, the young preacher-rhetorician approaches these moral and metaphysical claims with suspicion and satire. Neither knowing nor doing (both of which assume the form of an action) can adequately grasp the universal element of religion at the heart of Schleiermacher's argument. The book's famous second speech makes a case for regarding "intuition of the universe" and "feeling" as more central to a sense of the reality of the organic and metaphysical world than are knowledge or morality.[68] In his hands the aesthetic and poetic sensibility of nascent romanticism assaults the moralism of Kant as represented most immediately in Schleiermacher's world by the speculative idealism of J. G. Fichte.

Thus it is the case that Schleiermacher and Mendelssohn are directly opposed on the topic of natural religion. Yet that fact ought not to obscure the reality that, like Mendelssohn in *Jerusalem*, Schleiermacher defends the view that religion is universal. Humans by nature have a

67 See Arkush, "Mendelssohn and the Religious Enlightenment," 179–85; Arkush, *Mendelssohn and the Enlightenment*. In reviewing this book, Michael Zank writes, "Arkush's Mendelssohn is an Enlightenment philosopher who happened to be Jewish," and "Without saying so, Arkush's essay is a farewell to Mendelssohn, or at least a challenge. Unless your defense against Spinoza, Locke, and Reimarus is better than Mendelssohn's – that is, unless you can retrieve what it means to believe in revelation – you may as well admit that your Judaism is mainly pragmatic and consists in resisting the pressures exerted by the majority culture," *Journal of Religion* 77 (1997): 660.
68 *OR* (Crouter), 22: "It does not wish to determine and explain the universe according to its nature as does metaphysics; it does not desire to continue the universe's development and perfect it by the power of freedom and the divine free choice of a human being as does morals. Religion's essence is neither thinking nor acting, but intuition and feeling."

religious capacity. The poetic and aesthetic sense of awe and wonder that gives rise to "intuitions of the universe" and "feeling" is seated in our nature as human beings, just like the sense of God, virtue, and immortality that mark the Enlightenment creed of his Jewish predecessor. Because of this element of *On Religion*, its author's position is sometimes characterized as "generic."[69] Stressing this same universality, Hermann Timm maintains that "Schleiermacher has given the name 'religion' to this metacritical sphere of totality."[70] Like the twentieth-century theorist of religion, Mircea Eliade, Schleiermacher holds that humans have a natural capacity for religion.

A person is born with the religious capacity as with every other, and if only his sense is not forcibly suppressed, if only that communion between a person and the universe . . . is not blocked and barricaded, then religion would have to develop unerringly in each person according to his own individual manner.[71]

Teachers of *On Religion* have had the experience that students occasionally picture him as a kind of "free thinker" or "Buddhist from Berlin," based upon the deeply experiential, yet universal, arguments of the second speech. At the same time, even in its famous second speech what looks like a universal system of mystical self-reflective insight is qualified at several levels by a radical turn from nature to the particular experience of human communities in historical time and place. The Garden of Eden functions for Schleiermacher as a peopled garden, where human interaction creates the potential for experiencing the sacred.[72] We shall return in a moment to analyze how the ending (and overall movement) of *On Religion* resolves the tension between the particularity of our experience and its relation to universal claims about religion. Against our first impressions, Schleiermacher's attack on the natural religion of his era leads him to plead for a form of universal religion that is locally anchored in the human condition. In that sense, he and Mendelssohn are working out an argumentative strategy that is cognate, if not identical in content.

---

69 Wilfred Cantwell Smith, *The Meaning and End of Religion* (New York: Harper and Row, 1978), maintains that *On Religion* "would seem to be the first book ever written on religion as such – not on a particular kind or instance and not incidentally, but explicitly on religion itself as a generic something" (45).

70 *Die heilige Revolution: Schleiermacher – Novalis – Friedrich Schlegel* (Frankfurt-on-Main: Syndikat, 1978), 24.

71 *OR* (Crouter), 59.

72 Ibid., 37, "Since the deity recognized that his world would be nothing so long as man was alone, it created for him a partner, and now, for the first time, living and spiritual tones stirred within him."

In part 2 of *Jerusalem*, which is a third longer than part 1, Mendelssohn turns to the task of defending the specifics of Judaism as historically viable in a manner consistent with his account of natural religion in the work's first part. Like *On Religion*, the text moves from the more general to its specific exemplification in the author's personal religious tradition.[73] The interpretation of Mendelssohn's apologetic work hinges on how well he is able to knit his account of Judaism into the preceding endorsement of natural religion, with its corollary insistence on the noncoercive nature of authentic religion. The initial specific task of part 2 of *Jerusalem* is thus to address the issue of whether the right of excommunication should continue to exist within the Jewish community, a point which Mendelssohn denied, though Dohm affirmed in *On the Civil Improvement of the Jews*. Mendelssohn thus begins with the political circumstances that lie behind his work. To endorse an element of lawful power, not just over but within religion, would be to adopt the tools of the state and to leave open the issue of the state's power to interfere, suppress, or persecute Jews in the future. The opening of part 2 (77–83) shifts to a more immediate, personal rhetoric; Mendelssohn speaks to the cluster of issues raised by the Dohm treatise, while responding directly to Cranz, who had pointed out that Mendelssohn's deistic views of religion contradict the obviously statutory dimension of the "faith of his fathers," in which "Moses connects coercion and positive punishment with the nonobservance of duties related to the worship of God."[74]

In developing his response to this crucial point, Mendelssohn acknowledges that many of his coreligionists agree with Cranz' points.[75] It would seem difficult to deny the obviously coercive theocratic nature and legally binding character of ancient Judaism. Mendelssohn's strategy is to appeal to a different sense of the Judaic past, which requires a significant reinterpretation of the tradition. Rather than speak directly to Cranz' and many coreligionists' views – which can hardly be denied as a matter of history – Mendelssohn develops a different account of the Jewish origins and the Torah traditions that were given at Sinai.

---

73 The task of reconciling Jerusalem parts 1 and 2 parallels that of reconciling speeches 2 and 5 of *On Religion.*

74 *Jerusalem*, 85. Mendelssohn quotes the text of *The Searching for Light and Right*, "Ecclesiastical law armed with power has always been one of the principal cornerstones of the Jewish religion itself, and a primary article in the credal system of your fathers. How, then, can you, my dear Mr. Mendelssohn, remain an adherent of the faith of your fathers and shake the entire structure by removing its cornerstones, when you contest the ecclesiastical law that has been given through Moses and purports to be founded on divine revelation?"

75 *Jerusalem*, 85.

On Mendelssohn's account, revelation understood in a traditional sense as a literal, independent word captured in speech and given for all time to the Jewish people on Sinai is superseded, though he does not say this in so many words. In its place, according to Mendelssohn, is a set of formulations of the Torah as a "revealed legislation." For Mendelssohn, the fact of the original history – the historical founding of the community that experienced this event – constitutes the most sacred foundation of the tradition. Truths of reason and those of direct observation bear a kind of immediate authority.

Historical truths, however – those passages which, as it were, occur but once in the book of nature – must be explained by themselves, or remain incomprehensible; that is, they can only be perceived, by means of the senses, by those who were present at the time and place of their occurrence in nature. Everyone else must accept them on authority and testimony. Furthermore, those who live at another time must rely altogether on the credibility of the testimony, for the thing attested no longer exists.[76]

We have already noted Arkush's view that Mendelssohn's endorsement of the Enlightenment religion of God, virtue, and immortality imperils his Jewishness. For Arkush, Mendelssohn simply denies revelation covertly; his exposition of and appeal to a received historical tradition as grounding the believing and practicing community has little weight.[77] It is as if the sections of part 2 of *Jerusalem* were intended to placate his Jewish compatriots while concealing an essential sellout of the tradition. Mendelssohn's actual teaching remains wrapped lock, stock, and barrel in the credo of Enlightenment reason and religion. Following the Locke interpretation of Leo Strauss, and more recently of Michael P. Zuckert, Arkush views the English philosopher as dissimulating with respect to the truth of Christianity, while allowing these beliefs to stand in order to blend into the assumptions of his age and gain a hearing for his cause.[78] Arkush imputes a similar strategy to Mendelssohn; what appears as a benign virtue in Locke, becomes a troubling fault in Mendelssohn. In the case of Locke, concealing one's real belief is practical, humane, and sensible; in Mendelssohn's case, it marks a moral weakness that is unstable and dangerous in view of later developments within German Jewry. It is as if dissimulation on the part of a nonbeliever can be approved, but not

---

76 Ibid., 93.   77 Arkush, "Questionable Judaism."
78 Arkush, *Mendelssohn and the Enlightenment*, 247–54.

on the part of a believer. But one can ask whether the logic of both positions does not resist that way of reading.

While summing up his argument near the end of *Jerusalem*, Mendelssohn turns to the Psalms for support. His significant rendering of the Psalms into German was published the same year. What strikes the reader is how he appeals directly to the Psalms (a traditional source of revealed truth for Jews) to undergird the contention of part 1 that nature and the earth illustrate the majesty of deity. "The heavens declare the majesty of God."[79] It even looks as if the one who denies revelation nonetheless seeks to anchor his philosophical teaching through the authority of received scriptural teaching. One must ask what Mendelssohn is doing at this point. What does the appeal to scripture accomplish within his argument? And how can one who denies revelation still appeal to scripture? Arkush maintains that this is mostly sleight of hand and that the references to Old Testament texts are mere gestures that do nothing to address the underlying issues posed for Judaism by its most severe critics, most notably Spinoza in the seventeenth century. Here again, however, another way of reading might argue that the teaching of natural religion is itself, for Mendelssohn, concealed within the hidden resources of the sacred text.

In his own recapitulation of the argument in the last speech of *On Religion*, Schleiermacher maintains that religion in general is an artificial construction of philosophers that ought not to be mistaken for real, lived religion. Authentic religion arises from the particularities of human experience, including ceremonies, rituals, and practices that seem antithetical to reason. *On Religion* chides the naïveté of this popular deism and natural religion.

So-called natural religion is usually so refined and has such philosophical and moral manners that it allows little of the unique character of religion to shine through; it knows how to live so politely, to restrain and accommodate itself so well, that it is tolerated everywhere. In contrast, every positive religion has exceedingly strong features and a very marked physiognomy, so that it unfailingly reminds one of what it really is with every movement it makes and with every glance one casts upon it.[80]

For Schleiermacher, so-called natural religion is decidedly against nature, understood as all that is natural to human experience.[81] A contrast is drawn between living religion and the superficial antihumanism of deism.

---

79 *Jerusalem*, 126.   80 *OR* (Crouter), 98.   81 Ibid., 98–100.

If we want to find religion, he maintains, we must look for it within the religions. As we have noted, interpreters of *On Religion* frequently compare the second and fifth speeches, and ask whether Schleiermacher succeeds in moving from abstract "intuitions of the universe" to anything resembling the mediation of the traditional Christ at the end of the book. Yet the progressive force of the argument, as it moves relentlessly from the greatest to the least level of abstraction, anchors "intuition and feeling" experientially within an explicit appropriation of Christian meaning, where the figure of Christ stands as central.[82]

In the end, Schleiermacher sees the Christ as "religion raised to a higher power" and endorses the fundamental historically manifest intuition of Christianity as the inability of the finite to capture the infinite.

Even while the finite wishes to intuit the universe, it strains against it, always seeking without finding and losing what it has found; ever one-sided, ever vacillating, ever halting at the particular and accidental, and ever wanting more than to intuit, the finite loses sight of its goal.[83]

Original Christianity, for Schleiermacher, "must everywhere disclose all corruption, be it in morals or in the manner of thinking, and above all in the irreligious principle itself."[84] This insight of constantly seeking renewal, developed by twentieth-century theologian Paul Tillich as "the Protestant principle," is the counterpart within the fifth speech of the "intuition of the universe" of the second speech. It also has its requisite feeling that is awakened within the Christian soul in the form of "holy sadness."[85] Schleiermacher's earliest effort to interpret the Christian religion parallels the sense of unfulfilled longing of the early German Romantic circle. Yet it also arguably seeks to reconcile a specific level of particularity with a universal claim about religion (as "intuition and feeling") that in its universality bears the stamp, if not the same content, of the Enlightenment.

Judged by its rhetoric and style, Schleiermacher's *On Religion* can be seen as a headstrong, even at times an impetuous book. Its author writes enthusiastically in the first person and draws from his experience to tease

---

82 The intuition of Christ, which symbolizes the clash of the infinite with the finite of speech 5, constitutes a specific, concrete exemplification of an intuition of the universe of speech 2 that is mediated through the historic community of the Christian church.

83 *OR* (Crouter), 116.

84 Ibid., 117.

85 Ibid., 119. "Holy sadness" (*heilige Wehmut*) is the counterpart within Christian feeling of the experience of unfulfilled longing as the fundamental intuition of the Christian faith.

readers into examining their assumptions about religion and its status in the world. Yet its argument against explicit dogma and doctrine partially veils Schleiermacher's true position. If one takes everything at face value, then his admonitions against knowledge and morals raise a host of difficulties. How can a book that is against knowing make any claims upon a reader's intellect? How can a writer who honors human morality appear to undercut it in favor of aesthetic and subjective values? One is invited to see that a living pulse of religion lies beneath the encrustations of dogma. A subversive twist in the argument gives the book a dynamic quality and allows its young author to state questions relentlessly. His strategy is first to get the reader's attention, and then to dislodge some measure of the smugness and certitude that readers often bring to their habits of reading. Like Simonides of Greek legend, Schleiermacher only reluctantly comes to speak about his topic. This is preferred to the glib depictions of religion that were widespread among his contemporaries.

Direct appeal to scripture occurs even less frequently than in Mendelssohn. Nowhere is the dialectic of assertion and concealment so evident as it is in the manner that *On Religion* incorporates scriptural passages into its argument. Virtually none of Schleiermacher's biblical allusions are identified. To do so would play into the hands of the cultured despisers of religion who have long since broken with a habit of validating religious argument by the authority of scripture alone. In Schleiermacher's hands scriptural meaning is internalized, beginning with the text's appeal to scriptural metaphor and simile as against literal meaning.[86] Beginning with his ecclesiastical superior, F. S. G. Sack, interpreters have repeatedly charged Schleiermacher with undermining Protestant Christian teaching and introducing a form of religious naturalism. But in truth Schleiermacher never renounced his youthful work, even though he revised it in 1806, again in 1821, and lightly in 1831. As the book evolved, it took on theological tones and coloration; its arguments became fleshed out to complement his dogmatics set forth in *The Christian Faith*. The book's language and rhetorical strategies were thereby deepened more than abandoned.[87] Revision of his work allowed Schleiermacher to ward off further misunderstandings. We can never know what might have emerged if *Jerusalem* had been written at an earlier point in Mendelssohn's life, so that similar editing and self-clarification might have taken place. At the same

---

86 *On Religion* has many references to the "dead letter." Viewed as a tract against literalisms, the work plays into Protestant Christianity's age-old stereotypes of Judaism.
87 See below, chapter 10.

time, it is doubtful that we need that kind of evidence. If we bear in mind that *Jerusalem* is itself a composite of arguments that draw from the range of Mendelssohn's commitments and career, then it stands as a finished work that reflects these layers of personal history.

REVELATION AS SUBJECTIVE AND HISTORICAL EXPERIENCE

Neither Mendelssohn nor Schleiermacher stands uncritically within his respective religious tradition. Both writers seek to draw forth new levels of insight and meaning while reconfiguring cherished biblical, and, in Mendelssohn's case, rabbinic texts, they have inherited from their predecessors. Mendelssohn argues for his Jewishness in part 2 by providing a personal account and explanation of how the Torah, as revealed legislation, was once and for all time given through a historical event. This depiction of the legacy of Judaism remains controversial among Mendelssohn specialists. Yet the teaching of *Jerusalem* in part 1 as well as in part 2 includes numerous points where the human experience of religion, and arguments in support of this experience, strongly emerge.

Writers on Mendelssohn, including Altmann, Sorkin, and Arkush, agree that there are idiosyncratic elements in his approach to the question of revelation.[88] Altmann has noted that Mendelssohn gives a unique account of revelation in *Jerusalem* and that his final work, *Morning Hours*, which gives his most mature philosophical defense of religion and religious belief in God, develops an argument that links the sense of human insufficiency with the necessary postulate of belief in a God. Yet the sense of human insufficiency – not a typical Enlightenment theme – is also present in *Jerusalem* and links that apologetic text to Mendelssohn's final work. At several crucial points in its argument *Jerusalem* expresses a sense of the fragility and poignancy of individual moral choice. In a passage on subjectivity that is almost Kierkegaardian, Mendelssohn asserts that

since man's capacity is limited and therefore exhaustible, it may occasionally happen that the same capacity or goods cannot simultaneously serve me and my neighbor . . . since I am obliged to make the best possible use of my powers, everything depends on a choice, and on the more precise determination as to *how much* of what is mine should I devote to *benevolence?*[89]

---

88 Altmann, *Essays in Jewish Intellectual History*, 119–41.
89 *Jerusalem*, 48. A similar line of thought occurs at the end of Kierkegaard's "Diary of the Jutland Priest," where religious smugness is concealed by the inner satisfaction of thinking "I've done what I can." In fact, no one can ever be sure that he or she has done enough, since an absolute

The heart of Mendelssohn's defense of religious freedom is seen in his respect for the utter independence of each individual person. In his words:

No one has a compulsory right to prescribe to me how much of my powers I should employ for the good of others and upon whom the benefit of my labors should be conferred. It must be left solely to my discretion to determine the rule by which I am to settle cases of collision.[90]

With respect to external actions of religion, Mendelssohn puts forth the strict view that "religion buys nothing, pays nothing, and allots no wages."[91] It seems that for Mendelssohn religion arises out of a sense of human vulnerability. He decries both atheism and Epicureanism, since neither the godless nor the hedonistic-naturalist perspective shows proper respect for the precariousness of life. Mendelssohn is well aware of the Hobbesian view that the social order depends upon fear of God. Unlike Hobbes, however, Mendelssohn holds that each person, not just the monarch, is morally motivated by fear. For him, each individual, not just the sovereign ruler, relates directly to deity. Like Schleiermacher, Mendelssohn held that religion has its primordial seat within the free unfolding of individual lives.

These traces of epistemological reflection in *Jerusalem* are related to the overall line of argument about God's existence from his final work, *Morning Hours*, especially section 16, which treats "Explanation of the concepts of necessity, contingency, independence and dependence – Attempt of a new proof for the existence of God from the incompleteness of self-knowledge."[92] Although Mendelssohn was still a rationalist at the end of his life, his philosophizing has an original flair that stresses the element of contingency in all knowledge in ways that defy the metaphysical certitude of his Enlightenment models, Wolff or Baumgarten.[93] And while he claimed not to have grasped Kant's magnum opus, *The Critique of Pure Reason* (1781), the work appears to have nudged Mendelssohn

---

standard of measurement is not at hand in political-moral life. Søren Kierkegaard, *Either/Or*, part II, tr. Howard V. Hong and Edna H. Hong (Princeton: Princeton University Press, 1987), 346: "So every more earnest doubt, every deeper care is not calmed by the words: One does what one can."

90 *Jerusalem*, 49.

91 Ibid., 61.

92 *Gesammelte Schriften*, III/2, ed. Leo Strauss (Stuttgart–Bad Cannstatt: Frommann–Holzboog, 1974), 138–47.

93 Ibid., 144: "Und gleichwohl ist der Inbegriff aller menschlichen Kenntnisse voll von diesen anscheinenden Widersprüchen, von Möglichkeiten, Anlagen, entfernten oder nahen Vermögen, größern oder kleinern Fähigkeiten, Talenten u. s. w., wodurch wirklich vorhandene Dinge bezeichnet und von einander unterschieden werden."

somewhat away from a confident and robust rationalism. Admittedly, it is difficult to show all the links between Mendelssohn's philosophical views and his commitment to Judaism. But the rich appreciation of the given-ness of a revealed historical tradition arises precisely because of his insistence that human life is not wholly autonomous or self-made. An allegiance to biblical truth goes hand in hand with the truth of Judaism; together, both levels of insight serve to hedge his rationalism.

If beliefs and convictions necessarily arise from free choice, it follows that contracts or agreements in the form of public oaths regarding religion are illicit. No one can be required to make a public statement of an inner conviction in a manner that conveys its permanence. "We are putting conscience to a cruel torture when we question them [i.e., persons] about things which are solely a matter of the *internal sense*."[94] Mendelssohn's frequent acknowledgment of a private, internal sense is commensurate with Kierkegaard and Romantic literary theory in acknowledging the irreducibility of one's innermost being and the ways that our mental life (thus our religious beliefs and convictions) fluctuates and never attains stability. Mendelssohn asserts that "The perceptions of the internal sense are in themselves rarely so palpable that the mind is able to retain them securely and to give them expression as often as it may be desired. They will slip away from it at times, just when it thinks it has taken hold of them."[95] He then gets directly to the point of religious freedom: "Many things for which I would suffer martyrdom today may perhaps appear problematic to me tomorrow."[96]

Although this language may appear lacking in the robust canons of Enlightenment reason, Mendelssohn's view rests upon a foundational insight concerning contingency, privacy, and inwardness.

My neighbor and I cannot possibly connect the very same words with the very same internal sensations, for we cannot compare them, liken them to one another and correct them without again resorting to words. We cannot illustrate the words by things, but must again have recourse to signs and words, and finally, to metaphors; because, with the help of this artifice, we reduce, as it were, the concepts of the internal sense to external sensory perceptions. But, given this fact, how much confusion and indistinctiveness are bound to remain in the signification of words, and how greatly must the ideas differ which different men, in different ages and centuries, connect with the same external signs and words![97]

94 *Jerusalem*, 66.
95 Ibid.   96 Ibid.   97 Ibid.

This heightened awareness of the fragility of language and the power of lived experience is perfectly consistent with Mendelssohn's insistence in part 1 on the personal risk in religious adherence. This level of grounded, contingent insight into human knowing thus serves as a framing principle that unites the arguments of parts 1 and 2 of *Jerusalem*.

Instead of being cast in two parts of a sequential argument, Schleiermacher's book unfolds in a five-act drama in which each speech analyzes a particular problem while goading the reader to think about religion by satirizing popular as well as Enlightenment views.[98] Neither work is systematic or didactic; each contains meandering sets of reflections that speak directly to contemporary issues and sensibilities. Only in the end does one have the possibility of standing back and asking questions about these two famous interpretations of religion in modern Europe.

On Religion approaches the topic of revelation not as a separate source of religious truth but as a religious person's deepest awareness of the discovery of the action of deity in the world. "What is revelation? Every original and new intuition of the universe is one, and yet all individuals must know best what is original and new for them."[99] The insight put forth in 1799 by Schleiermacher is further developed in *The Christian Faith* (1830–1), where he writes:

every original ideal which arises in the soul, whether for an action or for a work of art, and which can neither be understood as an imitation nor be satisfactorily explained by means of external stimuli and preceding mental states, may be regarded as revelation.[100]

As understood by Schleiermacher, revelation has a strong element of what M. H. Abrams calls "the natural supernatural" of Romantic literature.[101] His mature work wrestles at length with the problem of how to depict an original awareness that guides our lives but which is neither generated solely from within oneself nor explainable as based solely on external influences. This is a far cry from classical definitions of revelation in Catholic tradition, where authority is granted to a body of truth that is suprarational. In the thought of Schleiermacher – however one weighs the adequacy of his formulations for today – there can be little doubt that the

---

98 See below chapter 9, on the work's rhetorical design.
99 *OR* (Crouter), 49.
100 *CF*, §10, 51.
101 M. H. Abrams, *Natural Supernaturalism: Tradition and Revolution in Romantic Literature* (New York: W. W. Norton, 1971).

experience of Christ as revelation stands at the center of his teaching.[102] Older forms of propositional truth, which put stock in the precise articulation of formula, have simply yielded to an account that attends self-critically to the experience and effect of religious claims upon the lives of their practitioners.

"JERUSALEM" AND "ON RELIGION": AN UNLIKELY KINSHIP

The premier Mendelssohn scholar of the last generation, Alexander Altmann, warns readers of *Jerusalem*:

Those who merely glance at it superficially may deceive themselves into believing that they have taken the measure of the book. Those who are serious in undertaking its study will realize that there is far more to it than meets the eye.[103]

At the time of writing, Mendelssohn was an honorary member of the prestigious Wednesday Society, a distinguished circle of scholars, preachers, writers, and government officials who met weekly to debate issues of the day between 1783 and 1798.[104] His argument reflects the thorough engagement with this political and social elite. Easily overlooked in this comparison is the fact that both Mendelssohn and Schleiermacher were lucky in their friends. We are most aware of the need of Mendelssohn, who arrived in Berlin at age 14, to have made his way through that society with the assistance of patrons and well-placed supporters who saw his promise. Something of the same can be said of Schleiermacher, whose rise through the ranks of Berlin society was helped immeasurably by his associations with nobility, statesmen, artists, scientists, and writers. In the spirit of Altmann's admonition, I have at least discovered some elements of surprise in Mendelssohn's *Jerusalem*. It is not my aim to argue that Mendelssohn is a precursor of Romanticism. Nor do I wish to dismiss the uniquely romantic elements in Schleiermacher and reclaim him as purely an Enlightenment thinker. Rather, I hope only to have shown that certain of Mendelssohn's fundamental attitudes, that is, towards the human self, towards knowledge claims, and towards religion, have striking affinities with Schleiermacher.

---

102 Consider *CF* §13, 62: "The appearance of the Redeemer in history is, as divine revelation, neither an absolutely supernatural nor an absolutely supra-rational thing."
103 "Introduction and Commentary," in *Jerusalem*, 29.
104 See Günter Birsch, "The Berlin Wednesday Society," in *What is Enlightenment?*, 235–52. With the exception of Mendelssohn and the publisher Friedrich Nicolai, all were civil servants, including names prominent in debates about Jews in Prussia, such as Wilhelm Abraham Teller and Christian Wilhelm von Dohm.

There remains for me one other, arguably even more compelling reason for wishing to juxtapose *On Religion* with *Jerusalem*. The two books are the Jewish and Protestant Christian religious classics par excellence in the modern period. Within their troubled and contested histories of interpretation, these texts have often determined the repute of their respective authors. A comparison of the two books has religious and cultural resonance that echoes the past, while reaching to the present day. *Jerusalem* and *On Religion* suffer the identical fate of being viewed simultaneously as charters that sell out their respective traditions and as foundations for the survival of each religion into the nineteenth century and beyond. Neither work is cast as a formal philosophical treatise, even if Mendelssohn's book comes closer to that mark. The literary form of these religious books defies the stereotyped view of Enlightenment philosophy as a didactic and argumentative treatise. For all their meanderings, each work argues in defense of its author's religious views in a manner that yields a result that is consistent overall, even if interpretive problems remain for posterity.

In view of all this, some positive levels of insight result from looking at *Jerusalem* and *On Religion* together. However much both writers are involved in the revolution of thought associated with Kant, neither the Haskalah Jew nor the romantic Protestant is a happy and uncritical recipient of that teaching, or thinks he can apply it directly to the task of defending his tradition against a rising cultural indifference. Unlike the young Schleiermacher, Mendelssohn was known and admired by Kant.[105] Readers of both works invariably note that both writers bring deep appreciation of history to the task of depicting and defending religion. Although we may associate the recovery of a sense of history with the Romantics, this sense is obviously at work in part 2 of Mendelssohn's *Jerusalem*.[106] For his part, the entire progression of Schleiermacher's argument towards his fifth speech is an assertion that draws its power and plausibility from the contingencies of historical experience.

---

105 On Kant's meeting with Mendelssohn in Königsberg in 1777, see Paul Mendes-Flohr and Jehuda Reinharz, eds., *The Jew in the Modern World* (Oxford: Oxford University Press, 1995), 61, and Arnold M. Eisen, *Rethinking Modern Judaism: Ritual, Commandment, Community* (Chicago: University of Chicago Press, 1998), 24–30, on Kant's ambiguous reception of *Jerusalem* and lifelong strictures against religious Judaism.

106 It is instructive to note that Mendelssohn's appeal to history is more existential than it is progressive. *Jerusalem*, 95–6 sharply criticizes the rationalized view of history and revelation of Lessing's *Education of the Human Race*.

Of course, seasoned readers of *On Religion* are all too aware of the apparent pejorative reading of Judaism as a "dead religion" of the fifth speech.[107] If Moses Mendelssohn took pains not to give offense to the majority Christian culture in writing his work,[108] Schleiermacher did not show a similar restraint in positioning his work with respect to Judaism. His comments on Judaism reflect the age-old stereotypes of legalism that had long informed Protestant teaching. It would be an interpretive leap if we were to try to guess just how Moses Mendelssohn might have regarded these pronouncements of his younger Romantic contemporary. One must imagine that they could not have been passed over without great pain. In his *Essays in Jewish Intellectual History* Alexander Altmann suggests that the rabbis of Berlin's German-speaking synagogue had turned to Schleiermacher for tips on preaching.[109] Though evidence to back up that claim may not be at hand, Schleiermacher's sensibility towards Berlin's assimilated Jews, beginning with the circle around Henriette Herz, was more nuanced than the few lines from his 1799 book would suggest.[110]

It is ironic that these two intentionally history-laden texts by Mendelssohn and Schleiermacher should be so burdened by the subsequent history of each text's reception. Just as Schleiermacher has been decried for failing to uphold orthodox Christian teaching, so Mendelssohn is today often viewed by experts within Judaica as having failed at the task of preserving an authentic expression of Judaism within eighteenth-century Germany. In Schleiermacher's case the pendulum is swinging in more positive directions, while the repute of Mendelssohn hangs in the balance, depending upon the respective theological or historical biases of contemporary scholars. If we attended to the repute of Mendelssohn in German anthologies from 1929 that celebrate his bicentenary, we could

---

107 *OR* (Crouter), 113–14. See below, chapter 5, for Schleiermacher's discussion of Jewish emancipation.

108 This is one reason why natural reason is emphasized as common ground, while explicit references to the absurd propositions of Christian dogma are largely reserved for private correspondence.

109 Altmann, *Essays in Jewish Intellectual History*, 195–6.

110 For example, Schleiermacher praised the dean of Enlightenment preachers in Berlin, Johann Joachim Spalding, for his "impartial dealings with Jews." Beutel, "Aufklärer höherer Ordung?," 361. What Schleiermacher says in speech 5 about Judaism being dead is at odds with the more general position of speeches 2 and 5 that each religion has a foundational intuition that shapes the tradition as it unfolds in history. If it were carried forth consistently, that line of thought would approximate the argument of *Jerusalem*, part 2.

scarcely imagine that his contribution to Jewish learning could ever fall out of favor.[111] His work, not just as philosopher of Judaism but also as Bible scholar and translator, is applauded by Franz Rosenzweig in 1929 upon the bicentenary of Mendelssohn's birth.[112] A pattern of assimilation of the conventional interpretation has been subject to criticism in the light of the Holocaust. Writing in 1967, Michael A. Meyer in *Origins of the Modern Jew* characterizes Mendelssohn's position as "an ephemeral solution."[113] In US Jewish studies scholarship in the 1990s the interpretive possibilities are framed by the contributions of David Sorkin and Allan Arkush.[114]

Writing as historian of modern Judaism, David Sorkin has made an eloquent case that the "Mendelssohn myth" – the philosopher's thorough Germanification – has been shaped by scholars who are largely unfamiliar with Mendelssohn's writings in Hebrew on the way the early Haskalah draws from internal (not external German) Judaic sources.[115] Because of this scholarly lacuna, Sorkin maintains that extant accounts of Mendelssohn, including that of the late Alexander Altmann, are incomplete. Sorkin brings these Hebrew materials to bear on the study of *Jerusalem* and shows how those teachings present a Mendelssohn who is more complex than the legendary friend of Lessing and of the German Enlightenment. For Sorkin, the two Mendelssohns (the Judaic loyalist and the Enlightenment accommodator) are actually one and the same. But the translator of *Jerusalem*, Allan Arkush, maintains flatly that Mendelssohn's efforts to defend Judaism in his book were unsuccessful, while further claiming that Mendelssohn knew that this was the case. Arkush argues that Mendelssohn dissimulates, does not adequately defend Jewish tradition (especially against the attack of Spinoza), and capitulates

111 *Gedenkbuch für Moses Mendelssohn*, ed. Verband der Vereine für jüdische Geshichte und Literatur in Deutschland (Berlin: Verlag von M. Poppelauer, 1929); *Moses Mendelssohn: Zur 200 Jährigen Wiederkehr seines Geburtstages* (Berlin: L. Schneider, 1929); Moses Mendelssohn and Bertha Badt-Strauss, *Moses Mendelssohn: Der Mensch und das Werk* (Berlin: Heine-Bund, 1929).
112 Franz Rosenzweig, "Der Ewige: Mendelssohn und der Gottesname," in *Gedenkbuch für Moses Mendelssohn*, 96–114.
113 Meyer, *Origins of the Modern Jew*, 29–56. In the long term, of course, the products of history and culture, including monuments of religious thought, appear ephemeral and unstable, since they are subject to divergent readings.
114 Arkush, *Moses Mendelssohn and the Enlightenment*; Arkush "Questionable Judaism of Moses Mendelssohn," 29–44; David Sorkin, "The Case for Comparison: Moses Mendelssohn and the Religious Enlightenment," *Modern Judaism* 14 (1994): 121–38; "Sorkin, Mendelssohn Myth and its Method," 7–28; Sorkin, *Mendelssohn and the Religious Enlightenment*. See also Arkush's review of Sorkin's 1996 book in *Modern Judaism* 17 (1997): 179–85.
115 Sorkin, "Mendelssohn Myth and its Method," 7–28.

to the dominant cultural pressure of Kantian philosophy and Protestant Christianity by abdicating any responsibility for the commandments as a revealed Judaic teaching. Clearly Mendelssohn did not write the book that Arkush wanted him to write. Yet the way of reading with utter suspicion of Mendelssohn's stated views and arguments also has a cost: in this case it runs the risk of riding roughshod over a truly historical sense of Mendelssohn's place within German Jewry.

In *Rethinking Modern Judaism*, Arnold Eisen brings the tools of social science and anthropology to bear on *Jerusalem*. On this view "divine script" and "revealed legislation" become viable ways for Mendelssohn not just to cling to but to defend Jewish practice, while still being acculturated within the German setting. Eisen's account draws from a postmodern conviction that universal canons of reason cannot be developed.[116] Eisen's Mendelssohn develops a defense of Judaism that rests on recognizing its mythic force through community-building rituals. If Eisen is correct, debates about the rationality of religious belief are far less central than we are accustomed to think. Other ways of validating one's foundational life choices were also at hand, including the idea – seen in Schleiermacher as well as Mendelssohn – that religion is not just a "set of ideas" but is anchored in communal-historical existence.

Similar vagaries and shifts in the history of interpretation apply to Schleiermacher's *On Religion*.[117] Its fate at the hands of readers has always been varied. Like the interpretation of *Jerusalem*, the reasons for this situation have to do with the originality and design of the work as well as with the fact that it does not fit neatly into an established genre of religious expression. Neither strict philosophical argument nor a merely edifying document, *On Religion* has the twin marks of instability as well as durability. The same holds for *Jerusalem*. The instability of such texts constitutes an invitation to readers to return to them again and again, seeking to puzzle out their meaning. The fact that we continue to pour over such illustrious pieces of religious writing accounts for their durability. Neither Mendelssohn nor Schleiermacher can be considered an unassailable interpreter of his respective Jewish or Christian tradition. But each writer touches on the classical issues that make the study of such texts worthwhile.

---

116 Eisen, *Rethinking Modern Judaism*, draws from the reflexive sociology of Pierre Bourdeax and expresses suspicion about imposing the canons of Enlightenment rationality on the deeds and behavior of religious communities, in this case Judaism.
117 See chapter 11 for an analysis of these patterns of interpretation.

CHAPTER 3

Hegel and Schleiermacher at Berlin:
a many-sided debate

What separates both Hegel and Schleiermacher is still more often felt, or considered under relatively subordinate viewpoints that are governed by special interests, than it has been expressed with conceptual clarity.

Hermann Glockner (1920)

The differences between them here were not clear-cut logical disagreements but more matters of temperament and emphasis, differences which however have been historically decisive, as is clear from the development of German thought after their time.

Richard B. Brandt (1941)

Anyone who seeks to interpret the debate between Hegel and Schleiermacher would be well advised to issue a few qualifying remarks. When we decide to approach them in relation to each other we confront formidable interpretive obstacles, three of which I wish to mention at the outset.[1]

The first level of difficulty to be confronted by an interpreter of Hegel and Schleiermacher lies in the sheer complexity of their thought, which demands the utmost intellectual exertion. To this day settled interpretations of their work scarcely exist. Both figures have been interpreted, in quite opposite ways, as having advanced as well as having undermined the cause of Christian belief and Christian theology in the modern period.

A second set of difficulties might be called philological or textual. Both thinkers expressed themselves on relevant topics in a large number of texts, not all of which were published, some of which were revised more

---

1 Several major works of Hegel scholarship, which appeared since the original publication of this essay, are especially pertinent for this chapter. Peter C. Hodgson, ed., G. W. F. Hegel, *Lectures on the Philosophy of Religion*, vols. I–III, tr. R. F. Brown et al. (Berkeley: University of California Press, 1984–7); Cyril O'Regan, *The Heterodox Hegel* (Albany: State University of New York Press, 1994); Terry Pinkard, *Hegel: A Biography* (Cambridge: Cambridge University Press, 2000).

than once in their lifetimes, and for some of which there are as yet no truly adequate critical editions. Relevant material like Schleiermacher's *Dialektik* or Hegel's *Vorlesungen über die Religionsphilosophie* went through significant changes and alterations when delivered in lecture form. In both cases extant editions are based largely on student transcripts and editorial reconstructions. But it is not just the problem that some of the key materials needed for a full-scale, substantive comparison are inadequate for our purposes. In fact, there are no texts by Schleiermacher in which a critical review (and thus a potential refutation) of Hegel's work is given. Works that bear on their view of each other's work are more oblique than direct confrontations. In thirteen years of association at the same university, 1818–31, neither figure engaged the other in public debate or wrote a major critical review that names the other figure. We shall see that Hegel comes closer than Schleiermacher in publicly acknowledging the presence of the other figure by offering an explicit written critique. Though I shall argue that this criticism is significant and by no means a mere afterthought, such references constitute mere footnotes on the corpus of Hegel's work, taken as a whole. For his part, Schleiermacher's asseverations against Hegel are largely reserved for private communications, especially correspondence with fellow theologians in the German universities.

In addition to these difficulties (the sheer weight of their thought and the disparate nature of the sources at our disposal), further obstacles arise from the fact that their apparent differences are virtually institutionalized among working philosophers and theologians. Analyses of the Hegel–Schleiermacher relationship are, more often than not, marred by relatively uninformed prejudice and one-sided judgments. This is perhaps the strongest reason for attempting to clear the air by exploring their relationship in its historical setting. All too rarely does anyone approach them with equal enthusiasm and a sense of impartial objectivity. The reasons for this situation are perhaps obvious. For one thing, no metasystem is available to the philosophical or theological critic from which to launch a full-scale comparative analysis. More often than not Hegel's thought is used as a framework for the analysis of Schleiermacher. For example, Hermann Glockner, who is sympathetic towards Schleiermacher, takes Hegel's thought as the basis for the comparison since it is more systematic and conceptually clearer.[2] Lacking an appropriate framework or

2 Hermann Glockner, "Hegel und Schleiermacher im Kampf um Religionsphilosophie und Glaubenslehre," (1930) *Hegel-Studien*, Beiheft 2 (1965): 246–71.

metasystem, the tendency is to use the thought of one figure as the basis for criticism of the other. Given this approach, predictable conclusions emerge. This is all the more the case at points where we do not find analogous interests, for example, Hegel's lack of appreciation of a concern with the living church as community and practical theology and Schleiermacher's lack of concern with the finality of a system based on a dialectical logic.

What, then, is one to do in wishing to engage in comparative judgments about their teaching and work? By taking a historical approach to their relationship I hope to build a *prima facie* case for the impingement of the thought of the one figure on the thought of the other. This can be seen as a first step towards sorting out the thorny intellectual issues that divided them. I do not wish to argue that the substantive differences between them can be reduced to their individual biographies or, in the words of Richard Brandt, to their respective "temperaments."[3] We shall see that matters of taste, personal temperament, and bias enter strongly into their relationship at any number of points. But far from attempting to reduce their differences to these factors, what I am seeking to accomplish is to get clear on how the biographical-historical setting relates to their substantive differences.

The degree to which either Hegel or Schleiermacher had a genuine influence on the other figure is still today a moot question. In one sense I think it is clear that they did not influence each other. Neither thinker depended in a substantial way on the thought of the other in coming to his own position; in both instances they were fully formed and committed to their views prior to the call of Hegel to Berlin in 1818. Yet in another sense I believe there may well be a significant influence between them. In the decade of the 1820s each figure served tacitly as the intellectual foil for the work of the other. At the height of their careers it was virtually impossible for either figure to express his views on religion or philosophy without implicitly confronting the thought of the other figure.

In both instances their debate is filtered through other contemporaries. Each writes for an audience of theologians and philosophers that encompasses, but is not directly targeted at, the opposite figure in Berlin. Hegel's repeated criticism of philosophies of feeling and intuition is primarily aimed at F. H. Jacobi and J. F. Fries. But his need to refute their teaching

---

3 Richard B. Brandt, *The Philosophy of Schleiermacher* (1941) (Westport: Greenwood Press, 1968), 326.

is urged on by the belief that his Berlin colleague holds similar views. Conversely, during the 1820s Schleiermacher was frequently involved in debates (concerning liturgy, theological method, and dogmatics) with Philipp Marheineke. One suspects that his quarrel with Hegel was more directly expressed with his Hegelian colleague in his own department (with whom he shared the pulpit of the Trinity Church) than with Hegel himself. For want of space this secondary level of the confrontation is largely omitted from the present essay.

Faced with these obstacles, one might argue that the relationship between Hegel and Schleiermacher is virtually an irresolvable puzzle and should simply be let well alone. On this view they were like ships (albeit large and impressive ones) passing in the night. Such a stance, however, strikes me as unsatisfactory for several reasons, the chief of which is that the masters of these ships knew that, far from just passing, they were contending for the same open seas. We do well to remind ourselves that, despite their problematic relationship and many-sided differences, Hegel and Schleiermacher held certain views in common that are today often called radically into question or viewed with indifference. Both figures are part of that "new epoch" admirably sketched by Charles Taylor in his book on Hegel.[4] Their commonly held beliefs include: first, that the university is not only a significant place of learning but also a major force in shaping and not just in reacting to currents of modern culture; second, that there could and must be a new accommodation between traditional religious and Christian teaching and modern thought, including humanistic as well as natural scientific inquiry; and third, that the work of Immanuel Kant, which sought to reconcile us to the world by defining the limits of pure reason, was incomplete and must be supplanted by new efforts at synthesis and system-building. By disavowing knowledge of things in themselves, full comprehension of the world and of one's relationship to the world, not to mention knowledge of God, was denied to humanity.

In view of these shared assumptions Hegel and Schleiermacher appear to have disagreed more about means than about ends or goals. The sibling nature of their rivalry must be kept in mind as we go about the task of relating them to each other and assessing the nature of their differences.

---

4 Charles Taylor, *Hegel* (Cambridge: Cambridge University Press, 1975), 3–50.

EARLY ENCOUNTERS AND FORESHADOWING OF DIFFERENCES

As nearly exact contemporaries Hegel and Schleiermacher were vitally involved in the wave of German intellectual reassessments that followed the French revolution and Napoleonic conquest of Europe. Central to this reassessment were questions about the role and meaning of religion in the modern world and its relationship to traditional Christian teaching. Wilhelm Dilthey, who wrote on the young Hegel as well as the young Schleiermacher, maintains that their views in the period around 1800 were not so far apart.[5] Dilthey calls attention to a passage in the fragmentary essay from the Frankfurt period, the "system-fragment of 1800," in which Hegel says that religion "makes no claim to be rational or reasonable." By acknowledging that there is a dimension of religion that is not to be fathomed by rational categories Hegel seems to be at one with the young Schleiermacher. But this commonality is illusory. The context of the remark makes it clear that Hegel has something else in mind. Though religion by itself may "make no claim to be rational or reasonable," it would be folly for philosophy to make such a claim on behalf of religion. Hegel foreshadows his mature position when he argues that "divine feeling, where the infinite is felt by the finite, is only completed by the fact that reflection is added to it and holds sway over it."[6] By asserting not just that religion is rooted in the nonrational but that reflection and reason must be added for its fullest expression, Hegel points to and anticipates his later criticism of Schleiermacher.

At the same time, however, Dilthey is not entirely mistaken in arguing that the two thinkers shared a great deal in that early period. Each sought to address the same set of issues: the relationships between religion, philosophy, politics, ethics, and the arts. Both thinkers enjoyed long scholarly apprenticeships during part of which they served as house tutors for the aristocracy. It is natural for us to ask when they first became aware of each other and what their initial reactions were.

In his early theological essays Hegel was searching for a view of religion as the inner power of communal forms of life that would unify a modern political community much as the Greek polis was illumined and shaped by Greek myth. Not surprisingly, he came to criticize the author of *On Religion* along similar lines in his first philosophical publications. Though

---

5 Wilhelm Dilthey, *Die Jugendgeschichte Hegels* (Leipzig: B. G. Teubner, 1921) [*Gesammelte Schriften* 4], 149f.

6 G. W. F. Hegel, *Werke 1: Frühe Schriften*, ed. Eva Moldenhauer and Karl Markus Michel (Frankfurt-on-Main: Suhrkamp, 1971), 423.

Schleiermacher's speeches on religion were originally published anonymously, the author's identity was widely known. What Hegel thinks of the speeches is expressed in the preface to his first published essay, *The Difference between Fichte's and Schelling's System of Philosophy*, written in Jena (1801):

> A phenomenon such as the *Speeches on Religion* may not immediately concern the speculative need. Yet they and their reception – and even more so the dignity that is beginning to be accorded, more or less clearly or obscurely, to poetry and art in general in all their true scope – indicate the need for a philosophy that will recompense nature for the mishandling that it suffered in Kant and Fichte's systems, and set reason itself in harmony with nature, not by having reason renounce itself or become an insipid imitator of nature, but by reason recasting itself into nature out of its own inner strength.[7]

Far from being critical, Hegel views the youthful work of his contemporary as an important expression of the age's longing for an adequate understanding of religion and the relationship between man and nature. Hegel is also aware that the first book of Schleiermacher was having a mighty reception among his contemporaries. He believes that *On Religion* confirms the direction of his own work and points to the need for his own philosophy. Hegel cites the text the way a philosopher might call attention to a contemporary literary statement that, to some extent, corroborates his view of the situation that they share as thinkers. He is not overtly hostile, accords a certain respect to *On Religion*, and tacitly acknowledges a common goal.

Yet even at this early stage caveats distinguish Hegel's position from that of Schleiermacher. One must imagine that Hegel gave the speeches a more critical reading during the next year. In *Faith and Knowledge* (1802) his remarks about the speeches are circumspect and point to their subsequent parting of the ways. At the end of a section in which he criticizes the intuitional philosophy of F. H. Jacobi, Hegel expresses concern about Schleiermacher's reliance on intuition and the individuality of the subject-knower who has these intuitions.[8] He correctly sees that *On Religion* argues for a full-blown religious personality that embodies individual genius, talent, artistry, and a dialectical mode of aesthetic and religious creativity. His basic point is that Schleiermacher's notion of religion is

---

7 G. W. F. Hegel, *The Difference between Fichte's and Schelling's System of Philosophy*, tr. H. S. Harris and W. Cerf (Albany: State University of New York Press, 1977), 83.
8 G. W. F. Hegel, *Faith and Knowledge*, tr. H. S. Harris and W. Cerf (Albany: State University of New York Press, 1977).

rooted in a subjective experience that is in danger of never attaining an adequate objective embodiment. If the analogy with the arts is taken seriously, and Hegel does perceive that Schleiermacher means it to be taken seriously, we are in a situation in which "art is supposed to be forever without works of art; and the freedom of the highest intuition is supposed to consist in singularity and the possession of personal originality." By pressing the artistic analogy Hegel hopes to show that Schleiermacher's synthesis is inherently unstable. The religious individual as artist has his own soul, but no manifest work of art. Yet the world of culture requires not just souls but works of art as their objectification. The connection with nature and the universe seems tenuous if no adequate public embodiment of private religiosity exists. Hegel apparently reads the fourth speech as positing religious communities as passive entities that require the active virtuosity of a preacher or poet for their sustenance and inspiration.

Hegel's interpretation of *On Religion* is plausible and has some basis in the text. Yet it overlooks the crucial point, that Schleiermacher in fact considers the sermon as the embodiment of a Christian art form. A good sermon, for him, is itself a religious work of art and, against Hegel, it occurs in a publicly manifest church as a worshipping community. For all of Schleiermacher's individualism in *On Religion*, the social and communal dimensions are necessary links between the second and fifth speeches. Hegel's charge of an unwarranted subjectivism reflects a different view of how religious community relates to politics. For Schleiermacher, the church as true religious community has its own reason for existence as an institution of human redemption that, as a matter of principle, is independent from the state.[9] Schleiermacher was later often at odds with the established church of Prussia as well as with Hegel (and his theological colleagues) on just this point. By contrast, Hegel emphasized the public role of religion in the context of the educative and moral life of the state. In Hegel's initial reception of *On Religion* we can glimpse levels of criticism that later became more pronounced. For his part we do well to remind ourselves that Schleiermacher never disassociated himself from *On Religion*. Rather than renounce it as a "youthful work," Schleiermacher chose to update it (revised in 1806 and 1821; reissued in 1831) by modifying its language and adding explanatory notes that relate its content to his current reflection. In his own later scheme for ordering theological

9 Robert M. Bigler, *The Politics of German Protestantism: The Rise of the Protestant Church Elite in Prussia 1814–1848* (Berkeley: University of California Press, 1972), 161f.

studies, *On Religion* falls into the category of "philosophical theology."[10] But for the present we must remain with their early encounter.

Since the early Hegel associates Schleiermacher with Jacobi's philosophy of feeling, we may pause here to examine this association and to ask whether it has any basis in fact. Jacobi appears to have made no formal reply to Hegel's attack on his teaching in *Faith and Knowledge*. Writing to his fellow philosopher in Kiel, K. L. Reinhold, he complains that Hegel has attempted to characterize his work as "romantic" by mentioning Herder and Schleiermacher, whereas Jacobi saw his work as having a more strict philosophic interest.[11] Hegel's juxtaposition of *On Religion* with Jacobi was not without a private reaction from Schleiermacher. Commenting to his lifelong friend Karl Gustav von Brinckmann, Schleiermacher regrets that Jacobi did not respond to Hegel's remarks.[12] He is interested in knowing how Jacobi sees *On Religion*, tells Brinckmann that he likes Jacobi very much, and regrets that his admiration is not reciprocated. Schleiermacher appears to admire Jacobi and even sees himself as the proper heir (though also the reviser) of a "philosophy of faith." At the time Jacobi was an established man of letters, better known than Hegel or Schleiermacher, who stood in the vanguard of German culture. Schleiermacher's admiration appears not to have slackened in this early period. This is not to say that he sought to make himself a slavish imitator of Jacobi. At one point he complains about Jacobi's desire for a circle of worshipping disciples (*Jüngersucht*) and asserts that a desire for true followers creates a situation of intellectual slavery.[13] But Schleiermacher nonetheless admires Jacobi for his genial manner of philosophizing and for making Hume's English empiricism known in Germany.

Schleiermacher had hoped to dedicate the first edition of his dogmatics, *The Christian Faith*, to Jacobi, but dropped the idea when Jacobi died in 1819.[14] By 1818 Schleiermacher's self-confidence had emerged so that he could now engage Jacobi directly in an exchange of views on the relationship between faith and philosophy. Hans-Joachim Birkner warns against our making Schleiermacher's much-cited letter to Jacobi (March 30, 1818) into a programmatic statement of how its author views the relationship

---

10 Hans-Joachim Birkner, "Theologie und Philosophie: Einführung in Probleme der Schleiermacher-Interpretation," (1974) in *Schleiermacher-Studien*, ed. Hermann Fischer (Berlin: Walter de Gruyter, 1996), 174.
11 Nicolin, #65.
12 Ibid., #74.   13 Ibid., #77.
14 Martin Redeker, ed., Friedrich Schleiermacher, *Der christliche Glaube*, vols. I–II (Berlin: Walter de Gruyter, 1960), I, XXVI.

between theology and philosophy.[15] Personal letters ought not to carry the weight of formal expressions of thought. But in view of our interest in his relationship to Jacobi, and Hegel's criticism of him in this regard, the letter deserves scrutiny.

The occasion for the letter to Jacobi was an earlier response in which Jacobi sought to explain his philosophic stance to Schleiermacher. Jacobi sent along part of a letter to K. L. Reinhold in which he claims that he is a pagan with his understanding but a Christian with his feeling, thus swimming between two seas, which he does not wish to unify out of fear of self-deception.[16] Schleiermacher's rejoinder reveals his thought on this question at the time he was writing the first edition of his dogmatics.

Schleiermacher's position attempts to avoid the dualism that led Jacobi to say that he is a pagan with his understanding but a Christian with his feeling. He also wishes to avoid moving towards a speculative philosophical synthesis in the manner of Hegel. Against Jacobi, Schleiermacher asks, "If your feeling is Christian, how can your understanding interpret in a pagan manner?" Just as feeling and understanding cannot be merged, they can also not be held apart. Both are on an equal footing as they stand in the field of religion and they make equal claims. Religiosity or piety is a matter of feeling, he writes further, but in contrast, what we call religion, which is always more or less a matter of dogmatics, only arises through the interpretation of understanding which rests on this feeling. To Jacobi's admission that "I am a pagan with my understanding," Schleiermacher asserts, "I am a philosopher with my understanding." For him philosophy is a neutral category and constitutes an interpreting and translating agency for the claims of religious feeling, but not so distinct from this feeling as to be in opposition to it. Even Hegel, in 1802, was aware of distinctions between the two thinkers. He rightly saw that Jacobi orients the capacity of understanding around material, finite objects, whereas Schleiermacher has a higher conception of the capacity of understanding to assist in the reconciliation with nature and with the universe as a whole.[17]

Against Hegel, Schleiermacher wishes to be conscious of a divine spirit within him that is other than his own reason and against Jacobi he claims he "will never give up seeking out this [spirit] in the deepest depths of the nature of the soul."[18] Schleiermacher admonishes Jacobi not to be alarmed

---

15 Birkner, "Theologie and Philosophie," 183–5.
16 H. Bolli, ed., *Schleiermacher-Auswahl* (Munich: Siebenstern Taschenbuch Verlag, 1968), 116–19.
17 *Faith and Knowledge*, 150–2.
18 Bolli, *Schleiermacher-Auswahl*, 117.

by the apparent duality of human experience; such oscillations between polarities of our experience are real and present to us, yet are not to be viewed as respectively pagan and Christian. Foreshadowing the mature formulations of *The Christian Faith*, Schleiermacher writes that there is "an immediate consciousness" out of which both our feelings and our understanding flow. Oscillation is characteristic of finite life. His first speech in 1799 argues against the expectation of a false equilibrium between the "opposing forces" of the universe.[19] Now, in 1818, he makes the same point against Jacobi by saying that his dogmatics and his philosophy will never be completed, even though they are gradually defined ever more closely together. When Jacobi proposes that we exist with a view of nature as deified or opt for a Socratic-Platonic anthropomorphism as mutually exclusive alternatives, Schleiermacher responds by arguing that even in Jacobi a deification of consciousness occurs. Schleiermacher stops short of acknowledging the necessary involvement of deity in our experience at the point where we try to define and conceptualize this involvement. "We cannot conceive of a real idea of the highest being," he writes,

All real philosophy consists only in the insight that this inexpressible truth of the highest essence lies at the basis of all our thinking and experience, and the development of this insight is itself that very thing which, according to my conviction, Plato construed as Dialectic. I don't believe we can get further than this.[20]

Though he does not wish to unify the two seas of human experience, Schleiermacher, unlike Jacobi, is not pained or troubled by the apparent bifurcation of reality. "Understanding and feeling also remain for him alongside each other, but they touch each other and form a galvanic pile."[21] The metaphor of a galvanic pile may fall a good deal short of the comprehensive grasp of the self-unfolding divine spirit that lies at the heart of Hegelian dialectic. Yet Schleiermacher, by appealing to such a unity and a synthesizing activity (at some level of human consciousness) and by his avowed interest in following the divine into the depths and nature of the human mind, takes a position against Jacobi that

19 *OR* (Crouter), 5.
20 Bolli, *Schleiermacher-Auswahl*, 119.
21 The image of electricity generated from a galvanic pile was fresh in Schleiermacher's day, the procedure having been invented around the time of his birth by the Italian anatomist Luigi Galvani. On Schleiermacher's use of physical metaphors, see Terry H. Forman, "Schleiermacher's 'Natural History of Religion': Science and the Interpretation of Culture in the Speeches," *Journal of Religion* 58/2 (1978): 91–107.

acknowledges the legitimacy of the fundamental tendency of Hegel. Schleiermacher, it appears, has the same difficulty defining his position over against current philosophies of feeling and intuition that he has in differentiating himself from his romanticizing literary colleagues. The fact that he does have this independence of mind makes his relationship with Hegel all the more interesting and all the more difficult to define.

HEGEL'S CALL TO BERLIN

A gymnasial rector in Nürnberg in 1814, Hegel hoped that he might soon obtain a regular university appointment. His friend and fellow student in the Tübingen-Stift, Heinrich Paulus, wrote to him about the vacant chair of philosophy and the divided mind at Berlin over the appointment of a successor to Fichte.[22] Paulus reports to Hegel that de Wette, a popular colleague of Schleiermacher who taught biblical exegesis and historical theology, favored his old teacher J. F. Fries for the position. The pejorative image of Schleiermacher's work is readily apparent from Paulus' remarks to Hegel:

de Wette has decided in favor of Fries' doctrine of faith and presentiment, but he [Fries] has so much scholarship that it would be hard for him to play in the hands of Schleiermacher's religion without morality and without belief, notwithstanding the fact that presentiment [*Ahnen*] could be for both of them a comfortable commonplace that they could mutually share.

Apart from Fries (whose work is known today mainly through Rudolf Otto), the other chief contender for the chair of philosophy was Hegel, whose reputation, based on the *Phenomenology of Spirit* and *Logic*, was already becoming well established.

As maneuvering towards the appointment progressed, de Wette wrote to his teacher, Fries, about how his colleague in theology, Philipp Marheineke, was trying to get Hegel invited as Fichte's successor.[23] Meanwhile, Schleiermacher's close associate and eventual successor, August Twesten, wrote to him (in June 1815) complaining about the lack of intelligibility of Hegel's Objective Logic (part one of the Logic).[24]

Schleiermacher responds to the observation that Hegel's logic is a piece of legerdemain (*Taschenspielerei*) by saying that he has not yet seen it himself but that, judging by reviews, he has a similar impression.[25]

22 Hoffmeister, #236.   23 Nicolin, #176.   24 Ibid., #168.
25 Ibid., #16.

Though aware of the work of Hegel, the extent to which Schleiermacher ever actually read and studied the key philosophic works is, as far as I can tell, still an open question. When contemplating Hegel as a future colleague in 1815, Schleiermacher had reason to see in him a challenge to his own mode of thought and his sense of the tasks of theological teaching in relation to philosophy.

One must take care, however, not to exaggerate the differences between them or their status relative to each other at this moment in their careers. It is difficult to imagine that the remarks Hegel made about *On Religion* were damaging in a sense that would cause Schleiermacher difficulty. Schleiermacher was well aware of the rhetorical nature of that work and had already taken care to revise the work considerably; in a few years he would give it a still more "scientific" cast and relate its teaching directly to his dogmatics. More germane to the Hegel appointment is the fact that, as early as his March 1810 acceptance speech as a member of the Berlin Academy of Sciences, Schleiermacher maintained that the academy was better suited to study philosophy historically and critically than it was for establishing new systems of philosophy.[26] Yet there is no evidence that Schleiermacher wanted to ban systematic philosophy from the university. Such a stance was contrary to his liberal conception of the university set forth in his programmatic paper of 1808, at the time of the founding of the University of Berlin.[27]

Hence, despite indications that there were serious intellectual differences between himself and Hegel, Schleiermacher, much to the displeasure of his friend and colleague de Wette, voted to call Hegel to the chair of philosophy.[28] At the same time there is little doubt that Schleiermacher's action was intended as much to head off Fries' chances as it was from genuine enthusiasm for Hegel. Since there was an apparent need for speculative philosophy to be represented at Berlin, Hegel was the most promising candidate for the job. Schleiermacher was at the height of mid-career and continued to attract more and more theological students. His colleagues consisted of de Wette, A. W. Neander in church history, and Marheineke, his colleague in theology who, to Schleiermacher's disappointment, emerged among the theologians a firm champion of Hegel.

The faculty senate proposed Hegel's name on January 4, 1816, but by October the appointment had not been officially approved. Schleiermacher

26 *KGA*, I/11, *Akademievorträge*, ed. Martin Rössler, 5.
27 See below, chapter 6.   28 Nicolin, #174.

suggested to a friend that the Minister of Culture would have to bear the blame if they should lose Hegel, adding, "God only knows what is to become of our university if it continues to lack philosophers."[29] During this time of vacillation on the appointment Hegel received and accepted a call to Heidelberg, so that it was another two years before the move to Berlin took place. In March 1818 Schleiermacher wrote (with apparent pleasure) to a friend: "Now it's decided, we're getting Hegel and a very strong possibility also of getting A. W. Schlegel. I'm curious to see how both of them will make out."[30] Schleiermacher mused in private over the imagined relationship between Hegel and A. W. Schlegel; but Schlegel eventually went to Bonn. Meanwhile, others were preoccupied with similar imaginings, but focused on his own relationship with Hegel. Having failed to win the appointment for his old teacher, de Wette wrote to Fries in April 1818: "Hegel is coming here. I'm not afraid of him. I now have too much influence among the students of my faculty, and Schleiermacher certainly eclipses him too much."[31] The remark is revealing. It illustrates de Wette's concern for his personal security as well as a belief that Schleiermacher would be more than a match for Hegel. In Heidelberg, Hegel's old university, his former colleagues wondered about how his relationship with Schleiermacher would develop.[32]

The actual stage for the coming together of Hegel and Schleiermacher in Berlin was set as much by the Ministry of Culture under Karl von Altenstein as it was by rival parties within the faculty. Altenstein was aware of a close-knit faculty group that was gathered around Schleiermacher and other colleagues who had been present at the inception of the university. He wished to bring to Berlin a strong philosopher of independent views who would serve as a counterbalance to this group of professors. In this aim Altenstein clearly succeeded. Hegel appears to have known nothing of this underlying administrative plan.[33] Meanwhile, Schleiermacher's faithful friend Twesten, always a persistent "Hegel-watcher," complained again to Schleiermacher about Hegel's Logic, adding, "What a completely different spirit there is in your dialectic than in this logic!"[34]

POLITICAL DIFFERENCES

Published correspondence and the memoirs of contemporaries permit us to glimpse the unfolding drama that began in 1818 with Hegel's arrival in

29 Ibid., #191.   30 Ibid., #256.   31 Ibid., #262.   32 Ibid., #281.
33 Ibid., #316 and #709.   34 Ibid., #306.

Berlin, the stronghold of Schleiermacher's theological influence. I have noted that Hegel's early view of *On Religion* foreshadows a difference in political attitudes. These issues came almost immediately to a head at a time when Hegel was completing the *Philosophy of Right*, his major work of moral-political teaching. Politics thus provided the occasion for the first overt rupture of an outwardly cordial, though always official, relationship.

It is worth recalling that in their youth both figures directly witnessed the power unleashed by the French revolution. Each taught briefly at a university that was forcibly closed when overrun by Napoleon (Halle and Jena in 1806). Each knew the revolutionary ferment of his age at first hand, felt the lack of national culture and unity of the German people, and sought throughout his life to relate his teaching and writing to the service of German culture.

The theme of Hegel and the modern state has been much discussed by scholars, and a full airing of it lies beyond our present interests. It will suffice to observe that Hegel must be acquitted of the older charge of being the father of modern political absolutism. It is not my aim to give currency to this charge if I point out that, relatively speaking, Hegel's view of the power and authority of the state and its bearing on religious life is more conservative than Schleiermacher's. Early in his publications Schleiermacher, reflecting his early upbringing among the Moravians, saw that religious life needs a degree of independence in relation to the state. Though his personal confession was Reformed, his teaching on church and state at times approximates a sharply delineated version of Luther's two-realms doctrine. There must be some basis for religious values, as well as for a religious community whose life is inviolable and allowed to freely unfold in relationship with, but not subordinated to, the state. Such themes occur early in his work, are vigorously attested to by passages from the third and fourth speeches, and remain throughout his lifetime. By contrast, Hegel sees religious life more tightly bound up with the state, virtually as the realm of inner meaning and spiritual direction of the nation. If we differentiate them by asking what each thinker takes as the primary community to which his thought is directed, then I believe that the church occupies the place in Schleiermacher that the state eventually assumes for Hegel.

The immediate setting for the public rupture of their relationship was the political activity of professors and students in the wake of tendencies towards reaction that followed upon Napoleon's stunning victories. Schleiermacher promoted the far-reaching reforms of Baron von Stein that envisaged eventual representative power in a political assembly under the monarchy, the emancipation of the Jews, and other measures. But the reform movement of Stein was short-lived and fell on deaf ears after 1812. Student gatherings of fraternities and gymnastic clubs were suspected of promoting romantic and radical political thinking and rekindling the original impetus of the revolution. Professors who associated with the student movement also came under suspicion. In this setting a situation developed as a result of which de Wette, the liberal colleague of Schleiermacher opposed to the call of Hegel, came to be dismissed from the university.

In his *Philosophy of Right* (1821) Hegel, a son of Swabia, criticized the rise of student fraternities in Prussia. He focuses his attack on the philosophy and political activities of Fries, who took part in a student festival on the Wartburg and actively encouraged radical sentiment among students. In his analysis of these events Schlomo Avineri writes that Hegel "attempts to point out how a subjectivist philosophy may lead to romantic political terrorism and the loss of any rational criterion for the discussion of public and social life."[35] Underscoring the point that the German student fraternities were not harmless social clubs, Avineri notes that

The truth of the matter is that in their ideology and actions these fraternities prefigured the most dangerous and hideous aspects of extreme German nationalism. To present their aim as merely agitation for German unification is simple-minded: they were the most chauvinistic element in German society. They excluded foreigners from their ranks, refused to accept Jewish students as members and participated in the antisemitic outbursts in Frankfurt in 1819.[36]

Thus, it was not as an alarmist or reactionary that Hegel engaged in criticism of these clubs. In this situation, a member of a Jena fraternity named Karl Sand, who was also a student of theology, murdered the journalist and poet August von Kotzebue, whom the students suspected of being a Russian agent. The case inflamed passions on all sides. What began as a student affair quickly became an affair of state that encompassed the universities. Immediate demands for action against the student movements were heard within the Prussian court and educational ministry.

35 Schlomo Avineri, *Hegel's Theory of the Modern State* (Cambridge: Cambridge University Press, 1972), 119.
36 Ibid.; see also Pinkard, *Hegel*, 435–47.

As a sympathizer of the student cause (though without wishing to condone an act of murder), the Berlin theologian de Wette wrote a letter of condolence to Sand's mother in which he suggested that Sand's motives were pure. Such were the events in progress as Hegel finished the *Philosophy of Right*. It was natural for Hegel to take a stand on these events in the preface to that work, where he blames both Fries and de Wette for fomenting student extremism and for advocating a romantic and subjectivist ethic.[37]

By implication, Schleiermacher also came in for criticism, first, because of his close association with de Wette and the student movement and, second, because of his defense of Friedrich Schlegel's experimental novel, *Lucinde*, a work that appeared to assault the moral order by claiming that true romantic love may be sufficient grounds for legitimating sexual relations.[38] Though tame by today's standards, Schlegel's *Lucinde* is among the first modern books in which a known author reveals his own behavior in the bedroom. Kierkegaard found it quite obscene and distasteful and I suspect it may have formed part of the material upon which Kierkegaard drew when he conceived "The Diary of the Seducer" in *Either/Or*.[39]

Amid this cluster of interrelated issues the main lines of a confrontation between Hegel and Schleiermacher were drawn. In fact, during his Heidelberg professorship Hegel had been a champion of student clubs. One student even reports that in Berlin Schleiermacher, Hegel, and de Wette were all three present at a student festival where wine-drinking and singing alternated with speeches and vigorous discussion of the Kotzebue affair. On this occasion a young Hegel student took the position that while there would be no raising of their glasses in honor of Sand, one should nonetheless "let evil fall where it shall, only without a dagger."[40] The professors are said to have been quite as jubilant as the students. If we judge by his subsequent actions and attitudes, Hegel must have been quite uncomfortable in that setting. In official circles such gatherings were coming increasingly under suspicion. The days of revolutionary fervor were now met with a more forceful hand.

---

37 *Philosophy of Right*, tr. T. M. Knox (Oxford: Clarendon Press, 1952), 5–6 and paragraphs 126, 140; See Hoffmeister, II, 218–19.
38 On this topic see below, chapter 4.
39 *Philosophy of Right*, 263; Søren Kierkegaard, *The Concept of Irony*, tr. Lee Capel (Bloomington: Indiana University Press, 1965), 302–16.
40 Nicolin, #295 and #296.

For his questionable judgment in the Kotzebue affair the theologian de Wette was dismissed from the faculty by the government (September 1819). A storm of protest ensued, with Hegel defending the right of the university to dismiss him on the grounds that a professor as a state official can hardly be allowed to condone an act of murder. Hegel insisted, however, that de Wette be permitted to draw a portion of his salary. When this failed to materialize a number of professors, including Hegel and Schleiermacher, contributed towards de Wette's support during the first year of his dismissal.

Differences over the dismissal of de Wette occasioned a note-worthy public exchange between Hegel and Schleiermacher in which Schleiermacher charged his colleague with having shown a pitiful (*erbärmlich*) attitude towards de Wette. Sharp words were exchanged on a social occasion. Schleiermacher, realizing he had been intemperate, sent a conciliatory note to Hegel that also contained the address of a good wine merchant (at least one substance they could agree upon as being of the highest significance). Schleiermacher added his hope that they could continue the dispute at the point where it stood before his own harsh words and Hegel's rejoinder were uttered, "For I have too much esteem for you not to want to reach an understanding with you on a topic which is of such great importance in our present situation."[41] In his response, Hegel writes:

I thank you, my esteemed colleague, in the first place for the address of the wine merchant contained in your note of yesterday; – as well for the expression, which, in putting aside a recent unpleasant incident between us and transmitting the response that arose in my own excitement, has left me with a decided increase in my admiration of you. It is, as you note, the present importance of the subject that led me to initiate a dispute on a social occasion, which to be able to continue with you and bring our views into an accommodation can be nothing else than interesting.[42]

The formal expressions of cordiality, however, did not translate into a meeting of minds. The outburst of hostility signaled to their contemporaries that there was little possibility for substantive agreement between them.

Among their respective students, the divergence of the masters' positions was acutely felt. Tension between them could hardly go unnoticed.

41 Hoffmeister, #361, see also #362.
42 Karl Rosenkranz, *G. W. F. Hegels Leben* (1844), third edition (Darmstadt: Wissenschaftliche Buchgesellschaft, 1971), 326.

In addition to the actual clash of positions taken in their lectures, the university was rife with rumors about their relationship. Writing home in November 1818, Richard Rothe reported, "Hegel is said to be very much down on Schleiermacher, but Schleiermacher is supposed to have provided the immediate occasion."[43] In government circles and at court there were rumors that Hegel and Schleiermacher had come near to a duel during their exchange of words. Report of open hostility between them was sent from as far away as Breslau by one of Schleiermacher's friends. Writing from Weimar after his dismissal, de Wette complains to Schleiermacher about the negative references in Hegel's *Philosophy of Right*, adding that as far as Fries is concerned, he is sorry that Schleiermacher and other well-intentioned persons have done him an injustice.[44] The tone of his letter suggests that de Wette now expects Schleiermacher to regret having voted in favor of Hegel's appointment. De Wette's early anxiety in regard to the coming of Hegel to Berlin was more than justified by subsequent events. Whatever may have been the personal or intellectual shortcomings of de Wette – it does not seem germane to attempt to estimate them – his dismissal from the theological faculty left Schleiermacher without the support of a valued colleague. When we reflect that the eventual successor to his position was the conservative biblicist Ernst Wilhelm Hengstenberg, it appears that Schleiermacher also emerged on the losing side of the Kotzebue affair.

THE ACADEMY OF SCIENCES

Schleiermacher's role in excluding Hegel from the Berlin Academy of Sciences, possibly even more than their political differences, contributed to Hegel's ill will towards him. The exclusion of Hegel from this august group was no momentary affair; its effect was felt throughout his career and tended to freeze his problematic relationship to Schleiermacher by the erection of a significant institutional barrier.

As noted, Schleiermacher's March 1810 acceptance speech before the academy spoke against systematic philosophy and in favor of the historical-critical approach to philosophy as appropriate to be represented in the academy.[45] At the time of Hegel's arrival in Berlin this sentiment was shared by a majority of academy members. His influential colleague in classical philology, August Boeckh, rested the case against speculative systems of philosophy on two grounds: (1) the nature of speculative

---

43 Nicolin, #309.   44 Ibid., #332.   45 *KGA*, 1/11, 1–7.

88   FRIEDRICH SCHLEIERMACHER

philosophy is such that it is more self-contained than other disciplines and
thus has no need of collegial work, the fostering of which is the stated
purpose of the academy; and (2) where philosophy should be represented
in the academy, it can already be represented in the philological and
historical disciplines.[46]

In his magisterial history of the academy, Adolph von Harnack maintains that the hostility between Hegel and Schleiermacher did not
occur until after Hegel's arrival in Berlin and takes pains to point
out that Hegel was named Ordinarius in the summer of 1818 at the
behest of Schleiermacher, who was then rector. Harnack believes that
Schleiermacher's opposition to Hegel's admission to the academy rests
more on the earlier stated policy of members (a policy established in
the days of Fichte) than on personal antipathy or rivalry. Yet once both
were together in Berlin, Schleiermacher was firm in his resolve to keep
Hegel out of the academy. Whatever motives we may attribute to
Schleiermacher, the exclusion of Hegel from so significant a body of
scholars was sure to have major repercussions within the faculty. This
was especially the case since Altenstein, acting as minister of culture, had
assured Hegel of membership in the academy when arranging the call
from Heidelberg. Altenstein protested in vain about the exclusion and the
formal means of bringing it about by abolishing the philosophical division of an academy that was honored to have had G. W. Leibniz as its
first president.

Consistent with the principles invoked against Hegel, Schleiermacher
dropped his own membership in the philosophical division and hence-
forth presented his papers (on Greek philosophy, ethics, and the New
Testament) in the historical and philological sections. He had been
flexible on the original appointment. But he drew the line on the
question of Hegel's participation in the academy. According to Harnack,
"Schleiermacher feared the despotism of Hegelian philosophy and at least
the Academy was to be kept free of it."[47] There may indeed be more to
the story yet to be uncovered. But it would seem as if an academy of
sciences must want to be open to all perspectives in the university if it
hopes to fulfill its purposes of contributing to an advancement of learning. One can only imagine the sorts of questions that Hegel would have
raised about the dominance of historical-critical and philological inquiry,
had he been able to be present on those occasions.

46 Adolph von Harnack, *Geschichte der königlich preussichen Akademie der Wissenschaft zu Berlin*, 1/2
   (Berlin: Reichsdruckerei, 1900), 692–3.
47 Ibid., 785.

From the point of view of Hegel's impact on the university and his following among students, his exclusion from the academy had no real effect. In the next decade he engaged in a countermove by founding a scholarly society that published the *Journal of the Society for Scientific Criticism.*[48] Though not intended as an alternative to the older, prestigious academy, this organization soon constituted a rival group of scholars (some with dual memberships) with Hegel as its acknowledged leader. Activities of this new scholarly society differed from the academy in two ways. First, it was under the Ministry of Culture rather than the university, and second, it sought to be more active than the academy in promoting scholarly views on questions of importance. Since the society was not related to the university, its membership was not restricted to Berlin.[49] By January 1828 the society included Wilhelm von Humboldt, A. W. Schlegel, Goethe, and Hegel's former Heidelberg colleague, the mythologist F. W. Creuzer.

When the name of Schleiermacher was proposed for membership Hegel said that he would withdraw if Schleiermacher were admitted.[50] Such a response was not unexpected in view of Schleiermacher's part in excluding him from the academy. If we ask what light their mutual exclusions throw on the overall relationship between Hegel and Schleiermacher, one point stands out clearly. The rival groups of scholars functioned as formal barriers between the two thinkers and were a continuous source of friction. Since persons in Hegel's society were held together by their mutual enthusiasm for Hegelian philosophy, Schleiermacher's suspicion about the imperialism of speculative philosophy was doubtless reinforced. The episode also illustrates that Schleiermacher's natural affinity was with the historians, linguists, and philologians. In his effort to exclude Hegel he appears to have acted in defense of an honorable concept of the university as an open, pluralistic marketplace of competing viewpoints. It is ironic that Schleiermacher's action and that of the other academy members erected a barrier that worked against his concept of the university as an open, inclusive scholarly community.

HEGEL'S CRITIQUE OF SCHLEIERMACHER'S DOGMATICS

Shortly after Hegel's arrival in Berlin, Schleiermacher was earnestly at work on his dogmatic theology (*Glaubenslehre/The Christian Faith*),

48 Max A. Lenz, *Geschichte der königlichen Friedrich-Wilhelms-Universität zu Berlin* (Halle: Verlag der Buchhandlung des Waisenhauses, 1910), 291–312.
49 Nicolin, #486.   50 Ibid.

intended as a system of Christian teaching for the United Evangelical Church of Prussia. His colleagues de Wette and Marheineke had already published their dogmatics and Schleiermacher's friends in the theological world urged him to get his work into print.[51] Due to the novelty of his treatment that he fully recognized, Schleiermacher fell far behind his original estimates of time needed to complete the project. Over a year elapsed between the publication of parts 1 and 2 of the first edition, issued in May 1821 and August 1822.[52] Publication of part 1 of the *Glaubenslehre* was the occasion for an impassioned outburst from Hegel that makes their debates over student fraternities and the Berlin academy seem tame by comparison.

When a former student, H. Fr. W. Hinrichs, asked Hegel to write a preface for his *Religion in its Inner Relationship to Science*, the philosopher penned one of his strongest polemics.[53] Hegel waited over a year after being asked to write, apparently expecting that part 2 of Schleiermacher's dogmatics would soon emerge from the printer.[54] Though Hegel's preface does not mention Schleiermacher by name, its target was immediately known from the caustic references to "absolute dependence" and "one who raises Plato to his lips." The preface appeared in May 1822, three months before part 2 of the dogmatics.

It does not appear accidental that Hegel first began to lecture on philosophy of religion in April 1821, just after reading the first part of Schleiermacher's dogmatics and while he had the request for a preface to Hinrichs' book in hand.[55] The sequence of events directly connects the inception of his lectures on philosophy of religion to the work of his colleague in theology. Though his earlier works, including the unpublished youthful manuscripts, the *Phenomenology of Spirit*, and the

51 W. Gass, ed., *Fr. Schleiermacher's Briefwechsel mit J. Chr. Gass* (Berlin: Reimer, 1852), 117, 159f., 164.
52 See Hegel to Daub, May 9, 1821 (Hoffmeister, #387), which reports that Schleiermacher's dogmatics is being printed, and Hegel to Hinrichs, April 7, 1822 (Hoffmeister, #410), where Hegel reports that he has read part 1. Part 2 was finished on or about August 13, 1822, *Schl Briefe*, IV, 297–9.
53 See F. G. Weiss, ed., *Beyond Epistemology: New Studies in the Philosophy of Hegel*, tr. A. V. Miller (The Hague: Martinus Nijhoff, 1974), 221–44; Kipton E. Jensen, "The Principle of Protestantism: On Hegel's (Mis)Reading of Schleiermacher's *Speeches*," *Journal of the American Academy of Religion* 71/3 (June 2003): 405–22; and Eric von der Luft, ed. and tr., *Hegel, Hinrichs, and Schleiermacher on Feeling and Reason in Religion: The Texts of their 1821–22 Debate* (Lewiston, NY: E. Mellen Press, 1987).
54 Hinrichs requested a preface from Hegel on October 14, 1820 and Hegel returned the manuscript on April 21, 1822; the book appeared in May 1822.
55 Hodgson, ed., *Lectures on the Philosophy of Religion*, I, 3.

Encyclopedia, all address the status of religion in relation to philosophic thought, this set of lectures (repeated in differing versions in 1824, 1827, and 1831) was wholly devoted to that subject. It would go too far if we were to claim that Schleiermacher's theology was the actual cause of Hegel's decision to start lecturing on philosophy of religion. I imagine that Hegel would have wished to lecture on religion as a means of rounding out his system even if he had remained at Heidelberg. But his correspondence with friends and the timing of these concerns show how vitally disturbed he was by Schleiermacher's work. He chides Karl Daub (his Heidelberg colleague) as a theologian about the fact that Schleiermacher's dogmatics is believed to be appropriate for the Prussian church and expresses the hope that Daub and other colleagues would speak directly to Altenstein about the direction of theology in Berlin.[56] These references show that, in addition to completing the treatment of religion in Hegel's philosophical system, the immediate local significance of his lectures is that they were designed to put what he called "Berlin theology" (theology under the sway of Schleiermacher) out of business.

Symbolic of the final rift between the two thinkers is the remark of Hegel in the Hinrichs preface to the effect that if religion is defined as the feeling of absolute dependence, "a dog would be the best Christian for it possesses this in the highest degree and lives mainly in this feeling."[57] This polemical saying has embittered countless Schleiermacher students towards Hegel, beginning in their own day. To compare the consciousness of absolute dependence to an animal feeling seems manifestly unfair as an interpretation of the introductory paragraphs of *The Christian Faith*.[58] Any careful reader of Schleiermacher knows that the feeling in question presupposes a capacity for self-consciousness that is only possessed by humans. No matter how dependent a dog may feel, it is doubtful whether the ultimacy or finality of any dependence is felt. But there is little reason to be shocked that a rationalist like Hegel can enliven his argument with a polemical stroke.[59] Displays of biting irony and sarcasm often endear philosophical writers like Kierkegaard and Nietzsche to their readers. That Hegel as a rationalist can be mean and partisan in argument merely indicates that he is mortal and passionately concerned

---

56 Glockner, "Hegel und Schleiermacher," 249; Hoffmeister, #410.
57 Weiss, ed., *Beyond Epistemology*, 238.
58 On Hegel's misreading, see O'Regan, *Heterodox Hegel*, 35.
59 On Hegel's mean-spirited sarcasm toward Schleiermacher, see Pinkard, *Hegel*, 515, 527.

about the truth of the matter under discussion. In this contest played out before colleagues and students the stakes were running very high.

What, then, stood behind Hegel's openly hostile, sharp attack? If we attempt to synthesize Hegel's mature objections to Schleiermacher we can identify the core of his criticism and see the features that set him resolutely against his colleague. One can classify Hegel's philosophical opponents in one of three camps.[60] There are: (a) those older metaphysicians of dogmatic abstraction who directly identify concepts and things; (b) those who are Kantian in placing strictures on the unifying powers of the intellect – the concepts we have of things are not the things themselves; and (c) those who soar beyond the Kantian limitation of knowledge but do so illicitly through a flight of mystical intuition and feeling. Summed up by catchwords: Hegel's opponents are philosophical dogmatists, empiricists, and advocates of mystical intuition. In Hegel's mind there was a progression through these three camps in recent thought, with each building upon and attempting to overcome the preceding school's inherent weaknesses. The third position, which embodied its own weaknesses as well as those of the preceding Kantianism, is generally where he places Schleiermacher. Put broadly, Hegel sees Schleiermacher as being too uncritically Kantian. On his view, Schleiermacher accepts the reduction of knowledge to the realm of finite objects but then seeks to get beyond this reduction at the level of intuition and feeling. For his part, Hegel attempts to get beyond Kant through a more thoroughgoing effort at describing and identifying all the antinomies of thought. Hegel's philosophy of spirit is an attempt to heal the breach between the external world, self-consciousness, and our consciousness of the world. Kant's self-limitation of knowledge is admired for its modesty and clarity, but it has the disadvantage of leaving the realms of nature and human selfhood unintelligible. Thus the way is left open for romanticists, poets, mysticizing philosophers, and theologians of feeling and intuition to produce an incoherent and arbitrarily unified view of the world. This is Hegel's resounding charge against this third school of contemporary thought. Lacking intellectual nerve and an ability to overcome Kantianism, this approach falls victim to an unwarranted arbitrariness of thought and runs the risk of being subjective.

What Schleiermacher wanted to accomplish in *On Religion* was honorable enough in combating the intellectualism and moralism of

---

60 The threefold characterization of Hegel's philosophical opponents is drawn from his *Logic*, second edition, tr. W. Wallace (Oxford: Oxford University Press, 1892), chs. 4–5.

Enlightenment views of religion that had persisted beyond the age of the Enlightenment. But his position leaves the problem of knowledge and of the active self-consciousness unresolved. In Schleiermacher reason is one-sidedly understood to consist of the discriminating intellect. Reason has the office of dividing and dissecting, while the drive to unify our experience is left in the hands of immediate consciousness and feeling. The price paid for this alleged independence of religion from philosophy is too high for Hegel. Against this view Hegel argues that reason is a ubiquitous and never-ceasing feature of our experience. Even the most basic theological claim of the Christian religion – that humans are sinners in need of redemption – requires a rational act of recognizing one's being in a state of sin. Hegel's point is that reason cannot be systematically excluded from the deepest and holiest moments of our experience. If it is, we reduce ourselves to something less than human and the remark about the dog (from the Hinrichs preface) is not then inappropriate. The price paid for immunizing religion to the attack of its cultured despisers is too high. A theology that seems to be invulnerable can be so only at the cost of its own intelligibility. In the end, the paradox of mysticism continues to haunt the work of Schleiermacher. He uses dialectical argument to fend off objections without seeing that this process of argument commits him to tacit positive claims of his own about the office of reason and rationality. He too uses reason systematically and constructively, even when he describes this use in his theology as didactic or rhetorical.

Another problem that Hegel has with Schleiermacher is the continuous appeal to history and historical experience as if this appeal can cut off counterargument. Hegel must have seen the first proposition of the dogmatics of 1821 (later moved to §19) as a historicizing of religious truth. In this famous theological definition of dogmatics Schleiermacher writes: "Dogmatic theology is the science which systematizes the doctrine prevalent in a Christian Church at a definite time." Taken at face value, the statement sounds like Schleiermacher is willing to take as theologically true the level of opinion prevailing in the church at any given time. In that situation religious truth would be more a matter of sociological research than the science of divine and eternal things. Such practice, if carried out, would reduce the eternal to the level of insight of any given era, be it good, bad, or indifferent. In pointing out these things in the Hinrichs preface, Hegel is not in the position of minimizing the importance of history and a historical understanding. On the contrary, his works amply show that historical consciousness plays a prominent role in the developing awareness of truth. We see this in the Hegelian adage that "philosophy is its own time, apprehended in thought," a formulation that appears to parallel Schleiermacher's thesis about theology from the dogmatics. Thus we must inquire further into what separates them on the question of the place of history and historical consciousness. What is lacking in Schleiermacher's teaching about history that is made good in Hegel's?

When the question is put this way it appears that in Hegel's view the entire basis of truth in Schleiermacher appears to be determined by the historical way of knowing. There was no part of Schleiermacher's work available to Hegel (the lectures on *Hermeneutics* and *Dialectics* were never published) in which he could see the canons of truth that operate for Schleiermacher independently of the realm of historical insight. (This is not to imply that Hegel would have been satisfied with those works.) Hegel seems to have sensed that the full problematic of the historical approach to knowing was not fully felt by Schleiermacher, for whom historical insight and eternal truth (e.g., the impact of the Johannine Christ on the life of faith) could still work easily hand in hand. Hegel seems to have been prescient in seeing that the dominant mode of dealing with religion and religious consciousness in the modern period would consist of the external approach of historical-critical studies or the leap inward based on personal confession and intuition. As Hegel put it in the Hinrichs preface, modern theologians deal too exclusively with what "spirit has left behind." In modernity "the products of the earnest efforts of scholarship, of industry, of acumen, etc., are likewise called truth, and an ocean of such truths are brought to light and propagated."[61] Such historical truths are not the truths that satisfy the longing of the human spirit for a wisdom that is not of this world. In saying this Hegel anticipates Kierkegaard's as well as Nietzsche's strong pronouncements against mere historical vantage points, which vitiate an encounter with a living truth.

For Hegel, an uncritical reliance on history or tradition making the case for religion leads to an untenable historical relativism. If the fortunes of religion rest only or mainly on historical experience and not on a sense of truth that transcends history, the modem era will inevitably outgrow the present phase of human religiousness. The peace between reason and revelation, if it is so constructed, is a hollow peace. Unlike the synthesis of faith and reason of the medieval schoolmen, this peace is based on a final indifference in which the two sides do not come into substantive

---

61 Weiss, ed., *Beyond Epistemology*, 236.

contact. In the hands of Schleiermacher the contract between philosophy and religion is more rhetorical than conceptual. For Schleiermacher, religion and philosophy share language but talk about different things. Philosophy does not have it in its power to think the thoughts of a transcendent reality; one can only speak of transcendent reality through the life of faith that is based upon an "immediate consciousness of God." For Hegel there is shared thought and an identical divine content for religion and philosophy. They do not merely coexist but mutually need each other for their completion.

Another difficulty that Hegel has with Schleiermacher is related to everything said thus far. In his suspicion of the mediation of our experience by thought, Schleiermacher makes relatively short shrift of the doctrine of the trinity. For Hegel, the trinity was the mirror in Christian language of philosophic truth, virtually the first article of a rational faith in a divinely unfolding dialectic.[62] Because of his emphasis on the immediacy of religious experience, Schleiermacher views the trinity as a secondary articulation of faith, arising more from speculation than from the needs of faith. From his perspective it is difficult to imagine how one would ever attain an immediate feeling of the inner distinctions in the godhead. The doctrine is only treated in the final three propositions of *The Christian Faith*. The reason for this is that religious experience and Christian self-consciousness are immediate and prior to the mediating power of thought.

When the matter is put this way we can identify the problem of immediate knowledge as the intellectual core of the differences between Schleiermacher and Hegel. It is a misunderstanding of Hegel to claim, as is sometimes done, that he is against immediacy. This is simply not the case. The transitions of the *Logic* rest on and give an account of immediacy. The question is whether any reflection on immediacy can recapture the immediate and attain what the French philosopher Paul Ricouer calls a "second naïveté." Hegel is convinced that there is nothing that exists in heaven, in nature, in mind or in any aspect of our experience, which is not mediated as well as immediate.[63] Immediacy simply cannot stand by itself unmediated. When we talk as if this is the case we simply create a breach between what our thought posits and refers to and what our thought actually does in its own explication. The split between the object referred

---

62 See O'Regan, *Heterodox Hegel*, 287–326, on Hegel's spirit "as fully inclusive trinitarian articulation of divine subjectivity."
63 G. W. F. Hegel, *Science of Logic*, tr. A. V. Miller (London: Allen and Unwin, 1969), 68.

to and the thought doing the referral is irrevocable. The very act of pointing to immediacy requires us to say how immediacy is mediated, through what acts of consciousness we have this direct sense of utter dependence. The alternative is to remain mute in the face of one's private experience. This alternative is, for Hegel, as unthinkable for theology as it is for philosophy of religion. Against Schleiermacher, Hegel argues that the mind that knows that it has an experience of utter dependence must be a free, independent mind. If our experience is paradoxical, then the paradoxes of the heart must be taken up into our mind and intellectual experience. Only with an active mind or spirit that is aware of its own moments of dependence can one enter the kingdom of heaven.

POSTSCRIPT — AN UNFINISHED COMPARISON

In presenting the main lines of Hegel's critique of Schleiermacher's dogmatics I have slightly simplified matters in order to get a number of critical issues out in the open. I have not attempted to formulate a rejoinder, a task that would necessarily draw from the full range of Schleiermacher's work. It is noteworthy that Schleiermacher issued no response. He felt himself to be quite unscathed by the attack, even though in his words "it was not exactly pleasant."[64]

Both thinkers drew a continuous stream of students to Berlin in the decade of the 1820s. Schleiermacher's lectures on dialectics attracted at least as many, and in some semesters more, students than did Hegel's on logic.[65] His lectures on philosophical topics did not suffer the fate of an Arthur Schopenhauer, who was unable to attract students alongside Hegel in the same period.

It is painfully obvious that the interrelated lives of these two illustrious Berlin colleagues reveal some ordinary human sensibilities (as well as prejudices) on both sides of the relationship. By offering a narrative of events I have sought to bring out their fundamental attitudes and the complex, human side of the situation in which they encountered each other's teaching. The tensions and poignancy of their struggle were

---

64 Writing to de Wette (summer 1823) Schleiermacher says: "For his part Hegel continues to grumble about my animal-like ignorance of God, just as he already did in the preface of Hinrichs' philosophy of religion and in his lectures, while recommending Marheineke's theology exclusively. I pay no attention to it, but still it is not exactly pleasant" (Nicolin, #391).

65 In the summer of 1822 Schleiermacher had 188 students in "Dialectics" while Hegel had 74 in "Logic-Metaphysics" and in 1828 Schleiermacher had 129 in "Dialectics" while Hegel had 138 in "Logic" (Hoffmeister, 743–9).

enhanced by the fact that each figure saw himself as the defender of a proper philosophical (and scientific) stance in the university as well as the bearer of an interpretation of the Christian religion vitally needed by the age.

Hegel's contemporary biographer, Karl Rosenkranz, says of the relationship between the two thinkers:

It was fortunate for Berlin that the Hegelian element with its thorough and compartmentalized systematic and its insistence on method stood in the way of the Schleiermacher element with its versatile flexibility. But also for Hegel and his school it was good fortune that Schleiermacher's scholarship, spirit, wit, presence, and popular power did not let it grow up too quickly and made it take shape gradually.[66]

Rosenkranz, who stood close to his teacher Hegel, acknowledges that Schleiermacher was a significant obstacle in the development of a Hegelian school. Schleiermacher was as unwilling to let Hegel have the final say in philosophy as Hegel was unwilling to abandon theology and religious teaching to Schleiermacher. Though we are familiar with the revolt of the later nineteenth century against Hegel, we are insufficiently aware that the revolt was anticipated, if not precipitated, by a teacher of theology at his own university. Schleiermacher is the original harbinger of the revolt against Hegel, subsequently undertaken by Kierkegaard in the name of an existential religiousness and by Karl Marx as a quest for a just social order. To be sure, Schleiermacher had voted to call Hegel to the Berlin professorship, but really only to block someone else's chances. At the time his attitude was, if we must have speculative philosophy at Berlin, then we might as well get someone good.

66 Rosenkranz, *Hegels Leben*, 327.

CHAPTER 4

Kierkegaard's not so hidden debt to Schleiermacher

At age 64 and at the height of his fame Schleiermacher journeyed to Copenhagen where he was accorded full academic honors.[1] This festive and elegant affair, which occurred on September 22–9, 1833, less than five months before his death, must have been extraordinary. The *Copenhagen Post* of 28 September vividly describes the German theologian's considerable achievements by observing:

A troubled Christendom has found in him an enthused proclaimer no less than an intellectual freedom in relation to superstition, fanaticism, and literalist authority. The mutual relatedness and well-executed connection of the various sciences are brought to expression in his personality as in his writings and no one has developed the limits of individual sciences with greater clarity or strength, especially the autonomy of theological science and its independence from an excessive speculation. His entire effectiveness manifests the union of science and life. It is no exaggeration if one considers Schleiermacher in many respects as the most significant theologian of our time in the Protestant church, whose uncommon spiritual power and originality are in innermost connection with a deep mind and living feeling. It is also no exaggeration if one believes that the church has had no greater theologian from the time of Calvin down to the present day.[2]

After mention of Schleiermacher's masterful contributions to Plato studies and the study of ancient philosophy, it is further noted that "his whole effectiveness is so significant and influential, that he would have to be an object of interest for anyone, who did not wish to hold himself aloof from the most important movements of the age."[3]

The visit to Denmark's capital must indeed have been extraordinary. Religious and secular figures, luminaries from university and civic circles

---

1 For a vivid account of the visit that includes source documents, see Jon Stewart, "Schleiermacher's Visit to Copenhagen in 1833," *Zeitschrift für Neuere Theologiegeschichte/Journal for the History of Modern Theology* 11/2 (2004): 279–302.

2 *Schl Briefe*, II, 502–3.   3 Ibid., 503.

gathered around a festive meal in Schleiermacher's honor. The Romantic poet Adam Oehlenschläger (1779–1850) composed a Danish song for the occasion, and deftly put it into German for the guest's benefit. By giving Plato and Socrates to the Germans Schleiermacher had connected the Baltic Sea with the Archipelagos and had become the Melanchthon of his age. Following a toast "to the thinker, the preacher, but especially to the man," Schleiermacher arose to respond. Scarcely able to speak from emotion, he suggested that his hosts had not touched upon "what he had become but what he would have wanted to become, or perhaps might have been able to become."[4] Following the Danish national hymn and standing in the presence of the king, Schleiermacher expressed his heartfelt wishes for Denmark and its people.

As the serious mood became ever more ebullient with speeches and song, Schleiermacher spoke some words of encouragement directly to the younger theologians present. Some one hundred and fifty theological students, mostly persons who were not members of fraternities (the others had celebrated with Schleiermacher the previous evening) adjourned to the garden of the hunting lodge amid music and torchlight. More songs were presented and genial discussion ensued, after which Schleiermacher reminded his youthful admirers that a man's name can have validity for an era when he works for his times with fidelity and devotion, but that only the divine spirit has lasting duration, and he hoped that the spirit would rest in them and make their work fruitful for future years.[5]

In September 1833 the 20-year-old Søren Kierkegaard was about to begin his fifth semester of theological studies. Despite the sure sense we have that Kierkegaard had to have been aware of the Schleiermacher festivities, direct evidence to that effect does not exist. The young Kierkegaard's theological, literary, and philosophical studies had only recently begun. His prolonged struggle to get to grips with the impasse between the pietistic orthodoxy of his father's house and the reigning forms of supranaturalism and rationalism in theology would shortly unfold. His meticulous journal writing, where we might expect notice of the event, only began later. Both recent German commentators Wilhelm Anz and Henning Schröer pass quickly over the visit in their respective 1985 essays that treat the Kierkegaard–Schleiermacher relationship.[6] An argument

---

4 Ibid.   5 Ibid., 505.
6 Wilhelm Anz, "Schleiermacher und Kierkegaard Übereinstimmung und Differenz," *Zeitschrift für Theologie und Kirche* 82/4 (1985): 409, and Henning Schröer, "Wie verstand Kierkegaard Schleiermacher?," *Internationaler Schleiermacher Kongreß Berlin 1984*, 1/2 (Berlin: Walter de Gruyter, 1985), 1147.

about how Kierkegaard came to view Schleiermacher, and to express a not inconsiderable debt to him, must begin with his subsequent published works and journals.

Yet noting the Copenhagen visit heightens our sense of the general esteem and high regard with which Schleiermacher was held in Danish letters. Kierkegaard's teachers, F. C. Sibbern, A. Oehlenschläger, and H. N. Clausen, were among those most involved in the visit.[7] In early summer 1834 the young student signed on with another teacher, H. L. Martensen, for a tutorial on Schleiermacher's *The Christian Faith*. As a concrete historical point of departure the 1833 visit places their connection in its context and anchors our puzzling (methodological and substantive) question about how, and the degree to which, Kierkegaard is related to Schleiermacher. To characterize the state of this discussion today is daunting and can easily be viewed with a measure of skepticism.[8] A look at the evidence and extant scholarly literature leads to inconclusiveness with significant agreements and sharp disagreements with Schleiermacher duly noted in the Kierkegaardian œuvre. In recent comments on this material (Anz and Schröer as well as a bibliographic note by Howard and Edna Hong) the matter seems almost like a draw.[9] Schleiermacher was an important figure for Kierkegaard, highly influential in some respects, but pointedly criticized in others. To be sure, a major sustained discussion of Schleiermacher by Kierkegaard does not exist. Scholars are reduced to argument about allusions, individual comments in the journals, and an occasional paragraph of substantive commentary. Kierkegaard's high praise alternates with sharp critique in a way that easily baffles. The most recent account of Schleiermacher's overall impact in Denmark, despite the impressive 1833 visit, is no more promising. Contributers to the 1984 Copenhagen Colloquium on German Literature, where Wilhelm Anz' paper originated, seem strained to show that Schleiermacher had a significant influence on Danish theology as a whole, not just in the case of Kierkegaard. Writing on "Schleiermacher and Danish Romanticism" Helge Hultberg virtually denies the role of Romanticism in Demark's Golden Age and characterizes the intellectual climate in the first decades

---

7 Niels Munk Plum, *Schleiermacher i Danmark* (Festskrift udgivet af Københavns Universitet Anledning af Hans Majestaet Kongens Fødelsdag 16. September 1934) (København: Bianco Lunos Bog Trykkeri A/S, 1934).

8 Interest in the two figures continues to increase. An international conference, sponsored by the Danish Kierkegaard Society and the German Schleiermacher Society, was held in October 2003 in Copenhagen on the theme "Truth and Subjectivity."

9 See *Schl briefe*, II, 505 and *JP*, IV, 626–7.

of the nineteeth century as a "synthesis of the Enlightenment, Christianity, and moderate Platonism" in which "the monistic tendencies" of the young Schleiermacher could have no effect.[10] Hultberg maintains that "The Danes found Schleiermacher simply too bold, too much convinced of the possibilities of the human spirit."[11]

STRANGE BEDFELLOWS

Certainly if the two figures were less prominent or otherwise had nothing in common, the matter might well be abandoned. Yet because of their weighty individual contributions to the history of modern theology scholars rightly still pursue such projects. No full monograph exists on the topic, though Hermann Fischer's 1963 book on sin comes somewhat close in this regard.[12] Among persons in a position to write that monograph, Emanuel Hirsch provides pertinent observations in annotations to his German translation as well as in his *Kierkegaard-Studien*, where he traces Kierkegaard's youthful development.[13] His comment about the two thinkers in the *History of Modern Protestant Theology* repays careful study.

It cannot be denied that Kierkegaard with his claim that truth is subjectivity takes up and carries further in its most pointed form the central idea of Schleiermacher concerning how religion relates to knowledge and piety to dogmatic statements. To this extent, Kierkegaard in his generation is the only authentic pupil of Schleiermacher.[14]

Yet no settled historical account of their intellectual relationship within nineteenth-century theology is at hand. Though Schleiermacher stands at the start of the century, summed up by the catchwords "Romanticism," "liberal theology," or "mediating theology," Kierkegaard is much less well understood as related to the development of theology in his own time and place. Bruce H. Kirmmse's fine historical account goes far towards

---

10 Helge Hultberg, "Schleiermacher und die dänishe Romantik," in *Schleiermacher im besonderen Hinblick auf seine Wirkungsgeschichte in Dänemark*, ed. Hultberg et al. (Copenhagen: Fink, 1986), 125.

11 Ibid., 126; for a companion piece that compares Schleiermacher and Grundtvig, see Theodor Jørgensen, "Schleiermachers und Grundtvigs Verständnis vom Heil in Bezug auf die Versöhnungslehre unter besonderer Berücksichtigung ihrer Bestimmung des Bösen," in Hultberg et al., eds., *Schleiermacher im besonderen Hinblick*, 82–101.

12 Hermann Fischer, *Subjektivität und Sünde: Kierkegaards Begriff der Sünde mit ständiger Rücksicht auf Schleiermachers Lehre von der Sünde* (Itzehoe: Verlag "Die Spur," 1963).

13 *Kierkegaard-Studien* (Gütersloh: Verlag C. Bertelsmann, 1933), II, 21–4 .

14 Emanuel Hirsch, *Geschichte der neuern evangelischen Theologie* (Gütersloh: Verlag C. Bertelsmann, 1949), V, 453–4.

placing Kierkegaard amid Danish contemporaries, but does not treat the ways in which the Danish world of Kierkegaard relates to mainstream European philosophy, theology, or letters.[15] Claude Welch's *Protestant Thought in the Nineteenth Century, 1799–1870* puts Kierkegaard into its final chapter as if he epitomizes the movement of the century's religious thought towards subjective understandings of religion.[16]

It is one thing to acknowledge that Kierkegaard had no influence at all on nineteenth-century theology. It is quite another to act as if he lacks immediate antecedents or contexts for his life's work. An exception to the general failure to integrate Kierkegaard into the mainstream of nine-teenth-century theology, Hendrikus Berkhof argues that the two thinkers have similar goals but pursue different methods:

> Can one not say even that, fundamentally, Schleiermacher and Kierkegaard aimed at the same goal? Both of them sought to make intelligible for their cultured contemporaries the renewal of humanity through the work of God. The first strove to attain this goal by the way of harmony (though not by that way alone, as we saw); the second by way of conflict (with the tools of contemporary language and psychology). Schleiermacher, and following him liberalism and the theology of mediation, sought to make apologetic use of idealism in order to lead it in priestly fashion to its secret Christian goal; Kierkegaard sought to unmask it prophetically as a form of the never-ending scandal over the paradox of the gospel. In the cultured world of the educated both men remained solitary figures. Schleiermacher was adopted, in domesticated form, in the church and assimilated in the theology of mediation. Kierkegaard attacked precisely this theology as the mediating ideology of the church establishment and was, accordingly, rejected also by the church.[17]

On Berkhof's view differences abound amid arguably common aims. These differences reflect their personal-biographical choices. Schleiermacher was married and preeminently engaged in the social world of church and university, while Kierkegaard was the quintessential private citizen, aloof from official institutions, whether the university, the church, or marriage. These orientations to public life mirror the sets of problems addressed in their thought. Yet neither thinker can be explained by his personal social and institutional choices. One would scarcely wish to

15 Bruce H. Kirmmse, *Kierkegaard in Golden Age Denmark* (Bloomington: Indiana University Press, 1990).

16 Claude Welch, *Protestant Thought in the Nineteenth Century, 1799–1870* (New Haven: Yale University Press, 1972), 1, 292, "And in his turn to 'subjectivity' Kierkegaard was the paradigm of a main tendency of the century as a whole."

17 Hendrikus Berkhof, *Two Hundred Years of Theology: Report of a Personal Journey* (Grand Rapids: William B. Eerdmans, 1989), 78–9.

argue that Kierkegaard fails to deal with "the university, the church, or marriage." The larger contours of these themes constitute shared terrain. Schleiermacher's life mediates, as do his hermeneutics, dialectics, and theology; Kierkegaard attacks mediation at the outset and never deviates from this position. But whether positively or negatively, the theme of mediation (and its problematic aspects) is a basic preoccupation of both writers. To give weight to Berkhof's portrayal is to emphasize how each thinker construes the overall aims of theology more than to elucidate their detailed insight into particular issues that inform this task.

Yet if the history of theology is to attend to foundational issues that shape the cultural expression of theology, and not just to fragmentary citations or a set of likely but wholly conjectural influences, a more basic encounter with the possibility of Schleiermacher having had a significant impact on Kierkegaard must be undertaken. In what follows I maintain that, despite their different social locations and the ambiguous reception of Schleiermacher set forth by Kierkegaard, *a set of formal as well as substantive concerns unites far more than it divides the two thinkers and that this constitutes Kierkegaard's debt to Schleiermacher.* The argument partly rests on recognition of the powerful movements of shared intellectual thought in the context of which Schleiermacher functions as mentor and pathfinder, not as constant beacon of light or even of truth. Here I have in mind German Romanticism, its aesthetics, its discovery of Otherness and the inexpressibility of Being; the heightened quarrel with various Kantianisms, including the views of Fichte; the turn to Platonic dialogs, and especially to the figure of Socrates as a model of thinking and discourse; a keen sense that dogmatics must be recast in a way that will preserve the time-honored autonomy of theology in a form that relates to the immediacy of lived experience; and, of course, the ever-present shadow of Hegel and speculative thought as a means of appropriating the Christian tradition. One is tempted to paraphrase the adage about politics and say that "anti-Hegelianism" also makes a strange bedfellow. The debt that I describe is often indirect and diffuse; it takes the form of a mutual indebtedness to the legacy of Romanticism as this shaped the major projects of both writers.

Of course, continued interest in pairing these two theologians is virtually assured by the received version of modern theology. This story, shaped as it is by Barth's polemics against theological liberalism, places Kierkegaard and Schleiermacher at opposite ends of a spectrum. Schleiermacher's heavily romanticized interpretation of religion's essence marks him as a defender of *homo religiosus*, while Kierkegaard's radical critique of immanental religion (aesthetics generally and Religion A of *Concluding Unscientific Postscript*) restores divine otherness and the mystery of Christian belief to its proper perspective. If the line from Schleiermacher leads to Feuerbach and religious humanism, the line from Kierkegaard leads to Barth and to a renewed interest in ingenious theological (and today also philosophical) defenses of Protestant orthodoxy. In *The Word of God and Theology* (1922) Barth writes with characteristic verve that "the ancestral line on which we have to orient ourselves, if the thoughts developed from the nature of the case are to be decisive, runs from Kierkegaard to Luther and Calvin, to Paul, to Jeremiah . . . In order to be completely clear, I wish expressly to point out that the name Schleiermacher is missing from the ancestral line that is here recommended."[18] A recent one-volume account of twentieth-century Christian theology oriented around the themes of immanence and transcendence sees Kierkegaard mainly as a spur to dialectical theology.

Themes announced by the nineteenth-century Danish philosopher – the transcendence of the God who speaks the ineffable divine truth to the individual in the moment of divine encounter – became the foundation on which the theologians of neo-orthodoxy in the twentieth century built and the theses that they expanded in their theological deliberations.[19]

Though they have a kernel of truth, the one-sided and misleading nature of such statements reflects theological polemics more than the task of getting to grips with a historical understanding of the forces of modernity that lie behind and continue to shape Christian theology.

AMBIGUOUS EVIDENCE

A look at the overt references to Schleiermacher in Kierkegaard's œuvre will prepare us for what follows. In the Hongs' edition of *Søren Kierkegaard's Journals and Papers* (*JP*) some 27 entries pertain directly to Schleiermacher. By way of comparison, there are some 30 for Kant, 10 for J. G. Fichte, 20 for his son, I. H. Fichte, 40 for Goethe (not including 12 more to Goethe's literary works), 49 for N. F.S. Grundtvig, 46 for J. G. Hamann, 135 for Hegel, 51 for J. L. Heiberg, 40 for Lessing, 235 for Luther, 67 for Plato, 19 for Schelling, 26 for F. Schlegel, 28 for Shakespeare, and 217 for Socrates. (These figures are compiled from the

18 Cited in Schröer, "Wie verstand Kierkegaard," 1148.
19 Stanley J. Grenz and Roger E. Olson, *Twentieth-Century Theology: God and the World in a Transitional Age* (Downers Grove, IL: Intervarsity Press, 1992), 65.

index, plus enumerating nonindexed entries that are listed under proper names). None of these figures includes cross-references within the main body of Kierkegaard's work. Their enumeration only provides impressions that are of marginal significance. Very likely the figures confirm in some fashion what a reader may already guess as to the relative weight of influences on the overall thought of Kierkegaard. At least these seem to be the main points of reference in his thinking, excluding explicitly biblical figures and themes that I have not listed.

In their bibliographic note on the journal references to Schleiermacher the Hongs are most circumspect, claiming only that in reading the works of Schleiermacher Kierkegaard "received considerable stimulation for the solution of issues important to him."[20] Though bland, this assertion largely accords with, even if it understates, what I wish ultimately to argue. In their two-page summary the Hongs do not pinpoint the nature of this stimulation or show how it fits into an overall picture of Kierkegaard's development. With two exceptions – Kierkegaard's praise of the *Confidential Letters* as "masterful" and the utterances in *Concept of Anxiety* about Schleiermacher's "immortal service to dogmatics" – one might well conclude that Kierkegaard saw Schleiermacher more as theological enemy or nemesis than as a profound influence.[21] Most journal entries (e.g., number 3843 of *The Christian Faith*) read more like "student notes" than like final or even rounded pronouncements, though disturbing questions are raised about "the feeling of absolute dependence" for example, "If the feeling of absolute dependence is the highest, how is this related to prayer?"As the young Kierkegaard struggled with notions of predestination he saw Schleiermacher as putting undue stress on divine determinism. Entry number 3848 says cryptically: "Schleiermacher as Stoicism reborn in Christianity." Kierkegaard associates "the romantic" with free creativity and openness to miracles, which he contrasts with

---

20 *JP*, IV, 626.
21 The famous "immortal service to dogmatics" reference to Schleiermacher, Kierkegaard, *The Concept of Anxiety: A Simple Psychologically Orienting Deliberation on the Dogmatic Issue of Hereditary Sin*, ed. and tr. Reidar Thomte in collaboration with Albert B. Anderson (Princeton: Princeton University Press, 1980) 20, is treated in Richard Crouter, "More than Kindred Spirits: Schleiermacher and Kierkegaard on Repentance," in *Schleiermacher and Kierkegaard: Subjectivity and Truth*, ed. Niels Jørgen Cappelørn et al. (Berlin: Walter de Gruyter, 2006). See Philip Quinn, "Does Anxiety Explain Original Sin," *Nous* 24/2 (1990): 227–44, and Walter E. Wyman, Jr., "Rethinking the Christian Doctrine of Sin: Friedrich Schleiermacher and Hick's "Irenaean Type," *Journal of Religion* 74 (1994): 199–217. Here I have only sought to make a plausible case for the elements of Romanticism and Plato interpretation that make Schleiermacher a significant figure for Kierkegaard, quite apart from their positions on the doctrine of sin or other theological issues.

both Hegel and Schleiermacher.[22] Referring to Schleiermacher's phrase "the Christian consciousness," and noting that Neander associates it with the Reformation, Kierkegaard writes: "That may be all right, but there is something very dubious about it" and relates the notion to the Christian diffusion and collective consciousness "that is supposed to be Christianity – no thanks."[23] In an 1837 entry Kierkegaard vents the age-old suspicion that Schleiermacher teaches religious pantheism,[24] while in 1850 he holds the view that Schleiermacher "represents everything in the sphere of being, Spinozian being."[25] Elsewhere he states in 1850 that Schleiermacher "treats religiousness in the sphere of being," and adds the undated marginal note:

This also explains Schleiermacher's stipulation of the feeling of absolute dependence as the principle of all religion, for this is again a condition of religiousness in the sphere of being. As soon as the question becomes ethical, consequently a question of the becoming of this condition, how it comes into existence, what I have to do in order that it can come into existence, also how it is to be maintained or how I am to be maintained in it, which also is becoming, then the mark of religiousness is changed. I think it is precisely in this way that Schleiermacher may be said to have falsified Christianity, because he had conceived it esthetically-metaphysically merely as a condition, whereas Christianity is essentially to be conceived ethically, as striving. S. conceives of religiousness as completely analogous to erotic love. But this is a misunderstanding. Erotic love essentially has nothing to do with a striving. But Christianity is in the sphere of becoming. As soon as this is understood, every single Christian qualification is characterized differently than in S. And not only this, but only then do the most decisive qualifications of Christianity appear, and they are lacking in S., or in S. they lack the decisive quality.[26]

This last evidence in particular, even if sporadically attested, suggests a reception and interpretation of Schleiermacher that is decidedly unfavorable in ways that are not easily explained away. The received Barthian understanding of the difference between Schleiermacher and Kierkegaard

---

22 JP, II, 207 (#1563): "It is obvious that in time the romantic gradually declines more and more, precisely to the same degree as necessity is advanced (Hegel), in such a way that Christianity does not remain romantic at all (for example, Schleiermacher, a necessary development). To what extent does the antique, which thus enters in, resemble so-called actual antiquity. The present tense of beauty."

23 JP, III, 251–2 (#2822).

24 Ibid., IV, 13 (#3849): "That pantheism constitutes a surmounted factor in religion, is the foundation for it, seems now to be acknowledged, and hereby also the error in Schleiermacher's definition of religion as remaining in pantheism, in that he makes the extra-temporal fusion factor of the universal and the finite – into religion."

25 Ibid., 14 (#3852).

26 Ibid., 14–15 (#3853).

seems virtually vindicated. At the very least, a significant burden is put on those who would argue a contrary case.

In his paper "Schleiermacher and Kierkegard: Agreement and Difference," Wilhelm Anz starts by reciting this same evidence and notes how the critique of "absolute dependence" and identification of religion with a form of inwardness seem to accord with the critique of Schleiermacher of dialectical theology. Given these explicit disagreements on specific issues, Anz (in a move similar to that of Berkhof) turns to the larger framing issues:

> But the discussion that I believe we must lead with both figures cannot make progress if we do not recognize and hold on to the common situation in which both figures stand and the agreement in essential intentions that results from this.[27]

Anz then seeks to show that Schleiermacher and Kierkegaard share a sense of existential dialectic that lies behind all their theological work and connects it with the lived world of believers. The touchstone of his discussion is found in Kierkegaard's remark in *Concept of Anxiety* about Schleiermacher's "immortal service to dogmatics." Here Schleiermacher is said to be a thinker "in the beautiful Greek sense, a thinker who spoke only of what he knew."[28] In the end, for Anz, despite the overall agreement of intentions, the differences can scarcely be explained away.

> But the fact remains that Kierkegaard did not change his judgment that Schleiermacher had misconstrued Christianity in essential respects. The difference retains its weight; the restlessness of dialectical theology on this point is not without ground. (In order to clarify it adequately, there must first be agreement concerning the commonality of both figures.)[29]

Anz' motivating interest is more theological than historical. He wishes to challenge dialectical theology's view of the matter by suggesting that the commonalities will outweigh an eventual close reading of the details.

In his contribution to the 1984 *International Schleiermacher Congress* entitled, "How did Kierkegaard understand Schleiermacher?,"[30] Henning Schröer similarly reviews evidence from the journals. Like Anz and the Hongs, Schröer does little to historically contextualize a reading of these fragmentary entries from the journals. As an aside one can note that this situation is not easily corrected by a user of the Hongs' English edition of

---

27 Anz, "Schleiermacher und Kierkegaard," 417.
28 Kierkegaard, *Concept of Anxiety*, 20.
29 Anz, "Schleiermacher und Kierkegaard," 429.
30 Schröer, "Wie verstand Kierkegaard," 1147–55.

the journals, which breaks with a chronological layout in favor of a series of encyclopedia-type catchword entries. The arrangement virtually defies using the English edition of the journals to reconstruct the actual theological debates of Kierkegaard in his development.[31] (The inclusion of extensive journal citations as appendices to individual volumes of the new Princeton edition of *Collected Works* partly compensates for this situation.) Compelling and nuanced interpretations of individual paragraphs are especially difficult to make apart from the intellectual and historical context of journal entries. Only when we are aware of the cluster of issues running through the mind of Kierkegaard at a distinct period of his life are we able to see a living Kierkegaard at his writing table and to assess how he actually sees and reads his contemporaries. Of *The Concept of Irony* Schröer writes:

> This writing contributes little to the question before us. That Kierkegaard mainly attaches himself to Schleiermacher there in a philological sense shows his high regard. The line of demarcation with respect to Hegel . . . also allows Schleiermacher's merits to appear. At best the distinction in their respective views of Socratic dialectic is of interest. While Schleiermacher finds a positive knowledge in Socratic ignorance, for Kierkegaard it is much more a *via negativa*, which expressly brings out the existential dialectic of Socrates as personality . . . One can see that a noteworthy difference exists between Schleiermacher and Kierkegaard in their conceptions of dialectic. For Schleiermacher dialectic is the art of conducting a conversation, but also the art of knowing, while for Kierkegaard it is grasping the contradictoriness of existence, the art of paradoxicality in order to produce existential seriousness and come into the state of becoming Christian.[32]

Yet to so judge *Concept of Irony*, while technically correct, seems to mistake the trees for the forest, while missing the thick underbrush that nurtures the forest. Like Anz and Berkhof, Schröer appeals to overarching aims, intentions, and commonalities, including the true, though in this instance unilluminating, fact that Barth, Schleiermacher, and Kierkegaard are united in opposition to speculative theology in the sense of Hegel.[33]

To judge these sporadic references to Schleiermacher clearly requires some standard by which to sift and to weigh evidence. Taken at face value, the issues seem to be moot, and the overwhelming positive judgment of

---

31 For a new level of sophisticated reconstruction of the Danish Hegelianism around Kierkegaard, see Jon Stewart, *Kierkegaard's Relations to Hegel Reconsidered* (Cambridge: Cambridge University Press, 2003).

32 Schröer, "Wie verstand Kierkegaard," 1150–1.

33 Ibid., 1155.

Confidential Letters and the overt praise of Schleiermacher in *The Concept of Anxiety* do not fit well with the mixed evidence at hand.

SCHLEIERMACHER'S 'CONFIDENTIAL LETTERS'

What is required, I think, is greater recognition of the historical matrix that lies behind the scholarly efforts to identify commonalities between Kierkegaard and Schleiermacher. It is not, after all, just perchance that such agreements arise. The matrix in question involves the legacy of Romanticism and the convergence of an understanding of the world, of texts, and of oneself transmitted from this source, along with the rediscovery of Plato. The actual significance of Schleiermacher for Kierkegaard lies along this axis. To put the matter that way is to sense how the dual features that run through Kierkegaard's master's dissertation, *The Concept of Irony with Continual Reference to Socrates* (1841)[34] – Romanticism and Socratism – are both fed by Schleiermacher. The task of critiquing the former from a perspective steeped in the latter had been prefigured in the work of Schleiermacher. We do well, too, to remind ourselves of the origin of these elements in the works of the *Athenaeum*, literary organ of the Schlegel brothers, along with Novalis and Schleiermacher, and that the work that Kierkegaard considered "masterful" without qualification, the *Confidential Letters on Schlegel's "Lucinde,"* arose in this immediate context. These works, after all, decisively shaped Kierkegaard's mature views; the pseudonymous projects largely determine the teaching of Kierkegaard for his readers. Kierkegaard's imaginative, lifelong appropriation of Socrates rested on the Plato revival, including philological notes and philosophical commentary, initiated by Schleiermacher. As Plato scholar Schleiermacher is, after all, the emulator of dialogical thinking. This is seen not just in the rhetorical art form of *On Religion: Speeches to its Cultured Despisers* (1799, 1806, 1821) but also in the *Letters on the Occasion of the Political-Theological Task and the Open Letter of Jewish Householders* (1799) on David Friedländer and Jewish emancipation in Prussia,[35] *On the Liturgical Right of Evangelical Princes: A Theological Reflection* by Pacificus Sincerus (1824), *Conversation about Scripture of Two Self-Preeminent Evangelical Christians. Luther with Respect to the New Prussian Order of Worship: A Last Word or a First* (1827)[36] on

34 Ed. and tr. Howard V. Hong and Edna H. Hong (Princeton: Princeton University Press, 1989).
35 See below, chapter 5.
36 *KGA*, 1/9, *Kirchenpolitische Schriften*, ed. Günter Meckenstock with Hans-Friedrich Traulsen (Berlin: Walter de Gruyter, 2000), 211–69, 381–472; the works are not available in English.

liturgical controversies within the Prussian Church Union. Each of these works, plus the better-known translated work *The Celebration of Christmas: A Conversation* (1806), makes use of anonymity, pseudonymity, and fictional voices to gain a hearing for distinctive points of view that deeply reflect Schleiermacher's engagement with his contemporaries.[37] It bears recalling that Schleiermacher, the Plato scholar and philologist as well as the Protestant Christian theologian, was being feted in Denmark in September 1833.

In passing, too, I wish to observe that it is not necessary for my argument for us to think that Kierkegaard (any more than Schleiermacher) would have been comfortable with the label "Romantic." Indeed, Kierkegaard came to view this older generation of contemporaries as the very people who had liberated the world intellectually but who had, at the same time, ushered in a world of aestheticism that gravely threatened authentic Christian existence. By primarily associating Schleiermacher with the classic (and the recovery of Greek antiquity), Kierkegaard obscures the ways in which they both are part of the same large stream of European thought that first brought together heightened literary sensitivity and self-reflexive philosophical criticism.[38]

Schleiermacher's *Confidential Letters Concerning Schlegel's "Lucinde"* attracted the attention of Kierkegaard, then a university student, when it was reissued by the 24-year-old poet and writer Karl Gutzkow (1811–78) to celebrate Schleiermacher's boldness on the first anniversary of his death.[39] In his journal from October 1835, Kierkegaard refers to Schleiermacher's "Lucinde Letters":

37 Available in English as *Christmas Eve: Dialogue on the Incarnation*, ed. and tr. Terrence N. Tice (San Francisco: EM Texts, 1990).
38 It is increasingly recognized that early German Romanticism is a philosophical as well as a literary movement. See Manfred Frank, *The Philosophical Foundations of Early German Romanticism*, tr. Elizabeth Millán-Zaibert (Albany: State University of New York Press, 2004); Terry Pinkard, *German Philosophy 1760–1860: The Legacy of Idealism* (Cambridge: Cambridge University Press, 2002), writes of the romantic appropriation of Kant; Philippe Lacoue-Labarthe and Jean-Luc Nancy, *The Literary Absolute: The Theory of Literature in German Romanticism*, tr. Philip Barnard and Cheryl Lester (Albany: State University of New York Press, 1988).
39 An advocate of the *Junges Deutschland* movement's critique of political absolutism and bourgois society, Gutzkow republished Schleiermacher's controversial treatise after hearing that it was not to be included among the theologian's Collected Works. Gutzkow's passionate foreword presents the work as a "token for love to lay upon the winter snow of the grave" (*Schleiermachers Vertraute Briefe über die Lucinde* [Hamburg: Hoffmann and Campe, 1835], v), while his youthful remembrances of Schleiermacher (*Berliner Erinnerungen und Erlebnisse*, ed. Paul Friedländer [Berlin: Das Neue Berlin, 1960], 280–3) give a vivid portrait of the preacher and lecturer.

These letters are written about a book, *Lucinde,* published at one time by F. Schlegel. It is not known for sure whether or not this book is by Schl. [eiermacher], but Gutzkow puts the burden upon everyone to prove that it is not by him. Surely on the basis of internal evidence alone it is incontestable; the characteristically Schl. dialectical-polemical language is unmistakable through-out, just as in, for example, "*Versuch über die Schamhaftigkeit*" ["*Essay on the Sense of Shame*"]. It is probably a model review and also an example of how such a thing can be most productive, in that he constructs a host of personalities out of the book itself and through them illuminates the work and also illuminates their individuality, so that instead of being faced by the reviewer with various points of view, we get instead many personalities who represent these various points of view. But they are complete beings, so that it is possible to get a glance into the individuality of the single individual and through numerous yet merely relatively true judgments to draw up our own final judgment. Thus it is a true masterpiece.[40]

It will repay us to try to tease out of the *Confidential Letters* what it is that Kierkegaard so very much admires in this way of writing. It *was* an interesting way to write, and it behooves us to ask what Kierkegaard found so attractive in it, before we weigh the idea that Schleiermacher's work may have served as the inspiration for the pseudonymous masks of Kierkegaard's project of indirect communication. In what ways do the "Lucinde Letters" constitute a form of indirect communication? What truths about oneself, and about one's relationship to Friedrich Schlegel and the projects of Romanticism, are concealed in this form of writing? This wholly fictive work both defended and criticized his friend Schlegel's *Lucinde,* a book that shocked its German contemporaries with its raptur-ous celebration of erotic love between Schlegel and his (married) friend, Dorothea Veit. In the end we can judge that Schleiermacher is less rhapsodic than Schlegel and puts realistic limits to Schlegel's ecstatic utterances about a new religion of love, as a fusion of "spiritual voluptu-ousness and sensual beatitude."[41] Yet to assert that directly does less than justice to the topic at hand. The very form of these fictive letters under-scores what I am saying. The idea that you can engage in telling criticism by *concealing* your own persona was an unusual and startling notion of Romantic literary theory. As a term, "Romantic" still has connotations

---

40 Cited in *The Concept of Irony,* 425. In commenting on this work in the context of Kierkegaard's studies in 1835, Emanuel Hirsch writes: "His own pseudonymous authorship later does the same in a deeper sense. One may venture the thesis that the literary form of the first part of *Either-Or* is largely an imitation of [Schlegel's] *Lucinde,* in its second part an imitation of Schleiermacher's *Lucinde* letters" (Hirsch, *Kierkegaard-Studien,* II, 33, n. 6).

41 *Friedrich Schlegel's "Lucinde" and the Fragments,* ed. and tr. Peter Firchow (Minneapolis: University of Minnesota Press, 1971), 44.

that derive from the German *Roman* or novel, where authors invent
characters. As the *Athenaeum* (Critical Fragments number 26) puts it:
"Novels are the Socratic dialogues of our time."[42] In the language of the
day the young Schleiermacher was being novelistic in his *Confidential
Letters*.

In attempting to identify the literary connection between Schleiermacher
and Kierkegaard we may remind ourselves that Schleiermacher was considered by contemporaries to hold uncommon insight into human life.
Discussing his "Essay on the Sense of Shame," later incorporated into the
letters, with Henriette Herz on April 16, 1799, he writes:

> Actually I believe I know a good deal about the human, especially about his inner
> being, which is where I have a clear intuition; but in that which one calls the
> world, in practical knowledge, in routine and its little tricks, there I am an awful
> bungler.[43]

Writing in July 1800 to his friend and confidante Karl Gustav von
Brinckmann, Schleiermacher observes that his "Lucinde Letters" are
"more about love than about Lucinde" and downplays their significance,
while expressing interest in his friend's perception of their form. "On the
whole they aren't very significant, and so you can allow yourself time to
read them when you have nothing better to do. On the style of the letters
and the form of the effort I would eventually like to have your opinion."[44]

It is, indeed, the work's form that deserves discussion if we are to
fathom what attracted Kierkegaard to the letters. As a basis of comparison
with Kierkegaard's pseudonymity, a reader would do well to become
better acquainted with this work of the young Schleiermacher. Characteristic of the Schlegels' movement, the work is a mélange of literary forms.
Typical, too, is the way that literature and art take actual events into the
world of letters and reproduce interpretations of them at a higher level.
Here, the events are the publication of *Lucinde* and the *de facto* social
notoriety of its bedroom discussions in the world of 1800; later, the ninth
letter makes direct allusion to other actual works by Schlegel, published in
the *Athenaeum*. Thus a real world situation is addressed at a level that is
aesthetically removed from the conflict; hypothetical space is, as it were,
created in which, as Kierkegaard recognizes, various viewpoints come to
unfettered expression.

---

42 Ibid., 145.
43 *Schl Briefe*, 1, 219, cited in *KGA* 1/3, *Schriften aus der Berliner Zeit 1800–1802*, ed. Günter
   Meckenstock with Hans-Friedrich Traulsen (Berlin: Walter de Gruyter, 1988), LI.
44 *Schl Briefe*, IV, 74, cited in *KGA* 1/3, LVII.

The anonymously published letters begin with a fictional editorial introduction that establishes a tone of ironic distance towards the project. The collection is presented to an unknown friend, being unsure what possible use he might make of them. Tentativeness is especially warranted, since the second half of *Lucinde* had not yet even appeared. The editor (later we learn he is called Friedrich) professes neutrality with respect to his project and chides his unknown friend about "having something up his sleeve in wanting to publish the letters" (144, 30–1).[45] Certainly one should not expect the letters to "mediate between the work [*Lucinde*] and the universal tumult against it" or "to convert or instruct people; according to their manner of origin and nature these letters are not suited to that end" (144, 36–145, 2). He contemplates writing a couple of letters of his own against these letters and also against *Lucinde*, but decides that it will avail nothing to try to speak reasonably with people "for whom the simplest and most natural concepts teach nothing" (145, 18–19). Yet since a reader may want to hear a single voice in the matter he makes their publication by his correspondent conditional upon printing at the outset a "Dedication to the Uncomprehending," addressed to "friends and citizens in the world and in literature" (146, 4–9). Here, the editor writes, "I dedicate these pages to you, being confident of your holy zeal to characterize the most wanton book and to expose the most dangerous assaults" and ends with an ode to resurrected love that shall animate a new life and "supplant the empty shadows of imagined virtues" (147, 21–2).

There follows a collection of nine letters, not conceived as a straightfoward series but set in an arrangement whereby their authors, Friedrich (the editor), Ernestine (his sister), Karoline (Ernestine's daughter), Eleonore (the editor's lover), and Edward (a male friend) have different relationships to Schlegel's work as well as to one another. At two points the epistolary form is broken up, first by a formal treatise ("Essay on the Sense of Shame"), an earlier piece by the editor which he gratuitously attaches to the letter from Ernestine, and second by a series of fragmentary aphoristic thoughts on *Lucinde* and love that are appended to a letter sent to the editor by his Eleonore.

---

45 In what follows parenthetical page references are given to *KGA* 1/3. Ruth Drucilla Richardson, "Schleiermacher's 'Vertraute Briefe': A Momentary Aberration or a Genuine Schleiermacherian Ethical Treatise?," in *Schleiermacher und die Wissenschaftliche Kultur des Christentums*, ed. Günter Meckenstock (Berlin: Walter de Gruyter, 1991), 455–72 compares the treatise to Schleiermacher's ethics and does not treat the work's origin and impact within Romantic thought; for a thoughtful discussion of *Vertraute Briefe* in its literary context, see Julie Ellison, *Delicate Subjects: Romanticism, Gender, and the Ethics of Understanding* (Ithaca: Cornell University Press, 1990), 17–44.

The first letter to Ernestine accompanies a copy of *Lucinde*, recalls their earlier discussion of love, and seeks her opinion. When no response is forthcoming he sends a scolding second letter in which he accuses her of prudery and suggests she should go to England (154, 15; 158, 8; 159, 13). Heady ideas are contained here, including the thought that "even if one might not know an author, or a book had no author, it [a work] nonetheless has spirit and character" (155, 25–7). Appealing to her directly for a response, he notes that "his sister is a noble lady . . . the whole world knows she understands love and is one of the few chosen people who lives in a true marriage" (155, 42–156, 4). In language reminiscent of Plato's *Symposium* he, of course, acknowledges the difficulty of philosophy as a vehicle for examining the nature of love. But in the end he really just cannot abide the "false modesty, which is natural to most of you [women]" and he chides her without mercy with the thought that, though man denies the gift of abstraction to woman, "in matters of love her imagination is more than equal to the task of portraying love in its innermost mysteries" (157, 13–21).

Responding sharply to his provocation, Ernestine in the third letter rejects any suggestion of prudery and asserts that he could have spared himself his second letter. His reflections on shame, which they had talked about earlier, are more to the point than this silly talk about prudery. If she must write, however, she will offer the critique that the *Lucinde*'s view of love is "a bit too much turned in on itself." "I would prefer," she writes, "that it would move rather more outward into the world and accomplish something clever" (162, 23–163, 2). In her response to her brother, Ernestine celebrates the wholeness and divinely given mystery of love. She insists on making a distinction between love generally and the love of Julius (Schlegel's male persona) in *Lucinde* (166, 11–12). Near the end of her letter she asks how one can possibly go about "properly classifying and spinning out a theory regarding the sense of desire?" (166, 31–2). "If one really believes in the universality of jest and seeks irony in everything, then the task naturally arises of also making both a jest of love and even of the lovers themselves" (167, 11–14).

Where a reader expects a direct response to the awaited letter the editor inserts a copy of his own "Essay on the Sense of Shame" to which Ernestine has alluded, thus distancing himself for a moment being from her querulous response to Schlegel's book (168, 3–178, 24). This mini-treatise (itself more than twice as long as the longest letter) on a sense of self as it relates to a sense of personal modesty and shame interrupts the flow of the letters. Kierkegaard regarded its "dialectical-polemical language" highly; its placement constituted just the sort of literary trick and jarring textual dislocation that he would later utilize, ironically describing a dialectically serious discussion as an appendix, while placing it in the middle of a work.[46] In a veiled way an editorial voice is covertly reclaimed while it is also formally disavowed. The immediate effect is ironic; Ernestine has just taken a stand against undue theorizing, even while admitting that she liked this treatise. The little essay provides just that occasion for Schleiermacher to delineate the inner meaning of personhood by pondering what gives rise to a sense of shame. His aim is "to get acquainted with each person . . . to know where his freedom is least fortified and most vulnerable in order to protect it right at that point" (172, 40–3).

Proceeding immediately to the fourth letter (from Karoline, Ernestine's daughter) – which was enclosed in her mother's third letter – we hear a young girl's perspective on these matters. She rejects the view that she must actually read the book to form an opinion, long passages of it having been read aloud to her by her mother. Despite (or because of?) this partial reading Karoline raises the sharpest critique yet of its male hero Julius and by implication of Schlegel. This one-sided conquering male ego constitutes "an annoying gender despotism" and exemplifies the "horrible egoism of men" (183, 3, 9). The author may understand women, but he obviously knows nothing about young girls (183, 14–15). Though only in the ninth letter (the last of the series) does the editor respond to Ernestine, the fifth letter responds directly to the enclosed message from her daughter, Karoline. As expected, she is chided for only selectively hearing the work and forming her judgments apart from entertaining the work as a whole. Maidenhood, in Schlegel's view, is a time "when everything still hovers in the attractive magic of dark intimations in a state of graceful confusion" (184, 19–25). He gently urges her to experiment with life and suggests that a "holy shyness" (which by implication she has) is better and higher than "common shame and decorum."

A sixth letter to a male friend, Edward, directly challenges this friend's view (which we have not read) that *Lucinde* is full of immorality. Such a judgment ill becomes a work of art, which must be grasped from within its various parts. Here the strongest defence is given of Schlegel's "religion

46 See, for example, *Philosophical Fragments*, ed. and tr. Howard V. Hong and Edna H. Hong (Princeton: Princeton University Press, 1985), "Appendix: Offense at the Paradox (An Acoustic Illusion)," which follows chapter 3 (49–54), or the notoriously difficult "Interlude" between chapters 4 and 5 (72–8).

of love and its deification" (193, 34). Edward is bluntly told that "Anyone who has not looked into the inner side of this deity and of humanity and is incapable of grasping the mysteries of this religion is not worthy of being a citizen of the new world" (194, 13–15). Whereas the other voices have been more nuanced and ambiguous with respect to Schlegel's book, the response to Edward takes the form of deep sympathy with the Romantic project.

As if to confirm Friedrich's sympathetic sixth letter, Eleonore (his lover), in the seventh letter, expresses the most passionate and internalized response to *Lucinde*. She sees her own and Friedrich's love mirrored in the work, even as she expresses some doubts about the way that *Lucinde* distinguishes between the roles of friendship and love in male and female relationships. Her critique of Julius' love is that he acts as if love is onesidedly derived from woman, while in the case of their own love everything is both cause and effect in a truly mutual manner (199, 7–9). Lucinde's experience needs to be shown more completely, just like Eleonore's, "since women who love are open earlier and more unlimitedly than men" (200, 21–2). The lyrical style of Eleonore's letter contrasts sharply with other letters as well as with the editor's voice. As enclosures, she sends random thoughts to her Friedrich in the form of aphorisms, brief reflections while reading *Lucinde*. Here we see that while the first interruption of the letter form was a philosophically nuanced minitreatise, the second interruption consists of fragmentary insights, the preferred vehicle of the makers of the *Athenaeum*. By only enclosing a sample of her thoughts, Eleonore leaves the reader to ponder what remains unexpressed between them. The last enclosure ends on an ecstatic note of the harmony of love, "of which there is no higher wisdom or deeper religion" (206, 1–2). Responding to his lover in the eighth letter, the editor suggests that their love should be so stimulated by *Lucinde* as to constitute a companion piece. Such, at any rate, is his fantasy (212, 2–9). He ends by reflecting on the poetry of their love, "which reflects the immediacy of nature and the heart, which for us will always be the source of the tenderest and most beautiful in life" (212, 18–21).

Lastly in the series the editor turns in the ninth letter to respond to his sister, Ernestine, whose opinion he had so earnestly sought at the outset. The letter is gentle but carefully phrased. He sends it along with other works by Schlegel from the *Athenaeum* ("Stanzen an Heliodora" and marked passages from the "Ideen") as a means of showing how unfair she has been. Such further works will put Schlegel's ideas of love into a wider perspective. He agrees with her that a man should not and cannot separate from the bourgeois world, but maintains that this idea is neither suggested nor expressed by the work. Friedrich maintains that "[the work] is only abstracted from the bourgeois world and its conditions since they are so bad, and this is absolutely necessary in an artistic work that sanctifies love" (214, 2–5).[47] She vastly underestimates what love has been set forth in the world by Julius' art. There may be grounds for criticism, Guido and Antonio [in *Lucinde* Schlegel's code name for Schleiermacher] are enigmatic figures and cannot be grasped, the work's form excessively intensifies and torments the imagination, and she may occasionally even be right about too much theorizing. Yet she must admit that for an artist to whom everything must be art, one must move from quarreling over details to a sense of the whole (215, 34–216, 9).

A MODEL FOR KIERKEGAARD

We can expect that the exact way and the degree to which the *Confidential Letters* served as a model for Kierkegaard's indirect communication will continue to be debated. Novice readers of Kierkegaard, who are invariably baffled by his literary tricks, need only to steep themselves in the aesthetic theory of early German Romanticism to realize that the techniques were not made up in Copenhagen out of whole cloth. What is suggested here is that there are specific reasons why he came to admire Schleiermacher's literary stratagems. The inventions of his "true masterpiece" are "complete beings" through whom "it is possible to get a glance into the individuality of the single individual and through numerous yet merely relatively true judgments to draw up our own final judgment."[48] Thus the integrity of the act of personal appropriation is preserved in the art of an engaged reading and criticism. In their 1983 and 1985 essays on the trilogy of Schlegel, Schleiermacher, and Kierkegaard, neither Hans Dierkes nor George Pattison treats the ways in which Kierkegaard draws immediate literary inspiration from Schleiermacher.[49] Both writers dwell more on

---

47 Tension between Schlegel and Schleiermacher arose very soon on the point of how art is related to life. See Hans Dierkes, "Friedrich Schlegel's *Lucinde*, Schleiermacher and Kierkegaard," *Deutsche Vierteljahrschrift* 11/3 (1983): 437; Jack Forstman, *A Romantic Triangle: Schleiermacher and Early German Romanticism* (Missoula: Scholars Press, 1977); Sabina Wilke, "Authorial Intent Versus Universal Symbolic Language: Schleiermacher and Schlegel on Mythology, Interpretation, and Communal Values," *Soundings: An Interdisciplinary Journal* 74/3–4 (1991): 411–25.
48 See quotation above, 111.
49 Dierkes, "Friedrich Schlegels *Lucinde*," 431–49, and George Pattison, "Friedrich Schlegel's *Lucinde*: A Case Study in the Relation of Religion to Romanticism," *Scottish Journal of Theology* 38 (1985): 545–64.

the task of differentiating the three thinkers' distinctive appropriations of Romanticism. Yet by being steeped in the work of Schleiermacher, Kierkegaard had the advantage of drawing from Romanticism while engaging in an extended critique of Schlegel's teaching on irony.

It takes us too far afield to comment extensively on the appeal to Schleiermacher in *Concept of Irony*. That work, however, cannot be understood apart from the work of Schleiermacher on Plato. Granted, Schleiermacher's understanding of Socratic dialectic may end with a doctrine of knowledge that, on Kierkegaard's reading, is more positive and less paradoxical than his own.[50] A full discussion of dialectic in both writers remains to be undertaken. But on the issue of delineating the philosophical significance of Socrates they are in basic accord, even if on Kierkegaard's reading the emphasis is put on what Gregory Vlastos calls "the strangeness of Socrates."[51]

In what precedes I have sketched the actual historical matrix related to Schleiermacher in which I believe Kierkegaard's work is most fruitfully understood. I have sought to move the discussion beyond a general assertion that their common aims outweigh actual differences. To have a model for indirect communication is more than having an aim; it points to an intellectual practice that runs very deep. Whether formal influence on the art of writing constitutes the Archimedean point around which all other discussions of their relationship must be oriented requires further argument. Kierkegaard's journals reveal differences in detailed judgments having to do with religion and theology that set him apart from Schleiermacher. Debts and influences are arguably most profoundly felt when the temper and quality of another person's mind is felt to be so attractive that one must create one's own position over against the model of the master.[52]

In some respects the matter resembles the case made by Ronald M. Green in *Kierkegaard and Kant: The Hidden Debt*. Green argues that Kantian thought is brilliantly turned against itself at the hands of

---

50 Schleiermacher's aim in writing "On the Worth of Socrates as Philosopher," ed. Charles Anthon, *Xenophon's Memorabilia of Socrates* (New York: Harper and Bros, 1848) 443–57, was to quarrel with contemporary German classical philologists who asserted either that Socrates belonged to the end of the previous age of philosophy (Krug) or that he stood as precursor to Plato, though not as a significant thinker in his own right (Ast).

51 Gregory Vlastos, *Socrates: Ironist and Moral Philosopher* (Cambridge: Cambridge University Press, 1991). Vlastos' asides regarding Kierkegaard's reading of Socrates suggest how very much the paradoxicality of Socratic thought in the hands of Kierkegaard is nurtured by Romantic sources (43–4).

52 The anxiety of influence theme articulated by Harold Bloom is taken up in chapter 11.

Kierkegaard.[53] Yet in this present instance Kierkegaard's debt is only partially hidden, owing to the fact that overt criticism of Schleiermacher exists side by side with expressions of significant admiration. I would add that I do not think the position I have taken contradicts Green's recent efforts to depict Kant as the chief spur behind the Kierkegaardian corpus. It does, however, further contextualize the argument of Green by pointing out that Kierkegaard owes Schleiermacher a formal debt having to do with the art of writing in a concealed manner and a substantive debt of modeling a standard of intellectual integrity and objectivity in the interpretation of Plato. Subject to further review, including the examination of explicitly theological texts and arguments that are not taken up in this chapter, this is how I construe their relationship.[54]

53 Ronald M. Green, *Kierkegaard and Kant: The Hidden Debt* (Albany: State University of New York Press, 1985).

54 See Richard Crouter, "Revisiting Kierkegaard's Relationship to Schleiermacher," in *Kierkegaard and his German Contemporaries*, ed. Jon Stewart (in press), in the Kierkegaard Research: Sources, Reception and Resources of the Kierkegaard Research Centre at the University of Copenhagen series.

PART II

Signposts of a public theologian

CHAPTER 5

Schleiermacher's Letters on the Occasion *and the crisis of Berlin Jewry*

Just how and why Jewish emancipation into civil society came to be addressed in a set of six fictive letters by Friedrich Schleiermacher forms a complex but compelling story. How did a rising young Christian theologian within the Berlin Romantic circle come to use his gifts of satire, irony, and substantial insight into religion to address a sociopolitical situation with immense implications for Christians as well as Jews? If comparable moments exist in the history of Christian theology where a major theologian so directly (and constructively) engages the religious teaching and sociopolitical striving of contemporary Jews, they must be few in number.[1] Of course, Schleiermacher's life (1768–1834) coincides with the era of democratic aspirations. The quest for universal rights of late eighteenth-century Europe, epitomized by the neighboring French revolution, had a great impact on Prussian, with a Jewish population many times that of France. Though French Jews (mostly living in Alsace) were emancipated in 1790 and 1791, it would take Prussia another eighty years to grant full civil and political rights to its Jews.[2]

Eventually known as the premier theologian of modern Protestant liberalism and the translator of Plato into German, Schleiermacher served

---

1 One thinks of Reinhold Niebuhr in this regard as a possible analogy. See, e.g., "The Relations of Christians and Jews in Western Civilization," (1958) in *The Essential Reinhold Niebuhr: Selected Essays and Addresses*, ed. Robert McAfee Brown (New Haven: Yale University Press, 1986), 182–201.
2 The "Law of the Equality of Religions as Regards Common and State Civic Rights in the North German Confederation" was passed in July 1869 in the movement towards German unification; see Michael Brenner, "Between Revolution and Legal Equality," in *German-Jewish History in Modern Times*, ed. Michael A. Meyer (New York: Columbia University Press, 1997), III, 297; Werner E. Mosse, "From 'Schutzjuden' to 'Deutsche Staatsbürger jüdischen Glaubens': The Long and Bumpy Road of Jewish Emancipation in Germany," in *Paths of Emancipation: Jews, States, and Citizenship*, ed. Pierre Birnbaum and Ira Katznelson (Princeton: Princeton University Press, 1995). In addition to other essays in *German-Jewish History*, I–IV, ed. Meyer, see Meyer, *The Origins of the Modern Jew: Jewish Identity and European Culture in Germany 1769–1824* (Detroit: Wayne State University Press, 1967), and David Sorkin, *The Transformation of German Jewry, 1780–1840* (Oxford: Oxford University Press, 1987).

123

with distinction as teacher at the University of Berlin from 1810 until 1834. His youthful 64-page pamphlet, *Letters on the Occasion of the Political-theological Task and the Open Letter of Jewish Householders* (July 1799) has received modest attention in the scholarly literature.[3] His involvement in German–Jewish and Jewish–Christian relations in Berlin is all the more striking since there is little doubt that Schleiermacher – like most Christian theologians – maintained the supersessionist view that Christianity's truth had supplanted that of Judaism.[4] Christian anti-Judaism (prejudice based on religious commitments) and its relationship to anti-Semitism (racial hatred) is well established by a myriad of recent studies.[5] In addressing the religious and political aspirations of his acculturated Jewish contemporaries in Berlin Schleiermacher was walking on perilous ground, ground which is further haunted by our knowledge of the subsequent fate of German Jewry. It is the contention of this writer that we still have much to learn from this and similar moments of authentic interreligious dialogue.

SETTING OF THE 'LETTERS ON OCCASION'

The direct spark for Schleiermacher's *Letters on the Occasion* was an exchange of views between David Friedländer (1750–1834), silk merchant, intellectual, and spiritual heir of Moses Mendelssohn in the Berlin Jewish community, and Wilhelm Abraham Teller (1734–1804), Provost of the Berlin Protestant Church. Friedländer and Teller were both deeply under the spell of Enlightenment ideas about universal reason, human dignity and morality, and both wished for a progressive political-religious life where, as Jew or Christian, these values could be fostered. To bring these voices to life through the eyes of Schleiermacher is to revisit the religious

---

3 Hans-Joachim Birkner, "Der politische Schleiermacher," in *Schleiermacher-Studien* (Berlin: Walter de Gruyter, 1996), 137–56, does not mention this controversy; Joseph W. Pickle, "Schleiermacher on Judaism," *Journal of Religion* 60/2 (1980): 115–37; Kurt Nowak, ed., Friedrich Schleiermacher, *Briefe bei Gelegenheit der politisch theologischen Aufgabe und des Sendschreibens jüdischer Hausväter* (Berlin: Evangelische Verlagsanstalt, 1984), 67–86; Gunter Scholtz, "Friedrich Schleiermacher über das Sendschreiben jüdischer Hausväter," in *Judentum im Zeitalter der Aufklärung*, ed. Vorstand der Lessing-Akademie (Bremen, Wolfenbüttel: Jacobi Verlag, 1977), 297–351 is especially thorough and suggestive.
4 This position is reflected in his notorious remark in the fifth speech of Schleiermacher's *On Religion*; see note 12 (this chapter) and accompanying text.
5 Paul L. Rose, *Revolutionary Antisemitism in Germany: From Kant to Wagner* (Princeton: Princeton University Press, 1990), like the older work by Nathan Rotenstreich, *Jews and German Philosophy: The Polemics of Emancipation* (New York: Schocken Books, 1984) does not include Schleiermacher in its treatment of the German intellectual tradition's attitudes towards Jews.

conflict and political-social pain faced by Berlin's Jewish community in the era of the French and American democratic revolutions.[6]

Wilhelm Abraham Teller had served since 1767 as Provost or head of the Protestant Church in Berlin. In the 1790s he was recognized as a leading Enlightenment theologian of that city. His influential publications sought to square Protestant Christianity's age-old dogmas with Enlightenment moral-religious teaching. Indeed, *The Religion of the Perfect* (1793, second edition) as well as his earlier *Dictionary of the New Testament for Explaining Christian Doctrine* (1785, fourth edition) attempted to separate the "Jewish-Oriental," that is, sacrificial, elements of Christian teaching on reconciliation from what he took to be universally acceptable as Christian. Here Teller espouses the view that it would suffice for Jewish converts to confess Jesus as the founder of "a better moral religion."[7] Without advocating Jewish emancipation but appearing open to a Christian missionary agenda, Teller set the stage for Friedländer's political-religious overture.

Teller's liberal Enlightenment views might be described as a form of eighteenth-century deism with a Christian flair. These views, plus his considerable influence, made him a natural recipient for Friedländer's *Open Letter to His Most Worthy, Supreme Consistorial Counselor and Provost Teller at Berlin, from some Householders of the Jewish Religion* (April 1799). More treatise than letter, Friedländer's 86-page document provides its readers with a thoughtful reflection of Haskalah (Enlightenment) Judaism in Berlin. Jews and Christians alike have pilloried Friedländer's proposal for urging conversion to Protestant Christianity as the vehicle for Jewish emancipation into Prussian civil society. Even with its main qualification (refusing to confess Jesus Christ as Son of God) few persons, then or now, can see merit in quasibaptism as a vehicle for attaining civil rights.

A close reading of Friedländer's treatise reveals a remarkable mind in great turmoil. Here was a human plea for understanding and dignity in the face of the marginality of German Jewish existence under the growing commercial and political conditions of modernity. However little merit we may see in linking political rights to church membership, Friedländer's dignified tone and rhetoric tell a nuanced story that reveals this disciple of

---

6 The relevant texts are now available in Friedländer et al. translated from *KGA* I/2, *Schriften aus der Berliner Zeit 1796–1799*, ed. Günter Meckenstock (Berlin: Walter de Gruyter, 1984), 325–69, 373–413, and from Wilhelm Abraham Teller, *Beantwortung des Sendschreibens einiger Hausväter jüdischer Religion an mich den Probst Teller* (Berlin: August Mylius, 1799).
7 *Religion in Geschichte und Gegenwart*, third edition, vi, 678.

Moses Mendelssohn's keen intelligence and pride in his Jewishness (even amid his severe quarrels with Orthodoxy and its rabbis). Published anonymously, the document set off a firestorm of some twenty-three pamphlets (including Schleiermacher's), plus ten newspaper or journal articles.[8] Despite the work's anonymity, readers quickly associated it with Friedländer and his circle,[9] along with the March, 1799, 11-page essay, *Political-theological Task Concerning the Treatment of Baptized Jews.*[10]

In April 1799 Schleiermacher had just completed his celebrated early book, *On Religion: Speeches to its Cultured Despisers.* Here he argues that religion arises from a distinctive "intuition of the universe" and "whether we have a God as a part of our intuition depends on the direction of our imagination."[11] Indeed, one infers from the apparent liberalism of such passages that their author was well beyond thinking that one religion can be truer or better than another. Given this perspectival view of truth, readers are invariably startled by reading in that work's fifth speech: "Judaism is long since a dead religion, and those who at present still bear its colors are actually sitting and mourning beside the undecaying mummy and weeping over its demise and its sad legacy."[12] The description of Judaism seems so prejudicial and dismissive (not to mention its being patently false) as to raise many questions about how and why its author would publish an anonymous pamphlet that same summer that engaged the living aspirations of a faith he considered dead.

Since February 1799 Schleiermacher had been in Potsdam in an interim post as preacher to the court, though his regular position was that of hospital chaplain at the Berlin Charité. His romanticist friends, the Schlegel brothers, Henriette Herz, and his earlier friend Alexander von Dohna had urged him to write *On Religion*, which he did between

---

8 Ellen Littmann, "David Friedländers Sendschreiben an Probst Teller und sein Echo," *Zeitschrift für die Geschichte der Juden in Deutschland* 6 (1935): 92–112.

9 After first denying any involvement, Friedländer acknowledged writing the *Open Letter* in 1819; see Littmann, "David Friedländers Sendschreiben," 93.

10 See above, note 6.

11 *OR* (Crouter), 53. For Schleiermacher, religion arises from intuitions of the universe and is more closely aligned with poetry and feeling than with metaphysics and morals, as well as with his defense of positive religion in contrast with the natural religion of the eighteenth-century Enlightenment. By contrast Friedländer's deist principles (God, immortality, virtue, and dignity of humankind) rested on the older rationalism of Moses Mendelssohn.

12 The passage continues, "Moreover, I speak of it, not because it was somehow the forerunner of Christianity; I hate that type of historical reference in religion. Its necessity is a far higher and eternal one, and every beginning in it is original. But Judaism has such a beautiful, childlike character, and this is so completely buried, and the whole constitutes such a remarkable example of the corruption and total disappearance of religion from a great body in which it was formerly found" (*OR* (Crouter), 113–14).

February and April 1799, while remaining in close touch with these friends. Though surely too neat and schematic, the three spheres of literary expression (Friedrich Schlegel), Jewish life (Herz), and government service (Dohna) all have an impact on the fictive letters. The son of a noble family in Schlobitten, East Prussia, where Schleiermacher earlier served as a tutor, by the late 1790s Alexander von Dohna held a position in the Prussian government and had ushered Schleiermacher into Berlin's social circles, including the Jewish salon of Henriette Herz frequented by the von Humboldts and other persons among the cultural elite.

His correspondence shows Schleiermacher discussing the *Political-theological Task* with Henriette Herz (March 16, 1799) and pledging to respond to it in the Berlin journal where it appeared. In addition, a letter to Herz (April 9, 1799) speaks of receiving and exchanging materials pertaining to Jewish emancipation from Alexander von Dohna.[13] Having already begun the task of translating Plato's dialogs, Schleiermacher was well aware of the power of indirect discourse when treating topics that resist simple resolution. This skill worked to his advantage in addressing the thorny issues surrounding Jewish emancipation. Taking an indirect, literary approach enhanced a sense of dispassion and distance while enabling him to relate the political and religious issues to matters he had just presented at length in *On Religion*. The very next year he would again use the literary form of an exchange of pseudonymous letters to defend another unpopular work: Friedrich Schlegel's *Lucinde*, a notorious self-revelation of Schlegel's love life with the daughter of Moses Mendelssohn, Dorothea (Veit) Schlegel.[14]

The *Letters on the Occasion* are artfully conceived as letters from a concerned preacher to an editor and political leader in Berlin. The letters read as if Alexander von Dohna had collected and published letters from Schleiermacher; their artistry is seen in the way that the politician's views are only inferred from the preacher's responses, while the fact that a politician collected and presents the letters gives their ideas presumed status in the eyes of the state. A sharp call for political responsibility on behalf of Prussia's Jews had just been made by the anonymous, satirical *Political-theological Task*, which appeared in a Berlin journal of art and culture. In turn, these fictive letters frame and analyze theological, moral, and historical arguments in light of this denial of full political rights to

13 *KGA* I/2, LXXXII–LXXXIII. That Schleiermacher's first fictive letter is dated April 17, two days after
    he finished *On Religion*, further links the two projects.
14 See chapter 4 of this book.

Prussia's Jews. No stranger to the use of a sharp tongue, wit, and satire, Schleiermacher's *On Religion* delights in turning contempt towards religion back in the face of religion's cultured despisers; his *Letters* take delight in needling the state for failing to confront directly its widespread and malicious contempt towards Jews. A lovely ruse is exhibited in the politician-recipient's cover letter (with its "prefatory reminder" of how they came into being), as well as in the dating of the letters, which purport to have been written from the 17th of April to the 30th of May, while the war of pamphlets was in process. Such detail enhances verisimilitude and underscores the realistic voice assumed by Schleiermacher. In what follows these literary inventions by Plato's young German translator are frequently cited simply as "the preacher" and "the politician."

THE ARGUMENT OF SCHLEIERMACHER'S LETTERS

In the first letter Schleiermacher chides his politician friend's arrogance for doubting that writers, who only work with words, could have anything useful to say about a matter of practical politics. He contrasts the purely rhetorical appeal of *Political-theological Task* with the *Open Letter*, a more somber work that puts an actual proposal on the table. The preacher acknowledges that the *Open Letter* is beautifully written and notes its acknowledgment of mysticism as the seed of piety and religion – a view that permeates Schleiermacher's recently completed *On Religion* – yet chides the author for not integrating this aspect of religion into his work as a whole (82/333).[15]

It is a moot question whether, at the time of writing, Schleiermacher knew Friedländer was the author of the *Open Letter*. Most interpreters think he must have known.[16] If Schleiermacher did know, his pitting of the "splendid Friedländer" against the anonymous author of *Open Letter* was an especially brilliant rhetorical ploy. Yet caution is urged in view of Schleiermacher's random jottings on Jewish emancipation in his *Gedanken* (youthful notebooks).[17] Private entries on the *Political-theological Task* and on Friedländer's earlier *Akten-Stücke* on emancipation do not directly link Friedländer with the *Open Letter*, where we might have expected them to do so. What is not in doubt, however, is that Schleiermacher

15 Parenthetical page references refer to the English texts in Friedlander et al. with German references to *KGA* 1/2 provided after a forward slash.
16 Littmann, "David Friedländers Sendschreiben," 92–112.
17 None of the three entries that touch on the *Sendschreiben* mention Friedländer's name; one entry ironically speculates that the *Sendschreiben*'s author might be a Christian because of its tendency to split hairs in an argument in a crypto-Jesuitical manner; *KGA* 1/2, 45–8.

connects Friedländer's earlier publications with the 1799 emancipation debate. It seems reasonable to think that Schleiermacher must have surmised that Friedländer was somehow behind the *Open Letter*. But since the Teller letter's dual proposals regarding (1) quasi-conversion and (2) dropping ceremonial law both went against Friedländer's (not to mention Mendelssohn's) earlier published views, it would have been difficult to name him as their author.[18]

Schleiermacher identifies the *Open Letter*'s call for "quasi-conversion" (83/334) to Protestantism as the plot of the drama, which requires direct action by the head of Berlin's Protestant community, Provost Teller, and by the Prussian state. By contrasting the current document with Friedländer's previous efforts in the *Akten-Stücke* the preacher's political realism is seen (84/335). The *Open Letter* writer is chided (1) for acting alone in 1799, unlike the earlier situation that had broader backing, and (2) for breaking with Mendelssohn, who wished to retain the ceremonial law.[19]

The core of Schleiermacher's position on Jewish emancipation, which echoes the sharp distinction between church and state of *On Religion*,[20] is set forth clearly:

Reason demands that all should be citizens, but it does not require that all must be Christians, and thus it must be possible in many ways to be a citizen and a non-Christian – which surely any number of them already have become – and to discover among them those who are suited to our situation and the case at hand; that is the task that no one can escape who wishes to speak openly about this matter, and that thus far has not been treated such that one might let it rest as settled. (85/335)

Being Christian and converting to Christianity are by no means necessary conditions for full and effective citizenship. Here Schleiermacher speaks directly to the polemical satire of *Political-theological Task*. In agreement with that document's satire he playfully assaults the "lazy reason" of statecraft, which avoids thinking of new solutions and falls back on old, settled understandings as a (false) means of solving problems. "How should it not be a case of irresponsible cowardice to give up on that very thing that is known to be not only desirable but necessary?" (85/336).

---

18 The *Open Letter* further veiled its origin by purporting to have been written by a group of Jewish householders.

19 That Schleiermacher had read and known Mendelssohn's argument from *Jerusalem* is apparent not only from the First Letter but also from Schleiermacher's unfinished work (1796–7) on the nature of contracts, *KGA* 1/2, 62–4.

20 *OR* (Crouter), 90, "Away, therefore, with every such union of church and state!"

Whoever does not wish to contribute to the final and satisfactory solution of this task directly by making new proposals or by seeking to resolve difficulties that one could not overcome until now, must – if one doesn't just tell him that he ought to remain silent – at least make an indirect contribution. He must tackle things in their present situation, bring forth the incoherence and inconsistencies in the present conduct of so-called Christian states, and place things in some kind of new light; he must apply some kind of stimulus to tease them out of their laziness so that they finally begin to make proposals from their side and – which they alone are capable of – proceed at the same time with the work at hand. (85–86/336)

In light of this statement the *Letters* attempt to tease the state out of its laziness while stimulating some useful proposals, perhaps along lines of the recently enacted "New East Prussian Regulation of the Jews" (1797). The state cannot be reluctant solely on the economic grounds that it receives "protection money" (*Schutzgeld*) from Jews, a view of an unenlightened government that Schleiermacher rejects. Rather, the preacher strongly associates himself with the view of the *Task* and *Open Letter* that critiques the dogma that "the inner corruption of the Jews" makes it "dangerous to accept them into civil society." This view he finds "very widespread among men of your estate. God knows how this belief may have been shaped into a full-blown theory in the matters they have thought and written about in their official duties, about which little is ever reported to the public" (87/337). Schleiermacher critiques the *Open Letter* for failing to present a more historical account of the dogma of a corrupt Jewish character, and the *Task* for not interrogating the state's assumption of this dogma more severely.

In his second letter Schleiermacher chides his politician friend for taking issue with the rage and indignation of the task-giver's tract, while knowing that the state's policies regarding conversion and citizenship are utterly inconsistent. His friend's objection to the *Task*'s argument against proselytism on grounds that it disrupts families is technically correct, but limited and not realistic because it minimizes the power of the natural bonds of social sentiments. It is wrong to dislike the sarcastic and angry tone of the honest satire when the cold reasoning of the state has been so inadequate. On the preacher's view, the sarcastic tone could even be sharper, "for I am concerned that many persons will think the author has adopted the political option [mass conversion of the whole Jewish nation] in earnest." But the preacher agrees with his friend's emphasis on the *Open Letter*'s seriousness and dignity, even if there are annoying features in the letter: (1) The presumption of an opposition between mysticism and enlightened reason is viewed as a typically Jewish position, as if it could not arise among Christians; (2) suggesting that the "authentic meaning" of ceremonies pertain solely to priests; and (3) showing a "restrained bitterness" when the work engages directly in discussions of how the state relates to Christianity (91/340). On the whole, for an anonymous document where no prior knowledge of an author can shape a favorable opinion, it is all the more remarkable that the *Open Letter* has received such praise.

Yet the sense of bitterness towards Christianity and the state is in conflict with the work's "obtrusive, unwarranted expectation" of a demand for conversion to Christianity. Here Schleiermacher identifies the contradictory impulse that runs between the *Open Letter*'s apparent aversion to Christianity and its willingness to embrace the larger tradition (albeit it for political ends). The preacher sees how steeped the letter is in Judaism's basic truths, how it even seeks precedents in Moses and the rabbis for abolishing law while aligning its position with the teachings of the Psalms and the prophets; how Christianity's basic truths are depicted only as faith claims, while Judaic truths are viewed as rational convictions (92/341). By contrast, certain phrases praise Christianity's openness to the hilt. How is one to weigh these apparent contradictions? In the preacher's words:

All of this taken together brings me to the thought that the author cannot be serious even by half in the way he proposes conversion to Christianity; rather that his intention is only to proceed in such a way as to make it obvious that such a half-way transition is the most that could be demanded of a reasonable and educated man, quite apart from the fact that one should not require anything of the kind. This secret meaning will satisfy the Jewish nation, which is so clever in matters of interpretation, whereas the letter and the appearance of peace and dignity is for the Christians; the former to embarrass them, the latter to keep them in a good mood. (92–93/342).

On this view the *Open Letter* engages in a secret meaning, perceptible to its Jewish readers, which undercuts Christian claims to truth while purporting in some fashion to wish to join the Protestant church. Here lies the sharp edge of disagreement between the preacher and open letter writer; the latter insists on the sheer incompatibility of modern reason with Christological dogma, whereas the former took pains to come up with an arguably reasonable yet normative understanding of Christ in *On Religion*.[21] The second letter does not consider the nuanced reasoning of Friedländer regarding the phrase "Son of God" in a confession that will earn Jews Christian approbation and citizenship.

---

21 *OR* (Crouter), speech 5, 115–21.

In his third letter the preacher's grounds and motivation for involvement surface. His politician friend has apparently wondered how a Christian could object to Jewish conversions, as if that were the supreme goal of all right-thinking Christian theology. The preacher explains that his fears lie in just this sphere, coupled with the view that if the *Open Letter* has no effect and fails to get the desired notice, then the disruptive practice of conversion will continue. As a convinced Christian the preacher takes the conversion of Jews "to be the worst thing that can happen" (95/344). Twenty or thirty years earlier such a gulf separated Jews and Christians that – apart from occasional marital ties – the problem did not arise. Yet even if not harmful to the state, the mixed motives and political end of Jewish conversions will surely do great harm to the Christian church. "By far most of those whom we can expect among us will be the sort of persons who are wholly indifferent towards anything having to do with religion" (96/345). They are ruled by worldly sentiments or are convinced Kantians who equate their own morality with religion.

Here we see Schleiermacher's roots in Moravian pietism, with its teaching about an experiential faith, views endorsed in *On Religion* with the sensibility of the early Romantic poets. There is too much external adherence to religion as it is, and this has been aided and abetted by political compacts like the Peace of Westphalia (1648), which reenforced the territorial religious settlement of the Peace of Augsburg (1555). The argument here contains a strong critique of the *Open Letter*'s truths of reason, which the preacher relegates to a form of Kantian moralism that equates morality with religion itself. Schleiermacher appears to conflate the *Open Letter*'s endorsement of quasibaptism with the *Task*'s satirical and ironic call for a time of education (*Bildungszeit*) to follow mass baptism as a means of overcoming the faults of Jewish character. Even if the latter extends twenty years, the preacher asserts, it would still remain inadequate. The idea of proposing a time of education seems wrongheaded to Schleiermacher, since misunderstood irony might encourage the view that such a time is actually needed.

But the underlying religious insulation of Jewish and Christian communities appears most generally to rest on Schleiermacher's romanticist view of positive religions as virtually organic entities:

It is impossible for anyone who really has a religion to accept another one; and if all Jews were most excellent citizens, not a single one of them would be a good Christian; but they would bring along a great many peculiarly Jewish elements in their religious principles and convictions which, just for this reason, are anti-Christian. (97–98/347)

Since this teaching would appear to allow no growth or transference between religions, one might wonder how any new religion could ever arise. The point reflects Schleiermacher's considered teaching that each religious awakening is unique and, once awakened, becomes so all-consuming and set in the fabric of existence that it cannot be replaced. Most abhorrent to him is the idea that one might traffic in religions just as one trades on the commodities market! His political objection to conversion is then supported by a more specific stance that argues against law-based religion as a form of works righteousness: "Indeed, a Judaizing Christianity would be the true disease with which we should infect ourselves!" (98/347). For Schleiermacher, this theological issue was resolved in Paul's letters in Christian antiquity (e.g., Galatians 2–3), which defend the freedom of the Christian life against positions that would place law at the center of religion.[22] There is no point in just trying to put a good face on a process as onerous as wanting to convert Jews and make them into Christians.

In the third letter the preacher continues to pose other explicitly Christian objections to the conversion of Jews. In coming to a decision on these matters his politician friend should take to heart objections coming from within the believing traditions. Far from welcoming Jews into its midst, the church should resist this process, "for if it endures this all-the-more decadent governmental courtesy even longer, it will pay, much too dearly indeed, for this politeness with its complete ruin" (99/347). This is the case, even though Jews increasingly take part in the process of German education in ways that approximate those of Christians. If the *Open Letter* has a plea for Teller, the preacher's plea is that Teller will realize that the church "should decisively declare itself to this effect: that it request the state to put an end to such an oppressive course of action" (i.e., conversion). Rather than encourage baptisms of Jews, the church, although it cannot prescribe to the state, can "declare before the whole world that it has nothing at all against" allowing Jews "into the unlimited enjoyment of civil liberty" (100/348). On the related matter of matrimony between Jews and Christians the preacher argues that, though it may not be advisable – for various practical reasons – nothing within religion speaks against it; the practices of the early church obviously sanctioned it, and nothing in sacred scripture speaks against it.

---

22 *On Religion* frequently appeals to the contrast between letter and spirit; see Schleiermacher's sermon "Evangelical Faith and the Law," in *Servant of the Word: Selected Sermons of Friedrich Schleiermacher*, ed. and tr. Dawn DeVries (Philadelphia: Fortress Press, 1987), 136–51.

Though Schleiermacher conceives of religions as self-contained, if not exclusive enclaves of meaning, the allowance of interfaith marriages tempers that insight with realism.

In opening the fourth letter the preacher complains that his politician friend has mistaken his desire not to have Jews in the church for enmity towards Jews, or perhaps a secret belief in their "moral degradation." In a sharp retort the letter writer reminds his friend that he also wishes that "the greatest portion of Christians," including good friends and the politician himself, were not in the church. But he chooses not to defend himself further, urging this nonresistance on the grounds of his being a Christian (102/351). When the politician appears to have pressed him for more practical solutions and suggestions, the preacher responds that his discussion partner simply has not paid attention to the previous letters. This remark, however, in no way prevents the preacher from becoming more specific in his recommendations and ideas. In passing, a reader soon realizes that Schleiermacher's preacher has already studied the earlier Jewish reform efforts led by David Friedländer with care.[23]

The fourth letter specifically maintains that (1) ceremonial law is a political hindrance, and that (2) the current method of naturalizing Jews as citizens requires a cumbersome, tedious, and unfair investigatory process. In not requiring that Jews should "completely reject ceremonial law but only subordinate it to the laws of the state" (103/352) the preacher's demand is less stringent than that of the *Open Letter*. In agreement with the *Open Letter* the preacher also requires Jews to re-nounce the hope for a messiah, while wryly noting that Friedländer's *Akten-Stücke* complains about Jews being treated as foreigners, but refers to the Jewish people as a nation and reenforces the idea that their allegiance may belong to some entity other than the German state. Even if belief in future nationhood has "few true followers," "as long as it remains a public confession, the state cannot treat them other than by assuming that they believe in it." Acknowledging the need for a smooth working relationship with society, the preacher notes that a level of moral corruption that inhibits assimilation can even occur among his own people: "Who would wish to deny that our own common people are well inclined to deceive foreigners?" He observes the social cohesion that German society feels in the Jewish community and defends it by saying: "Only for this reason do the Jews separate themselves from other fellow

23 The fact that Friedländer's documents from that period (the *Akten-Stücke)* are cited several times points to Schleiermacher's involvement with the issue of Jewish emancipation prior to 1799.

citizens, so that when the time of departure comes, they may be as little entangled as possible while being bound together as much as possible" (104/353).

Schleiermacher's final requirement in response to the politician's challenge to become more concrete is that Jews "constitute a special ecclesiastical society" (105/353). This would establish an "altered Judaism" in the form of a state-recognized (Reform or Enlightenment) Judaism that embodies the two prior conditions of (1) subordinating ceremonial law, to German civil law, and (2) giving up the hope in a messiah. In both instances, citizenship requires accepting the full legitimacy of the state and its lawfulness as well as sharing in its maintenance and well-being. Recognizing that even the *Open Letter* stops short of proposing full organic union with the church and (against initial appearances) seeks a way to preserve one's Jewishness, the preacher paraphrases Saint Paul to write that "if one in accord with law has to destroy the law for the sake of the eternal, one still remains under the law, i.e., in Judaism" (106/354–5).[24] In effect, the passage wishes to suggest that the choice of subordinating (outmoded religious) law to (living) German law creatively ensures the survival of one's (truly religious) Jewishness through the use of law.

Though the fourth letter rejects the idea of Jews attaining civil liberty via the church, it argues strongly for a non-Christian alternative that would parallel the *Open Letter*'s proposal to Provost Teller. Far from polemicizing against the *Open Letter*, Schleiermacher believes he has "shown that it is full of the spirit of Judaism and of love for the same and that the conversion to Christianity is a false deed that does not belong in it" (105/354). Against reader expectation, and against the expection of his fictionalized interlocutor, the preacher thinks he has captured not just the spirit of the *Open Letter* but even improved on that document by denying any need to ensure Jewish civil liberties through church membership. Only an evil demon could have driven its author to want to unite with the church in order to have an assured place in the society; if this aim can be granted short of conversion, that is an improvement for both Jew and Christian.

Once one has wholly excluded its false elements, the *Open Letter* contains everything that the state can demand from the Jews and is the true codex of a new Judaism, capable and worthy of political existence in every respect. You see how little I am against the *Open Letter* when I allot it this place! I see the *Task*

---

24 Adapted from Galatians 2:19: "For through the law I died to the law, so that I might live to God."

and the *Open Letter* as necessary and complementary pieces and believe that, taken together, both contain everything that the Jews have to do for their benefit: the former indirectly by provoking the state to depart from its accustomed way; the latter directly by opening a new way to it. (106/355)

This statement unambiguously endorses both of the Judaic documents to which Schleiermacher responds through his preacher. Thus Schleiermacher as Christian theologian, who might well have taken a strongly anti-Judaic line on religious grounds, uses his *Letters on the Occasion* to support the proposals that derive from Friedländer's circle of Haskalah Jews. He ends the fourth letter by challenging his imaginary political interlocutor, and thus his readers, to come up with valid objections to what he proposes.

It remains only to characterize the fifth and sixth letters in light of the preceding arguments. The fifth letter constitutes an effort to make the proposal for a new Jewish sect more plausible in view of the natural skepticism of political realism. The preacher first seeks to disarm potential objections to new recognition of a Jewish sect based on the 1648 Peace of Westphalia's strictures against the creation of new religions. This older imperial law (of the Holy Roman Empire) is less important than the immediate matters at hand and the needs of Prussia. (Indeed, the old empire did come to an official end in 1806.) In addition, he maintains that having a new sect of elite, educated, and enlightenment Jews will have practical benefits; among these, the natural bonding within the Jewish community will not cease to help poorer classes of Jews who remain in Orthodoxy, and will serve as a leadership group to counterbalance the interests of Orthodoxy, among whom there are also persons of wealth. If the Orthodox continue to grow and fan the flames among the poorer class of Jews, this will "support hatred of Christians and the fatherland far more strongly than is the case up to now" (108/357). If there had been such "a select group of the Jewish nation" (here Schleiermacher also uses the term "Jewish nation") at the time of the earlier reform efforts, something salutary would have happened, at least for these people. Granted, one might simply institute a new Jewish regulation on the model recently enacted in East Prussia.[25] But then "even less would be achieved towards that which our German Jews want and what I as a Christian have wished for them" (110/358).

25 *Das General-Juden-Reglement für Süd- und Neu-Ost-Preußen* from 17 April 1797 is printed in Ludwig von Rönne and Heinrich Simon, *Die früheren und gegenwärtigen Verhältnisse der Juden in den sämmtlichen Landestheilen des Preußischen Staates* (*Die Verfassung und Verwaltung des Preußischen Staates*, vol. 8/3) (Breslau: G. P. Aderholz, 1843), 292–302.

Letter 6 stands apart from the debate pursued thus far and responds to other reactions to the *Open Letter* that the politician has sent the preacher. At the outset I mentioned that Friedländer's letter to Teller set off a firestorm of reactions and protests in the Christian world. It was largely to counter these reactions that Schleiermacher produced his own pamphlet of fictive letters. Letter 6, dated 30th May 1799, is especially concerned to mock a particularly obnoxious, anonymous reaction to the *Open Letter* signed "by a preacher *in* Berlin."[26] His own work "by a preacher *outside* of Berlin" constitutes a direct rejoinder to this document. Schleiermacher goes to great lengths to attack this document, while sarcastically wondering why more sensible Protestant clergy in Berlin have not become involved. His personal motivation is clear when he writes: "I am ashamed when I think it is possible that worthy Jews, who, however, know so few clergy, and hardly have a proper idea of this class of persons, might draw inferences about the others from this one" (111/360). The sixth letter's final paragraph ends the exchange by noting that Mr. Teller's response, which had been written in the meantime, is instructive and gracious: "He casts aside all worldly considerations in order to clarify, according to his insight, only that about which he's been asked "(112/361). In fact, Teller denied the baptism proposal but remained open to full Jewish civil rights. In the perspective of Friedrich Schleiermacher the cycle of debate had now run its course.

CIVIL ACCOMMODATION AMID RELIGIOUS DIFFERENCES

What, then, is one able to conclude with regard to this exchange of views? Basically, two quite fundamental and interrelated points emerge from careful study of the *Letters on the Occasion*. First, these consist of the fact that Schleiermacher's views as a Christian theologian who is antithetical to Judaism on religious-theological grounds remain fully in place. (These were subsequently reenforced by his dogmatics [*The Christian Faith*], his sermons, and his writings on the history of the Christian church.) Evidence points to the reality that Schleiermacher, whose New Testament faith emerged from German pietism, had a lifelong aversion to Hebraic religion, that is, what he takes to be legalistic religion of the Old Testament. Second, a distinction must be made between intraconfessional theological agreement (which is never achieved) and the fact that

---

26 [Anonymous,] *An einige Hausväter jüdischer Religion, über die vorgeschlagene Verbindung mit den protestantischen Christen. Von einem Prediger in Berlin* (Berlin, 1799).

theological agreement is not a prior condition for (a) civil discourse about
theology or (b) granting practitioners of diverse religions civil rights under
a common polity. Schleiermacher's teaching regarding the relative independence of church and state is reflected in the work. His fictive letters
recognize the likely devastating consequences if the call for Jewish emancipation is either completely blocked or allowed to drift, and he combines
this rational appeal with an appeal to the powers of human empathy. On
balance, one must conclude that the justifiably restrained bitterness of
both Judaic documents found as deep a resonance in him as it did among
his Jewish friends in the circle around Henriette Herz.[27] With these
associations in mind, the demand for emancipation (with minimal conditions) looked not just reasonable but long overdue. Here, as elsewhere, Schleiermacher's realism and progressive political temperament[28]
was profoundly shaped by his generation's experience with the French
revolution and the distantly admired American case of church and state
separation.

In a situation where Friedländer saw the temptations of conversion on a
daily basis, and the social as well as political benefits that flowed from
being assimilated, he had to act. Far from Friedländer selling out his
tradition to Christianity, he desperately sought to resolve an intolerable
situation that was, as it turned out, too messy for immediate social and
political resolution. At a time when conversions seemed inevitable and
began to happen more frequently among educated Jews, Friedländer
sought an accommodation; once within what he genuinely took to be a
largely deist Protestant community, at least his Jewish existence and that
of like-minded Jews (and their progeny) could be preserved without
having to confess Christ as savior. If this reading of the document (which
goes beyond Schleiermacher's reading) seems extreme, that is only because it requires us to step further into Friedländer's world. The Jewish
horror not just of giving up one's own people with its shattering of family
and other ties, but of confessing Christ as savior is poignantly expressed in
the *Open Letter* and its precursor, the *Political-theological Task*. Though
not uncritical of their details, Schleiermacher enters deeply into these

27 For the impact of the Jewish salons on Schleiermacher's Berlin, see Deborah Hertz, *Jewish High
   Society in Old Regime Berlin* (New Haven: Yale University Press, 1988), Steven M. Lowenstein,
   The Berlin Jewish Community: Enlightenment, Family, and Crisis 1770–1830 (Oxford: Oxford
   University Press, 1994); Peter Siebert, *Der literarische Salon: Literatur und Geselligkeit zwischen
   Aufklaerung und Vormaerz* (Stuttgart: Metzler, 1994).
28 See below, chapter 7.

Judaic works and ends by defending them as necessary, useful, and complementary.

On this reading Schleiermacher's *Letters on Occasion* constitute an extended footnote to the negative comments on Judaism of the fifth speech of *On Religion*. They reflect the beliefs and aspirations of Schleiermacher's circle of Jewish friends, who were deeply alienated from their roots in Talmudic tradition, in a situation where, as Friedländer puts it, knowledge of Hebrew was "diminishing daily." The proximity of *On Religion* and the *Letters* in 1799, plus evidence that Schleiermacher was pondering work on the latter while writing the former, tie the two works together in the life of their author.[29]

Indeed, if *On Religion* was written especially against the background of the Enlightenment with his early Romantic literary friends in mind, the *Letters* are written against this same background but with his Jewish friends, especially the circle around Henriette Herz, in mind. In effect, life in the salons constituted the Judaic side of the early Romantic movement, where openness to new literature and new politics was mixed with healthy respect for Enlightenment rationality. To modern religious reformers like Friedländer and Schleiermacher, the claims and practices of Orthodox Judaism were indeed perceived as "long since dead." However biased and short-sighted that belief may have been, in their day or in ours, the words take on new meaning in light of the 1799 debate. To Schleiermacher's credit, he saw that citizenship requires no religious test and that civil society can retain its bonds amid acute religious differences. Two-hundred years later the human community continues to struggle towards a just civil and political order in the face of irreconcilable religious rivalries and their immense social tensions.

---

29 See Günter Meckenstock in *KGA* 1/2, LXXXII–LXXXIV; Jacob Katz' classic account of the movement of Jews into civil society *Out of the Ghetto: The Social Background of Jewish Emancipation 1770–1870* (New York: Schocken Books, 1973), 120, has the order of publication reversed: "*Speeches on Religion*, published shortly after he had taken a stand on the Jewish issue, did a great deal to rescue religion from its subordination to rationalism."

CHAPTER 6

A proposal for a new Berlin university

It may surprise English-speaking specialists in modern religious thought to discover that in Germany the name Friedrich Schleiermacher resonates so strongly within the fields of educational theory and practical pedagogy. As a theologian-educator reflecting on the nature of a university, his work compares with John Henry Newman's *The Idea of the University* in Great Britain and the US.[1] Hundreds of German monographs, papers, and conferences testify to Schleiermacher's contributions to *Pedagogik*.[2] Among these works, *Occasional Thoughts on the Universities in the German Sense* became a standard text on universities in its author's lifetime, even if today it is more often cited than studied in depth.[3] Schleiermacher's contribution to founding the University of Berlin is virtually without precedent. Few professors have lectured at a university, the ethos and structures of which they had shaped so formatively.[4] In hindsight we can see that *Occasional Thoughts* is a pivotal document in his intellectual biography; it drew from all that preceded, even as it shaped his subsequent

1 For the classic text with commentary and bibliography, see John Henry Newman, *The Idea of a University*, ed. Frank M. Turner (New Haven: Yale University Press, 1996).
2 See Michael Winkler and Jens Brachmann, eds., *Schleiermacher Texte zur Pädagogik: Kommentierte Studienausgabe*, i–ii (Frankfurt-on-Main: Suhrkamp Taschenbuch, 2000), as well as Jens Brachmann "The Literature on Schleiermacher's Pedagogical Lectures and Writings," http://www2.uni-jena.de/erzwiss/win/bibliographie.html for an extensive bibliography. Edwina Lawler, "Neohumanistic-Idealistic Concepts of a University," in *Friedrich Schleiermacher and the Founding of the University of Berlin: The Study of Religion as a Scientific Discipline*, ed. Herbert H. Richardson (Lewiston: Edwin Mellen Press, 1991) only treats Schleiermacher briefly, 26–36; see Thomas Albert Howard, *Protestant Theology and the Making of the Modern German University* (Oxford: Oxford University Press, in press); for essays that relate Schleiermacher's pedagogical world to North American discussions, see Ian Westbury, Stefan Hopmann, and Kurt Riquarts, eds., *Teaching as Reflective Practice: The German Didaktik Tradition* (Mahwah: Lawrence Erlbaum, 2000).
3 *KGA* i/6, *Universitätsschriften*, ed. Dirk Schmid (1998), xxiii–xxiv.
4 By comparison, his participation in the debate on Jewish emancipation in 1799, treated in the previous chapter, was episodic, and led to no immediate institutional changes.

career. It is ironic that one of Schleiermacher's most accessible and relevant treatises should be examined so infrequently.

If we have generally not thought of Schleiermacher as the maker of institutions, perhaps out of a mistaken sense that romantics do not do that sort of thing, the time is ripe to think differently. Theodore Ziolkowski has compellingly argued that the energies unleashed by the Romantic movement contributed to institutional life in fields that include mining, the law, insane asylums, and museums, in addition to universities.[5] At the time Berlin was comprised of some 150,000 private citizens, including 700 persons associated with the court, some 3,600 civil servants, and twelve casernes that garrisoned 13,500 officers and soldiers.[6] Since the time of Friedrich the Great the city had been the cultural center of northern Germany ("Athens on the Spree"). By 1800 it was a protoindustrial city, with 50,000 persons who worked in factories or manufacturing, especially of textiles, but including tobacco, gold, silver, leather, and sugar processing.[7] During the debates about a new university French forces occupied Berlin. Napoleon had easily conquered Prussia and Saxony in the battles of Jena and Auerstedt (October 1806). With the signing of the Peace of Tilsit (1808), Prussia took a 50 percent loss in territory, was restricted to land east of the Elbe, and lost the University of Halle, where Schleiermacher taught from 1804 to 1806. It was a time for reexamination and new beginnings.

In what follows I first characterize Schleiermacher's setting and involvement in founding the new university. Having located in Berlin after the closing of Halle, he was without portfolio and eagerly entered the debate about the educational needs of Prussia and the German nation. Second, I analyze Schleiermacher's *Occasional Thoughts* in ways that bring out the distinctive tensions of his proposal, including how it relates to the liberal humanistic classicism of Wilhelm von Humboldt as well as to the rival philosophical proposal of the philosopher J. G. Fichte, which cast loose from existing models and sought to reinvent the university *de novo*. In these matters Schleiermacher is much closer to Humboldt than to Fichte. Like Humboldt, he wrestles with the issue of how state authority and prerogatives relate to a model that includes teachers, learners, and researchers, who are united only by the pursuit of truth. Like Fichte, he sees

5 Theodore Ziolkowski, *German Romanticism and its Institutions* (Princeton: Princeton University Press, 1990).
6 Theodore Ziolkowski, *Berlin: Aufstieg einer Kulturmetropole um 1810* (Stuttgart: Klett-Cotta, 2002), 35.
7 Ibid., 31–32.

the new university as a living organism that places philosophical inquiry in the forefront, while fostering a desire and love of teaching and learning that affects students' lives. But unlike Fichte, Schleiermacher recognizes that the drive for knowledge of a university must be brought into some semblance of harmony with practical civic needs and historic institutions of learning. His views address a range of issues that include university governance, the nature of teaching as it relates to learning, and how the university relates to the demands of pure research. Finally, I end by reflecting upon the reception of *Occasional Thoughts* and weigh its significance as a mirror of its author's times, a strong echo of his liberal democratic and social-ethical teaching, and a body of reflection that has for too long been submerged behind his more formal contributions to the history of Christian theology.

THE SETTING OF OCCASIONAL THOUGHTS

Despite being dispirited by the presence of French forces, Berlin in 1807 was a propitious setting for a debate on higher education.[8] Its public-spirited civil servants and educated classes eagerly participated in the city's literary salons, music, theatre, and scientific societies, to form a vibrant cultural life. Theodore Ziolkowski notes the rarity in cultural history of a situation where so many significant writers and intellectuals engage in such intense discussion of public affairs and the spirit of *communitas*.[9] If the arts and sciences had a public face, the same was true of theology. By attending Henriette Herz' salon, contributing to the early Romantics' *Athenaeum*, writing *On Religion,* and preaching at the Trinity Church, Schleiermacher's Berlin persona was well established. Overly tidy categorizations of public engagement may seem unneeded in the case of Schleiermacher. But several distinct forms of public intellectuality can be identified in his work. There is, first, the act of an author publishing his intellectual work, thereby submitting those views to public scrutiny.[10] By

---

8 The debate began in 1802 with a memoranda by Johann Jakob Engel (1741–1802), gymnasial professor, teacher of Wilhelm and Alexander von Humboldt, and director of the National Theatre, and a book on education by Johann Benjamin Erhard (1766–1821), practicing physician and self-taught devotee of Kant; see Ernst Müller, ed., *Gelegentliche Gedanken über Universitäten* (Leipzig: Reclam-Verlag, 1990), 5–42, 312, 316, which contains texts pertaining to the debate by J. J. Engel, J. B. Erhard, F. A. Wolf, J. G. Fichte, F. D. E. Schleiermacher, K. F. Savigny, W. v. Humboldt, and G. W. F. Hegel.
9 Ziolkowski, *Berlin*, 26.
10 For Kant the public use of reason is "that use which anyone makes of it *as a scholar* [*Gelehrter*] before the entire public of the *reading world*;" see Immanuel Kant, "An Answer to the Question: What is the

appealing to reason's neutrality, Enlightenment rationality shaped the realm of public discourse. In this sense, each essay, review, book, or sermon that Schleiermacher published is a public act.[11] A narrower sense of public intellectuality arises when a writer disseminates ideas in books, journals, symposia, or newspapers that treat controversial issues of civic and public policy, especially where action is pending on the part of the state.[12] Such works are typically designed to advance a particular social or political agenda.[13] His part in shaping the new university falls into this type of public intellectuality, where written discourse and action meet a pressing social-political concern. Another sense of public intellectuality focuses on a writer's actual deeds. Here a scholar steps beyond the halls of ivy into direct political involvement. For a time Schleiermacher functioned this way as editor and war reporter (June–September 1813) for *The Prussian Correspondent*, to which he submitted 106 articles or reports during the war of liberation.[14] The same year saw him lecturing on pedagogy and ethics at the university and delivering his famous lecture *On the Various Methods of Translating* (June 24, 1813) to the Academy of Sciences.[15] But nowhere was Schleiermacher's lasting institutional impact greater than in his proposal regarding a new university in Berlin.[16]

Enlightenment," in *What is Enlightenment? Eighteenth-Century Answers and Twentieth-Century Questions*, ed. James Schmidt (Berkeley: University of California Press, 1996), 60.

11 Manuscripts developed from his lectures, but not published by Schleiermacher, would not fit this category, though the publication of such texts in a critical edition is making them public today. In this sense a very private individual (e.g., Kierkegaard, to take an extreme case) can be newly discovered and made a public intellectual by posterity.

12 Reinhold Niebuhr counts as an American public theologian in this second sense; see Charles C. Brown, *Niebuhr and his Age: Reinhold Niebuhr's Prophetic Role and Legacy* (Harrisburg: Trinity Press International, 2002); Schleiermacher's church-political papers fall into this category of public engagement; as written public documents, they are enacted within and for the sake of the institution he served; see *KGA* 1/9 for his church-political works.

13 Of course, successful political engagement does not necessarily depend upon academic talent. See Max Weber's famous essay "Science as Vocation" (*Wissenschaft als Beruf*), ed. H. H. Gerth and C. Wright Mills, *From Max Weber: Essays in Sociology* (Oxford: Oxford University Press, 1958), 150: "Please, consider that a man's value does not depend on whether or not he has leadership qualities . . . The qualities that make a man an excellent scholar and academic teacher are not qualities that make him a leader to give directions in practical life or, more specifically, in politics."

14 See Hans-Joachim Birkner, "Der politische Schleiermacher," in *Schleiermacher-Studien*, ed. Hermann Fischer (Berlin: Walter de Gruyter, 1996), 145, and *KGA* 1/14, *Kleine Schriften 1786–1833*, ed. Matthias Wolfes and Michael Pietsch (1980), CXLI–CLXXXI, 397–500.

15 See *KGA* 1/11, *Akademievorträge*, ed. Martin Rössler with Lars Emersleben (2002), XXXII–XXXIV, 65–93; Adam Schnitzer, "A History in Translation: Schleiermacher, Plato, and the University of Berlin," *Germanic Review* 75/1 (winter 2000): 53–71, fruitfully relates the view of discourse and communication of the university treatise to the text on translating.

16 Schleiermacher's impact on German cultural institutions through the formation of the University of Berlin is arguably as great as the impact of his theology. See Daniel Fallon, *The German*

At the time it was by no means obvious that a new university would be founded in Berlin to compensate for the catastrophic loss of Halle. Rationalist and enlightened circles at court and in the Berlin administration shared in a widespread European suspicion of universities as institutions in decline. In France universities were closed in favor of *écoles spéciales* (1794); more than half of the German universities were closed by Napoleon. Discussions had ensued in 1795 in the prestigious Wednesday Society about whether the educational goals of Prussia might be best served by Berlin's existing institutions. In addition to its Academy of Sciences (1700), Berlin had a College of Medicine and Surgery (1724), a mining academy (1770), a veterinary school (1790), a school for military doctors (1795), a building academy (1799), and an institute for agriculture (1806).[17] Libraries, theatres, singing academies, the opera, and public lectures flourished in a city that also had five *Gymnasien*, 34 bookstores, and 32 publishing houses.[18] It wasn't self-evident that Berlin would be better off to consolidate elements of these disparate institutions into a university and risk diminishing established traditions. If we simplify the extreme positions in this debate: one party would leave Berlin's educational institutions relatively extant, while another, led by the philosopher J. G. Fichte, would reinvent a university for the city in which all university disciplines would be guided by the teachings of his own system of Idealist philosophy. Building upon his own thought, which paralleled Humboldt's humanism on the cultivation (*Bildung*) of individuals, Schleiermacher assumed a stance between these extremes.

Occasional Thoughts was written at a pivotal moment in his biography. In Michael Winkler's view the work has "paradigmatic significance," both for its place in Schleiermacher's literary-biographical development and for its presentation of his mature social philosophy.[19] His studies in the immediately preceding years fed creatively into the challenge at hand. Work on the first volume of his Plato translation (published in 1804)

University: A Heroic Ideal in Conflict with the Modern World (Boulder: Colorado Associated University Press, 1980), "Schleiermacher's model university structure became the basic organizational pattern for all German universities up to the present time," 36; "Schleiermacher's strong advocacy of the university's right to nominate a slate of three candidates for each vacant professorship eventually prevailed over the ministry's claim for unilateral authority of appointment," 37; see also, Frederic Lilge, *The Abuse of Learning: The Failure of the German University* (New York: Macmillan, 1948), 19–20.

17 Ziolkowski, *Berlin*, 156.
18 Ibid., 38–39.
19 Michael Winkler, "'Zu einem anmaßenden Ich, worüber so viel Geschrei ist, hat man es noch gar nicht gebracht': Friedrich Schleiermacher und das Problem der Bildung in der Moderne," in *Dialogische Wissenschaft: Perspektiven der Philosophie Schleiermachers*, ed. Dieter Burdorf and Reinold Schmücker (Paderborn: Ferdinand Schöningh, 1998), 207.

honed his reflection about the nature of philosophy, claims of knowing, and forms of effective teaching. Though Schleiermacher does not explicitly cite his prior studies of moral theory (on Aristotle, Kant, or the *Outlines of a Critique of all hitherto Moral Theory* from 1803), those studies nonetheless inform the university treatise. At the time Schleiermacher longed to cultivate a public presence. On Christmas Day 1808, soon after turning 40, he wrote to his fiancée, Henriette von Willich, about this aspiration: "If I could still somehow enter into an activity for the state, even if only temporarily, then I know I would not wish for anything else."[20] He continues:

> Science [*Wissenschaft*] and church, state, and domestic life – there is nothing further for a human in the world, and I would be among the few happy men, who had enjoyed everything. To be sure, it is only in this most recent time when men divide and separate everything that such a joining of interests is rare; at other times every able man was fearless in everything, and so it must also become, and our entire effort is aimed that it might be so.

As Schleiermacher penned these words, the manuscript of *Occasional Thoughts* was at the printer. The life for which he longed would unfold soon enough in all four spheres of social and political existence.[21]

In the aftermath of Prussia's humiliating defeat and Napoleon's attaching of Halle to Westphalia, King Friedrich Wilhelm III began to entertain thoughts regarding prospects for a university. When he charged his chief cabinet officer Karl Friedrich von Beyme to proceed with plans for developing a new university,[22] Beyme requested memoranda from five former professors from Halle, including the philologist Friedrich August Wolf, as well as three Berliners, including the philosopher Fichte.[23] Schleiermacher was noticeably absent from the list, despite the fact that Beyme had spoken with him about being on the new institution's theological faculty. A letter to a friend suggests that Schleiermacher felt Beyme had never particularly liked him.[24] *KGA* editor Dirk Schmid surmises that

---

20 Cited from Heinrich Meisner, *Friedrich Schleiermachers Briefwechsel mit seiner Braut* in Birkner, "Politischer Schleiermacher," 137.

21 Testimony to his impressive public persona is especially evident in the astonishing procession of mourners, including the King and Crown Prince, who attended his February 1834 funeral procession; see above, chapter 7, n. 71.

22 When a delegation of former Halle professors called upon the King to insist that their university be reopened in Berlin, Friedrich Wilhelm is reported to have said, "The state must replace with intellectual strength what it has lost in material resources." Fallon, *German University*, 9; Ziolkowski, *Berlin*, 157.

23 Dirk Schmid, ed., *KGA* 1/6, xv.

24 *Briefwechsel mit J. Chr. Gaß*, ed. W. Gaß, (Berlin, 1852), 72f., cited in Andreas Arndt, ed., *Friedrich Schleiermacher Schriften* (Frankfurt-on-Main: Deutscher Klassiker Verlag, 1996), 1195.

Schleiermacher heard about these overtures from his Halle colleague, F. A. Wolf.[25] Schleiermacher felt strongly about educational as well as political reform in a new Prussia. Accordingly, he wrote the treatise between October and early December (1807) and published it with Georg Reimer near end of March 1808.

At the time Fichte's reputation was better established than Schleiermacher's. He had published a significant, though to many people obscure, post-Kantian system of Idealist philosophy, *The Science of Knowledge* (1794), as well as popular works, the *Vocation of Man* (1800), *On the Nature of the Scholar* (1804), and the *Addresses to the German Nation* (1808), which calls for a new German education from which "the regeneration and recreation of the world" will spring forth.[26] Both figures were known and respected by the even-tempered and aristocratic von Humboldt. Schleiermacher never names Fichte directly in his treatise on the university, and it would be a mistake to focus unduly on their rivalry. But that *Occasional Thoughts* was meant to oppose the views of Fichte is not in doubt. Despite their mutual association with Friedrich Schlegel, Schleiermacher viewed Fichte's "transcendental philosophy" as a system of thought in which Idealism trumps the reality of the world in ways that produce a culturally impotent philosophy.[27] By appearing as a book and not as a private memorandum, Schleiermacher's unsolicited proposal for a new university was assured a wide readership and vigorous discussion. His publisher, Georg Reimer, had insisted that it appear under the theologian's own name, presumably for marketing purposes.

But the book's publication and arguments would not alone have carried the day for Schleiermacher. During the next year the debate about education in Berlin moved beyond the circle around Beyme, to include the influence of statesman, classicist, and diplomat Wilhelm von Humboldt, who had begun service in the Prussian government at age 22 and who had written *The Limits of State Action*, a work that subsequently provided the epigraph for Mill's *On Liberty*, at age 24.[28] Humboldt's

---

25 Dirk Schmid, ed., *KGA* 1/6, xv–xvi, believes that the slighting of Schleiermacher led him to publish his views on universities in general with an appendix on the prospects for the one under consideration in Berlin.

26 Johann Gottlieb Fichte, *Addresses to the German Nation*, ed. George A. Kelly (New York: Harper and Row, 1968), 215.

27 *OR* (Crouter), 20, 22–4, 26; see his satirical review of Fichte's *Vocation of Man* (*Bestimmung des Menschen*) in August Wilhelm Schlegel and Friedrich Schlegel, ed., *Athenaeum: Eine Zeitschrift*, II, ed. Berhard Sorg (Dortmund: Harenberg Kommunikation, 1989), 1017–31.

28 See Wilhelm von Humboldt, *The Limits of State Action*, ed. J. W. Burrow (Cambridge: Cambridge University Press, 1969), a translation of *Ideen zur einem Versuch die Grenzen der*

soberly balanced view of the responsibilities as well as the abuses of government, and his arguments on behalf of freely cultivating individual humans (*Bildung*) commended his work to Mill.[29] From 1792 to 1801 Humboldt lived in Jena and Weimar, then in Paris and Spain, where he studied literature and published literary criticism.[30] He was again in government service, stationed in Rome, from 1801 to 1808, before returning to Berlin, where he served sixteen months (February 20, 1809–June 14, 1810) in the Interior Ministry as privy councilor in charge of culture and public instruction.[31] In those months Humboldt introduced a thorough reform of Prussian secondary education based on the new humanistic classicism and launched the path towards founding the University of Berlin.[32]

When Humboldt returned abruptly to Italy in June 1810, he established a four-person commission that included Schleiermacher to draft provisional statutes for the university. None of the other commissioners had labored so intensely on matters at hand. Schleiermacher was thus positioned, as secretary and chief draftsman, to press his ideas forward, while drawing upon the ideas in his published treatise. The king approved the final report on October 2, 1810 and the university got under way, though final approval did not occur until April 26, 1817, following the conclusion of the Napoleonic wars and the Congress of Vienna.[33]

As noted, there is reason to view Fichte as a window into the overall stance of Schleiermacher's university proposal. Fichte's own memorandum, a *Deduced Plan for erecting an Institution of Higher Learning in Berlin, which has the requisite connection to an Academy of Sciences*, was

---

Wirksamkeit des Staats zu bestimmen. The Humboldt epigraph picked up by John Stuart Mill is relevant to the present dicusssion: "The grand, leading principle, towards which every argument hitherto unfolded in these pages directly converges, is the absolute and essential importance of human development in its richest diversity" (51). Written in 1791–2, Humboldt's classic statement of liberal German political philosophy was not published until after his death.

29 Among other passages admired by Mill: "Whatever does not spring from a man's free choice, or is only the result of instruction and guidance, does not enter into his very being, but still remains alien to his true nature; he does not perform it with truly human energies, but merely with mechanical exactness"; Humboldt, *Limits of State Action*, 28.

30 Fallon, *German University*, 15.

31 See Karl-Ernst Jeismann, "Wilhelm von Humboldt als Chef der Sektion für Kultus und Unterricht in Berlin und seine Bedeutung für die Bildungsreformen in Deutschland," in *Berlin im Europa der Neuzeit: Ein Tagungsbericht*, ed. Wolfgang Ribbe and Jürgen Schmädeke (Berlin: Walter de Gruyter, 1990), 99–111.

32 Horst Siebert, "Humboldt and the Reform of the Educational System," in *Wilhelm von Humboldt: Politician and Educationist*, ed. Joachim H. Knoll and Horst Siebert (Bad Godesberg: Inter Nationes, 1967), 28–51.

33 Fallon, *German University*, 34, 36.

presented to Beyme on October 8, 1807.[34] Two months later he delivered his public lectures, *Addresses to the German Nation*.[35] Fichte's extended memorandum was not made public until 1817, though its general content reflects ideas from other of his works that were known to Schleiermacher. Fichte's proposal insists on deriving all structures and procedures of the university from pure reason. Compared to Schleiermacher's vision, Fichte's was that of a purist community.[36] If ever enacted, his version of the university would have combined the zeal of a monastery with the intellectual drive of Plato's academy.[37] Alongside Fichte's "deduced" (*Deduziert*) view, the term "occasional" (*Gelegentliche*) in Schleiermacher's *Occasional Thoughts* cloaks his systematic intent with an ironic touch of unpretension. It goes beyond my present purposes to examine how Fichte's proposal relates to his complex body of earlier work.[38] Not insignificantly, however, in the winter of 1805/6 he had already drafted a proposal for the internal organization of the university at Erlangen.[39]

The argument of Fichte's *Deduced Plan* consists of sixty-seven sections divided into three chapters.[40] If we put aside certain negative stereotypes of Fichte's flamboyant character, the proposal is not unattractive. Its insistence is that philosophy be central within the curriculum, that students should be well removed from the anxieties of the world, and that the community should form a "household with board and lodging"

34 Johann Gottlieb Fichte, *Deduzierter Plan einer zu Berlin zu errichtenden höhern Lehranstalt, die in gehöriger Verbindung mit einer Akademie der Wissenschaften stehe*, cited in Arndt, ed., *Friedrich Schleiermacher Schriften*, 1197; Schleiermacher had already known of Fichte's *On the Nature of the Scholar* (1804) and of the Erlangen proposal (1805), *KGA* 1/6, 41.

35 Fichte, *Addresses to the German Nation*, xxvii. The lectures, which began on December 13, 1807, were delivered on Sundays between noon and 1 p.m. in the amphitheatre of the Berlin Academy; on Fichte's political-educational stance, Kelly remarks that the philosopher "came to place his political trust in the peremptory rule of the wise, a kind of ethical technocracy doubled by strong feelings of social egalitarianism" (xvi).

36 Although named the first rector of the new university, Fichte remained so only for four months and had a falling out with his colleagues, including Schleiermacher, when he tried to take university action against students who wished to settle their disputes through dueling; see Ziolkowski, *Berlin*, 156–8.

37 It is not accidental that, for Fichte, the dress of students and faculty would distinguished their roles, and that the main circle of students were to be called "regulars," whereby the students of greatest ability would constitute a "college of regulars," thus echoing the medieval nomenclature for clergy attached to religious order; R. H. Turnbull, *The Educational Theory of J. G. Fichte* (London: University Press of Liverpool, 1926), 209–17.

38 On Fichte's early work, see Anthony J. LaVopa, *Fichte: The Self and the Calling of Philosophy, 1762–1799* (Cambridge: Cambridge University Press, 2001).

39 Excerpts given in Turnbull, *Educational Theory*, 259–62.

40 Ibid., 170–259; the three chapters treat (1) "General Idea of an Academy Demanded by the Needs of the Time" (170–90), (2) "How the Proposed Idea can be Realized in the Given Circumstances of Time and Place" (190–242), and (3) "Of the Means Whereby our Scientific Academy shall Obtain Influence over a Scientific Universe" (242–59).

that should resemble a college more than a larger, less personal university.[41] There would be no "religion requirement," since religious teachings have been thoroughly sublimated within conscience, where the human will meets the demands of the moral law.[42] Frederic Lilge states the main principles underlying Fichte's lengthy proposal under six theses (which I slightly amend):[43]

1. To study philosophy is to raise thinking to the level of conscious artistry.
2. To teach in a philosophical spirit is to stimulate students to become creative thinkers.
3. Philosophy has a right to the free, rational critique of the assumptions and principles of all other disciplines.
4. A university shall not assume the burden of professional training (in theology, law, or medicine).
5. Certainty of knowledge depends upon teaching a single system of philosophy.
6. The intellectual and political unity of the nation requires a single university for the education of its elite.

If we align the six Fichtean postulates with Schleiermacher's proposal, we can see that Schleiermacher does not disagree with the first three Fichtean claims, even if he understands these postulates differently. A more mediating sense of what constitutes proper philosophic thought – more indebted to Plato's dialogic mode of inquiry than to a deductive system – causes Schleiermacher to assume a decidedly different stance with respect to the last three propositions. As we shall see, Schleiermacher is concerned to argue that even professional education (theology, law, medicine) can and must itself be permeated by philosophic inquiry, that certainty of knowledge is obtained through open-ended dialog and not through a deductive philosophical system, and that multiple German universities will serve a diverse people better than a single elite institution. Where Fichte's proposal appears acerbic and radical, *Occasional Thoughts* is mediating and reformist. In varying degrees both figures were patriots and nationalists, but Schleiermacher's hermeneutical approach to

41 Ibid., 208.
42 See Fichte, *Addresses to the German Nation*, 33, which maintains that there is "no need of religion to regulate life. True morality suffices wholly for that purpose."
43 Lilge, *Abuse of Learning*, 43–52. Worth noting is the fact that the American scholar Lilge saw Fichte's philosophy as having contributed to the rise of National Socialist ideology in Germany, while the earlier British work, R. H. Turnbull's, *Educational Theory*, viewed Fichte's thought as the basis for renewal of German higher education in the Weimar period.

philosophy reflects a more democratic political spirit. Still, Schleiermacher's proposal shares many concerns with Fichte, just as it does with Humboldt, even while resolving these issues in its own fashion.

SCHLEIERMACHER ON THE NATURE OF THE UNIVERSITY

We have seen that what might have been a mere position paper by Schleiermacher came to be a substantive educational proposal. In the original edition the book consists of 176 pages. At age 40 Schleiermacher could draw from his experience as house tutor, participant in a Berlin Gymnasial teaching seminar, as well as teaching for two years at Halle (October 1804 to October 1806).[44] His reflections on education had been honed by studies of moral theory, Greek philosophy, theories of sociability, translating Plato, problems in extant schools of moral teaching, and the issue of how individual autonomy relates to human community.[45] *On Religion* had already pitted humanistic values of *Bildung* against "practical men of reason and understanding," code words for the German counterparts of Bentham's utilitarianism.[46] The preface of *Occasional Thoughts* informs readers that the work seeks to mediate between new and old forms of learning.

For even where something new is to be formed, it is of the greatest importance to know what was essential or accidental in what existed before and what was perhaps even founded in error or misunderstanding and is thus objectionable, as must constantly be discovered in all branches of human activity.[47]

He writes "not only for the few who are to create, transform and govern in this area but for all those who take a lively interest in the subject" (2/20). The treatise's seven sections cover: (1) the relationship of the scientific association to the state; (2) how schools, universities, and scientific academies are related; (3) the general shape of the university; (4) its faculties; (5) the morals of students and their oversight; and (6) the

---

44 See Nowak, *Schleiermacher*, 48–63. By his own definition of the professorial life cycle, Schleiermacher was at the height of his intellectual powers: "If philosophers did not ordinarily shrink from determining the proper, natural beginning and end of generative power, it could certainly be established even for this talent that as a rule it begins to develop between the twenty-fifth and thirtieth years and quickly rises to its finest flower, also that one who has left one's fiftieth year behind can expect its rapid decline" (*OT* 47; *KGA* 1/6, 66).
45 Nowak, *Schleiermacher*, 63–162.
46 *OR* (Crouter), 63–4.
47 *OT*, 1–2; *KGA* 1/6, 20; in what follows parenthetical page references are given to the English *OT* (tr. occasionally emended) with the German critical edition, *KGA*, following a forward slash, e.g., (1–2/20).

conferral of scholarly degrees. The work concludes with an appendix (less than one-fifth of the treatise) that speaks directly to questions about Berlin as the home of a new university. As a thoroughly principled discussion of higher education, the work does not betray its author's vested interest in the debate's outcome. Its rhetoric of persuasion interweaves lofty goals of educational philosophy with practical concerns (student morals in the city, uniting disparate existing institutions into one body, integration of the aims of schools, university, and research academy) that were on the minds of Berlin's administrative and political elites.

As in his formal works that strive for coherence and consistency, Schleiermacher is concerned to relate parts to their whole and vice versa, while nudging a reader to see the need for mutual interdependence (of ideas as well as structures) in his ideal university. The life of the mind is necessarily communal, but it cannot be dictated by external forces: "The appearance of any scientific scholar's living solitarily in one's labors or pursuits, and exclusively for one's own sake, can only be an empty one . . . The most varied modes of communication together with the community of all pursuits, must be formed strictly from the drive to know, wherever it has truly awakened" (3/22). An inherent drive to know must assume communal forms, for knowing requires conversation with others for its confirmation. Education is grounded in the human heart and fostered within families, prior to its being formally structured in ways that might be susceptible to state interference. Indeed, as Michael Winkler has noted, the fundamental problem of education for Schleiermacher requires him to explain how a "pedagogical event," which is finally elusive, can be described as accessible in an organized form.[48] In addressing that challenge Schleiermacher's realism causes him to seek out structures and procedures for the proposed university that will serve best to form individuals within a scholarly community, while preserving relative autonomy from the Prussian state.[49] He had done something quite similar in 1799 when delineating the proper conditions for cultivating religion in institutions.[50]

---

48 Winkler, '"Zu einem anmaßenden Ich,"' 209.
49 On the comparable ideal of *Bildung* in Humboldt, compare Horst Siebert, "Humboldt and the Reform of the Educational System," who writes that Humboldt "was convinced that the human personality could remain untouched by technical and social developments. There can now be no question that this optimism was mistaken" (47).
50 Not surprisingly, the problems faced in institutionalizing education parallel those in Schleiermacher's thought about the elusive act of communicating religion. See *On Religion*, speeches 3 and 4.

HE DRIVE TO KNOW AS IT RELATES TO THE STATE

Schleiermacher begins his section on how the university relates to the state
by announcing several basic premises that bear on human nature, human
community, and the life of the mind. Since a desire to have knowledge
(*Kenntnisse*) is universal among humans, scholarship and science are
required in order to provide "intelligible justifications" that move beyond
a mere appeal to instinct and authority. A society that rests upon appeals
to earlier authorities must acknowledge that the earlier authorities themselves rest on still higher principles. It is self-evident that scholarship and
science cannot be "brought to fruition or fully possessed" by any one
individual. Since "each is dependent on all the rest and can by oneself
possess only an isolated fragment and that very incompletely," science
must be communal (2/20). In the domain of knowing, everything inter-
relates with everything else; something presented for itself alone "is found
to be distorted and incomprehensible." In turn, every effort to attain
knowledge arises from communication, which flows from a primary law
within human nature. Nature has "enunciated this law in the impossibility of scientifically producing anything exclusively without language."
Rightly understood, institutions rest upon and arise from this primary
human drive to know, which is "something original, having arisen out of
inner impulse, out of free inclination" (3/22).

When the primordial drive to know becomes institutionalized and
more extensive, the state is needed to protect its goals as a "moral person"
that has come together in the interest of science (4/22). Just as the German
state supports any number of citizen groups (*Vereine*), as long as these are
not politically disruptive, so it is with scholarly associations. But when the
state sees certain groups as useful it "appropriates and absorbs" them for
its own purposes, while obscuring the fact that they arise freely. The
appearance of being integral to the state is so strong that it is difficult to
realize that anyone could ever wish to pull back from the state, even
though it is "actually alien to them." With these words Schleiermacher
recognizes that there is "no lack of striking opposition on the part of the
scientific association against such a tight connection to the state" (4/23).

Potential for misunderstanding with state authority is compounded by
the fact that scholarly pursuits each "participate in the special nature of a
language" (4/23), by which he means that a variety of disciplinary
domains obtain in the academy. The task of overcoming these different
domains is the highest aim of science, even if it is never fully accomplished (5/23). This goal of achieving mutual understanding enables

various alliances within the university to form a moral community ruled by common standards of argument. No matter how small a state may be, it still requires knowledge and, like individuals, seeks to bring the disparate knowledge claims into some "general sensibility" (5/24). The state can only progress when these knowledge claims are justified by rational argument. The state is "self-seeking through and through; thus it tends not to offer support to science, except on its own terms, within its own boundaries." Yet "concern for understanding and cooperating with each other" arises despite the fact that "the state works only for itself" (6/24).

If I read him properly, Schleiermacher gives the Prussian authorities yet another reason to protect a relatively autonomous academic community. For him language, which is crucial to knowing, is not coextensive with the state but extends into the larger German nation.[51] Science functions within this larger linguistic-cultural community, just as it does within a state. In his words:

What, then, could be a more amenable, trustworthy, natural means preparatory to this end than to establish the most heterogeneous, authentic, least jealous community in the scientific domain, which stands in just as exact a reciprocal relation with the state as it does with language? (7/25)

With these words Schleiermacher appeals to the pride in a Prussia that longs to wield greater cultural influence in the German nation.[52] Just as the drive to know is inherent and originates with individuals, so its linguistic nature aligns it with a broad cultural community, the bounds of which exceed that of the state. Though crucial to the scientific association within its polity, the authority of the state is relativized by being dependent upon an even larger linguistic culture. Here the argument is not intended to minimize the role of the state, so much as to explain how the pursuit of knowledge and the practice of statecraft are mutually dependent upon language and culture. Schleiermacher warns against an intellectual chauvinism in which larger German states dominate smaller ones: "True independence [among German states] . . . can exist only if each amply contributes proportionately toward maintaining and extending the common good" (7/26). He warns against the state trying

51 The theme looms even larger in Fichte's *Addresses to the German Nation*, 62–77, which speak about the primordial significance and power of the German language as continuously evolving and less artificial than the neo-Latin tongues (romance languages).
52 John Michael Stroup argues against the view that Enlightenment clergy were uniformly subservient to government, "Protestant Churchmen in the German Enlightenment – Mere Tools of Temporal Government?," in *Lessing Yearbook* 10 (1978), ed. Richard E. Schade and Jerry Glenn (Munich: Max Hueber Verlag, 1978), 149–89.

to prevent citizens from taking part in the scholarly and scientific activities of neighboring German states; such hegemony, seen in Catholic Germany, is "a dark, deplorable sign of bigotry" (8/26). Even if politics is an art, and heads of state are more like artists than scientists, that government is best whose leaders have a capacity to "look at facts and experiences scientifically or at least how to use presentations of them that have this purpose" (8, 27). Those who pursue the craft of politics introduce real improvements only when they grasp the true idea of the state, the history of their particular state, and know how to use examples from the whole domain of history, "so that in every instance coming to govern well requires coming to know truly" (9, 28). The danger lies in the fact that the state prefers information that it can measure, amass, and use for its own ends, while scholars voluntarily unite for the sake of science, the aim of which differs from amassing information. In its quest for knowledge the community of scholars must aim at more than mere endless questioning. It seeks to cultivate informed perspectives in individuals as well as in a field of study based upon underlying principles; when that is done, creative intellectual discovery and the pursuit of knowledge through original research (*Lehrfreiheit*) parallels the freedom of students to learn (*Lernfreiheit*).[53]

Without minimizing the competing interests of university and state, *Occasional Thoughts* argues that the tensions are outweighed by their mutual concern for the larger good of the culture and nation. Clearly self-interested by nature, the state does not easily promote the free intellectual pursuit of knowledge: "The state works only for itself, historically it is chiefly self-seeking through and through; thus it tends not to offer support to science except on its own terms" (6/24). Persons who govern universities come from all walks of life, that is, are not necessarily the most learned. Such government officials act by "evaluating and dealing with everything according to its immediate effect on the state – and, as experience also teaches, certainly not to the advantage of intellectual improvement" (22/40). Conversely, within the scholarly community a tendency to act oblivious to state interests and to withdraw from politics is also evident. Whereas Fichte sees the ideal university led by a modern

---

53 Under "freedom to learn" (*Lernfreiheit*) Schleiermacher includes not only students' intellectual freedom but their freedom to experiment with Bohemian and other styles of life as a process of their natural growth in awareness of self and world. In contrast with Fichte's aspiration of moral purity among students, Schleiermacher accepts a degree of "lamentable" conduct, which makes students burdensome to their neighbors in the city. See *OT*, 49, which begins the section on student morals and their oversight (49–60/68–79).

philosopher-king, appointed by the state, Schleiermacher recognizes a permanent tension between the academy and the state but believes that rational and just decisions can be made by persons who are responsible for both spheres of interest. If, like Fichte, Schleiermacher has a utopian aspiration, his vision nonetheless gives greater weight to the practical workings of institutional structures.

BETWEEN SCHOOLS AND RESEARCH ACADEMIES: THE GERMAN SENSE OF A UNIVERSITY

Though many of the principles behind Schleiermacher's idea of the university have triumphed as an ideal in our world, such a triumph was not obvious at the time he wrote. Whereas other nations, such as France, had developed excellent special higher schools and research institutions, the "German sense of a university" must necessarily stand in the middle, while relating both to schools and to research academies (15/34).

It could even be claimed that the whole type displayed therein is originally German and follows exactly the cultural example of other relationships that have also come out of Germany: the school as the being together of master and apprentices, the university as being together of master and journeymen, and the academy as the gathering together of masters. (11/31)

Differentiation of the three levels of education occurs not just through the respective roles of teachers and students but by how each level relates to the task of knowing. Schleiermacher believes that two elements – having special talents and pursuing the spirit of systematic philosophy – run through all of education. The former is typically encountered in the schools, while the latter belongs by its nature to the academy of sciences. Youth are particularly gifted in certain areas, and rapidly accumulate knowledge in mathematics, in grammar, building vocabulary, and factual historical knowledge. But "without this systematic spirit of philosophy even the most remarkable talent will not attain independent status" (12/31). Schleiermacher agrees with Fichte that rigorous mental training in the schools must move beyond mechanical learning towards a sense of philosophical inquiry.[54] Through an inspired art of teaching (*kunstmäßige Behandlung*) schools must inculcate a philosophic quest for knowledge as

---

54 Cf. Turnbull, *Educational Theory*, 176, where Fichte writes: "Artistic skill can be formed only by the pupil working under the teacher's eye according to some definite plan adopted by the latter and practising the art, of which he is to become a master, in its different stages from the beginning onwards to mastery, progressing regularly and without omitting anything."

a basis for study at the university and later in the research academy. Schools are gymnastic in character (hence their name), as places where "intellectual powers are exercised for knowing" (14/33). Such exercises do not prepare products for publication, as in the academy of sciences, but concentrate on the process of learning how to learn.

For its part, the research academy consists of a community of master scholars ruled by persons who treat their own disciplines "in a philosophical spirit": "Only as this spirit, similarly present in all, is wedded to the distinctive talent of each member can anyone become a true member of the association" (16/35). The university, whose *raison d'être* lies in awakening this spirit, is uniquely suited for the task of being guardian over the development of this "wholly new intellectual process of life" (16/35). A philosophically inquiring mind does not arise in one's sleep, as if it needs no breeding or inculcation. Developing a capacity "to investigate, to contrive, and to give account" goes well beyond the mere assembling of information.

Rather, the totality of knowledge is to be presented, accounted for, and in this manner the principles and, as it were, the fundament of all knowing are brought into perspective so that each person gains what it takes to become acquainted with every area of learning. (17/35)

Students need less time at the university than they did in schools, since their thinking and capacity to integrate new perspectives is now greater.[55] Schleiermacher's lofty idealism is evident when he writes: "Only one moment is actually spent at the university, only one act is completed: the idea of knowledge, the highest consciousness of reason, awakens in the person as a regulative principle" (17/35-6). The capacity of reason to carry inquiry in every direction distinguishes the university from both the schools and the research academy.[56]

For reasons that differ from the situation in schools, the research academy puts pure speculative knowledge and concern with its overall unity into the background. A research academy emphasizes "elaborating the particular in a completely accurate and exact manner in the domain of all real sciences" (17/36). It is not the case that particular products of research are devoid of a philosophic spirit, but that "if the sciences are,

---

55 "Learning how to learn can be accomplished in a shorter time" (17/35).
56 Schleiermacher views the textbook as a means of probing inquiry and the characteristic book of a university. By their design textbooks relate parts to wholes within a given discipline and foster a rounded and complete sense of a given discipline or subject matter (17/36).

in academic fashion, to be furthered as a common effort, then there everything of a purely philosophical nature must already have been settled so that almost nothing is left to be said on the subject" (18/36). For Schleiermacher the difference seems to be that while the university is a place of endless debate, a research academy must necessarily set aside certain metaphysical differences and find common cause by appealing to reason across their discplines and fields of study. The underlying idea appears to be that if metaphysics is too difficult for the schools, it can be too divisive and distracting for a research academy. Such an approach differs significantly from Fichte, whose ruling philosopher in the academy derives true principles of knowing for the entire community, even to the point of instructing other faculty members on how to incorporate a proper philosophical perspective into their disciplines.[57] For Fichte a system of speculative philosophy is tied to a single starting point and requires no collegial reflection for its implementation. Schleiermacher rejects the view that there is only "one philosophical mode of thinking among a given people." His point is that historical and critical treatments of philosophy have exposed the falsity of that position (18/37).

Fichte and the philosopher K. L. Reinhold (1758–1823)[58] are Schleiermacher's apparent targets when he objects on principle to "transcendental philosophy."

Indeed, the scholarly and scientific spirit as the highest principle, as the immediate unity of all knowledge, cannot be represented and exhibited for itself alone – in ghostlike fashion – in sheer transcendental philosophy . . . Probably no more vapid a philosophy is thinkable than one that extracts itself so purely and expects that real knowing, as something lower, should be given or taken from a totally different source . . . Only in its lively influence on all knowing does philosophy admit of being presented; only with its body, with real knowing, does its spirit admit of being grasped. (19/37)

Knowledge must interpret the real empirical world as well as the thought constructions that we bring to this world. Philosophical seminars and practical institutes should be retained within the university and not (with Fichte) relegated to an academy of sciences. Only such integrated programs of study can build up the confidence of apprentice scholars. Schleiermacher decries the academic arrogance that causes schoolteachers

---

57 The point relates to Schleiermacher's stance against including Hegel in the Academy of Sciences, a topic treated in chapter 3, and is also expressed in his acceptance lecture before the Academy of Sciences, May 10, 1810, *KGA* 1/11, 1–7.
58 *KGA* 1/6, 37, editor's note.

to view professors as nothing more than "presumptous ingrates who often destroy the better portion of what the school teacher has built." Gymnasien need really good directors, who have the same "scientific perspicacity, the same unalloyed spirit of observation, as one who works to advance science" (21/39).

Returning to the question of the state's role, Schleiermacher notes that state interests and prerogatives have the potential to exacerbate the tensions between the three levels of the educational system and to view the freedom of universities with suspicion. He expresses scorn for those who "hold back all their students from any civil activity," thus taking another swipe at Fichte's notion of a purist scholarly community that operates solely for its own sake (23/41). Schleiermacher's more pluralistic worldview allows the interplay of freedom to extend to empirical structures within the university and in its relations to the wider world. He is confident that nature will "regulate itself ever aright, and quite evenhandedly, the relation between those who devote themselves to science, pure and simple, and the rest" (23/42). As a committed democrat, he is confident that individuals will sort out and regulate a balance between the life of the mind and the needs of the civil order.

FURTHER (NON-FICHTEAN) THOUGHTS ON THE UNIVERSITY

In a section of his treatise called "A Closer Examination of the University Generally," Schleiermacher seeks to defend further his understanding of the university, while countering Fichte's more elitist proposal. He argues for the diversity and free play of the disciplines as well as for students of diverse talents as needed to constitute an ideal and well-ordered university.

The aims of the university Schleiermacher envisions are best realized by acknowledging that the selection and admission of students is more art than science. No one can fully predict how well a student will do at university based on achievements in secondary school. Elements like courage and energy may drive students to compete at the university who may be "unsuited for science in the highest sense" (25/44). As an educator who fosters individual human development (*Bildung*), Schleiermacher maintains that less talented students will always be admitted to universities: "Unavoidably many come to the university who are really unsuited for science in the highest sense" (25/44). Rather than decry that fact, he thinks it is "a dreadful and a terrible thought" to suppose one can fully decide who is entitled to study based strictly on preparatory achievement.[59] Even those less talented for scholarship and science gain much from studying at the university; they carry what they have gained on into their careers. To its great benefit the state draws a portion of such persons into its service (26/45). By pointing in more practical directions Schleiermacher wishes not just to resist Fichte's more abstract philosophical utopia, but to counter those voices that would simply retain Berlin's extant educational options (while retaining the provincial universities of Frankfurt/Oder and Königsberg on the periphery) or disperse the universities of Germany altogether and adopt the French model of turning them into *écoles spéciales*.[60]

The antielitism and democratic spirit of Schleiermacher's proposal defies certain stereotypes of German universities as Ph.D. factories with authoritarian bureacracies weighted towards research programs.[61] Such a model conflicts sharply with a view of *Bildung* that places individuals in a reciprocal process of teaching and learning. For him lecturing must incorporate a dialogical (Socratic) style of reflecting on the origins and methods of a field of study, not just dispense factual content.

Few understand the significance of using lectures; but, oddly enough, this practice has always persevered despite its constantly being very poorly done by the majority of teachers. This continuance is clear proof of how very much lecturing belongs to the essence of the university and of how greatly it is worth the trouble to reserve this form of instruction always for those few who, from time to time, know how to handle it correctly. Indeed, one could say that the true and peculiar benefit a university teacher confers is always in exact relation to the person's proficiency in this art.[62]

---

59 Based on his own modest class origins as son of a military chaplain, Schleiermacher is aware that social inequality will not be eradicated; but it can nonetheless be overcome when the ideal of *Bildung* is realized in the lives of individuals.

60 The passage in question (26/46) alludes to Stephani, *Grundriß der Staats-Erziehungs-Science*, 8, 148–50; Massow, *Ideen zur Verbesserung des öffentlichen Schul- und Erziehungswesens*, 126f., 252f.; Engel, [*Denkschrift über Begründung einer großen Lehranstalt in Berlin*] in R. Köpke, *Die Gründung der königlichen Friedrich-Wilhelms-Universität zu Berlin. Nebst Anhängen über die Geschichte der Institute und den Personalbestand* (Neudruck der Ausgabe Berlin 1860, Aalen 1981), 147–53, here 151f.

61 For a vigorous American and German discussion of the current status of German universities and their relation to the "Humboldt Mythos," see the essays in Mitchell G. Ash, ed., *German Universities Past and Present: Crisis or Renewal?* (Providence: Berghahn Books, 1997).

62 *OT*, 28; *KGA* I/6, 47; lectures are depicted as a sanctuary in which "dialogue can best awaken life from slumber and draw forth its first stirrings, as in this genre the marvelous art of antiquity still manifests the same results today" (29/48). "Amazingly enough, the erudition of a professor has become proverbial. To be sure, the more of it a professor has the better, but the greatest learning is useless without the art of lecturing" (30/49).

He sharply criticizes faculty members who dictate textbooks to their students without engaging them through a living encounter with the issues raised by their material.

A professor who repeatedly reads from a notebook, written down once and for all and for students to take down, quite inopportunely reminds us of that period when there was as yet no publishing and much value already attached to a learned man's dictating his manuscript to many people at once, a time when oral discourse also had to serve in place of books. (31/50)

Lectures that draw from the lecturer's own experience ("consciousness of his being together [*Zusammensein*] with the novices") connect best with one's listeners (30/49). Gifted teachers must combine "vitality and enthusiasm" with "reflectiveness and clarity" in order to make their enthusiasm effectual and understandable (30/49). "True vitality" is needed and not "incidental conceits and polemical attacks." When he calls for exchanges between teachers and students outside the lecture hall, Schleiermacher's words approximate the mission statement of an American liberal arts college: "Certainly the actual lectures must not be the teacher's only contact with students. To be stiffly reserved and unable to be something for one's youthful students beyond the lectern ordinarily accompanies the vices of lecturing already faulted" (31/50). Full engagement with the lives of students is required. If a faculty member is to reach those with weaker powers of comprehension, "other modes and levels of living with them [the students] must come to the teacher's aid" (31/50). The democratic spirit of the university always strives to be one, while embracing many elements. A complete balance and equilibrium will never be attained. This diversity of teachers and learners is highly valued and required; similarly, to have thirty-eight universities within Germany and not a central institution for the whole of the nation ensures lively competition between the various regions (33/52).

PHILOSOPHICAL (ARTS AND SCIENCES) VERSUS PROFESSIONAL FACULTIES

Among the contested points in late eighteenth-century European discussions of the university was the role of the, perhaps now outmoded, medieval faculties of theology, law, and medicine. Immanuel Kant's *The Conflict of the Faculties* (1798) echoed a widespread debate in Germany regarding how the faculty of philosophy (arts and sciences) should relate to the so-called "higher" faculties.[63] Kant's placing of the philosophical faculty at the heart of the university was followed by Schelling in *On University Studies* (1803), without either figure calling for the professional faculties to be banished altogether.[64] On this issue Schleiermacher aligns himself with Kant and Schelling against Fichte's plan to abolish the higher faculties. When *Occasional Thoughts* makes a plea for the coexistence of professional alongside liberal arts faculties, there is no doubt that the latter is the heart of the university. Just a few years later Schleiermacher's 1811 *Brief Outline on the Study of Theology* (treated in chapter 9 of this book) would make the case for the specific ways that theology relates to the larger university.[65]

While noting contemporary proposals to alter or abolish the three professional faculties of the university, Schleiermacher admits their "grotesque appearance" and calls for an approach that will "first try to understand aright the meaning of these forms, which have prevailed up to the present time" (33/53). The problem at hand relates back to the role and prerogatives of the state, which has a greater stake in the specialized professional faculties than in the philosophical faculty. The positive faculties of theology, law, and medicine were institutionalized over time in response to the needs of the church, the functioning of courts and administrative bodies, and the maintenance of citizens' health. They arose for the best of reasons to combat bad practices, while being united in one body in the spirit of scholarship and science. Though they aim at a practical end, these disciplines find their common ground in the inner connectedness of knowledge. Schleiermacher acknowledges that reform of the positive faculties is needed, and especially singles out faculties of law in this regard (35–36/55).

When it comes to ranking the four faculties Schleiermacher places the philosophical (arts and sciences) first, because (1) its autonomy does not allow it to dissolve into extraneous parts and (2) all members of

---

63 Immanuel Kant, *The Conflict of the Faculties*, in *Religion and Rational Theology*, ed. and tr. Allen W. Wood and George Di Giovanni (Cambridge: Cambridge University Press, 1996), 233–327.

64 F. W. J. Schelling, *On University Studies*, tr. E. S. Morgan, ed. Norbert Guterman (Athens: Ohio University Press, 1966), translates the 1803 *Vorlesungen über die Methode des akademischen Studiums*.

65 Schleiermacher's 1808 proposal does not speak to the matter of teaching Christian theology at the university versus the study of religion in a nonconfessional and pluralistic basis, wheras Fichte's plan called for supplanting the theological faculty with the historical study of world religions: "The task is more comprehensive than theology has understood it, since account must also be taken of the religious ideas of the so-called heathen" (Turnbull, *Educational Theory*, 206).

the university must be rooted in it, no matter to which faculty they belong. But pedagogical reasons also come into play in the ranking. The philosophical faculty is the first to be encountered by students at the university. As a proponent of general studies, Schleiermacher notes that "The old abuse of having boys in their cradle destined for a particular career is still not eradicated" (37/56). He calls for a year of free exploration of the various disciplines at the university before specialization occurs.

> It may still be hoped that the time will soon come when young people will be sent to the university only to pursue general studies . . . The disposition, love, and talent of these young people will develop most securely during this time. With less error, they will discover their proper calling and enjoy the great advantage of having found it on their own. (37/57)

Analogously to students who begin in the philosophical faculty and eventually participate in more than one faculty, the university will benefit from faculty members belonging to more than a single faculty.[66] Schleiermacher views "the mutual jealousy of the faculties" as "outmoded and ridiculous," since an authentic scholar who understands the nature of a science can pursue it in more than a single field (38/58). A teacher maintains vitality by developing varied approaches and sets of lectures. For its well-being the university ought to restrict the number of "nominal professorships" (we would say "adjuncts") who are repeatedly assigned to the same courses and fail to grow in a given field of study (39/59).

Having established the centrality of the philosophical faculty as the heart of the university, Schleiermacher offers further counsel on extant traditions. He defends the practice of receiving private student fees (in addition to salaries) as not inimical to the quality of instruction and as enhancing a professor's freedom to develop his own work (40/59). Seminars, which are especially prominent in medicine, theology, and the philological section of the philosophical faculty, often come close to the work of the research academies. Here students "step forward as producers while the teachers do not so much offer their own direct communication

---

66 "Any teacher of law or theology surely deserves to be ridiculed and excluded from the university who would feel no inner power and desire to accomplish something of one's own in the sphere of science, and with distinguished success, whether it be pure philosophy or ethics or philosophical consideration of history or philology" (38/57). In Schleiermacher's case the right to teach in the faculty of philosophy, in addition to theology, came to him with his membership in the Academy of Sciences; Nowak, *Schleiermacher*, 283.

as simply guide, support, and critique this student production" (41/60). Though they treat more particular content and have greater student participation, seminars are not necessarily more advanced than lectures, which are obliged to cover material in depth and remain open to a wider number of students. Between seminars and lectures he envisages discussion sections (*Conversatorien*) where "the student singles out what has been less easy to grasp in the lecture and gives it back to the teacher for recasting and clarification; and the student brings doubts and objections for resolution" (41/60). As if the contemporary resonances are not sufficiently startling, we can also note that Schleiermacher argues in favor of merit-based financial stipends as rewards for distinction. Monies bestowed earlier for excellence in the gymnasium are not to be carried automatically to the university, lest the individual who was an excellent pupil should turn out to be sustained as a mediocre student. Financial support should be distributed only to those who maintain a successful course of study.

Of course, all of these high pedagogical ideals will falter unless we can assume "that the teachers of the university are what they are supposed to be" (42/62). Schleiermacher recognizes that the recruitment of an excellent faculty requires judgment of a teacher's inner character. Though he does not dwell on the point at length, he leaves us viewing this task as one of discerning judgment. Though other forms of work may be motivated and sustained by external powers, "teaching can take place only through desire and love." He adds that without desire and love "even what the finest external rules and regulations may do can never become more than empty show" (43/62). Mistakes arise when appointments are not in conformity with the "idea and nature of the whole." Returning to the topic of state influence, he wrestles with the question of how best to balance the prerogatives of the state with the wisdom of a faculty's judgment in making appointments. Politicians – in Germany they have always had a hand in university appointments – lean towards "cultivating young people's thirst for knowledge only for what is deemed best for the state" (43/63). As a progressive reformist who builds from tradition, Schleiermacher suggests a practice that was eventually adopted in the nineteenth-century German universities and, in the main, continues today. In order to balance competing interests, the faculty presents the cultural ministry with a rank-ordered list of three persons from whom to choose, and the state ministry then makes the final decision (46/65).[67] As

---

67 Fallon, *German University*, 37.

he puts it: "Balance seems to be best secured through an arrangement of this kind, as modified especially for each university, and most untoward influences seem to be warded off" (46/65). The topic of faculty excellence leads Schleiermacher also to reflect on the need to maintain vitality in the professoriate over time. Here, the 40-year-old scholar observes that the generative power of philosophers rapidly declines after age 50.[68] He reasons that the decline of powers results not so much from repetition of lectures as from the age and experience gap between oneself and one's students.

Youth belong to an age group entirely different from their teacher's and the less one can assimilate them into one's thinking and can share a distinct love and joy with them, the more the inclination and skill of entering with them into a closer relationship has to subside and the more ungratifying and unfruitful the enterprise becomes. (47/66)

Here the realism of common sense combines with a romantic sense of human development to recognize all members of a university as living agents in a process of growth and change. For Schleiermacher the purposes of the university must reflect as well as respect the purposes of life. Issues of student life, teaching and learning, faculty appointments and governance all serve the goal of enhancing the life of the mind and contributing to the well-being of the larger community. In Schleiermacher's view the "scholarly and scientific disposition of our time" is "democratic through and through" (58/67).[69]

CONCLUSION

I have noted that the debate about higher education in Prussia did not occur in a vacuum. Undercurrents of discontent about the universities were dominant in Enlightenment thought well in advance of the Napoleonic period. At the end of the seventeenth century the philosopher Leibniz held that universities were antiquated beyond reform and preferred to associate himself with the Academy of Science.[70] By the late eighteenth century German universities were, in the words of Charles

---

68 See above, this chapter, n. 44.
69 It exceeds the bounds of this chapter to explicate the argument of two further sections (49–65/ 68–85), which treat "university morals and their oversight" and "the conferral of scholarly degrees." Both sections make recommendations in light of a principle of internal self-government that honors the spirit of scholarship and science that Schleiermacher takes to be crucial.
70 Lilge, *Abuse of Learning*, 2–3.

McClelland, "characterized by ongoing lethargy, decline, and frequent crises."[71] Many institutions were enfeebled by a sterile scholasticism in which "professors taught only what was in the books."[72] Theodore Ziolkowski reminds us that the background to the founding of the University of Berlin lies in the circle of Jena romantics, where dreams of a new kind of ideal university first began to turn the tide against the old German order.[73] In standing for that ideal, Fichte, who had lost his position in Jena as a result of the "atheism controversy," was more than an opponent of Schleiermacher. A reader of his *Deduced Plan* alongside of *Occasional Thoughts* is repeatedly struck by their shared dedication to common goals.[74] The enormity of the problems with Prussia's education system came to a head in the crisis brought on by Napoleon. Prussia's entire secondary school system had been overhauled during the time of Humboldt's tenure as minister in charge of education. The result was to normalize the classical Gymnasium, with its school-leaving certificate (*Abiter*) as the norm for future students in Germany.[75] A revival of university education would only be possible with newly strengthened schools. Building on that sentiment, Schleiermacher's proposal spoke directly to the need to coordinate the university not just with schools but with the research academy as well.

If we inquire into the relative weight to be given to Humboldt and Schleiermacher in the founding of the university, the answer is clear. It is best stated in the words of Kurt Nowak: "The chief person in the educational reform was not Schleiermacher, but neither was he some behind the scenes subordinate figure. Humboldt saw in him an adviser and co-designer who was full of ideas."[76] Schleiermacher shared deeply in Humboldt's sense of the classical cultivation (*Bildung*) of the individual. *Occasional Thoughts* blends that teaching with a romanticist's respect for how individuals relate organically to their communities and to the empirical details that inform their lives and choices within the larger society. At age 40 Schleiermacher was more experienced than a number of other

---

71 Charles E. McClelland, *State, Society, and University in Germany 1700–1914* (Cambridge: Cambridge University Press, 1980), 93.
72 Lilge, *Abuse of Learning*, 1.
73 Ziolkowski, *German Romanticism and its Institutions*, 218–308.
74 In his inaugural lecture as first rector of the university, Fichte proclaimed that "at no university in the world is this academic freedom more secure and more firmly grounded than here at our university," cited from Ziolkowski, *German Romanticism*, 303.
75 See Fallon, *German University*, 17–19.
76 Nowak, *Schleiermacher*, 216.

academic stars, who would join the new faculty in 1810. When they began at the university the legal scholar Karl Friedrich von Savigny was 31, the classical philologian August Boeckh was 26, and the historian Barthold Georg Niebuhr was 34 years old.[77] As the heir of Humboldt, surrounded by these and other outstanding colleagues, Schleiermacher participated in the university until his death in February 1834.

As a carefully reasoned piece of public reflection, *Occasional Thoughts* stands out in the Schleiermacher corpus. Understandably, its reception has been greater among educators and cultural historians than among theologians. Like much in Schleiermacher's theology, the document's strength lies in its ability to breath new life into old, inherited teachings and institutions. In that sense it conveys something of his romanticist respect for historical traditions. In his 1808 review of the book, Schleiermacher's soon-to-be colleague at the new university, the legal scholar and jurist Karl Friedrich Savigny (1779–1861), put matters this way:

It is especially gratifying that the author, while investigating the ideal situation of universities, has in no way been pulled away from evaluating existing institutions. He has succeeded overall in demonstrating the deep significance of old customs, concerning which the enlightened crowd had long been accustomed to view pityingly as outmoded forms.[78]

It may have taken a mind steeped in a romanticist respect for history to restore the German university to its Enlightenment critics.

The treatise's proposals on teaching and learning as well as on the structures and operations of the modern university are all couched in an ethical-social philosophy. Schleiermacher's confident optimism, keen political sense, and ability to take probing positions on issues of higher education would be the envy of many academic deans or provosts.[79] He was emboldened in this task, knowing that Wilhelm von Humboldt, who held the key ministerial post in this matter, held him in high esteem. When the collapse of Prussia at the hands of Napoleon unleashed a need for far-sighted renewal, Schleiermacher was eager to help the nation carve out a brighter future. For Schleiermacher, action and reflection worked hand in hand as Prussia debated its future.

---

77 Ziolkowski, *Berlin*, 175–6.
78 K. F. Saviny review, in Müller, ed., *Gelegentliche Gedanken*, 259.
79 In a book chapter that traces the vicissitudes of German universities 1810–1945, Rüdiger vom Bruch wonders whether the Humboldt–Schleiermacher university might not today be better preserved in North America; "A Slow Farewell to Humboldt?," in Ash, ed., *German Universities*, 27.

Occasional Thoughts attracted the attention of contemporaries through its well-crafted rhetoric and sense of balance between pragmatic concerns and substantive principles. Although didactic and expository, the work shows signs of Schleiermacher's commitment to philosophic inquiry and argument such as can only take place in the free and autonomous setting of a university. Though conversational and direct, the work has the internal consistency of a more formal book. At first glance *Occasional Thoughts* appears to differ from other Schleiermacher texts. It avoids the autobiographical and satirical tone of *On Religion* and the often hair-splitting, dialectical turns of mind of his theological magnum opus, *The Christian Faith.* Yet a drive to construct a self-consistent reflection on the nature, structures, and processes of a university remains intact. This is not unlike the reflection of his more formal magnum opus. Schleiermacher takes up views that are at apparent odds in ways that illuminate their partiality, while he seeks to obtain "a notion of the whole" (1/19). Here I have only alluded to sections of the work on the oversight of student life and on granting degrees, and not dealt at all with the concluding appendix that makes the specific case for locating the new university in Berlin. The suggestion of that appendix that the university might be provisionally situated in Berlin, and later evaluated, softened potential objections and shows his rhetorical-political skill. By placing the specific case for Berlin in an appendix the work invites readers to ponder the proposed ideal university without letting political objections of the urban administrators (increased financial burdens, disruptions caused by disorderly student life, diminishment of extant cultural and educational institutions) get in the way.

We have seen that the way forward for Schleiermacher had been well prepared by Wilhelm von Humboldt. In an era of Prussian recovery and longing for new prestige it was unlikely that those who wished to locate the university away from Berlin or simply revert to the status quo in the form of extant schools, professional institutes, and the Royal Academy of Sciences could resist the combined intellectual and institutional appeal of Humboldt and Schleiermacher. The Prussian king who began the deliberations arranged for the university to be opened in 1810 in a palatial residence that had belonged to Prince Heinrich, brother of Friedrich the Great, directly on Unter den Linden near the Opera. When the statutes were finally ratified in 1817, the university was appropriately named the Friedrich-Wilhelms-Universität, after the Prussian monarch. Only in 1949 under the East German socialist-communist regime did it receive its current name, the Humboldt University.[80] In the end, the success of Schleiermacher's treatise lies in the way it effectively addressed matters that were on the minds of the most thoughtful people of his day. Though born into a different social class from the aristocratic Humboldt, Schleiermacher must have made his mentor in matters of education and state policy exceedingly proud.

---

80 The name "Humboldt University" was bestowed in honor of both Alexander and Wilhelm von Humboldt; see John Connolly, "Humboldt Coopted: East German Universities 1945–1989," in Ash, ed., *German Universities*, 55, n. 1. There is abundant irony in the fact that the name of the most prestigious university of the statist regime of the German Democratic Republic came to bear the name of one of Germany's most stalwart champions of the rights and cultivation of the individual.

CHAPTER 7

Schleiermacher and the theology of bourgeois society: a critique of the critics

Ever since his death in 1834 the thought of Friedrich Schleiermacher has constituted a battleground of competing theological perspectives. His corpus, which touches on so many diverse aspects of human culture in the modern setting, continues to be the seedbed of rival interpretations and theories. This holds for the relationship between politics and theology. Though discussion of the political teaching of Schleiermacher has never attained the intensity of discussion of his theology, it is well known that much of his lifework focused on a theory of politics and society, including his ethics, his lectures on the state, occasional papers, and addresses before the Berlin Academy and other bodies, his Plato translations and prefaces (especially the *Republic*), not to mention the political dimension of numerous sermons or his direct involvement in the movement of Prussian Reform.[1] To this day few studies integrate the diverse strata of Schleiermacher's theological teaching into a full-scale treatment of his politics.[2]

The fact that several recent Schleiermacher interpretations take a political bent is to be lauded. The subject is worthy of investigation for its own sake but also because of its potential for throwing light on the relationships between political, economic, or social issues and present-day theological imperatives. By looking at familiar texts with a heightened political consciousness, a reader is forced to rethink fundamental positions of Schleiermacher's thought and to weigh perspectives that often reach into the fabric and aspirations of our own society.

---

1 Martin Redeker, *Schleiermacher: Life and Thought*, tr. John Wallhauser (Philadelphia: Fortress Press, 1973), 87–8.
2 The situation is now rectified by Matthias Wolfes, *Öffentlichkeit und Bürgergesellschaft: Friedrich Schleiermachers politische Wirksamkeit*, I–II (Berlin: Walter de Gruyter, 2004); see also Ted Vial's chapter on Schleiermacher and politics in the *Cambridge Companion to Schleiermacher*, ed. Jacqueline Mariña (Cambridge: Cambridge University Press, 2005).

The fresh challenge to Schleiermacher's thought makes the critique by the early twentieth-century "theology of revelation" (Karl Barth, Emil Brunner) seem modest in scope and parochial by comparison. This newer criticism is informed by a Marxian analysis of the human social order as well as by the penetrating insight of the sociology of knowledge that human ideas are, willy-nilly, shaped by networks of cultural forces and social interests that are hidden to the conscious intent of a writer. Students of Schleiermacher's teaching first faced this new challenge in the work of Yorick Spiegel, *Theologie der bürgerlichen Gesellschaft: Sozialphilosophie und Glaubenslehre bei Friedrich Schleiermacher* (1968); the challenge is continued, though in diverse ways, by Dieter Schellong, *Bürgertum und christliche Religion: Anpassungsprobleme der Theologie seit Schleiermacher* (1975), and by Frederick Herzog, *Justice Church: The New Function of the Church in North American Christianity* (1980).[3] The range of human sciences that come into play in these treatments is more vast than the standard divinity school problems we associate with theological methodology and the starting point of theological reflection. The direction of interpretation shows that theological criticism is not immune from fashions of cultural analysis that have already affected historical and social-scientific discussions.

It is not my intent to belabor the well-known Barthian criticism of Schleiermacher, even though its specter hovers over the formulations of Spiegel, Schellong, and, though to a lesser extent, Herzog.[4] Spiegel quotes Barth approvingly to the effect that Schleiermacher's theology is "wholly inward," while Schellong writes in a German journal (*Theologische Existenz Heute*) that seeks to perpetuate a Barthian theological perspective.[5] I argue that Schellong's and Herzog's versions of the new Schleiermacher interpretations, far from offering an adequate understanding of the relationship between Schleiermacher's theology and his politics, illustrate the intellectual bankruptcy of the sociology of knowledge when its insight is taken in lieu of judicious historical reflection as a means of understanding the past. These writers reflect an undue degree of present-mindedness (with its inadequately argued assumptions about the wholesale demise

---

3 Yorick Spiegel, *Theologie der bürgerlichen Gesellschaft: Sozialphilosophie und Glaubenslehre bei Friedrich Schleiermacher* (Munich: Kaiser Verlag, 1968); Dieter Schellong, *Bürgertum und christliche Religion: Anpassungsprobleme der Theologie seit Schleiermacher, Theologische Existenz Heute* (Munich: Kaiser Verlag, 1975); and Frederick Herzog, *Justice Church: The New Function of the Church in North American Christianity* (Maryknoll, NY: Orbis Books, 1980).

4 From the perspective of his call for a "justice church," Herzog views even Barth's theology as unduly intellectual, dominated by concepts (*Justice Church*, 100).

5 Spiegel, *Theologie*, 31, 87; Schellong, *Bürgertum*, especially 96–7.

and immorality of capitalism and the liberal social order). Since no metacritical standpoint is available, an interpreter's own frame of reference must be subjected to as much criticism as is leveled at the object of his study. Otherwise, historical study is reduced to an exercise in ideology that masquerades as a disclosure of the ideology of other persons.

After examining the new interpretations of Schellong and Herzog (whose Schleiermacher chapter in *Justice Church* is informed by the work of Spiegel), I next present a sketch of Schleiermacher's political thought. This section is necessarily tentative and preliminary; the topic reaches into what are as yet unmined veins in the Schleiermacher corpus. I argue that Schleiermacher's political thought arose directly from his experience of his revolutionary era and that amid this setting, with its competing options, he made political choices that must be judged to be on the side of progressive social change. I do not argue that Schleiermacher was an advocate of radical change or revolution. But it strikes me as an unwarranted and mischievous critical posture for the historical study of theology if we act as if the moral imperative of biblical faith should put the church on the side of revolution in all eras and circumstances.

In turning to Schleiermacher as political player and actor in my last section, I do not presume to resolve or to make a definitive or formal argument about the relationship between political theory and practice. The most astute writers within the sociology of knowledge (e.g., Karl Mannheim) are aware of the extreme theoretical difficulty in finding a definitive resolution of this relationship.[6] It seems odd that recent criticism, while presenting Schleiermacher's politics as rooted in bourgeois assumptions, should not first weigh his political action in its own setting, including the risks that were taken on behalf of causes that seriously challenged the status quo of Prussian privilege and power, before asking what Schleiermacher might teach us today about theology and politics. Schleiermacher was engaged in heated political controversy for much of his life; for a time he was virtually charged with treason against the king. What is so singular about the newer criticism is the way that it imputes a kind of "deductivism" to Schleiermacher, as if he, along with the German Idealists and Romantics among his peers, only thinks speculatively and abstractly, while missing the connectedness with social reality where change and real life take place. Against this, I contend that the shoe is on the other foot; if anything is "deductive" it is the habit, apparently on

6 Karl Mannheim, *Ideology and Utopia: An Introduction to the Sociology of Knowledge* (New York: Harcourt, Brace and World, 1936), 109–91.

the increase, of basing an analysis of Schleiermacher's theology and politics on anachronistic assumptions.

FROM CULTURAL ACCOMMODATION TO BOURGEOIS THEOLOGY

In the history of modern theology the name of Schleiermacher is virtually synonymous with theological liberalism. It was in sharp revolt against this liberalism that the Swiss theologian Karl Barth (d. 1968) launched his major assault on theological liberalism of the nineteenth century.[7] Barth convinced the theological world that nineteenth-century theology constituted an epoch of cultural accommodation, a tendency he called "cultural-Protestantism" (*Kulturprotestantismus*). In its overriding desire to remain relevant, Schleiermacher's theology departed from the classical teachings of the Christian tradition on human sinfulness and the free grace of the deity. Even at the outset there was always a political cast to Barth's suspicion of Schleiermacher; the young Swiss theologian wondered if the Berlin pastor would have signed the manifesto favoring the Kaiser's aims in World War One as readily as did Barth's own theological teachers.[8]

It is no new discovery to observe that the view of Schleiermacher as "cultural accommodationist," though stamped by Barth and Brunner, was partly shared by significant theologians of Protestant liberalism in the 1940s through the 1960s. So strongly was the "father of modern theology" burdened by the Barthian charges of subjectivism and cultural accommodation that H. Richard Niebuhr was unable to give a balanced account of Schleiermacher's teaching without making definite qualifications. In H. Richard Niebuhr's classic work *Christ and Culture* (1951) we find a strong echo of Barth's view, even though Barth's critique is qualified by being made to apply chiefly to Schleiermacher's youthful work *On Religion*. (The difficulty with this ploy lies in the fact that Schleiermacher never renounced the basic stance of his youthful work.) Niebuhr's fivefold typology of historic relationships between Christianity and culture continues to be among the most influential works of twentieth-century Protestant thought. By placing the early Schlelermacher in his category of cultural accommodation ("Christ of culture"), Niebuhr helped to

7 Barth's view of Schleiermacher is expressed throughout his corpus. See Karl Barth, *Protestant Theology in the Nineteenth Century* (Valley Forge: Judson Press, 1973), 425–73, as well as *The Theology of Schleiermacher*, ed. Dietrich Ritschl (Grand Rapids: Eerdmans, 1982).
8 Karl Barth, "Concluding Unscientific Postscript on Schleiermacher," *Studies in Religion/Sciences Religieuses* 7/2 (1978): 117–35.

perpetuate the interpretation of Barth. He writes in that work: "Perhaps Barth sees Schleiermacher as too much of one piece; but certainly in the *Speeches on Religion*, as well as in his main writings on ethics, he is a clear-cut representative of those who accommodate Christ to culture while selecting from culture what conforms most readily to Christ."[9] H. R. Niebuhr would himself only marginally qualify as a follower of Barth. He was, however, deeply aware of the path of liberal optimism as it captured the mind of American Protestantism in the modern period. His aphorism in *Kingdom of God in America* (1937) neatly summed up the shallow outcome of this theological direction: "A God without wrath brought men without sin into a kingdom without judgment through the ministrations of a Christ without a cross."[10] Niebuhr's credentials as a critic of the view he describes are as impeccable as Barth's, even though based on a different theological stance. There is irony in the fact that, of all recent Protestant theologians, a case can be made that Niebuhr's stance most nearly resembles that of his German predecessor. In his stress on divine oneness and radical monotheism, the need for an ethics that is broadly rooted in human sociality and a sense of history, as well as in the openness of theology to the pluralism of academic disciplines, Niebuhr stands close to Schleiermacher.[11]

The movement of Schleiermacher criticism launched by Spiegel in 1968 links Schleiermacher's theological liberalism directly with the socioeconomic liberalism of Adam Smith, the founder of the market theory of capitalism. Spiegel argues that the formulations of *The Christian Faith* are theological correlates of the free market system.[12] Both the model of exchange and reciprocal action (between relative freedom and relative dependence) and the inevitability of the hidden hand (the absoluteness of divine causality) are deeply embedded in Schleiermacher's work. There is much in Spiegel that deserves further discussion. But for reasons of space, I choose in this essay to treat the more recent works of Schellong and Herzog, each of which takes a line that is commensurate with Spiegel, even when not explicitly citing him.

---

9 H. R. Niebuhr, *Christ and Culture* (New York: Harper and Bros., 1951), 94.
10 H. R. Niebuhr, *The Kingdom of God in America* (New York: Harper and Bros., 1937), 193.
11 Paul Tillich's work might also be cited as a second example of ambivalence despite an underlying affinity with Schleiermacher's theological work. See *Systematic Theology* (Chicago: University of Chicago Press, 1951), 1, 41–2, and *Perspectives on Nineteenth-and Twentieth-Century Protestant Theology* (New York: Harper and Row, 1967), 90–114.
12 Spiegel, *Theologie*, 21, 49–55, 244.

In his German monograph *Bourgeoisie and Christian Religion: Problems of Accommodation in Theology since Schleiermacher* (1975), Schellong argues that Schleiermacher's theological enterprise wholly reflects the theologian's social class and privileged position in Prussian society. Curiously, Schellong asserts that Schleiermacher's actual "*political positions*" (his italics) are "relatively unimportant."[13] Rather than examine the explicit references to politics that run through the Schleiermacher corpus, Schellong seeks to find social and political positions that are unconsciously embedded in Schleiermacher's theology. Basic to Schellong's charge is the view that Schleiermacher's evolutionary view of the world entails a "naturalization" of the fact of evil. On that assumption hangs the charge of cultural complacency and a too ready acceptance of injustice and evil. It is true that Schleiermacher frequently acknowledges that nature offers us both good and evil; but Schellong's move from that insight to the inference that a lack of awareness of radical evil blinded the theologian to capitalistic exploitation is unsubstantiated.[14]

Schellong's Schleiermacher is the ultimate example of cultural impotence: "The theologian stands in a breathing space that has become narrow for the Christian religion. He cannot be creatively active; he is placed in a defensive situation. And Schleiermacher – equipped by nature for this task – accepted this situation and saw his task in an attempt to reconcile Christianity with the modern civil order then unfolding."[15] Readers of such a passage would scarcely guess that the figure under discussion was the active agent of political change in his era.

In a work that stands as an American parallel to Schellong's, Herzog's "Schleiermacher and the Problem of Power" in *Justice Church: The New Function of the Church in North American Christianity* (1980) adds to the renewed critique of Schleiermacher.[16] Though maintaining that his purpose "is not to berate Schleiermacher" and assuring the reader that even Barth allowed that Schleiermacher's "place in the history of Protestant thought is secure," Herzog asserts that his "point is rather to show how Schleiermacher appropriated a social order we also appropriate when we take over his theology."[17] In Herzog's words:

While seeming progressive in regard to science, in some respects he [Schleiermacher] stays very much within the old world of social privilege determining the function of religion. Today we face a much more radical task of world construction that does not stop at integrating merely the interests of science into the church.

13 Schellong, *Bürgertum*, 27.   14 Ibid., 44–5.   15 Ibid., 33.
16 Herzog, *Justice Church*, 55–71.   17 Ibid., 56.

The more one probes the Schleiermacher corpus the more one realizes that in spite of all the progressive features of his thought the new worldview he promotes is also the mainstay of the given social world of his day – and partly an attempt to legitimate it. Of course, there is no point arguing with history.[18]

Nowhere in his discussion of Schleiermacher does Herzog draw from or make reference to the theologian's interaction with his social milieu. Instead of an analysis of relevant passages from the political sermons, letters, or religious and philosophical works, we find allegations and assertions that rest on a few passages, often taken out of context. Herzog's trump card in this respect is a long quotation from a newspaper letter of 1831 in which Schleiermacher, responding to the way he was being lionized as a "man of the left" by adherents of the July Revolution in Paris, proclaims that he has always been a loyal subject of the king and shares the interests of the king in the public good.[19] It appears not to occur to Herzog to ask whether the theologian, then in his early sixties, protests too much. No mention is made of Schleiermacher's earlier relationship to the Prussian reform movement of Stein and Hardenberg, to the actual social privilege that the theologian is believed to have enjoyed, or to the task of weighing Schleiermacher's perspective alongside other influential voices, such as that of the philosopher J. G. Fichte, the linguist and educator Wilhelm von Humboldt, or his close associate in the early Romantic movement Friedrich Schlegel. Herzog's assertions are framed, though hardly made more plausible, by quotations from the Marxian philosopher Herbert Marcuse and the historian Herbert J. Muller on the interaction of Christianity with culture, as if their criticisms can automatically be applied to Schleiermacher.[20]

In advocating liberation theology in North America, Herzog's book assumes an honored place among the series of works on this topic published by Orbis Press. Herzog cites the well-known social gospel theologian Walter Rauschenbusch, where *A Theology for the Social Gospel* (1917) maintains that "the constructive genius of Schleiermacher worked out solidaristic conceptions of Christianity which were far ahead of his time."[21] On the same page, however, as if realizing that a senior patron of the contemporary liberationist movement has just commended Schleiermacher, Herzog cites a second passage by Rauschenbusch. Here we learn about "the professional theologians of Europe, who all belong by kinship and sympathy to the bourgeois classes and are constitutionally

---

18 Ibid., 57.   19 Ibid., 70, n. 38.   20 Ibid., 448–59, 68.   21 Ibid., 58.

incapacitated for understanding any revolutionary ideas, past or present"
and Herzog again acts as if the statement automatically applies to
Schleiermacher. A footnote to this passage informs the reader that "there
has been very little research of the historical background of Schleiermacher's
stance in this regard."[22] Yet this fact, even if it were the case, could hardly
warrant our saying whatever we want.

It is not necessary to review all the allegations of Herzog in detail for us
to see that they form an ideological pattern. The characterization in
question rests on the unsubstantiated claim that Schleiermacher holds a
wholly sectarian view of the church. "The most characteristic aspect of
Schleiermacher's view of the church is that it occupies a completely
spiritual sphere. It has to, because it is a modification of religion, which
is all by itself for Schleiermacher. The church exists alongside the
world. But its sphere is entirely different from the world."[23] To be sure,
Schleiermacher does exercise considerable dialectical ingenuity in writing
about the relationship between worldly and spiritual kingdoms. Herzog is
correct in sensing that they are not coextensive. Precisely because the
spiritual realm has a degree of cultural independence, the religious community provides Schleiermacher with a basis for launching a critique of
the politics of his era. In section 105 of *The Christian Faith*, where Herzog
cites the phrase "it is part alike of the purity and of the perfection of His
[Christ's] spiritual power that sensuous motives can have no share in it,"
Schleiermacher is concerned to argue that "Christianity is neither a
political religion nor a religious state or theocracy."[24] Political religions,
which would derive religion from civil legislation and, pushed far enough,
equate the life of faith with patriotism or nationalism, are rejected just as
are theocratic impulses to subordinate and control the interests of civil life
under a religious elite.[25] Herzog fails to see that the relative independence
of spiritual community and power in Schleiermacher's conception is the
very thing that protects the nineteenth-century theologian from a wholesale capitulation to his culture. By not explaining how the religious sphere
interacts with worldly interests, Herzog leaves us with a Schleiermacher
whose views are passivist and culturally unproductive.

Enough has been said here by way of indicating the resurgence of the
fashionable belief that Schleiermacher is a cultural accommodationist.

22 Ibid., 69, n. 10, which cites Robert M. Bigler, *The Politics of German Protestantism: The Rise of the
     Protestant Church Elite in Prussia 1815–1848* (Berkeley: University of California Press, 1972), 29, as
     an exception.
23 Herzog, *Justice Church*, 59–60.
24 *CF*, 472.   25 Ibid., 473.

Schellong's and Herzog's depictions of Schleiermacher as a theologian of bourgeois society are more problematic (doubtless because they lack subtlety) than were the initial charges formulated by Karl Barth. In his 1923–4 lectures on the theology of Schleiermacher, Barth writes in the light of his critical presuppositions, yet in a judicious analysis of the mature sermons writes of "the fourth of the principles which Schleiermacher's sermons proclaim in practice." "At this point we have to respect his insight and vision, for this principle is no other than that of social equality. Like the question of the absoluteness of Christianity, this is a theme that is constantly mentioned and discussed in these sermons, and to the best of my knowledge this side of his ethics has never been investigated or presented in context."[26] The desire of recent critics to use a "class analysis" approach in their theological work overrides careful treatment of historical evidence. It is doubtless the case that Schleiermacher, judged by hindsight, was involved in a variety of ways in processes of cultural accommodation. To the extent that accommodation to a social world operates unconsciously, the process cuts in all directions and includes the interpreters as well as the objects they study. The question remains, however, the degree to which these forces actually determine and shape the teaching of a given thinker. The new Schleiermacher criticism comes perilously close to affirming a social determinism, yet without drawing the consequences of this position.

SCHLEIERMACHER'S SOCIAL AND POLITICAL THOUGHT

The task of characterizing Schleiermacher's politics requires us to move into a matrix of historical events, the full complexity of which exceeds the bounds of this essay.[27] We may start with a text. Like all thoughtful contemporaries, the young scholar followed the revolution in France with keen interest. A letter by the 25-year-old to his father dwells on his attitudes towards the revolution, while commenting on the execution of the French king (Louis XVI) early in 1793. The letter discloses Schleiermacher's mind on the chief question of the day.

---

26 Barth, *Theology of Schleiermacher*, 37.
27 Frederick C. Beiser, *Enlightenment, Revolution, and Romanticism: The Genesis of Modern German Political Thought, 1790–1800* (Cambridge, MA: Harvard University Press, 1992) conveys a fuller picture of the political thought of the early Romantics, including Schleiermacher. Beiser writes that in its formative years Romanticism "attempted to be a middle path between liberalism and conservatism" and maintains that the organicism of the early Schlegel, Novalis, and Schleiermacher and their critique of civil society stood in service of protecting the Enlightenment ideals of liberty, equality, and fraternity (223, 232–44).

Had I not felt bound to preface my letter with an excuse, or at least an explanation to the nation, and had not the sermons been so intimately connected with this, I should before this have alluded to a subject which then absorbed my thoughts, and which still often recurs to me; I mean the wretched death of the King of France. I do not know how it has happened, that up to the present moment I have never written to you on these subjects; now, however, they occupy my mind too much to pass them over in silence. Being accustomed openly to communicate to you all my thoughts, I am not afraid of confessing that upon the whole I heartily sympathize with the French Revolution; although, as you will know from my character, without my telling you, I do not of course approve of all the human passions and exaggerated ideas that have been mixed up with it, however plausibly these may be represented as a natural consequence of the previous state of things; nor am I either seized by the unhappy folly of wishing to imitate it and of desiring the whole world to be remodelled according to that standard. I have honestly and impartially loved the Revolution, but this last act has filled my whole soul with sorrow, as I consider the good king quite innocent, and I utterly abhor every kind of barbarity.[28]

The letter exemplifies the searching of a young man for a set of secure beliefs about the relationship between politics and truth in a revolutionary context. That the king was condemned without being lawfully convicted of guilt mattered to Schleiermacher and affected his judgment of the revolution. A combination of critical involvement and distance to con-temporary events that is characteristic of his later political stance is foreshadowed here. In its entirety the 1793 letter shows that the young Schleiermacher was already aware of his ability to stir up heated controversy in politics as well as in theology. Throughout the period Schleiermacher's chief impact on contemporaries was through the spoken as well as the written word. His gift of communication is widely attested. Wilhelm von Humboldt noted to a friend that Schleiermacher's "strength lay in the deeply penetrative character of his words, when preaching or engaged in any other of his ecclesiastical functions."[29] As public speaker Schleierma-cher relished opportunities to make use of pulpit as well as university lectern. Sermons were carefully prepared during a time of intense concen-tration, but were delivered from a small slip of paper that listed only the main points. One writer has claimed that he was the "greatest political preacher in Germany since Luther."[30] His sermons, several editions of which were collected in his lifetime, frequently address the stance of the church as religious community on the public issues of the day. This is

28 LS, 1, 109 (14 February 1793).   29 LS, 2, 204.
30 R. F. Eylert, cited in Bigler, *Politics of German Romanticism*, 29.

especially evident during his preaching in Halle that followed the defeat of
the city by the forces of Napoleon in October 1806. When he first
reappeared in the pulpit, on November 23, his sermon "On the Use of
Public Catastrophes," on Romans 8:28 ("We know that in everything
God works for good with those who love him"), sets the direction for a
series of political sermons that address the tasks facing a defeated Prussia
from the perspective of the community of faith.[31] These sermons extended
into the new year of 1807 when he spoke on "What We Should and
Should Not Fear" and continue through a remarkable sermon on the
birthday of the former king, Friedrich the Great, on January 24, 1808,
"On the Proper Veneration in Regard to the Indigenous Greatness of an
Earlier Time," on Matthew 24:1–2, Jesus' prediction of the destruction of
the temple. Here Schleiermacher acknowledges that the present events
open up "wounds of the heart" and that "we find ourselves caught in a
destructive ambiguity of feelings," in which the splendid deeds of that
hero" are praised at the same time as the easy destruction of "almost
everything" he had produced is lamented.[32]

Politically engaged preaching continued throughout Schleiermacher's
career in Berlin. It was especially strong during times of acute political stress
and upheaval, as in 1813 during the resistance to Napoleon but also in 1831 in
response to the ferment of the Parisian July revolution of 1830 and its
repercussions in Germany. In his 1923–4 lectures on Schleiermacher, Karl
Barth calls attention to the ways in which Schleiermacher's sermons of the
later years, especially the "sermon on revolution" of the Tenth Sunday after
Trinity 1931, embodies the principle of social equality. The revolts of 1830
indicate the "great communal guilt" of the upper classes. In Barth's
summary of the sermon:

What have we done, he [Schleiermacher] asks, to remedy the results of the great
spiritual inequality among men which is caused by material relationships? Could
this oppressed portion of the brethren sink so low if we did not so often isolate
ourselves from it and regard it merely as an object of violent restraint? This has to
be changed, not by philanthropy, but by the establishment of spiritual fellowship
with this group, by the binding insight that we possess our spiritual advantages
on the basis of their external inequality, and that we are thus required to practice
all the more our equality with them before God.[33]

---

31 Friedrich Schleiermacher, *Predigten, zweite Sammlung* (Reutlingen: J. R. Ensslin'schen
   Buchhandlung, 1835), 81. This volume contains the three original collections of the sermons.
32 Ibid., 120–40, 218–40; the latter sermon is reprinted in Friedrich Schleiermacher, *Kleine Schriften
   und Predigten, 1800–1820*, ed. Hayo Gerdes (Berlin: Walter de Gruyter, 1970), 314–30.
33 Barth, *Theology of Schleiermacher*, 37.

Barth notes, too, that Schleiermacher's sermon on the Twentieth Sunday after Trinity 1831 suggests an even deeper awareness of the relatedness between the experience of divine grace and the churches' externally directed activity in God's kingdom.[34] Schleiermacher's political sermons were more aimed at what we today call nation-building (in this case of an effete and humiliated Prussia) than at comforting the upper classes, who were responsible for the debacle in the face of Napoleonic power or for ongoing social strife in a rebuilt German state.

It is more difficult to step inside the schools of politics, as they then existed, than it is to gain an idea of Schleiermacher as public speaker. If we simplify for the sake of analysis, there were three main political stances in the period. Dedicated liberals and apostles of liberty chose (at least rhetorically) to follow the principles of the French revolution, the cultural elite among the professoriate were too caught up in their arts and sciences to become involved in practical politics, while the Romantics emerge in the period as proponents of extreme nationalism and advocate rebuilding the state along lines of an organic and historical model.[35]

All three stances were represented among Schleiermacher's close associates at the university. As the self-proclaimed heir of Immanuel Kant, the philosopher J. G. Fichte was an unqualified liberal who never lost his enthusiasm for the principles of the revolution and their embodiment of personal moral freedom. In politics as in theology Fichte was the angry academic rebel of the day; his *Addresses to the German Nation* sought to rally the populace to national feeling while instilling the democratic virtues of the French model. From their earliest meeting, Schleiermacher and Fichte were at odds on substantive philosophical grounds as well as temperamentally.

Schleiermacher's colleague, the linguist and educator Wilhelm von Humboldt, exemplified the attitude of classicism towards politics. Humboldt, who stood closer to Goethe and Schiller than he did to the Romantics, picked Schleiermacher to assist him in the founding commission of the university, largely on the strength of Schleiermacher's 1808 work, *Occasional Thoughts on Universities in the German Sense.*[36] This

---

34 Ibid., 37–8. The sermon on the Twentieth Sunday after Trinity 1831 is found in Friedrich Schleiermacher, *Predigten*, III (Berlin: G. Reimer, 1843), 96–III.
35 Reinhold Aris, *History of Political Thought in Germany, 1789–1815* (London: Russell & Russell, 1936), 66; Beiser, *Enlightenment, Revolution, and Romanticism,* warns against overly facile labels for the era's political thought (13–14) and further differentiates the political thought of the early Romantics, including Friedrich Schlegel and Novalis, from generalizations about the conservatism of the Romantics (222–78).
36 See above, chapter 6.

document set forth an appropriate structure and procecure for conducting academic life in the new university. Humboldt exemplifies a true aristocracy of intellect; Aris maintains that his attitude towards practical politics was one of indifference.[37] The remark is puzzling in view of Humboldt's involvement in structures of power in Prussia and the leading roles he played at the behest of various ministries, including a position in the delegation to the Congress of Vienna. What Aris has in mind is that a figure like Humboldt took political power for granted; he was, as we might say, a member of the same club as the ruling class. Humboldt's chief emphasis in the university was on research and scholarship, those endeavors that would eventually bring fame to the institution.[38] Though Schleiermacher never wished to play down the importance of research, it was he more than Humboldt who stressed the significance of the new Prussian university in broadening and, in this sense, improving the leadership of the state. Though forming a "community of knowledge," the university was not to be controlled by the state apart from its legal and financial responsibilities; independence is claimed for the university in the self-regulation of teaching and learning.[39] In Humboldt we come closer to an encounter with the type of German academic, though in a more graceful and attractive form, which is under attack in the treatments of Schleiermacher that I have criticized in the previous section.

Alongside the politics of liberalism and classicism we have the not so easy task of sorting out Schleiermacher's affinity with the politics of the early German Romantics. Undeniably he shared deeply in the dreams and aspirations of these contemporaries, as they sought to develop a new beginning of culture. He also shared their national feeling for Germany and their mystical sense of identification with the nation. After Halle was taken by Napoleon in 1806 – an event he personally witnessed – Schleiermacher wrote to a younger friend, "I feel certain that Germany, the kernel of Europe, will stand forth again in a new and beautiful form."[40] But the disastrous consequence of the French attack on his native Prussia seared Schleiermacher's conscience like nothing he had previously experienced. As can be seen in the political sermons of the

37 Aris, *History of Political Thought*, 139–40.
38 On Humboldt and the research university, see the (postunification) symposium that revisits his legacy in German higher education, Mitchell G. Ash, ed., *German Universities Past and Present: Crisis or Renewal?* (Providence: Berghahn Books, 1997).
39 While defending the relative independence of a university, Schleiermacher writes: "The state works only for itself, historically it is chiefly self-seeking through and through; thus it tends not to offer support to science except on its own terms, within its own boundaries" (*OT*, 6).
40 *LS*, 2, 73.

Napoleonic period, its effect was to make him resolutely anti-French but also critical of the ill-prepared military and antiquated politics of the Prussian regime.

For an age like our own, which has experienced disasters that far exceed anything imaginable in Schleiermacher's day, the legacy of Romanticism in politics is in disrepute.[41] This is especially true, and not without good reason, for German Romanticism in its political forms. In the appeal to country, and to blood and soil, tones are sounded that strike fear even in a dispassionate student of the subject. We suspect the appeal to emotion of Romanticism because a considerable instability of mind appears to go along with this trait. But the lesson to be learned in taking a closer look at the Romantics is that they are by no means all alike. Though before the storming of the Bastille Romanticism worked predominantly to shape a politics of the left, after Napoleon's defeat it worked more in the opposite direction, towards a return to older authorities and traditions. In politics this meant a hardening of the authoritarian state. And in religion it often meant a rediscovery of Roman Catholic tradition and an idealizing of the Middle Ages. The *enfant terrible* among the early Romantics, Friedrich Schlegel, took this latter path in 1808.[42] In view of these divergent patterns, let us try to grasp Schleiermacher's precise relationship to this movement and the bearing of Romanticism on his political views and actions.

Though *On Religion* was a characteristically Romantic book and its author no ecclesiastical interloper but rather a full partner in the circle of Berlin friends, Schleiermacher nonetheless has definite reservations about the work of these friends, even in the work's first edition (1799). Schleiermacher speaks at length in his work about the aesthetic creativity of his associates. He has no problems with their tendency to view art and cultural creativity as forms of divine inspiration. But when their aesthetic zeal was presented as a substitute for religion and leads them to ridicule the institutional church, Schleiermacher saw in their work an inability to link their deepest aspirations with a moral community of authentic love. In a direct allusion to the work of Wachenroder and Tieck (*Herzensergiessungen eines kunstliebenden Klosterbruders*) he writes:

---

41 Beiser, *Enlightenment, Revolution, and Romanticism*, writes: "If we are to understand the politics of the Romantic movement, it is of the first importance that we must remove it from the shadow of Nazism" (226). For a summary of Schleiermacher's patriotism and its links to Romanticism, see Jerry F. Dawson, *Friedrich Schleiermacher: The Evolution of a Nationalist* (Austin: University of Texas Press, 1966).

42 On the young Schlegel's earlier relationship to Schleiermacher, see Jack Forstman, *A Romantic Triangle: Schleiermacher and Early German Romanticism* (Missoula: Scholars Press, 1977), 17–34.

Friendly words and outpourings of the heart always hover on their lips and return again and again and they are still not able to find the proper manner and final cause of their reflection and longing. They hope for a fuller revelation and, suffering and sighing under the same pressure, they see one another enduring, perhaps with inner sympathy and deep feeling, but yet without love.[43]

To his mind, the historic church, even with all its faults, still provided a viable alternative. He wrote the *Speeches* to convince his contemporaries of this fact. In their suspicion of institutionalized cultural forms, the "despisers of religion" were led more by Enlightenment anticlericalism than by a deep reverence for individuality and the glory of past traditions. While revising his speeches in 1806, Schleiermacher appended an "Epilogue" that warned his audience about wholesale conversions to Catholicism:

At present there are some who appear to rescue themselves from the Protestant into the Catholic Church. I am not speaking of those who in themselves are nothing and are dazzled like children by glitter and show, or are talked over by monks. But there are some to whom I myself have formerly drawn your attention who are somewhat able poets and artists who are worthy of honour; and a host of followers, as is the fashion nowadays, has followed them.[44]

Though aimed at diverse individuals, the "Epilogue" encompassed the mood of Friedrich Schlegel, who had originally urged Schleiermacher to write this book. With Prussia's capitulation to the French, Schleiermacher was prepared to assume official responsibilities as educator on behalf of a brighter future for the Prussian state; in 1808 Schlegel had moved out of Berlin and was in the process of converting to the Catholic faith. In the passage cited Schleiermacher does not rule out the possibility of authentic conversions; it went against his principles to deny an individual his freedom of choice. But if a conversion is authentic, then "surely traces of this natural constitution will appear in his whole life."[45] The difference with the Romantic school is that he has a sobriety of intellect that insists on making hard choices in life and that also embraces institutional forms of life, indeed relishes such opportunities for mediation. Viewed in light of the three dominant political options of his day, Schleiermacher's romantic sensibility insists upon individual liberty at all costs. He appears not to have shared the classicists' aloofness from and disdain for politics.

A formal statement of Schleiermacher's political philosophy was also made in 1814 in the form of a lecture before the Berlin Academy on the

43 *OR* (Crouter), 69.
44 *OR* (Oman), 268.   45 Ibid.

topic "On the Concepts of Different Forms of the State."[46] Several features of the lecture confirm our understanding of his politics. In the address Schleiermacher goes to great lengths to argue that the time-honored Aristotelian classification of political states as democracy, aristocracy, and monarchy eventually breaks down. Forms of government are more organic and natural and thus elude the categories of scientific scrutiny. In a dialectical perspective, a degree of interdependence exists among these inherited Greek categories. For example, since a king must in certain respects rely on others to assist him in the tasks of leadership or in fulfilling his will, he is dependent upon a kind of aristocracy, meaning by that term a group of natural or chosen leaders. In turn, democracy in a true form, if only because of the size of modern states, is unworkable and must assume representative leadership. A passage from the academy lecture testifies to Schleiermacher's romantic political stance with its predilection for the natural and organic:

The scientist in his endeavour to classify nature soon discovered that some of its products are more perfect than others, in which the essence of life is expressed more incompletely and developed to a lesser degree. This, however, could not deflect him from the natural course of Inquiry. Since the state, however, is a creation of man himself, it was thought as a result of this observation that a perfect state could be created by man himself proceeding from a theoretical model. We must declare this from the very beginning to be an illusion; for that which comes about through human nature is here erroneously mistaken for that which man makes. Never has a state, even the most imperfect one, been made; and in the sphere of unconscious activity all ingenuity can further both the spiritual and the physical aspects of nature only in an individual and subordinated manner. This illusion, however, was the cause of the fact that states were considered far too little as historical formations of nature, but always as objects upon which man has to exercise his ingenuity; thus their perfection and imperfection has been the main consideration. It may be argued that almost the whole of scientific study in this matter consisted of the endeavour to produce for the engineers of the state a single valid example of the state, in which all former phenomena remained only as attempts that have failed.[47]

In this statement Schleiermacher acknowledges the difficulty in developing a science of politics.[48] By its nature politics wishes to become the science of what is in process and living and thus can never be subject to

---

46 H. S. Reiss, ed., *The Political Thought of the German Romantics, 1793–1815* (Oxford: Basil Blackwell, 1955), 173–202; *Über die Begriffe der verschiedenen Staatsformen*, March 24, 1814, *KGA*, I/11, 95–124.

47 Reiss, ed., *Political Thought*, 175; *KGA*, I/11, 98.

48 On the substantive point, see Mannheim, *Ideology and Utopia*, 109–91.

comprehensive analysis in the manner of a formal science. What politics can do, however, is comparable to what Schleiermacher holds for theology as science. In both instances the main task is to describe and explore the richness of past human experience as fully and synthetically as possible as a basis for making choices in the present.[49] Like theology, politics is a hermeneutical field of inquiry that requires a sense of critical distance as well as contextual involvement. Seeing this helps us to distinguish Schlelermacher's stance from that of a present-day liberation theology in which the desire for a long overdue Christian praxis occasionally threatens to edge out balanced reflection.

In this section I have sought to place Schleiermacher's political thought amid the possible viable alternatives of his day. It remains to turn from Schleiermacher the thinker to Schleiermacher the player and political actor, a figure he refers to in the speeches as an "artist of politics."[50] Though the main spheres of Schleiermacher's activity and career alternate between the church and university, his direct involvement in the practical politics of his day is more considerable than is widely known. Contemporary awareness of this involvement supplements and adds credibility to his general political teaching.

THEOLOGIAN IN A TIME OF TURMOIL

Upon returning to Berlin in 1807 Schleiermacher championed the reforms set forth by the chief minister, Baron von Stein. These included the enactment of a representative assembly, freedom of the press, emancipation of the peasantry and of the Jews, and new regulations of taxation.[51] As his first contribution to cultural reform, Schleiermacher set down his thoughts on German higher education. His attitude was one of utter dismay when Stein was dismissed by the king in 1807. During a constitutional crisis in 1811, when things were going badly, he summoned the courage to write to the retired statesman whom he revered "most deeply among all public men."[52] Schleiermacher remarks that "nothing is more painful to me than the rumor circulating that your excellency, through

---

49 See, e.g., the tensions inherent in Schleiermacher's definition of dogmatics as "the science which systematizes the doctrine prevalent in a Christian Church at a given time," §19 in *CF*, 88
50 *OR* (Crouter), 83, 85 (*politische Künstler*).
51 See Walter M. Simon, *The Failure of the Prussian Reform Movement, 1807–1819* (Ithaca: Cornell University Press, 1955); Guy Stanton Ford, *Stein and the Era of Reform in Prussia, 1807–1815* (Princeton: Princeton University Press, 1922).
52 *Schl Briefe*, 4, 181–3 (July 1, 1811).

knowledge and approval, is taking part in all essential steps of the administration." He then adds a request to the letter, which reveals his intent in writing: "I am, to be sure, sufficiently hated by the chief persons of the court and the cabinet, but yet in many respects as good as unnoticed, and have various ways to discover much unobserved. I wish for nothing more ardently than that Your Excellency might use me in any manner pleasing to you to discover whether anyone is deceiving you, or to oppose false rumors."[53] That Schleiermacher had partial inside information about government affairs may derive from his longtime friendship with Alexander Dohna, who served from 1808 to 1810 as Minister of the Interior. Before taking up residence in Berlin, Schleiermacher had served as tutor and chaplain to the Dohna family in East Prussia.

Schleiermacher greeted the turn of events in 1813, when Prussia formed an alliance with Russia and entered the coalition against Napoleon, in a mood of exultation. If his reformist impulses were thwarted, his nationalistic feeling had not abated. Eager to contribute to the cause, he joined the historian B. G. Niebuhr and for several months worked as editor of a political newspaper, the *Prussian Correspondent*, which sought to rally popular support for the war against Napoleon.[54] In this work Schleiermacher needed to proceed cautiously; too much patriotic fervor among the peasantry or the middle classes would place unwanted political demands on the king. By this time Schleiermacher had sent his wife and children into the countryside of East Prussia, where they would be out of the areas of fighting. He complains vigorously to his wife about "quarrels with the government and the silly censorship."[55] Writing to his publisher and friend, Georg Reimer, Schleiermacher laments the lack of support he is getting for the paper, the difficulty in finding out what the government is doing, and the government threats and harassment as a result of an offensive editorial he had written.

My mishap has only served to amuse me; it is too absurd to cause me any real annoyance. Schuckmann [his superior in the Ministry of Interior Affairs], who had received a cabinet order to give me a severe reprimand, and to threaten me with dismissal, should I repeat the offence, began in the most angry and savage tone, and even accused me of high treason; but concluded with repeated assurances that he considered me a most upright man and sincere well-wisher to my country.[56]

---

53 Ibid.
54 See Schleiermacher's contributions to *Der Preußische Correspondent* (June–September 1813) in *KGA*, 1/14 (2003), 395–500.
55 *LS*, 2, 247.   56 Ibid., 248 (July 24, 1813).

In view of these difficulties and continued government interference, Schleiermacher resigned from the editorship the next year. It is a mark of the cosmopolitanism of the age that the man he most admired in politics, Baron von Stein, was by this time, after having been dismissed from Prussian service, in the service of Czar Alexander I of Russia as adviser on Prussian affairs.[57]

If we remain for a moment with Schleiermacher's enthusiasm for Stein, another angle of estimating his political philosophy is open to us. A widely read and learned statesman, Stein was himself a great admirer of the English parliamentarian Edmund Burke, whose lectures on the revolution in France were translated into German as early as 1793.[58] It would not be too far afield if we were to characterize Schleiermacher's politics as a form of "Burkean conservatism." Like Burke, he stood firmly on the side of individual liberty and worked for social reform and change while acting with a strong sense of historical examples. If Burke was, in the words of Frances Canavan, a "political theorist who mistrusted political theory," then Schleiermacher was his counterpart in theology.[59] To both men, the common experience of human life in civil society deserved prudent respect. What Canavan writes of Burke might just as readily apply to Schleiermacher's academy lecture on the state: "Burke's idea of a sound social order was not that of a monolith, but of a mixed and balanced constitution, in which the several parts of the state checked and restrained each other."[60] Since the parallel with Burke risks burdening Schleiermacher with yet one more label, it ought not to be pushed too far. But it does not strike me as obviously wrong-headed or un-Christian for Schleiermacher to have decided against the revolution in the form of the Napoleonic empire and to have sought a political stance that would resist the French, while not making an easy peace with the traditionalist landed interests and social problems of Prussia. What, then, can we conclude about the theologian in a time of turmoil? We have seen that Romanticism can lead to the left as well as to the right, and that the label gives us little

---

57 On Stein's "Russian exile," see Ford, *Stein*, 282–3.
58 Aris, *Political Thought in Germany*, 251; Beiser, *Enlightenment, Revolution, and Romanticism*, criticizes the Burke analogy: "Although the Romantics did insist that we should not change society wholesale according to some general plan, this should not be read as an affirmation of the more conservative politics of Burke. For they continued to stress the importance of gradual reform and evolution toward the principles of reason. Unlike Burke, they never endorsed a complete empiricism in politics" (239).
59 Francis Canavan, "Edmund Burke, 1729–1797," in *History of Political Philosophy*, ed. Leo Strauss and Joseph Cropsey, second edition (Chicago: Rand McNally College Publishing, 1972), 662.
60 Canavan, "Edmund Burke," 666.

guidance on Schleiermacher's actual politics. The same is true of a slogan like "cultural accommodationist." Since cultural forces are inevitably diverse and complex, we must always ask which forces are being joined and for what reasons and, also, against what other forces. If Schleiermacher accommodated himself to anything, it was to the reform efforts that failed but that challenged the prevailing prerogatives of aristocracy and crown in his nation. Failure of the reform movement and the enactment of the repressive Carlsbad Decrees was followed by increased persecution of government critics. Schleiermacher was under renewed suspicion in the early 1820s when letters of his expressing an abhorrence of government censorship and the secret police and condemning suppression of the student clubs (*Burschenschaften*) were found by the authorities during a search of the home of his brother-in-law (the nationalistic poet Ernst Moritz Arndt).[61] Schleiermacher's colleague on the theological faculty, W. M. L. de Wette, was dismissed from the university for having written a letter of condolence to the mother of a radical student who was charged with a patriotically inspired murder. For a time it seemed like Schleiermacher, too, would be dismissed from his position. He reported to Arndt in a letter dated March 21, 1820, "For longer than two weeks the whole city was again full of the news that I had been or was about to be dismissed."[62]

In the midst of this turmoil Schleiermacher produced his major systematic treatment of Christian theology, *The Christian Faith* (1821–2, rev. 1830–1).[63] He was also engaged in endless theological controversies involving Reformed and Lutheran church unity and liturgy,[64] plus the editing of his collected sermons and revising of earlier works. Towards the end of the decade of the 1820s Schleiermacher began to retreat from the heavy burdens of academy and church. He was less active than formerly in the customary squabbles of university life, with its endless committee work and professorial rivalries.

In view of these events and his own published statements it would be quite wrong to think of Schleiermacher as an antimonarchist. It was the politics of the king, not the monarchy, that troubled him. That the

---

61 Bigler, *Politics of German Romanticism*, 161. For Hegel's reaction to Schleiermacher's politics, see chapter 3 of this book.
62 *Schl Briefe*, 2, 373.
63 The first edition of the dogmatics is available in *KGA*, 1/7, 1–2, *Der christliche Glaube nach den Grundsätzen der evangelischen Kirche im Zusammenhange dargestellt (1821/22)*, ed. Hermann Peiter (1980, 1982).
64 Schleiermacher's church political publications (1808–30) are available in *KGA*, 1/9, *Kirchenpolitische Schriften*, ed. Günter Meckenstock with Hans-Friedrich Traulsen (2000).

Prussian state had a king was surely to his mind no automatic assurance of social injustice. As his academy lecture makes clear, what matters is the relationship that exists between the executive, judicial, and legislative functions of government. "These three activities must form the basis for a study of the state, so that the main principle of dissatisfaction is found in the question of whether all of these powers should be united in one moral person or distributed among several persons."[65] The best government was, in his view, not necessarily one that had overthrown a king; the best government was that which pursues wise policies and is attentive to the natural relationships of parts to whole, while allowing them to work together to represent the will of the people.

In a previous section I mentioned Frederick Herzog's use of a Schleiermacher letter from 1831 as evidence of Schleiermacher having been restricted by his class-consciousness. Now that we have rehearsed his role in Prussian politics of the era, we can take a closer look at that document. Herzog calls attention to the fact that the letter shows Schleiermacher's allegiance to the king.[66] But the letter in question, rather than illustrating cultural accommodation, is the work of a man who, though weary of fighting old battles, is not so weary that he will allow the French revolutionaries of 1830 to misrepresent his position. When the Parisian journal *Le Messager des Chambres* tried to represent his political position in a series of fictitious letters from Berlin, it was more than he could tolerate. The text of his open letter, which was then reprinted in German, reads:

Sir: As it has pleased one of your correspondents in this city to allude to me repeatedly, I trust that you will allow space in your columns for the subjoined answer to his remarks, if for no other reason, at least for the sake of your German readers.

First of all, I must disclaim the surname of great, as we Germans use this word so very sparingly that it can hardly be applied to a man like myself, except for the purpose of throwing ridicule upon him, which I am not aware that I have deserved.

Secondly. I am equally far from being "the most eminent Christian preacher in Germany" – I believe that was the expression used – and my sermons and discourses cannot possibly be models of eloquence, as I can never write them before delivering them. To attempt to be "sublime," as a preacher, would even be contrary to my principles; for the more sublime the Gospel, the more simple may the sermon be.

---

65 Reiss, ed., *Political Thought*, 176.
66 Herzog, *Justice Church*, 70 (n. 38).

Thirdly. We pray every Sunday that God will grant the king such wisdom as he needs for the fulfillment of the duties imposed upon him by God: but when doing this we are not aware that we express any other "wish of the people," than that it may lead a tranquil life under the rule and protection of the king, and ever draw nearer to the goal of Christian perfection. Such, sir, is the language of our Protestant church, and from this I have never diverged.

Fourthly, it is very true that I was "for a time forbidden to preach"; but it was from my doctor that the order emanated.

Fifthly. I belong to no party of the Left. Your expressions, right and left, right and left center, are quite foreign to our relations; and were your correspondent in truth a Prussian, he would not have made use of party appellations which, among us, no one would apply to himself. More especially, he would not have spoken of a party of the Left, secretly intent on revolutionary thoughts. We have made enormous progress since the peace of Tilsit, and that without revolution, without chambers, nay, even without liberty of the press; but the people have ever been with the king and the king with the people. Under these circumstances, must not a man be out of his senses who would pretend that henceforward we should progress more rapidly by means of a revolution? I, for my part, am always sure to be on the king's side, when I am on the side of the most enlightened men of the nation.[67]

It is a fascinating statement, not without traces of Schleiermacher's biting humor as he chides the French. Several factors are worthy of notice. For one thing, when Schleiermacher speaks about being "sure to be on the king's side," this is immediately coupled with "when I am on the side of the most enlightened men of the nation." From the preceding discussion, we think immediately of his having been on the side of the king's chief minister, Baron von Stein. Even more to the point is the fact that much of Schleiermacher's work shows disdain for the French. He saw in them the spirit of a rationalism that he opposed on philosophical grounds; in turn, the Roman Catholic nature of France, even more pronounced in the Restoration, was alien to him. Still a third factor shaped Schleiermacher's exchange with the French revolutionaries of 1830. Though long in disfavor with Friedrich Wilhelm III, Schleiermacher had shortly before been awarded the Order of the Red Eagle (third class), a decoration that recognized his lifelong service to the state.[68] In earlier days, amid storms of controversy, Schleiermacher had ridiculed his colleague, the Hegelian theologian Marheineke, for accepting such recognition. But after his long

---

67 *LS*, 2, 319–20 (March 8, 1831); the French original no longer exists; *KGA*, 1/14, cxx, 353–7.
68 *LS*, 2, 317; the award was also bestowed on Hegel in the same year. See Terry Pinkard, *Hegel: A Biography* (Cambridge: Cambridge University Press, 2000), 637.

years of service Schleiermacher was more than pleased to receive official recognition and graciously acknowledged it to the king. He wrote that the honor has "given me a proof of your favor that has earned me a degree of emotion such as few things could call forth, and that has arisen like a bright star over my old age, and will shed a luster over the future, the reflection of which will serve to dispel much of the gloom of the past."[69] It may yet be possible for someone to argue that Schleiermacher is a cultural accommodationist. But in 1831 Schleiermacher must have felt that the accommodating was on the other side. In these same last years of his life he was preaching the sermons that Karl Barth once noted for their social liberalism and teaching of social equality.[70] Schleiermacher never re-nounced anything he stood for and made no compromises to earn the favor of his king. It was Friedrich Wilhelm III who was moving, officially and personally if not politically, towards the theologian who had long been a troublesome figure in the state. There is little wonder that when Schleiermacher died, in 1834, the king decided to be in the procession along with thousands of other Berliners.[71] It was the sort of funeral that one would not have wanted to miss.

---

69 LS, 2, 317–18.

70 Barth, *Theology of Schleiermacher*, 17, 37–8, 133–4.

71 *LS*, 1, x–xi: "On the 15th February, 1834, a funeral procession was seen moving through the streets of Berlin, the like of which that capital had rarely before witnessed. The coffin, covered with a black pall and simply decorated with a large copy of the Bible, was borne on the shoulders of twelve students of the University, thirty-six of the most robust of whom had volunteered to perform, alternately, this pious service. After these came a train of mourners on foot, extending upwards of a mile in length, and these were followed by one hundred mourning coaches, headed by the equipages of the King and the Crown Prince. Along the whole line traversed by the procession, dense crowds of sympathizing spectators had gathered, while in the cemetery, beyond the gates of the city, similar crowds were assembled; and on every countenance might be read the fact that the individual borne to the grave was one of those representative men in whom are concentrated, as it were, in a focus, the moral and intellectual life of the nation and the period to which they belong, and who become, in consequence, centres of new light and diffusers of new and vivifying warmth. Such was, indeed, the case; for it was Friedrich Ernst Schleiermacher, whom, by a spontaneous movement, the capital of Protestant Germany was thus honouring in death."

PART III

Textual readings and milestones

CHAPTER 8

Schleiermacher's theory of language: the ubiquity of a romantic text

The challenge of locating the proper intellectual place of *On Religion: Speeches to its Cultured Despisers* within Schleiermacher's œuvre is especially daunting. An early romantic work that has repeatedly been relegated to its author's juvenilia, the text nonetheless accompanied Schleiermacher throughout his distinguished career as a theologian. In some manner, still difficult to determine, it claims a relationship to the larger contours of his theological imagination and academic work. Hans-Joachim Birkner knows the problem of locating *On Religion* better than most persons and has shown the pitfalls of approaching this Schleiermacher text (as well as others) with anachronistic notions of philosophy, theology, and their relationship in mind.[1] Of course, as Birkner notes, within his system of theological sciences Schleiermacher understood *On Religion* as "philosophical theology."[2] Elsewhere Schleiermacher speaks of *On Religion* in relation to the even broader category of "philosophy of religion."[3] Yet the disciplines of "philosophical theology" and "philosophy of religion" were in the process of formation in Schleiermacher's day, and the labels thus bear only a

---

1 Hans-Joachim Birkner, "Beobachtungen zu Schleiermachers Program der Dogmatik," in *Schleiermacher-Studien,* ed. Hermann Fischer (Berlin: Walter de Gruyter, 1996), 99–112; Hans-Joachim Birkner, *Schleiermachers Christliche Sittenlehre im Zusammenhang seines philosophisch-theologischen Systems* (Berlin: Alfred Töpelmann, 1964); Hans-Joachim Birkner, "Theologie und Philosophie: Einführung in Probleme der Schleiermacher-Interpretation," *Schleiermacher-Studien,* 157–92.
2 Birkner, "Theologie und Philosophie,"174, n. 20, citing *CF,* §3 and §10.
3 *OR* (Oman), 111. The 1821 "explanations" refer to the "*Glaubenslehre,* the Introduction of which contains the outlines of what I take to be the philosophy of religion, and therefore has many points of contact with this book"; *KGA,* 1/12, ed. Günter Meckenstock (1995), 140. This essay is best understood as an effort to examine the nature of these points of contact. On the revisions of the text, see the longer discussion on the work's revisions in Richard Crouter, ed. and tr., *On Religion: Speeches to its Cultured Despisers* (Cambridge: Cambridge University Press, 1988), 55–73, which are not included in the 1996 edition; see also Meckenstock, *KGA,* 1/12, VIII–XXVI.

semantic resemblance to the way these terms are used today.[4] As a means of estimating its relationship to his mature theology, we might raise the question of how *On Religion* fits into this system. Does the early work stand chiefly as an intellectual launching pad, which was substantively cast aside once the journey was begun? Or are there permanent insights within *On Religion* that unite it with its author's larger purposes? A fresh look at the critical orientation of *On Religion* can also shed light on the interpretive cul-de-sac that frequently surrounds the text's reception.[5]

To clarify the situation requires us to pay attention to Schleiermacher's effort, shared with his age, to construct a system of sciences in which the necessary components of scientific inquiry and learning are correlated with the enterprise of theology as a positive science. In view of *On Religion*'s *prima facie* status as expressing foundational insight, we can observe the way the terms "philosophical theology" and "philosophy of religion" apply to this work. In *Brief Outline*, where philosophical, historical, and practical theology constitute three interdependent divisions of theological inquiry, philosophical theology has several distinct meanings. It is viewed, first, as a critical discipline that is contrasted with disciplines that view material either "purely scientifically" or "strictly in an empirical fashion."[6] As a critical discipline philosophical theology seeks both to make logical clarifications through definitions and comparisons while drawing from and contributing to interpretations and descriptions of historical reality. In Schleiermacher's words,

philosophical theology utilizes the framework developed in philosophy of religion, in order to present (a) that perspective on the essence of Christianity whereby it can be recognized as a distinctive mode of faith, and at the same time (b) the form which Christian community takes, and (c) the manner in which each of these factors is further subdivided and differentiated.[7]

Each of these specific tasks is, in varying degree, evidenced in the argument of *On Religion*. The further specification that philosophical theology is general as well as Protestant Christian seems also to fit in with the argument of *On Religion*. The two-edged rhetorical stance of *On Religion*, which is aimed externally at a specific audience as well as internally at

---

4 *BO*, §24 and §29. On the development of and relationship between philosophy of religion and philosophical theology in Hegel, see Walter Jaeschke, *Reason in Religion: The Foundations of Hegel's Philosophy of Religion*, tr. J. Michael Stewart and Peter C. Hodgson (Berkeley: University of California Press, 1990).

5 On the reception of the work, see chapter 11 of this book.

6 *BO*, 29 (§32).   7 Ibid., 25 (§24).

misconceptions of religion and religious community, corresponds to the subdivisions of philosophical theology as "apologetics" and "polemics" (*Brief Outline*, §43–§68).

Granted, the interdependence of these two modes of arguing (*Brief Outline*, §63) is easily misunderstood in *On Religion*. As an exercise in the art of persuasive communication the text aligns religion ("sensibility and taste for the infinite"[8]) with its audience's poetic-aesthetic sense and its manifestations among individuals and historic communities. A rhetorical defense ("Apology") helps to "ward off hostility" (*Brief Outline* §39), and is needed in order for the work to get an initial hearing. The definitional problem of religion is addressed as well as a corrective issued with respect to how readers are to view its social embodiments. The external apologetic task of *On Religion* can succeed only in combination with a polemic that purifies the subject from within. Indeed, section 15.2 of *The Christian Faith* recognizes that the rhetorical "is directed partly outwards as combative and commendatory, and directed partly inwards, as rather disciplinary and challenging."[9] The two modes of argument are tightly interwoven in *On Religion*'s dialectical and rhetorical structure. An audience, presumed to be hostile to religion, is found to have a heightened capacity for it; a writer, who is presumed to be a staunch defender of the church, redefines its nature. The polemical intrachurch critique of religion lends credibility to work's argument by showing the author's independent position. Without the self-reflective critique of institutional and historical religion (speeches 4 and 5), the identification of religion as "intuition and feeling of the universe" (speech 2) too readily appears as a disembodied intellectual exercise. To be sure, in 1799 Schleiermacher expresses disdain for systems of theology and for the age-old confusion between religion and metaphysical systems.[10] "By its whole nature, religion is as far removed from all that is systematic as philosophy is by its nature inclined toward it."[11] Yet to write that "whoever only thinks systematically and acts from principle and design and wants to accomplish this or that in the world inevitably circumscribes himself"[12] does not belie the need for ordered rhetoric as a rational means of persuasion. The work consists of enthused speech and the living voice ("All this I know and am nevertheless convinced to speak by an inner and irresistible necessity that

---

8 *OR* (Crouter), 23; *KGA*, 1/2, 212.   9 *CF*, 78.
10 *OR* (Crouter), 13, 19–20; *KGA*, 1/2, 200.
11 *OR* (Crouter), 14; *KGA*, 1/2, 201.
12 *OR* (Crouter), 28; *KGA*, 1/2, 218.

Table 8.1. *Rhetorical structure of the five speeches*

	Problem	Oppositions	Resolutions
I	Foundational assumption	Two opposing forces	Demand for mediation (not a midpoint or equilibrium)
II	Intellectual definition	Manifest activity (thinking, doing) *versus* secret inactivity (feeling, intuition)	Intuition of the universe as mediatory
III	Personal formation	Outer forms (language, creeds, political constraints) *versus* personal, inward appropriation of truth	Indirect communication (Socratism)
IV	Institutional and social embodiment	Institutional with standard leadership (coerciveness) *versus* community (mutuality)	Reconceptualized ideal of religious community
V	Religious tradition	Natural religion (limited) *versus* historical religion (expansive/universal)	Christianity as universal religion; holy sadness as symbol of lack of finality

divinely rules me"[13]), and resembles in this regard the persuasive task of preaching.[14] But there is far more structure and dialectical argument in the work's rhetorical design than is commonly recognized.[15] A diagram representing the rhetorical structure of the five speeches makes these internal dynamics evident.

If we use categories from *Brief Outline* the diagram shows the problem addressed by each speech, the polarities in which a dialog with the reader ensues (apologetics), and a new mediating reality that is introduced as a result of recasting these tensions (polemics). Of course, the structure sketched here is concealed as well as revealed by the text. Much that is unsaid and unspoken is nonetheless expressed by a work that is thoroughly engaged in the task of mediation. "Holy silence" is required for

---

13 *OR* (Crouter), 4; *KGA*, 1/2, 190.
14 Christoph Meier-Dörken: "Zum Verhältnis zwischen Schleiermachers Predigten und seinen romantischen Schriften," in *Internationaler Schleiermacher-Kongress Berlin 1984*, 1/2 (Berlin: Walter de Gruyter, 1985), 661–79, argues against H. Gerdes' view that there is a decisive difference between the sermons and the romantic works.
15 *OR* (Crouter), xxix–xxxii.

speech to attain a hearing among its audience.[16] A level of unknowability stands in the background as counterpart of the speaker's direct appeal to seeing and hearing. When Schleiermacher says in 1821 that even a work with a rhetorical cast can make a literal point, he implicitly asserts that the distinction between literary and scientific categories as designations of writing in *On Religion* is not absolute.[17] The pervasiveness of his view that language has the capacity to speak the unspeakable cannot be emphasized sufficiently.[18] If it is the case that "everyone's philosophical theology essentially includes within it the principles of his whole theological way of thinking"[19] then we must be prepared to examine likely candidates for these principles within *On Religion*.

The issue of how language relates to its ground in reality comes to a head in the second speech's discussion of intuitions and feelings, where Schleiermacher writes:

Permit me first for a moment to mourn the fact that I cannot speak of both other than separately. The finest spirit of religion is thereby lost for my speech, and I can disclose its innermost secret only unsteadily and uncertainly. But reflection necessarily separates both; and who can speak about something that belongs to consciousness without first going through this medium?[20]

Reflection necessarily separates. Such an unavoidable separation immediately occurs not only in active reflection (speaking and writing) but also in our innermost self-reflection.[21] The theory of language articulated here reflects the self-consciousness that underlies the crucial and much analyzed introductory sections, *The Christian Faith*, sections 3 and 4. To recognize this level of being, which is presupposed in conscious self-awareness, is necessarily to move away from it. In the words of the "love scene" passage of speech 2, "That first mysterious moment . . . before intuition and feeling have separated . . . I know how indescribable it is and how quickly it passes away."[22] The description is well captured in Manfred Frank's formulation, "The cognitive ground of self-consciousness – its immediate being-transparent-to-itself – thus becomes peculiarly delayed in relation to the ground of its

16 *OR* (Crouter), 18; *KGA*, 1/2, 206.   17 *OR* (Oman), 110; *KGA*, 1/12, 139.
18 Rainer Volp, "Die Semiotik Schleiermachers," in *Zeichen: Semiotik in Theologie und Gottesdienst*, ed. Rainer Volp (Munich: Kaiser Verlag, 1982), 114–45, addresses the theory of language in Schleiermacher mainly in the later works.
19 *BO*, 39 (§67).
20 *OR* (Crouter), 31; *KGA*, 1/2, 220.
21 *KGA*, 1/2, 220–21.   22 OR (Crouter), 31; *KGA*, I/2, 220.

being."[23] The theme is reaffirmed in the 1821 "explanations" added to each address, where we read:

What I am conscious of or feel, must be imagined, and that is what I call the life of the object in me. But the infinite, meaning not something indeterminate, but the infinity of being generally, we cannot be conscious of immediately and through itself.[24]

In short, the rhetorical claim of *On Religion* regarding language and reality expresses the substantive teaching regarding the theory of language that Manfred Frank finds at the heart of *The Christian Faith*, the *Hermeneutics* and *Dialectics*. "The transcendence of being over the meaning, through which every linguistic community both reveals and conceals it immediately forces one to recognize the concept of an individuality which cannot simply be regarded as a deduction from or something subsumed under the semantico-syntactic system."[25] Here, in addition, Frank points to the irrepressibility of the subject as author of this insight, an observation that also applies to *On Religion* as a personal-rhetorical project. The quest for a common ground of reality, which Schleiermacher generally shares with German Idealism, is set forth in *On Religion* by a denial of the knowability of Being.[26] This teaching from 1799 remains in subsequent versions of the text, even if subject to complicated revisions, and stands at the heart of *The Christian Faith*'s famous paragraphs on self-consciousness in sections 3 and 4.[27] There, far from knowing being direct, one only becomes aware of this unity through the immediate self-consciousness. This "mediating link" (§3.4) includes the consciousness of being "utterly dependent," which stands as the denial of absolute freedom as the spontaneous source of being (§4.3). Linguistic expression (be it rhetorical, dialectical, didactic, or scientific) can never fully and immediately grasp reality. We should thus not be surprised to find the ubiquity of this romantic text in its theory of language. Near the end of speech 4, where

---

23 Manfred Frank, *The Subject and the Text: Essays in Literary Theory and Philosophy*, ed. Andrew Bowie, tr. Helen Atkins (Cambridge: Cambridge University Press, 1997), 7, which translates "Der Text und sein Stil," in *Das Sagbare und das Unsagbare: Studien zur deutsch-französischen Hermeneutik und Texttheorie* (Frankfurt-on-Main: Suhrkamp, 1989), 20.
24 *OR* (Oman), 103, tr. emended; *KGA*, 1/12, 130.
25 Frank, *Subject and the Text*, 18; *Das Sagbare*, 23–4.
26 Manfred Frank, "On the Unknowability of the Absolute," in *The Philosophical Foundations of Early German Romanticism*, tr. Elizabeth Millán-Zaibert (Albany: State University of New York Press, 2004), 55–75, traces the rise of this position among the early Romantics.
27 On *The Christian Faith* and language, see Reinhard Leuze, "Sprache und Frommes Selbstbewußtsein. Bemerkungen zu Schleiermachers Glaubenslehre," in *Internationaler Schleiermacher-Kongress Berlin 1984*, 1/2, 917–22.

the pathos of religious communities in their contest with political life is eloquently set forth, he writes: "Thus it is impossible to express and communicate religion other than verbally with all the effort and artistry of language, while willingly accepting the service of all skills that can assist fleeting and lively speech."[28]

Any estimate of the linguistic significance of *On Religion* cannot be isolated from the question of the text's revisions, which extended the work's horizons to meet new circumstances of time and place. Schleiermacher very likely stands among the most persistent and adroit self-redactors of the theological tradition.[29] The habit of engaging in self-interpretation and reassessments that lead to reformulations occurs not just in *On Religion*, but also in the *Soliloquies, Celebration of Christmas: A Conversation*, and *The Christian Faith*. With its three versions (1799, 1806, 1821), *On Religion* stands as a primary example of this extensive rhetorical process. An evolving, self-reflective pattern emerges in which Schleiermacher, faced with hostile criticism of his work, deepens arguments, develops new levels of insight, and clarifies problematic distinctions.

It is indeed confusing, if not bewildering, to try to walk in an author's footsteps, especially in so intimate a task as that of following a writer's editing revisions. To do this thoroughly obviously requires a lengthier investigation. In this regard Schleiermacher's reflection on the efforts of his predecessors to identify the core of Plato's teaching are sobering: to find ideas "reciprocally illustrated" in a corpus of work does not yet identify the project's central notions.[30] Yet working on these central notions is surely the task that awaits us if we take seriously the challenge of reading Schleiermacher in light of his hermeneutical principles. I have argued elsewhere that the revisions of *On Religion* are substantive as well as rhetorical and believe that, among other shifts and changes, this is especially evident in the elaboration of a "theistic reading" of the 1799 text in subsequent versions.[31] The dominant thrust of the original romantic text expresses profound indifference regarding the question of theism: "Whether we have a God as a part of our intuition depends on the direction of the imagination."[32] Among Schleiermacher's contemporaries, as well as among many present-day readers, a Christian view of God was

---

28 *OR* (Crouter), 74; *KGA*, 1/2, 269.
29 On the revisions of *The Christian Faith*, see chapter 10 of this book.
30 *Introductions to the Dialogues of Plato* (New York: Arno Press, 1973), 22–3.
31 *OR* (Crouter), 1988 edition (see above, note 3), 64–6.
32 *OR* (Crouter) 53; *KGA*, 1/2, 245.

believed necessarily to involve a personal deity. At the same time, the possibility of drawing out a theistic meaning of the ideas of *On Religion* is also present in the original text. The intentionality of 1799 admits of this reading, even if the original framing of the argument moves on a different track.

To be sure, students of the revisions often study them by moving backwards from 1821, while seeking traces of diminishing Christian orthodoxy as one approaches the 1799 text. The hermeneutic that informs such readings of Schleiermacher resembles an archaeological dig that is motivated by a preconceived line of questioning. While valid as a legitimate line of interrogation of the text, it cannot be maintained that the test of religious orthodoxy (a vacillating standard in the history of Christian teaching) is the sole or even the most telling way of assessing how *On Religion* relates to *The Christian Faith* and other mature works. In contrast with such an understanding, a more objective approach will ask whether *On Religion* has a theory of language that unites it with Schleiermacher's larger project. Compared with Wittgenstein (*Tractatus* and *Investigations*), Heidegger (*Being and Time* and *On the Way to Language*), or Barth (*Anselm* and the *Church Dogmatics*), there is no radical shift of direction in Schleiermacher's thought. Far from renouncing his youthful book, he took pains to elaborate, defend, and develop its fundamental meaning. Complicating this debate is, of course, Schleiermacher's well-known proclivity for fluidity of expression in *On Religion* as a rhetorical work:

This change of expression brings different sides of the matter to light, and I find it purposeful even in more scholarly lectures, if only the various forms match up and can be resolved into one other. Such a manner of writing seemed especially suitable in order to avoid the scrupulosity of too rigid a teminology.[33]

The preference for a flexible use of language is not arbitrary; it has a theoretical grounding in his reasoned view of the impossibility for finite humans to speak about Being in a manner untainted by distortion.

Indeed, the way of seeing *On Religion* as establishing a linguistic system of meaning sheds light not just on this earliest famous published work, but on his project as a whole. When one looks at Schleiermacher studies

33 *OR* (Oman), 103, emended; *KGA*, 1/12, 130; See *LL*, 38: "I think that everyone knows that I place little weight on definitive terminology so long as I am convinced that I mean the same thing as the other person";*KGA*, 1/10, ed. Hans-Friedrich Traulsen with Martin Ohst (1990), 316; see Hans-Georg Gadamer, "Semantics and Hermeneutics," in *Philosophical Hermeneutics*, tr. David E. Linge (Berkeley: University of California Press, 1976), 86, on the tension that exists between technical expressions and living language.

today, there appears to be new appreciation of the contemporary relevance of the hermeneutical and dialectical teaching.[34] The last word on this way of reading Schleiermacher has not yet been said and its theological implications will surely be drawn out further. Here, I have aimed only at the narrower question of how one might go about viewing *On Religion* in light of a newer appreciation of the role of language as a system of meaning in the hermeneutics. Numerous direct and indirect cross-references unite the work with *The Christian Faith*, far more than the annotations of sections 3 and 10 come into consideration.[35]

We can further test the argument by examining the utterances from Schleiermacher's explicit self-ruminations on the work. The 1821 "explanations," which correlate *On Religion* with the first edition of the dogmatics, are an understudied source of hermeneutical self-reflection. The explanations assume an external vantage point that distinguishes them from glosses that could readily be integrated within the text. They are best viewed as a set of metacritical remarks on the intentionality of *On Religion*, conceived at the time Schleiermacher was issuing the first edition of his dogmatics. They explain *On Religion* in the light of *The Christian Faith* (1821–2), and vice versa, but also comment on both works in the light of an evolving pattern of hermeneutical and dialectical reflection. As candid self-reflections on the intentions of his work, the explanations coincide with the first edition of *The Christian Faith*, just as the self-commentary of his *Letters to Dr. Lücke* postdate that work. The frank objectivity of his remarks may disarm readers, if they are willing to look beyond the suspicion that the comments are the face-saving effort of a theologian who has been placed on the defensive. When, by contrast, the explanations are read as perceptive metacritical remarks and hermeneutical signposts, they reflect and point to the cohesiveness of Schleiermacher's larger intellectual endeavor.

---

34 Manfred Frank, *Das individuelle Allgemeine: Textstrukturierung und -interpretation nach Schleiermacher* (Frankfurt-on-Main: Suhrkamp, 2001); *HC* is based upon Manfred Frank, ed., *F. D. E. Schleiermacher: Hermeneutik und Kritik* (Frankfurt-on-Main: Suhrkamp, 1977); Joseph Margolis, "Schleiermacher Among the Theorists of Language and Interpretation," *Journal of Aesthetics and Art Criticism* 45/4 (summer 1987): 361–8; Werner G. Jeanrond, "The Impact of Schleiermacher's Hermeneutics on Contemporary Interpretation Theory," in *The Interpretation of Belief: Coleridge, Schleiermacher, and Romanticism*, ed. David Jasper (New York: St. Martin's Press, 1986), 81–96.

35 The allusions and cross-references (substantive as well as rhetorical) to *The Christian Faith* and other works that occur frequently in the 1821 explanations attached to the speeches of *On Religion* deserve to be explored more fully with the relevant texts from *KGA* in hand.

The discovery that *On Religion* reflects an understanding of language that unites the work with Schleiermacher's mature perspective helps to explain the perennial interest in *On Religion* as a classic of modern western religious thought. A text written with youthful exuberance richly reflects its author's deepest predilections. According to Eva T. H. Brann, such a reinvention of tradition "consists of a conversation in which the participants listen to each other, circumvent, reinvent and echo each other, so that while temporal in its parts, it is timeless, or ever present, as a whole."[36] As a text, the book's reception (in and beyond the author's lifetime) exemplifies Gadamer's notion of the "consciousness of effective history." From Schleiermacher's earliest days the connection between a sense of history and religion is articulated. "History, in the most proper sense, is the highest object of religion."[37] Schleiermacher links theology with the distant past (e.g., allusions abound to scriptural and confessional teachings), while he states and restates his aims in the light of his and his readers' current horizons of meaning. Like Brann and Gadamer, present-day literary critics remind us that it is specious to expect a work to have a univocal meaning.[38] In fact, multivalent richness is the requisite feature of a classic text. Brann further observes:

The texts should be original, in the double sense of being the result of the author's own thought and of presenting the pursuit of a matter to its very origins. Texts of this underivative sort usually reveal themselves by the manner of their composition long before the student has gone very far in penetrating them: they are so subtly and artfully woven that the reader sees inexhaustibly many avenues to their meaning without losing faith that there is a meaning.[39]

On Religion meets Brann's criteria for a classic with its progressive unfolding of argument, subterfuges, audience anticipation, false starts, and irony, all of which contribute to the adventure of readers as they seek to puzzle out its meaning.

The historic designations of philosophical theology and philosophy of religion with which we began are themselves elusive, whether in the late eighteenth century or the late twentieth century. As philosophical theology, *On Religion* scarcely conforms to our twentieth-century expectation of a *theologia naturalis*, which typically seeks to demonstrate divine

---

36 "The Student's Problem," *Liberal Education* 54 (1968): 381.
37 *OR* (Crouter), 42; *KGA*, 1/2, 232–3.
38 Cf. in this regard the debate on intentionality between Jacques Derrida and John Searle, "Signature Event Context" and "Reiterating the Differences" in *Glyph* 1 (1977): 172–208.
39 "A Way to Philosophy," *Metaphilosophy* 6 (July–October 1975): 3–4.

existence or to prove the rationality of belief.[40] In Brann's words cited above, *On Religion* has "many avenues to its meaning." To maintain this claim requires us also to assert that such texts have "many avenues in their making," that is, they embody multiple purposes and intentions of a writer.

Schleiermacher's hermeneutics endorses this way of reading and understanding texts. Could one hope to divine the meaning of *On Religion* apart from considering its intertextual setting? Divinatory judgments, far from resting on the feeling of empathy (the misunderstanding of Schleiermacher on this point is widespread in English as well as German), rest on interpretive insights that arise from a reading at a point that eludes the rule-bound nature of judgments.[41] Here intertextuality means not just *On Religion* of 1799, but a fabric of meaning comprised of the revisions of 1806 and 1821, as well as the *Hermeneutics, Dialectics,* and *The Christian Faith.* Surely, if we take seriously the claim to "understand an author better than he understands himself," then we must consider his work "grammatically" and "comparatively" (i.e., textually) within its own linguistic horizons.[42] Even if we settle for a different (not a better) understanding, we need to pursue all possible angles. Indeed, the more one becomes aware of language as a theme that unites *On Religion* with other major texts, the more we are apt to see substantive relationships within the authorship. Once we are willing to break the spell of Hegel, Kant, Fichte, Schelling, Dilthey, Barth, or other (in varying ways) oppositional perspectives, as a basis of judgment, we can see that Schleiermacher gives testimony to a theory of language that significantly informs his work. Availability of the new Schleiermacher critical edition (*KGA*) will continue to spur interest in the wider reaches of the corpus and enhance our ability to emancipate the study of Schleiermacher from the preconceptions of other systems of thought.

---

40 Confusion on this point explains why English-speaking interpreters so frequently limit their concerns to debates about essentialist or foundationalist positions in his thought. See Ronald F. Thiemann, "Piety, Narrative, and Christian Identity," *Word and World* 3/2 (spring 1983): 148–59, and Ronald F. Thiemann, *Revelation and Theology: The Gospel as Narrative Promise* (Notre Dame: University of Notre Dame Press, 1985), as well as the critique of Thiemann, B. A. Gerrish's "Nature and the Theater of Redemption: Schleiermacher on Christian Dogmatics and the Creation Story," *Ex Auditu* 3 (1987): 128–32.

41 See Jeanrond, "Impact of Schleiermacher's Hermeneutics," 83–7, which draws on Manfred Frank's work.

42 On the formula, see Françoise Breithaupt et al., "Was heisst die hermeneutische Formel 'Die Rede zuerst eben so gut und dann besser zu verstehen als ihr Urheber,'" in *Internationaler Schleiermacher-Kongress Berlin 1984,* 1/1, 601–12.

To argue for *On Religion* in this manner doubtless invites further discussion. Schleiermacher's example of joining rhetoric with dialectic communicates a lesson as old as Plato's *Phaedrus*. For Plato, as well as for Schleiermacher, dialectical thought is never finally divorced from its foundation in the spoken and written word. In truth, not just theology but its cognate disciplines among the human sciences, linguistics, history, literary studies, and philosophy are today either involved in a quest for foundations or, failing in that pursuit, are preoccupied with the need to demonstrate their lack of need of such foundations.

In the end, then, the suggestion of this essay inevitably reverts to the vexed question of Schleiermacher's relationship to Romanticism. At least in the case of *On Religion* (in its various renderings and interrelated texts) the fervor about language and the conditions of understanding texts generated by the early German Romantics contributed greatly to Schleiermacher's mature teaching.[43] Whatever its value may be generally, Gadamer's insistence on the "questionableness of romantic hermeneutics" looks increasingly suspect as a characterization of Schleiermacher's place in the modern theory of texts.[44] The theologian's theory of language turns out to have more contemporary currency than is usually acknowledged. To the extent that, from the outset of his career, Schleiermacher maintained an independent mind, he presents a way of working as a theologian that can recast and partially overcome, even if not finally resolve, the epistemological and metaphysical problems posed for theology by the Enlightenment. To have a universal systematic view but not to equate this with a replication of reality in a single semantic-syntactic system required Schleiermacher to set forth his thought in a wide variety of interrelated texts. Though it is full of "fleeting and lively speech" that is shaped by ironic perspectives and biting satire, *On Religion* nonetheless counts as one of these texts.

43 See Ernst Behler, *German Romantic Literary Theory* (Cambridge: Cambridge University Press, 1993), especially chapter 6 on "Theory of Language, Hermeneutics, and Encyclopaedistics," 260–98.
44 Hans-Georg Gadamer, *Truth and Method*, tr. revised Joel Weinsheimer and Donald G. Marshall, second revised edition (New York: Continuum, 2002), 173–97.

CHAPTER 9

Shaping an academic discipline: the Brief Outline on the Study of Theology

> The fact that in such knowledge the knower's own being comes into
> play certainly shows the limits of method, but not of science.
>
> Gadamer, *Truth and Method*

Few theologians in the history of the Christian church have been as
rigorously self-reflective about the craft of theology as was Friedrich
Schleiermacher. Always a master teacher, Schleiermacher developed a
curriculum for Protestant theology that reflects a penchant for relating
thought and practice. In his hands, theological methods must be engaged
with actual history and the life of religious institutions. Of course, as an
intellectual pursuit a secure starting point for theology must be given. Like
Plato, arguably the favorite of his Greek predecessors, Schleiermacher's
architectonic cast of mind insists on linking matters of intellectual principle
and foundational insight to their specific, embodied details. Although less
philosophical in some respects, his preferred Reformation theologian, John
Calvin, exemplified an equally bold ambition and similarly systematic cast
of mind.

Not surprisingly, the question of theological method runs deep in
modern Christian thought. With the dawn of historical criticism and
Newtonian physics few verities of the Christian faith could any longer be
taken for granted. After the work of dramatist-critic Gotthold Ephraim
Lessing (1729–81) the gulf between accidental truths of history and eternal
truths of reason seemed permanent. At the end of the eighteenth century
rival theological camps staked out positions, none of which Schleiermacher viewed with satisfaction. The Kantian view, in which Jesus exemplifies the moral ideal of practical philosophy, set no store by Christian
doctrine, biblical theology, and the life of the church. That of a biblically
based supernaturalism, in which the Bible's miracles prove the deity of

Jesus, sought to shield this position from rational assaults. The speculative rationalism of Fichte and Hegel, Schleiermacher's successive philosophical colleagues in Berlin, subsumed the claims of theology beneath a dominant philosophical truth.

In contrast with these efforts Schleiermacher's lectures on theological encyclopedia address the issues at hand in a novel way. In his day, not unlike our own, theology as an intellectual discipline was poorly defined, its tasks and methods anything but self-evident. In his words, "One cannot tell what theology means from the name alone, because it has served up many aberrant meanings . . . Yet names cannot be changed arbitrarily; one can only precisely define how they are to be understood."[1] If the condition of theology has not improved today, and numerous intervening solutions have failed, we are nonetheless still challenged by his way of defining its component parts and illustrating their interrelationships. Schleiermacher's understanding of theology is philosophical while avoiding undue dependence on any specific school of philosophy, historical while not succumbing to historical relativism, and practical while placing its concern for lived religion squarely on the shoulders of a well-educated clergy. His theology has the avowed task of reconciling the substance of biblical and creedal teachings with a distinctively modern account of Christian consciousness. Schleiermacher thus launched a systematic program of theological inquiry that stands apart from those of his contemporaries. Whatever we may think of his achievement, he was right to remind us that "one cannot tell what theology means from the name alone."

In what follows I first offer a context for understanding what makes Schleiermacher's *Brief Outline* distinctive in the history of theology. Its groundbreaking tripartite division of theology (philosophical, historical, and practical) is examined in the next three sections of this essay. I then end by appraising certain issues within the work that continue to inform contemporary debates about Schleiermacher's theological method. Of course, the work provided a blueprint for the main principles of both editions (1821–2; 1830–1) of his magnum opus, *The Christian Faith*. This chapter does not explicitly address specific methodological issues that arise from within his dogmatics.[2] For the careful student of *The Christian*

1 *Th Enz*, 2.
2 See B. A. Gerrish's masterful essay, "Friedrich Schleiermacher (1768–1834)," in *Continuing the Reformation: Essays on Modern Religious Thought* (Chicago: University of Chicago Press, 1993), 147–77.

Faith, parallels with *Brief Outline*'s recommendations are readily apparent and well worth analyzing. Yet it seems salutary to focus our present attention on the program of theology as it is laid out in the *Brief Outline*.

CONTEXT OF THE "BRIEF OUTLINE"

By the end of the eighteenth century the term "encyclopedia" had begun to be used for texts that introduce the premises and contents of a field of knowledge in ways that are not necessarily arranged alphabetically. Hegel's *Encyclopedia of the Philosophical Sciences* (1817) produced such a work for his system of philosophy. It was largely to counter the influence of the text we are analyzing that the Hegelian philosopher Karl Rosenkranz produced his own *Encyclopedia of Theological Sciences* (1831).[3] Such introductions often surveyed rival positions and provided literature in the field, while advancing their author's views. In contrast with much of this literature the *Brief Outline* makes scant reference to the thought of others. Although it was lean and skeletal even in its second edition, the text challenges its readers, as future pastor-theologians of the German Protestant churches, to appropriate a boldly personal, self-consistent vision of the theological task.

In presenting his ideas, we do well to acknowledge that Schleiermacher's tripartite division of theology (philosophical, historical, and practical) draws from a time-conditioned idiom regarding the academic disciplines.[4] Aspects of the *Brief Outline* are unthinkable apart from definitions given elsewhere in his system of the sciences. Following the ancient Greeks, Schleiermacher contrasts "ethics" (as the "speculative science of reason") with "physics" (as the "speculative science of nature"), a usage that reflects Aristotle's notion of rational human beings who live in a world (ethos) that is distinguishable from nature. Ethics seeks to attain a coherent and consistent view of the abiding forms of the human world; history ("the empirical science of reason") strives to understand the actual unfolding of it. Ethics and history operate on distinctive planes; the task of analyzing and clarifying concepts is distinguished from the task of grasping the world as it develops. It is relevant for the discussion that

---

3 Karl Rosenkranz, *Enzyklopädie der theologischen Wissenschaften* (Halle: C. A. Schwetschke und Sohn, 1831), 4.
4 For a lucid account of these disciplinary definitions in *Brief Outline*, see Walter E. Wyman, Jr., "The Historical Consciousness and the Study of Theology," in *Shifting Boundaries: Contextual Approaches to the Structure of Theological Education*, ed. Barbara G. Wheeler and Edward Farley (Louisville: Westminster Press/John Knox Press, 1991), especially 104–8.

follows to observe that Schleiermacher further distinguishes between a *critical* theoretical discipline and a *technical* theoretical discipline or art, both of which relate contemplative to experiential knowing. Philosophical theology, as a *critical* discipline, connects what appears in history with the speculative task, while practical theology, as a *technical* discipline, consists of the art of relating what appears in history to practice.

These interrelated intellectual pursuits bear upon an analysis of the *Brief Outline* and inform its depiction of theological methodology. Yet caution is in order, since assumptions that inform his disciplinary matrix do not neatly translate into the disciplinary debates of our own day. Schleiermacher maintains that the materials of dogmatic theology, like those of history, are empirical, and insists that humanly experienced religious reality, whether past or present, must be explicated intellectually. Unlike some exponents and defenders of religious thought, Schleiermacher thinks theology arises from the bedrock of a personal conviction that does not directly stem from proof or argument. Consistently with that approach, theology is construed as a "positive science," whose organizing center lies outside itself in the practical tasks for which the science exists.[5] Theology functions to prepare leaders for service in the Christian church, much as one goes about preparing well-educated barristers or physicians.[6] Readers with skeptical inclinations will not approach the *Brief Outline*'s teachings empathetically within the circle of Christian witness, but are still capable of grasping how theology as an academic discipline relates to its own ends.

Schleiermacher does not hold the view, sometimes attributed to Max Weber, that objectivity is best reached through value-free inquiry.[7] For it to become real, knowledge requires a subjective moment of judgment through which it is personally appropriated. Section 101 of the *Brief Outline* acknowledges that historical studies "can never be wholly divested of the scholar's own particular viewpoints and opinions," even if we must

5 Hans-Joachim Birkner, *Schleiermacher-Studien*, ed., Hermann Fischer (Berlin: Walter de Gruyter, 1996), 104–5; B. A. Gerrish, "Ubi theologia, ibi ecclesia? Schleiermacher, Troeltsch, and the Prospect for an Academic Theology," in *Continuing the Reformation*, 255–8.

6 For a critique of the view that Schleiermacher's theology is held together by this functional aim apart from the formal definition of an essence of Christianity, see Markus Schröder, *Die kritische Identität des Christentums: Schleiermachers Wesensbestimmung der christlichen Religion* (Tübingen: J. C. B. Mohr [Paul Siebbeck], 1996).

7 Georg G. Iggers, "Historicism: The History and Meaning of the Term," *Journal of the History of Ideas* 56 (1995): 129–52, argues against the view that Weber's social scientific program rests upon value-free inquiry. Cf. Wolfgang Hardtwig, "Die Verwissenschaftlichung der neueren Geschichtsschreibung," in *Geschichte: Ein Grundkurs*, ed. Hans-Jürgen Goertz (Reinbeck bei Hamburg: Rowohlt Taschenbuch Verlag, 1998), 259.

try to keep our material free of these biases as much as possible. Like more recent students of historical epistemology, Schleiermacher holds that history seeks to make objective judgments about the past, even if "higher criticism carries out its task, for the most part, only by approximation" (§113).[8] Such approximations, however, are disciplined judgments, not just casual opinions. The commitment to grasping the human social world historically does not mean that Schleiermacher thinks we should, or even could, comprehend the human world as nothing but historical. By bringing reason to bear on the course of Christian history a student learns to "exercise his own discretion in matters of church leadership." "Nothing is more fruitless than a piling up of historical learning which neither serves any practical purpose nor offers anything for the use of others in its presentation" (§191). As the *Brief Outline* makes clear, dogmatics must be based upon a personal conviction of the Christian religion's truth. Like Nietzsche in *Use and Abuse of History for Life* (1874), the *Brief Outline* calls for a profound engagement, not just a scholarly encounter, with history. To study the Christian past chiefly for information or to establish a chronology remains useless. To analyze the meaning of theological teaching as it relates the essence of Christianity to the ongoing life of the church constitutes the agenda of the *Brief Outline*.

Intended to introduce beginning theology students to their discipline, the *Brief Outline* is the central work in which to probe Schleiermacher's approach to theological method. It was his first major book to appear in English, some seventy-eight years before his dogmatics was translated.[9] Perhaps owing to its shape as an outline, the impact of the book in Germany and in the English-speaking world has been uneven. Only in recent years has more attention been given to this theological charter alongside the more famous dogmatics that refines its principles even further.[10]

Schleiermacher first lectured on "theological encyclopedia" at the University of Halle (1805–6). He published the first edition of the book in 1811 and a revised version in 1830. He lectured on this material twice in Halle and nine more times in Berlin, including 1831–2, when the lectures were transcribed by David Friedrich Strauß, whose astute theological mind was already evident.[11] Schleiermacher himself acknowledged that

---

8 Unless otherwise noted, citations of *Brief Outline* are from *BO*.
9 *Brief Outline of the Study of Theology*, tr. William Farrer (Edinburgh: T. & T. Clark, 1850).
10 Theodore Ziolkowski, *Clio the Romantic Muse: Historicizing the Faculties in Germany* (Ithaca: Cornell University Press, 2004), ch. 3 puts the *Brief Outline* at the center of Schleiermacher's project of historicizing theology.
11 Birkner, *Schleiermacher-Studien*, 286.

his definition of dogmatic theology in the 1811 edition "is too short and aphoristic."[12] Although the stark expression of the first edition seems more cohesive to some readers than its 1830 revision, the later formulations embody his most mature thought. Since the 1811 and 1830 editions were published as mere adumbrations of classroom lectures, neither version conveys everything that Schleiermacher wished to communicate. It is fortunate that the David Friedrich Strauß transcript of these lectures has been available since 1987.[13] Strauß likened the task of taking notes on Schleiermacher's lectures to "photographing a dancer in full motion."[14] His meticulously transcribed text provides Schleiermacher's own commentary on the book's theses and explanations.

LOCATING AND DEFINING THE ESSENCE OF CHRISTIANITY

In addition to using ethics to signal the study of what is human, Schleiermacher's first division of "philosophical theology" bears slight resemblance to the term's usage today. Far from seeking to demonstrate the truth of Christian teaching, "philosophical theology" for Schleiermacher might be paraphrased as "philosophical reflection on the form and content of a religion in its givenness." It undertakes the crucial task of locating and defining the "religious consciousness" and "church community" that are the bedrock of Christian existence. This task is accomplished through the complementary pursuits of apologetics (*BO*, §43–§53), which looks outward and locates the church with respect to its origins in history, and polemics (§54–§62), which looks inward and analyzes the community's aberrations and afflictions. Although he never wrote a work under the name philosophical theology, *On Religion* as well as most of the "borrowed propositions" in the introduction of *The Christian Faith* fall into this category.[15]

When Schleiermacher published the first edition of his encyclopedia (1811) Hegel had not yet written his *Encyclopedia of Philosophical Sciences*, which seeks to ground the subfields of philosophy in a single principle.[16]

---

12 Friedrich Schleiermacher, *KGA*, 1/6, ed. Dirk Schmid (1998), LXVII.
13 See above, note 1.
14 Walter Sachs, ed., *Th Enz*, XXXIX, citing David Friedrich Strauß, *Gesammelte Schriften*, V, ed. Eduard Zeller (Bonn, 1876–8), 9.
15 See Birkner, *Schleiermacher-Studien*, 157–92; Martin Rössler, *Schleiermachers Programm der philosophischen Theologie*, Schleiermacher-Archiv 14 (Berlin: Walter de Gruyter, 1994).
16 "What is reasonable is actual; and, what is actual is reasonable." *The Logic of Hegel*, tr. William Wallace, second edition (Oxford: Oxford University Press, 1892), 10.

But the speculative rationalism of his contemporary German Idealists nonetheless influenced Schleiermacher's decision about how to use philosophy within theological inquiry. His dilemma was how to retain the dignity and power of a rational perspective, while allowing it to inform, and to be informed by, the contingencies of historical existence. Such a specific use of philosophical theology broke sharply with the indifference towards historic religion of Kant's rational theology and its sublation to philosophical reason of the German Idealists.

Schleiermacher is committed to the idea that human beings are religious by nature and find religious meaning within communities. "Unless religious communities are to be regarded as mere aberrations, it must be possible to show that the existence of such associations is a necessary element for the development of the human spirit" (*BO*, §22). Espousal of the view that religion is anthropologically necessary is today vigorously debated as a form of "religious essentialism."[17] Yet Schleiermacher appears to have been untroubled by such doubts; for him, "Christian consciousness" stands as a factual given. His unswerving insistence that the Christian instantiation of religion proceeds from the "concept of the pious community, not from the piety of the individual soul," seems to compete with his well-established individualism (*Th Enz*, 21 commenting on §22). Personal conviction is never absent from the theological task. The primary spiritual datum is the reality of the church in empirical history, a claim that is both normative and demonstrable through the study of history. "If we look into the matter of how Christian theology arose in the beginning, the Christian church was always already earlier, and thus even now for each individual the Christian church is earlier than theology" (*Th Enz*, 32). A given primordial communal piety is chronologically as well as logically prior to the need of the church to develop theology and produce handbooks on church leadership. Such definitional and practical needs arise only with the passage of time in an effort to adjudicate the claims of rival religious communities.

Everything in Schleiermacher's approach to theology hinges on this awareness of the church's religious reality and the need to give it intellectual definition. If, as Schleiermacher maintains, practical theology is the crown towards which theology moves, then philosophical theology

---

17 Wilfrid Cantwell Smith, *The Meaning and End of Religion* (San Francisco: Harper and Row, 1978) offers an antiessentialist critique of Schleiermacher that still clings to essentialism in the view of Talal Asad, "Reading a Modern Classic: W. C. Smith's *The Meaning and End of Religion*," *History of Religions* 40/3 (February 2001): 205–22.

is the root that identifies the reality of the church and thus gets the project off the ground.[18] This work of defining Christianity's essence philosophically, both in relation to other religions (apologetics) and with respect to its own aberrations (polemics), must be undertaken by every theologian. Schleiermacher directs our attention to "the two main points, the content of theology as the summation of all scientific elements, and the purpose of theology: the leadership of the Christian community," while adding that, "Christianity is a uniquely formed God-consciousness and a community that is founded upon it" (*Th Enz*, 20). The passage testifies to the reality of an original essence of Christianity manifest in history and of the pious community that mediates this content. Because of the need to clarify Christianity's content, inquiry into the essence of Christianity is required. Since the content of Christian consciousness is transmitted through a specific community, this historical resource must also be plumbed as a means of sustaining the original God-consciousness. If a degree of circularity appears in these claims, this is a price Schleiermacher appears willing to pay in order to avoid the pretension of deriving the content of theology from a single foundational starting point.

APPREHENDING THE CHURCH IN TIME AND PLACE

Schleiermacher's appeal to philosophical theology in the *Brief Outline* sets theology in motion by delineating the reality of the church, where Christian consciousness takes on geography and temporality. Historical theology, the work's second division, reaches from the age of the apostles through contemporary dogmatics. Although historical theology is analyzed more extensively (*BO*, §69–§256) than either philosophical (§32–§68) or practical theology (§257–§338), it is tightly interwoven with its corollary disciplines. Historical theology has the dual function of *confirming* philosophical theology, while *laying the foundation* of practical theology. "Since historical theology attempts to exhibit every point of time in its true relation to the idea of Christianity, it follows that it is at once not only the founding [*Begründung*] of practical theology but also the confirming [*Bewährung*] of philosophical theology" (§27).[19] Just how this

---

18 For the crown and root metaphors, see Heinrich Scholtz, ed., *Kurze Darstellung des theologischen Studiums zum Behuf Einleitender Vorlesungen* (1910) (Darmstadt: Wissenschaftliche Buchgesellschaft, 1973), 10, §26, "Die philosophische Theologie ist die Wurzel der gesamten Theologie," and §31, which reads, "Die praktische Theologie ist die Krone des theologischen Studiums."
19 *BO*, tr. altered; Scholtz, ed., *Kurze Darstellung*, 11.

works may be debated. But it seems reasonable to think that historical theology is assigned the task of confirming philosophical theology by examining how its definition of the essence of Christianity has stood up over time. Historical theology thus stands as a distinctive mode of inquiry that is intimately related to the other two divisions of theology.

Today it appears naïve to think that history can preserve meaning or somehow help to ground our moral choices. Historical study appears to be too much subject to revision to test our life choices effectively. But even in our day Schleiermacher's reasoning on the point has merit, provided that we share what we might call his realist approach to historical epistemology. This approach maintains that, despite the apparent vacillation of historical judgments, historical theology can reliably assay the reality of the Christian consciousness over time. This is so because historical reasoning preserves not just facts, but repeatedly makes and defends claims about the meaning of those facts.[20] As an empirical inquiry, history feeds our reflection with data that includes highs and lows in the story of the church. Where such reflection encounters more pain than pleasure, say in the era of the Crusades, a negative judgment of those events is rendered only by comparison with the positive teaching of Christ on the love of one's neighbor. On Schleiermacher's view, not to acknowledge the vital significance of a Christian consciousness in history requires a supreme indifference to Christianity.

Like the three main divisions of theology, which stand in dialectical and reciprocal relationships, the subfields of historical theology (exegetical theology, church history, and dogmatics) have tight internal correlations. Outwardly these subfields are related by chronological narrative. Schleiermacher differentiates between the epochs of Christian history. Earliest Christianity should be studied first; it alone provides source material through which philosophical theology can identify the distinctive contours of the church. Dogmatics should be studied last; it frames the issues that inform the mind of pastors as they lead the church in the tasks of preaching and church governance. But the life of the Christian faith past and present is grasped more as a living, quasiorganic entity than as a timeline of events. Since *all of historical theology* reflects the constitutive principle of theology as built on a living tradition of faith (*BO*, §81), biblical archaism and free contemporary spirituality both distort the truth of this tradition.

---

20 For a contemporary nonmetaphysical defense of historical truth, see Bernard Williams, *Truth and Truthfulness: An Essay in Genealogy* (Princeton: Princeton University Press, 2002). Whether Williams' approach would work in defending religious claims, however, remains to be argued.

As Schleiermacher puts it, since the present "can only be understood as a result of the past . . . the entire previous career of Christianity forms a second division of historical theology." Church history is not merely an auxiliary science for biblical exegesis but, "rather, both are related to church leadership in the same way, and are not in a subordinated but are in a coordinate relation to each other" (*BO*, §82). Historical theology draws upon the natural divisions of the modern study of history. Yet as a theological field historical theology is "the indispensable condition of all intelligent effort toward the cultivation of Christianity" and hence "all the other parts of historical study are subordinated to it" (§70). Schleiermacher goes to great lengths to rebut static views of the historical development of Christianity. He recognizes the period of the canon and the need for exegetical theology. But Christian meaning does not assume "definitive forms" just because of its *being in the earliest period*, and, however much there is a need for exegesis, the term is somewhat arbitrary, since the *interpretation of texts* goes on in all three divisions of historical theology (§88).

For church history, the second division of historical theology, the twofold development of the church, consists of the history of its common life (*BO*, §166–§176) and the history of its doctrines (§177–§183). Ethics and doctrine have not come into being merely for the sake of the present; they are bearers of the tradition in history. As historical theologians think about the course of Christian history, they must decide how doctrine relates to "the utterances of primitive Christianity" and correlates with philosophical propositions that "are not engendered by the Christian faith as such." Church teaching develops from this oscillating movement between primitive Christianity and philosophical thought. Here the complexity of this interpretive process can only be adumbrated. The methods of inquiry within church history are endless and no one person can master the whole field (§184). This creative historical engagement with the church in history leads Schleiermacher to take up dogmatics as the contemporary systematic application of this inquiry (§195–§222), which in turn leads to material on Christian ethics as the practical counterpart of doctrine (§223–§231).

In turning to dogmatics Schleiermacher was well aware of the novelty of placing this field of inquiry within historical theology. His preference for the designations "dogmatics" or "dogmatic theology" over "systematic theology" is related to this choice. Even though systematic theology rightly stresses that "doctrine is not to be presented as a mere aggregate of propositions, whose coherent interrelation is not clearly known," it nonetheless "conceals, to the detriment of the subject, not only the historical character of the discipline but also its aim in relation to church leadership." As a result, "numerous misinterpretations are bound to arise" (§97). The 1831–2 lectures elaborate:

One may thereby think that dogmatics is purely historical and the dogmaticians only express factual matters that have nothing to do with conviction. But if we return to the initial insight, this objection drops away, since no one would be a theologian except by virtue of his conviction about Christianity. (*Th Enz*, 99)

The term "dogmatics" puts emphasis on historic teachings that represent the common faith of the church. A church dogmatics is not a "truly scientific dogmatics or a rational theology," and it does not consist of the "private convictions" of the theologian, which might yield a "beautiful book, but not be dogmatics" (*Th Enz*, 99). The useful part of calling it systematic theology lies in showing that theology is not supposed to be just an aggregate of theological insights. But since "this is likewise the case with our designation and position" (*Th Enz*, 99, 100), dogmatics remains the preferred name for his craft.

Far from compromising Christian truth, Schleiermacher's rationale for placing dogmatics within historical theology links expressions of doctrine to the actual life of the church. Every theologian must form a coherent picture of the present teachings of the church, "even though after this period runs its course, perhaps it will occur to no one to take a measure of the church exactly at this point" (*Th Enz*, 181). Not surprisingly, dogmatic theology must be undertaken by every generation for very practical reasons. The practical emphasis of these choices is underscored by the way *Brief Outline* follows the discussion of dogmatics and Christian ethics with "church statistics" (*BO*, §232–§250), which inquires into the external conditions of the religious society.

His 1831–2 lectures show Schleiermacher contrasting his threefold arrangement of theology with the fourfold division that was standard in Germany, and subsequently in the English-speaking world.

In the usual arrangement of theology the chief points are exegetical theology, historical theology, systematic theology, and practical theology. Only two of these, historical and practical, are acknowledged here and the exegetical and the dogmatic are both subordinated to the historical. Here dogmatics thus appears as a part of historical theology, while it usually appears as coordinated with historical theology. The same holds for exegetical theology, about which far fewer objections have been made. (*Th Enz*, 182–3)

It remains for us to clarify further the reasoning that stands behind this significant shift in understanding how dogmatic theology relates to history.

Examined closely, we can identify three features of dogmatics that contribute to his position. First, for Schleiermacher, anchoring dogmatics firmly in history does not compromise the doctrinal statements or put them at risk. As a science, dogmatics requires the theologian to clarify and elucidate the ecclesial witness of the Christian consciousness. When Schleiermacher pursues dogmatics as historical theology, he does not abandon reason or personal conviction. Rather, the essence of Christianity (located by the apologetics and defended by the polemics of philosophical theology), lends underlying continuity to the church's historical, that is, developing, existence. Dogmatics differs from a mere account of church doctrine: "Whoever is not convinced of this doctrine, can of course provide a report about it, and about the manner in which its teachings cohere, but not preserve the value of this coherence by what he has established" (*BO*, §196).[21] As we have seen, historical theology serves to *found* practical theology and to *confirm* philosophical theology. As an example of an empty and unproductive system of theology Schleiermacher cites the work of Julius August Ludwig Wegscheider (1771–1849), whose system of rationalist Protestant theology does not help a reader "locate the connection of individual ideas" (*Th Enz*, 187). To locate ideas, for Schleiermacher, is to encounter them in history (past and present). The necessary element, alongside speculative and empirical uses of reason, is faith (hence a *Glaubenslehre* or "doctrine of faith"), formed in response to the proclamation of the Christian community.

Second, dogmatic theologians do not work out of their own resources and imaginative powers. The dogmatic theologian does not risk willfulness by speaking individually, but incorporates in his work the symbolic confessions and controversial interpretations that have arisen within Christianity, especially historic Protestantism. The historic symbols, which first arose from scripture, enable Schleiermacher to utilize the entire sweep of the Christian past as grist for his dogmatic mill. As a mature churchman Schleiermacher wrote an *Open Letter* (1831) to protest against the theology of contemporary Breslauer

---

21 Translated from Scholtz, ed., *Kurze Darstellung*, 75.

theologians Daniel von Cölln and David Schulz, who rejected the historic "symbolic confessions" and sought to impose their own confession on the church.[22] By contrast, a properly dogmatic Protestant theologian aims at a level of unity within Protestant teaching without insisting on uniformity. Whatever our judgments may be about the relative emphases and substantive choices offered by the details of Schleiermacher's dogmatics, his aim is to respect the historic expressions of the church's faith.

Third, being aligned within historical theology does not make dogmatic theology less argumentative. Theology must not smooth over controversy artificially. A merely external historical report ill-serves dogmatics; the same is true of a wholly irenic theology. Such efforts leave out "the middle terms necessary to form a truly demonstrative argument" and will also weaken "the precision in defining concepts necessary for winning confidence in the presentation" (*BO*, §197). Like philosophy, the discipline of a theology that draws from history must rigorously defend its claims. Even working historians pursue a similar goal, provided that their interpretations of the past are well argued and reach beyond mere chronicle.

These three interrelated foci (the necessity of a theologian's personal conviction, the fact that conviction draws from historic biblical and church tradition, thus avoiding idiosyncracy, and the argumentative nature and defense of this inquiry) make it reasonable to view dogmatics as historical theology. For Schleiermacher there is no better way to make it clear that "the present moment is the result of the entire past, but especially of the most recent epoch" (*Th Enz*, 217). By positioning the work of dogmatics within (not beyond or above) historical consciousness, Schleiermacher avoids the twin perils of a rank biblicism and of an idiosyncratic individual philosophy of faith. The former truncates Christian consciousness by ending it with the apostolic age, while the latter acts as if Christian truth and meaning is oblivious to its past expressions. For Schleiermacher, "There is a great difference whether we have to preserve each phrase of the canon, or whether we say, the manner

---

22 *Th Enz*, 185, n. 42, which cites Daniel von Cölln and David Schulz, *Über theologische Lehrfreiheit auf den evangelischen Universitäten und deren Beschränkung durch symbolische Bücher* (Breslau, 1830), and Schleiermacher's response, "An die Herren D. D. D. von Cölln und D. Schultz" (*Theologische Studien und Kritiken* [1831]: 3–29), printed in *KGA*, 1/10 (Berlin: Walter de Gruyter, 1990), 297–426.

in which each phrase of the canon is expressed is the sheer expression of our conviction." He continues:

This [the former of these views] is not at all possible, since our conviction results from the entire development that lies between us and the canon. If a theologian allows himself to move in a wholly natural manner, then he will not easily present his conviction in the field of dogmatics in biblical expressions, but in wholly other ones. The more scientific he wishes to be, the less the untreated expressions of the canon satisfy him; we have a history of the development of concepts before us, without reference to which we cannot adequately express our conviction. (*Th Enz*, 242–3)

Like Hans Georg Gadamer, cited above, Schleiermacher asserts that the claims of Christian theology are not less but more scientific, that is, conceptually coherent, for encompassing the theologian's own being and existence within history. In confronting biblical texts, their alien elements must be "referred back to the historical conditions under which language necessarily stands." But just as an adequate account of Christian theology's definitions of faith cannot merely be parroted from biblical phrases, it also cannot be reduced to the novel inventions of philosophy.

Even though dogmatics calls for one's own conviction, it still should not be taken apart from the connection with historical theology and presented as systematic theology, for an ambiguity arises in this expression, namely that dogmatics has been placed under the diction of philosophy in a different manner than has been done here, where the organization, juxtaposition, terminology have to be justified dialectically. (*Th Enz*, 243)

For Schleiermacher a "correct use of philosophy runs through the treatment of all the theological disciplines." By contrast, a wrong use of philosophy is "the death of exegesis and the death of history" (*Th Enz*, 244). All the reproaches against a "systematic dogmatics" – Schleiermacher uses the phrase one time in the Strauß lectures – rest upon a misunderstanding of these two uses of philosophy. "There is nothing of philosophical content in dogmatics, but what there is of philosophy in it is only the dialectical justification of the arrangement of the whole in its organization and further in its individual formulae" (*Th Enz*, 244). In the form of reflective and dialectical thinking philosophy provides an "intellectual location" and thus a warrant for religious meaning. In the end, for Schleiermacher, the potential misuse of a historical awareness is not nearly as great a potential enemy of dogmatics as the more popular alternatives of a biblical literalism or a rationalist system of theology.

LEADING AND GOVERNING THE CHURCH IN THE PRESENT

It remains for us to round out an understanding of Schleiermacher's theological program by exploring the idea of practical theology as its crown. His metaphor reminds us that practical theology is the place where the theologian's gifts yield fruit and exert leadership within the life of a congregation, the larger church body, and the world of human affairs.

Schleiermacher's commitment not just to the high and lofty status of practical theology but also to its role in implementing theology leads him to reflect even more on the limits of methodology within his proposals. Compared to philosophical theology, which is a *critical* discipline, and historical theology, which is *empirical*, practical theology is *technical*, an art or skillful craft (*Kunstlehre*, or *technē*, in the Greek sense) that links thought to practice. Schleiermacher distinguishes between his proposed theological methods and the task of putting them to effective use in the church. For him, all aspects of theology point towards the care of souls, where the mind of a pastor-theologian meets those of individuals within a congregation. And in the care-of-souls line of work "no other means whatever are applicable . . . than definite influences upon the hearts of people" (*BO*, §263). Thus although constructs, definitions, and admonitions are indispensable for a proper understanding of theology, even where methods and correct teachings are assimilated perfectly by a theologian, it is not methods but the mind of the theologian implementing the methods that influences individuals within the religious community.

In the end, everything in this positive science depends upon the natural talents and cultivation of persons who are drawn into the service of the church (*BO*, §336). Earlier in the *Brief Outline*, when discussing philosophical theology, Schleiermacher writes that "every theologian should produce the entirety of this part of his theology for himself" (§67; see also §89) and that "apprehending things historically is a talent" that must be practiced in each person's life (§155, §100). The most effective church leader not only "has most thoroughly and completely developed his philosophical theology," but also "the most appropriate methods will occur to the person whose historical basis for living in the present is the deepest and most diversified" (§336). True to his romanticist respect for individual ability and talent, Schleiermacher sees that implementing his theological method is hardly a matter of just having correct knowledge of theology. The highly articulated and coordinated theological methods and insight that he recommends require hermeneutical art for their enactment. Ministry is, in effect, the implementing side of theology, which rests on effectively communicating and mediating the meaning and truth of Christian faith. These themes, articulated when discussing practical theology, do not just arise in the book's final section. At its outset Schleiermacher expresses the need for passionate human engagement with theology. He writes: "No one person can perfectly possess the full compass of theological knowledge," and adds that "if one is to deal with any one of the theological disciplines in a truly theological sense and spirit, he must master the basic features of them all" (§14, §16). This tension between desiring mastery and recognizing one's limits reflects Schleiermacher's characteristic realism about the human condition. Practical theology works from a unity between an "ecclesial interest" and a "scientific spirit" (§257–§ 258), while bestowing deliberative order upon Christian dispositions and feelings. At the same time, no handbook on theological method – even one as erudite and well considered as the *Brief Outline* – can ensure its own success.

With respect to its actual contents, practical theology distinguishes between church service (*BO*, §277–§308) and church governance (§309–§334). Pastoral duties that function within a local congregation are contrasted with those in the wider church, in this instance, the German Protestant Church as it relates to the larger culture. Church service, for Schleiermacher, consists of the tasks of preaching (an individual expression of the theologian) and liturgics (a more communal expression). Elements of edification, which consist of rousing the religious consciousness, coexist with those of regulation, which consist of motivating Christian behavior (§293). At the level of practice, edification and regulation relate to the pursuits of dogmatics and Christian ethics within historical theology. Pedagogical tasks are central to this work, including catechetics as the task of educating children to be lively members of the ongoing body of the church. Missions reach out to those in the parish who have fallen away, become indifferent, or were never properly involved in the first place. The novelty of Schleiermacher's construal of "church service" lies not in his understanding of a pastor's duties but in his insistence that to enact these duties well one must draw from the insight and tasks of philosophical and historical theology.

Under church governance Schleiermacher places the necessary participation of the pastor-theologian in the affairs of the wider church, including synodal meetings and decisions regarding German Protestantism as a whole. Such admonitions are not intended to apply to Roman Catholic Christianity, and probably not even to non-German Protestant Churches. Yet his vision of church governance moves well beyond the quasipolitical committee work of ecclesial bodies. Teaching and writing, the chief activities by which Schleiermacher's legacy reaches us today, also contribute to church governance. Wolfgang Pleger doubtless overstates the fact when he writes, "Schleiermacher's philosophy in all its parts is a philosophy of practice."[23] Praxis, for Schleiermacher, is thoroughly informed by theory. Along with other parts of Schleiermacher's theoretical work, the encylopedia contributes to church governance by honing a curriculum for church leadership. Indeed, what are arguably Schleiermacher's most refined intellectual achievements, his published works on dogmatics and theological encyclopedia, have practical theology as their telos.

APPRAISING THE MODEL OF THEOLOGICAL STUDY

A review of these reflections on the *Brief Outline* might well begin with a warning and then issue a few reminders. First, the warning: it is a mistake to think that Schleiermacher's linear arrangement of his material should lead us to conclude that the methods and tasks of theology are sequentially valued. The carefully drawn correlations and cross-links within the encyclopedia are intended to serve the community of lived Christian faith that is presupposed as the *raison d'être* of such study. In this respect, *Brief Outline* resembles the *Christian Faith* in giving a highly intricate account of diverse yet interrelated teachings. Apart from the Strauß lecture transcript, the *Brief Outline* remains a mere sketch. Read sequentially, its 338 theses easily seem dull and rigid. Yet if the project is grasped dialectically, that is, in its multiple contending interrelationships, the life of the mind called theology is experienced as a reflective act that draws upon a vast array of materials. The challenge theology faces lies in its need to effect a balance between ecclesial and scientific interests. If we ask how Schleiermacher's encyclopedia differs from Hegel's, the answer is not that the former is less systematic or rigorous. The proper response is that Schleiermacher incorporates the lived religious community further into his discussion, while using that analysis to bestow order on the figurative and contingent dimensions of lived Christian existence.

We have seen that the realm of history looms large in his program. On this point his proposal remains controversial. For him, empirical historical work is not compromised when it is informed by certain normative claims about the tradition.

---

23 Wolfgang H. Pleger, *Schleiermachers Philosophie* (Berlin: Walter de Gruyter, 1988), 3.

No knowledge [*Wissen*] of Christianity is possible if one is satisfied only with an empirical approach and fails to grasp the essence [*Wesen*] of Christianity in contrast with other ways of faith and churches, and as the essence of piety and pious communities in relation to other activities of the human spirit.[24]

As B. A. Gerrish has said of historical theology, "it would be an impoverishment of the discipline to hold it strictly to the positivistic historical ideal of just ascertaining the facts."[25] By 1800 the study of history in Germany was moving from the realm of personal narrative and rhetorical persuasion towards becoming a science (*Wissenschaft*), an aspiration that is already looming within the work we have examined.[26] For Schleiermacher, taking a scientific, that is, disciplined academic, approach to explicating the meaning of Christianity requires this approach to frame interpretations of religious history that are compelling to persons with a subjective stake not only in the project but also in its overarching aims.

Certainly the most controversial issue in Schleiermacher's program is his insistence that dogmatics belongs under the umbrella of historical theology. Writing in 1963, Hans-Joachim Birkner called attention to the relatively modest place of dogmatic theology within Schleiermacher's theological program:

By arranging dogmatics within historical theology Schleiermacher, rather than having found successors, assured himself of many critics. The critics have conceived and rejected this arrangement mainly as a diminishment that seemed to prepare the way for, if not actually espouse, a consistent historicizing of dogmatics.[27]

Upon inspection, Schleiermacher appears to have legitimate reasons for his choices. He appears able to cast dogmatics under the umbrella of history because he holds the view that theological convictions of the community of faith are actually manifest in history. Today, such confidence that history and theology can flow so neatly together is widely thought to be lacking. Since "Schleiermacher's inclusive concept of historical theology signals the historicizing of theology,"[28] we may be assured that the debate will continue. But it does not follow from this last

---

24 Translated from Scholz, ed., *Kurze Darstellung*, 8–9 (§21).
25 B. A. Gerrish, cited in Mary Potter Engel and Walter E. Wyman, Jr., eds., *Revisioning the Past: Prospects in Historical Theology* (Minneapolis: Fortress Press, 1992), 302–3.
26 Hardtwig, "Verwissenschaftlichung der neueren Geschichtsschreibung," 245–60.
27 Birkner, *Schleiermacher-Studien*, 106; see also Hermann Fischer, *Friedrich Schleiermacher* (Munich: C. H. Beck, 2001), 74.
28 Engel and Wyman, *Revisioning the Past*, 3, drawing from B. A. Gerrish, *The Old Protestantism and the New* (Chicago: University of Chicago Press, 1982), 208–9.

observation that the turn to history in Schleiermacher led to a relativising sort of historicism. A profound confidence in the unity of reason prevents a slide into relativism. To be effective, a young vicar must combine a talent for dialectical thought with a sense of history and have sufficient powers of observation and empathy to interact effectively with the souls of his parishioners. For Schleiermacher, historical awareness is an indispensable part of being a theologian. Rightly delineated, it contributes mightily to the task of properly explicating the contents of the Christian consciousness.[29]

29 If Schleiermacher's theological method works for today, this can be the case only for those who share the key assumptions within his system of the sciences. To explore those assumptions further would require us to examine his unpublished lectures on ethics and dialectics as well as the introduction to the dogmatics, a task that reaches well beyond this essay.

CHAPTER 10

Rhetoric and substance in Schleiermacher's revision of The Christian Faith *(1821–1822)*

The search for the center of Schleiermacher's thought in *The Christian Faith* has long been a major preoccupation of Schleiermacher research.[1] Our efforts to grasp the precise nature of the relationship between Christian conviction and scientific or philosophical reflection in Schleiermacher's dogmatics continue to be a subject of scholarly controversy. At stake is the relative balance between its being a confessional work (Schleiermacher's Reformed side) and a philosophically grounded work (which in some respects approximates a natural theology). An interpreter must decide whether a Calvin or a Tillich is the proper model to have in mind when reading Schleiermacher or, if his work exemplifies a mixture of both tendencies, what constitutes its center – the linchpin that holds it together. This essay does not aim at final adjudication of the adequacy of Schleiermacher's dogmatics as much as at a preliminary issue: the bearing of his work as redactor on the theological substance of his thought. Such an inquiry can, I think, shed useful light on the origin and development of the seminal work of modern Protestantism.

It is odd that in an age of sophisticated literary detection the first edition of *The Christian Faith* (1821–2) has been so little studied.[2] At the turn to the twentieth century several German scholars called our attention to important differences between the original version and the 1830–1 edition.[3] But since that time there has been virtually no interest in

---

1 See W. Trillhaas, "Der Mittelpunkt der Glaubenslehre Schleiermachers," *Neue Zeitschrift für systematische Theologie* 10 (1968): 289–309.
2 Attention given to the first edition of *The Christian Faith* has subsequently been enhanced by availability of the 1821–2 work as *KGA*, 1/7.1–2, ed. Hermann Peiter, which contain the text, and *KGA*, 1/7.3, ed. Ulrich Barth with Hayo Gerdes and Hermann Peiter (1980), which contains Schleiermacher's marginalia and an appendix with excerpts from relevant reviews.
3 See M. Rade, *Die Leitsätze der ersten und der zweiten Auflage von Schleiermachers Glaubenslehre* (Tubingen: J. C. B. Mohr, 1904), 3: "Die erste Auflage der Glaubenslehre erwies sich als eine vortreffliche Interpretin der zweiten"; C. Stange, *Schleiermachers Glaubenslehre*, kritische Ausgabe,

comparing the editions, despite the fact that to compare an author's magnum opus with an earlier rendering of the same work requires little methodological ingenuity. It is remarkable that scholars working on Schleiermacher have not asked more questions about these texts. Are rhetorical changes substantive as well as formal and literary? And if they are substantive, do they alter or confirm his original intent? What clues do the revisions yield regarding shifts in Schleiermacher's thinking and the refinement of his theology in the face of criticism?

The most obvious explanation why such questions have not been raised by English-speaking theologians is the limited availability of the first edition. Even in German it only became widely accessible in 1984.[4] But whatever may be the reasons for neglect of the first edition, there is a widespread consensus to the effect that Schleiermacher's revision is purely rhetorical (having to do exclusively with literary form) and in no way bears on the substance and content of what he wished to say. By taking a fresh look at the question of Schleiermacher as redactor I hope to reopen the possibility that the first edition of the work provides important insight into the making of his mature theology.

In what follows I first attempt to probe the reasons for widespread acceptance of the above-stated view. I argue that even on the surface there are good reasons for not accepting the standard interpretation. Although it is true that all of Schleiermacher's changes do not constitute dramatic reversals of his thought, the accepted view is misleading, often based on second-hand or cursory impressions, and does not allow us to follow the evolution and deployment of his thought. In a second part I give examples of actual changes in the text (structural, rhetorical, as well as thematic) which show that the revisions, even when rhetorical and literary, are not without relevance for the substance and meaning of the work. They serve either (1) to deepen and clarify his original intent or (2) to revise certain basic formulations, thereby making the overall work more coherent and defensible. Underlying the present essay is the view that it is not necessary for changes to be blatant or to consist of reversals of one's thought for them to have a significant bearing on the content and meaning of a work. In this regard, the history of theology has much to learn from the insight

---

1. Abteilung: Einleitung (Leipzig: A. Deichert, 1910); H. Scholz, *Christentum und Wissenschaft in Schleiermachers Glaubenslehre* (Leipzig: Hinrichs, 1911); H. Mulert, "Die Aufnahme der Glaubenslehre Schleiermachers," *Zeitschrift für Theologie und Kirche* 18 (1908): 107–39.

4 See the two-volume study edition, *Der christliche Glaube 1821/22*, ed. Hermann Peiter (Berlin: Walter de Gruyter, 1984).

and approaches of biblical studies, where it has long been understood that redaction is a chief means of theological statement. Such an insight holds even more strongly in the case of self-redaction. Even where Schleiermacher's alterations appear to be offhand – I do not wish to deny that this is often the case – they go far towards revealing what he is thinking while reformulating this work in the face of criticism.

SCHLEIERMACHER AS REDACTOR

Chief responsibility for the fact that his revisions of *The Christian Faith* have been neglected must rest in part on Schleiermacher himself. In this as well as in other literary-theological efforts, the significance of his editorial work is consistently played down. Writing to his fellow theologian J. Christian Gaß he says: "Until now no paragraph remains completely as it was, but I am writing absolutely everything afresh. Of course in its substance everything remains the same."[5] Interpreters almost universally echo Schleiermacher's view that, though a large number of changes were made in the text, they do not affect the basic nature and content of the work. In his two-volume edition of the 1830–1 German text, Martin Redeker writes:

Schleiermacher had in point of fact formulated almost everything afresh in the second edition and thereby was still cognizant of the text of the first edition . . . In the first version he expresses more naturally and immediately what he actually has in mind and the structure of the first edition is more consistent and original than that of the second edition. In the later edition he considers the objections of his theological opponents and friends.[6]

Redeker initially appears to be an exception to the standard view outlined above. An appendix to his second volume gives a parallel list of the propositions from the two editions, and he does acknowledge real differences between the versions. But Redeker does not identify what is "more consistent" or "original" in the first rendering. Thus he does not actually take a stand on the question of whether we can or should trust Schleiermacher's self-commentary on his work as a redactor.

---

5 Wilhelm Gaß, ed., *Fr. Schleiermacher's Briefwechsel mit J. Chr. Gaß* (Berlin: Reimer, 1852) 219–20; similarly in a letter to Count von Dohna dated April 10, 1830; see H. Meisner, ed., *Schleiermacher als Mensch: Sein Wirken. Familien- und Freundesbriefe 1804 bis 1834* (Gotha: F. A. Perthes, 1922–3), 357.

6 Martin Redeker, ed., Friedrich Schleiermacher, *Der christliche Glaube (1830–31)*, 1 (Berlin: de Gruyter, 1960), 13, reprinted in a study edition (Berlin: Walter de Gruyter, 1999).

Similarly ambiguous or incomplete judgments are found in older as well as in more recent treatments. In his comparative edition of the introductions of the two versions, Carl Stange objected strongly to scholarly neglect of the first edition. He held the view that

> the structure of the second edition no longer lets us recognize the original intentions of Schleiermacher's system and at times even directly distorts it. This is to be explained on the basis of the peculiar manner in which Schleiermacher went about doing the revision . . . Thus it happened that the second edition everywhere deviates from the first in many details, both stylistic and systematic, while on the other hand even with the considerable innovations the memory of the first edition makes its presence felt.[7]

Although he contends that the original intention was obscured in the revision (at least in regard to the introduction), Stange does not work out the implications of these shifts or changes.

Nor has the question of Schleiermacher as redactor been taken up by English-language interpreters. The judgment of Richard R. Niebuhr in *Schleiermacher on Christ and Religion* is characteristic when he informs the reader that "What is implicit in the 1st edition is not revised but made more explicit. But no real alterations in direction or substance are evident."[8] More recently, the novelty of Schleiermacher's original formulations has been observed by Robert R. Williams' *Schleiermacher the Theologian: The Construction of the Doctrine of God.*[9] But Williams does not examine the full implications of the first edition for his thesis that Schleiermacher's theological method resembles a phenomenological approach to dogmatics.

Even in the abstract one might have reason to challenge a view that sees Schleiermacher's changes and alterations to his text as merely rhetorical, without any bearing on the work's content. It is doubtful whether form and content, even if not exact correlates, are ever wholly separable. In an age of sophisticated textual analysis we might wonder why we should think that a literary shift is ever a mere literary change. Since each change, however minor, reflects something new in the mind of an author, all have a potential bearing on the meaning of a work. Students of *The Christian Faith* are in the habit of drawing interpretive support from other published, and even from unpublished, texts by Schleiermacher. It seems

---

7 Stange, *Schleiermachers Glaubenslehre*, vi.
8 (New York: Scribner's, 1964), 138, n. 2.
9 Robert R. Williams, *Schleiermacher the Theologian: The Construction of the Doctrine of God* (Philadelphia: Fortress Press, 1978), nn., 17, 73, 99, and 139.

undeniable that the first edition of the same work might be studied towards the same end.

Against the prevailing view, I maintain that Schleiermacher's aims in revising his work are partly concealed by his self-commentary and that his performance tells us more about his intent than what he says about his work. The years 1821–2 were crucial years of productivity in midcareer. In addition to writing and publishing his dogmatics, he issued a third edition of his *On Religion* (thereby extending its life) as well as the *Soliloquies*, plus a second edition of his second volume of collected sermons. To ignore the first dogmatic effort of Schleiermacher is virtually to skip from *On Religion* (1799) and the *Brief Outline for the Study of Theology* (1810) to the final moment of his career in the early 1830s.

At this point a side glance at Schleiermacher as redactor of *On Religion* is illuminating. In this case also he expressed himself modestly and with pronounced understatement. In the preface to the third edition of that work (revised in 1821) he writes: "Thus the changes in the work are themselves not a few, but all only very external, almost only castigations of the writing style, in which it could not be my purpose to wipe out all traces of youthfulness" (April 1821).[10] Now the question of the interplay between rhetoric and substance in the revisions of *On Religion* has likewise not been fully resolved. But there is general agreement that, in this work, the changes were far more than cosmetic. The editor of the older critical edition of *On Religion* (1879), G. Ch. B. Pünjer, responds to what Schleiermacher says about his revision:

Yet this is not completely right. To be sure, many changes touch only the expression, serving partly to delete foreign loan words, partly to improve the style. Yet alongside these are many changes of a substantive kind. They treat especially the concept of religion and its psychological grounding, then also the concept of God and the relationship of God to the world, as well as the evaluation of historical Christianity.[11]

Few persons would argue that the changes in versions of *On Religion* are only rhetorical. Clearly a number of significant alterations and explanations are intended to give his thought a more orthodox Christian and less "romantic" cast. As a redactor, Schleiermacher is a master of understatement. Such a stance is consistent with his general mode of self-irony. For

---

10 G. Ch. Bernhard Pünjer, ed., *Friedrich Schleiermacher's Reden Ueber die Religion*, kritische Ausgabe (Braunschweig: Schwetschke, 1879), xiv.

11 Ibid., iii; on the revisions of *On Religion*, see F. W. Graf, "Ursprüngliches Gefühl unmittelbarer Koinzidenz des Differenten," *Zeitschrift für Theologie und Kirche* 75 (1978): 147–86.

humanly understandable reasons a writer may emphasize the continuity of his thought when that body of thought is under severe attack. On *prima facie* evidence we may thus wonder whether his commentary on *The Christian Faith* is any more reliable than what he says about *On Religion*.

More complex self-interpretations of his work as an editor are given by Schleiermacher in the *Open Letters to Lücke*, a lengthy two-part explanation of his intent upon reissuing the dogmatics in 1830–1. This explanation, at least on its surface, reveals a confident Schleiermacher who feels relatively unscathed by the critical reception of his dogmatics.[12] His critics, whether radically hostile or attempting to be constructive, attacked his theology from such diverse and diametrically opposed assumptions that their misinterpretations tend to cancel each other out. At the same time, the fact that he protests repeatedly about being badly misunderstood by contemporaries shows that he is not without being vitally affected and moved by their criticism.

Indeed, the first edition did meet with highly adverse reactions in the theological world. His dogmatics, a work intended for the United Evangelical Church of Prussia, was awaited with a sense of great expectancy. When the work appeared, critics were quick to take up their pens. It is not our task to review all the diverse critical remarks. Yet it is striking that contemporary appraisals of his theology stumbled over the same questions that have animated and befuddled Schleiermacher scholarship since his day. There is, first, the charge that his dogmatics is more philosophical and speculative than is appropriate for a substantive interpretation of Reformed Protestantism. A Reformed theology, to be true to its heritage, should hedge itself against natural theology in favor of a biblical, confessional perspective. In the second place, there is the related charge that Schleiermacher's Christ is more an ideal or abstract, intellectual construction than the living, historical founder and source of redemption. This second line of criticism, though potentially more damaging in its specificity, is really a subset of the first. Karl Barth apparently had this aspect of Schleiermacher's teaching in mind when remarking that Schleiermacher went to work on the image of Christ "like a sculptor working on a block of marble."[13] The implication is that, for all his christomorphic emphasis, Schleiermacher's Christ is too nimble and impressionistic to be the bedrock figure of historical tradition.

---

12 Mulert, "Aufnahme," 133–9.
13 Karl Barth, *Protestant Theology in the Nineteenth Century: Its Background and History* (Valley Forge: Judson Press, 1973), 461.

Even though Schleiermacher believed his critics erred, in the *Open Letters* he took seriously the fact that their criticism, reduced to essentials, aimed at these two fundamental points: the relationship of theology to philosophy (or, as he prefers to call it, "worldly wisdom") and the historical rootedness of his christology. Was he in fact too philosophical in the first rendering? In the 1821 introduction he asserts that dogmatics is not to be mixed with philosophy, and his entire method attempts to underscore this point.[14] Moreover, this alleged independence from philosophy is surely what animated the critique of his colleague G. W. F. Hegel.[15] Was his Christ rooted in historical revelation as the source of the church's faith? His basic understanding of dogmatics locates it as an intellectual enterprise that belongs to "historical theology."[16] Schleiermacher had good reason to believe that criticism on both points was unjustified. But he could not avoid feeling partly responsible for the large number of misunderstandings of his work. The process of revising put him in the position of having to face this body of criticism. It was natural for him to want to make his case more compelling and to communicate more persuasively with his readers.

Schleiermacher is more candid in the *Open Letters* than in personal correspondence. In contrast to assurances given to J. Christian Gass (cited above) that "in its substance everything remains the same," he openly acknowledges a series of distinctive changes in the editions.[17] He observes that his conception of the introduction must bear some of the blame for the work's unfortunate reception:

Has not the introduction with which I intended nothing other than a provisional orientation, which taken precisely, really lies beyond our proper discipline, been seen as the actual main part, as the proper core of the whole? And especially apparently the first part. On the basis of the character of propositions in the introduction it has been concluded that my dogmatics is actually philosophy and that it is intended either to demonstrate or to deduce Christianity, if indeed it is even worthy of this name.[18]

This passage, along with others, shows his intense disappointment with the reception of his work. But his comments also tacitly acknowledge the problematic nature of his first attempt to get his dogmatic theology off the

---

14 Schleiermacher, *Christliche Glaube* 1821: "Das Philosophisches und Dogmatisches nicht vermischt werden dürfe, ist der Grundgedanke der vorliegenden Bearbeitung" (*KGA*, 1/7.1, 14).
15 See above, chapter 3.
16 See above, chapter 9.
17 *KGA*, 1/10, ed. Hans-Friedrich Traulsen with Martin Obst (1990), 359, 370–3, 377–8; See *LL*, 56.
18 *KGA*, 1/10, 339.

ground. If he were not attempting to offer a philosophical justification of the Christian faith, how could so many diverse readers have misunderstood his intent? Although he would stand firm in his methodology and underlying convictions, it was impossible to ignore the fact that he was partly responsible for the misconceptions surrounding his work.

Schleiermacher reacted sharply to the suggestion that an unwarranted dependence on philosophy had led him away from historic Protestant teaching. If one wished to view him, as F. C. Bauer had done, as a gnostic, one would have to bring a similar charge against the Heidelberg confession.[19] It was crucial that his theology be seen as a reflection of the historic Protestant confessions, the living symbols of the church. Schleiermacher wrestled with his critics' allegations while attempting to see the possible connection between their two essential charges. It was difficult for him to see how his christological interpretations could have gone astray solely because of the work's structure. Thus he writes to Friedrich Lücke that the basic, underlying structure of the work will be retained. But the introduction was seen to be problematic. It was "the worst and most glaring misunderstanding" if one were to think "that [his] *Christian Faith* had a speculative tendency and rests on a speculative basis." This would have been avoided if "the dangerous introduction" had been "more strongly and expressly separated from the work itself."[20] Hence the chief aim of revision would be to make the introduction more independent and to delineate it more sharply from the main body of the work:

I cannot refrain from reproaching myself that, as most of my critics have been occupied predominantly with the introduction a majority of the most significant misunderstandings have arisen from the fact that they have considered the introduction too much as part of the dogmatics itself . . . Do I not therefore have reason enough to believe that even here the distinction between the introduction and the work has not been grasped sharply enough? But in the case of such men as these and others – for I could have an even greater list of examples – this cannot be encountered without it somehow being my fault, and therefore I have sought to locate this fault with the utmost sincerity. Though I have not found much, I have found enough to cause me to develop a significant reordering of material.[21]

Although Schleiermacher here speaks openly and candidly about his work, his self-explanation is still shrouded in considerable ambiguity. A reader must wonder why he felt compelled to issue this public apologia for his revision. Is he trying to explain in the *Open Letters* why he is

---

19 Ibid., 359.   20 Ibid., 342.   21 Ibid., 370, 376.

revising the work? Or is he trying to suggest that he has reason to be satisfied about the essential rightness of his theological position and thus explain why he is reissuing the work without making the major revisions that his critics wished to see? In either case, his relative dissatisfaction with his work, and especially with its introduction, is made clear.

REVISIONS OF THE CHRISTIAN FAITH

We may now examine Schleiermacher's revisions directly in order to explore the claim that, though some literary changes are purely stylistic, others also have an explicit bearing on the substance of the work and either (1) deepen and clarify the original intent or (2) revise certain basic formulations in order to bolster the coherence of the work as a whole. To repeat what was said above about the interplay of form and content, the removal of occasions for substantive misunderstanding arises from concerns for the content of an argument or position and is not adequately grasped if we see it as merely formal. If we place the two editions side by side we are confronted for the most part not so much by dramatic changes or reversals of thought as by subtle shifts and nuances in the argument. This holds for the work as a whole. But in the introduction, which he saw as the most troublesome part, the shifts and nuances are far more pronounced. To overcome what he saw as shortcomings of the first edition he engaged in making additions and deletions and in significantly reordering his material.

Schleiermacher's dogmatics had been long in the making. The work's inception goes back to his earliest days as a university teacher of theology. The mature shape and design of his theology thus took shape only gradually. Heinrich Scholz, in an older work, points out that Schleiermacher was more speculatively inclined in his younger days than in the period of his mature reflection.[22] Although not uncritical of the idealism of Fichte, Schleiermacher could write in 1805 that one would be able to measure the truth of his dogmatics solely on the basis of universal reason. At that time he was in search of his own resolution of the metaphysical and religious problems of German Idealism. His letter to the much admired F. H. Jacobi (March 1818) shows us a Schleiermacher who resists Jacobi's complete separation of feeling and understanding and calls for a synthesis of the two (at *some* level of consciousness).[23] Thus it may be

---

22 See Scholz, *Christentum und Wissenschaft*, 21f.
23 H. Bolli, ed., *Schleiermacher-Auswahl* (Munich: Siebenstern, 1968), 116–19.

surprising that there is no evidence of a direct rapprochement with any particular school of philosophy in the dogmatics of 1821–2. Speculative thought is formally excluded as the foundation of Christian teaching. It is not the case that the earlier version of his theology is in fact more "philosophical" in its orientation, while the mature version is more "confessional."

As best I can see, the most important differences in the two versions are undertaken in response to the two above-mentioned criticisms. The introduction is structurally recast in order to bring out the independence of dogmatics in relation to philosophic or other modes of nontheological reflection. To ensure this, a theory of language is adumbrated and the formal interdependence of certain propositions is coordinated with, but not subordinated to, the insight of philosophy. At the same time, in the introduction as well as at other crucial points (e.g., in his christological explanations) the ecclesiological and christological foundations of Schleiermacher's thought are stated more vigorously and unmistakably. As a self-consciously Protestant writer, Schleiermacher understands the doctrine of the church to rest on Christ and literally to owe its being to Christ. But before we examine specific changes that bear on these teachings it is important to establish the nature of the reordering and structural changes that took place.

Readers of Schleiermacher's *The Christian Faith* are familiar with its forbidding mode of presentation. Propositions in the form of theses are announced and commented upon in subsequent paragraphs, occasionally with an additional note at the end of a section. Although well suited for German lecturing and providing a framework for theological analysis, the procedure lacks immediate lucidity. Initial readers of Schleiermacher find themselves confronted by a morass of theses and, even with the refinements of the later edition (1830–1), often have difficulty in grasping the leitmotif of the work. The overall mode of presentation in the form of propositions and explanations is constant in both editions.

For example, the thirty-five propositions of the 1821–2 introduction are paralleled by thirty-one in the revision. In the earlier edition there are no intervening subheadings at all; the entire argument flows from the initial statement that "dogmatic theology is the science which treats the system of doctrine prevalent in a Christian religious community at a definite time." Hence the most obvious external signs of change in the later edition are seen in the relocation of the initial proposition at section 19 and in the rubrics and subheadings that are added to propositions 1–31. A summary cannot convey the complexity of the shifts within the introduction. But it seems that in 1821–2 the immediacy of religious affections and their temporal specificity form the bedrock from which all else derives, while the 1830–1 version is adorned with multiple levels of stage directions, explanations, headings, and subheadings that provide a greater intellectual context for the work. Such headings, none of which is in the 1821–2 version, can be seen at a glance as follows:

General statement
2–19   Explanation of dogmatics
  3–6   Propositions borrowed from ethics
  7–10   Propositions borrowed from philosophy of religion
  11–14   Propositions borrowed from apologetics
  15–19   Relationship of dogmatics to Christian piety
20–31   Methods of dogmatics
  20   Need for a rule for selecting and ordering dogmatic material
  21–26   On selecting dogmatic material
  27–31   On the formation and ordering of dogmatic material

We may briefly characterize the most obvious difference by saying that in the first version the scientific-intellectual (one is inclined to say methodological) dimension is brought forth implicitly from within the exposition of Christian piety, whereas in the more mature edition this relationship is reversed. What strikes a reader of the mature edition (which alone is available in English) is that Schleiermacher's introduction, if read in its entirety and not just paragraphs 3 and 4 that are most often anthologized, comprises a series of methodological injunctions and road maps to the terrain of Christian piety.

When we observe the overtly methodological consciousness of the revision, we may rightly wonder about its relationship to criticism of the initial work, in which severe doubts were aired as to whether it was sufficiently Christian in the sense of being rooted in the historical foundations of faith. The dilemma facing Schleiermacher as redactor was that he must deepen the scientific mooring of his dogmatics to meet the first charge (of an undue dependence on philosophical thought) but that, by so doing, he risked exacerbating the second charge (that his Christ is not rooted in the historical tradition). To fulfill the former demands of critics meant that on the surface of the work he would appear to move away from the immediacy of religious experience (including the immediacy of our historical experience) so vividly attested by the original structure and dynamic of the introduction. Indeed, the introduction of the "borrowed theses" (§3–§14) makes it seem as if Schleiermacher is confessing the dependence of dogmatics on external perspectives, a feature that thus compounds in a reader's mind the problem it is intended to obviate. In fact, virtually identical material was present in the first edition, but without any of these labels. Thus Hans-Joachim Birkner asserts that in these passages "a substantive alteration from the first [edition] does not occur."[24] The change, then, is one of providing informative labels and correlations. Schleiermacher does not thereby suggest that his dogmatics is dependent upon someone else's insights or some generalized, universally valid version of one of these subfields of inquiry. "Ethics," "Philosophy of Religion," and "Apologetics" are used as cross-references that serve to place dogmatics within his own system of theological sciences. Dogmatics is in his view (an insight that holds in both editions) not the telos or queen of theology so much as the synthesizing dimension of theology that is closest to contemporaneity and thus most vulnerable to criticism. As a result of a gradual maturing process the later Schleiermacher wishes to make clear that dogmatics is system-related in borrowing assumptions from cognate disciplines, while independent in allowing its form and content to arise from the task of explicating the Christian faith. As a field of theological inquiry, dogmatics draws from historical and biblical material (the three, taken together, constitute "historical theology"[25]) and is not reducible to a single-level system that is held together by a speculative or philosophical insight. These observations on the reordering of material may be summed up by noting that, roughly speaking, the material in paragraphs 15–19 of the latter work, now given the heading "The Relationship of Dogmatics to Christian Piety," is the starting point of the earlier version and sets the work in motion. In its new setting, as section 19, Schleiermacher's celebrated definition of dogmatics appears initially to be out of place. Neither of the immediately surrounding propositions appears to deal with the history-laden character of the theological enterprise. It seems odd that a clear-cut definition of dogmatics should not be stated at the outset. But in view of the dilemma facing its author, a decision was made to give priority to the external coordinates and issues of structure and method, while hoping to make clear internally

---

24 Hans-Joachim Birkner, *Schleiermacher-Studien*, ed. Hermann Fischer (Berlin: Walter de Gruyter, 1996) [original essay, "Theologie und Philosophie: Einführung in Probleme der Schleiermacher-Interpretation," (1974)], 182.
25 See above, chapter 9.

(within the expository paragraphs that comment on the propositions) that religion and Christian piety that originates in a historical proclamation still stand as the core. In addition to deepening its scientific foundation, the christological foundation needed simultaneously to be deepened and rendered more secure.

If we now hold in mind the newer, more explicit level of methodological self-consciousness of the later version, we see the tenor of the work set in motion by the new opening thesis: "The purpose of this introduction is, first, to set forth the conception of dogmatics that underlies the work itself; and secondly, to prepare the reader for the method and arrangement that followed it."[26] Numerous other propositions, even when echoing material from the first edition, also have a heightened level of didacticism. Many of these articles prove deadly to initial readers, since they so thoroughly suppress the reader's lived, first-order level of theological belief and conviction. Thus it is not surprising that paragraphs 3 and 4, which explicate the "immediate self-consciousness" and "absolute dependence," are often read apart from the rest of the introduction.

The tendency towards didacticism of the second version of the introduction may be seen in section 20, which (contrary to the impression given by the appendix of Redeker's edition) actually has no real analog in the earlier version.[27] In 1830 Schleiermacher writes:

Since every system of doctrine, as a presentation of dogmatic theology, is a self-contained and closely connected whole of dogmatic propositions, we must, with regard to the existing mass of such propositions, establish in the first place a rule according to which some will be adopted and others excluded; and in the second place, a principle for their arrangement and interconnection.[28]

The quest for criteria by which to structure a dogmatics is the ruling insight of the passage. By contrast, in 1821, the following proposition occurs at the same point:

The Christian system of doctrine is obliged to describe the pious affections, which occur in Christian life, so that the relationship to Christ as redeemer appears in the description in the measure to which it comes forth in feeling and so correlates it that its completeness is thereby illuminated." (§23)[29]

26 CF, 1.
27 Schleiermacher, Christliche Glaube, II, 506–7, which parallels §20 (1830–1) with §23 (1821–2).
28 CF, 94.
29 KGA, 1/7.1, 90.

In the revised proposition Schleiermacher is primarily dealing with a degree (*Mass*) of propositional theses, whereas in the earlier version the statement refers to the degree of relatedness to Christ as redeemer that steps forth in our feeling. Such a shift exemplifies the movement from the surface immediacy of the first edition to the more "scientific" texture of the second.

The essential key to the greater explicitness of theological method in the revision lies in the further development of a theory of language. His view that language consists of poetical, rhetorical, and dogmatic or didactic usages does occur in 1821–2. But it is not yet richly developed. By contrast, the significance of language is now brought out more thoroughly and dogmatic or didactic language presented as deriving from the poetic and rhetorical, the foundational levels of religious discourse. Rather than being hidden in the initial paragraphs, the theme of language is more deeply developed so that, leading up to section 19, it climaxes the section of the introduction that consists of an "Explanation of Dogmatics." For Schleiermacher, the independence of dogmatics from philosophy is grounded in a theory of language in which doctrine rests on and refers back to more immediate, preconscious levels of consciousness. Discussion of language follows the section that treats the "borrowed theses" of Christian reflection (§19; formerly §1). The impression of having created a historically relative mode of theological reflection in which theological insight grows out of a specificity of time and place is countered by an insight that rests on a structural and perennial claim regarding language.

In addition to the changes mentioned, there was considerable displacement of material and some deletion, to make room for the more self-conscious, scientific cast of the revision. The opening propositions, and their supporting explanations, which could not be worked into later propositions were simply dropped from the work. The best example of this is the deletion of section 6 from 1821, which reads: "In order to ascertain in what the nature of Christian piety consists, we have to proceed beyond Christianity and assume our standpoint beyond it in order to compare it with other types of faith."[30] Here again, the process of making revisions appears to be full of contradictory impulses. An avowedly methodological proposition is dropped, even though this general direction is augmented, in other ways, by the newer formulations. In its original setting, this proposition and section 7, which follows, introduce

---

30 *KGA*, 1/7.1, 20.

the section that, in the later rendering, comprises the "borrowed theses." In both instances Schleiermacher is making the same fundamental point. In order to get started, dogmatics is dependent on a frame of reference that lies beyond the dogmatic and confessional perspective pure and simple. The problem of determining the essence of Christianity and "the nature of Christian piety" must be settled before dogmatics proper can get under way.

Deletion of section 6 can hardly have been done because of its content. It is more likely that Schleiermacher, faced with criticism of his method, found the earlier formulation too misleading; it sounds as if an alien, perhaps even a non-Christian, perspective must be brought in at the outset. An identical passage from the *Brief Outline for the Study of Theology* (1810) was also dropped in that work's revision.[31] The reason for the deletion is thus more tactical than substantive. Schleiermacher's claim is that some such standpoint "beyond Christianity" is necessary in identifying the nature of piety if we are to avoid being trapped by the opinions of existing church parties. But such a stance does not necessarily lead to the adoption of a non- or anti-Christian perspective. This might be the case if the turn were to a perspective of worldly wisdom or philosophy, for this procedure would emphasize something other than that "which is historically given to us, on which task all similar undertakings, namely all so-called a priori constructions, have always shattered on the field of history."[32] This passage vividly attests to the history-laden dimension of Schleiermacher's entire project. Historical experience within the church as religious community speaks with more objectivity (in the sense of nonarbitrary reality) than do the rival and hotly contested systems of philosophical thought to which theology often has recourse. We may feel, by hindsight, that it is a pity that such a vivid passage was dropped, especially since Schleiermacher gives a lucid explanation in the earlier version of "why that which is meant had to be said."

If we place ourselves wholly within Christianity, then we think we are stimulated by pious Christian sentiment or ready to become so in every moment. But if that is the case we are not able to conduct ourselves with equal weight in relation to what is Christian and what is non-Christian that we wish to compare with it. But

---

31 The 1830 revision of the *Brief Outline*, *KGA*, 1/6, 256, drops §4 ("Der Standpunkt der philosophischen Theologie in Beziehung auf das Christenthum überhaupt ist nur über demselben zu nehmen") and clarifies the point in §33 by asserting that philosophical theology is beyond Christianity "only in the logical sense of the word" (*KGA*, 1/6, 338).

32 *KGA*, 1/7.1, 21.

the Christian element will delight and attract us and the non-Christian will put us off and be contrary to us. For this consideration we must allow our pious sentiment to rest because what matters is not that we should decide through our feeling what is true or false, for that we have already done a long time ago; what we must impress on ourselves is how the one and the other, the Christian and the non-Christian elements look and are constituted. When we have found that anew, then we again take up our standpoint within Christianity and affirm it with greater certitude.[33]

Far from suggesting neutrality of a final sort, the passage, and thus the procedure it recommends, insists upon attaining greater certitude regarding the objective basis of faith.

The foregoing remarks, though not exhaustive, are concerned to show the significance of Schleiermacher's reordering of material as well as the ways in which the introduction is recast to bring out more fully the scientific and methodological foundations of dogmatics. We may now look more closely at his response to the other major line of criticism, the charge that his theology is christologically inadequate. Despite the close alignment of dogmatic thought with historical tradition, numerous critics felt that his theology was not adequately rooted in Christ as historical redeemer. The best known of these critics, F. C. Baur, viewed Schleiermacher's Christ as gnostic and unhistorical. At issue is not the question of whether religious and Christian consciousness has a present historical dimension. That is never in doubt. The question is how Jesus of Nazareth as a past, historically given figure, is related to the current teaching of the church. Does Christ truly serve as historical redeemer in Schleiermacher's thought? Much of the Schleiermacher criticism of the twentieth century (especially as influenced by Brunner and Barth) was focused on this point.

Similarly to the case of theological method and the foundations of dogmatics, his work of revision is also a complex matter on this point. His concern is best made clear if we observe a small but significant shift of language in the revised work. Although the first edition is concerned to show the alignment and congruity between historical proclamation and doctrinal formulation (the latter, though secondary, must nonetheless reflect and be faithful to the former), such passages receive an expanded and pronounced treatment in the later version. In addition to speaking

---

33 *KGA*, 1/7.1, 22. See 23: "Sollen wir also andere Glaubensweisen in ihrer Wahrheit betrachten: so müssen wir auch um deswillen unser thätiges Verhältnis in Christentum für diesee Zeit ruhen lassen."

about the proclamation (*Verkündigung*) of the Gospel as the foundation of the church, this foundation is now, more than previously, set directly in the person and work of Jesus and referred to as the "self-proclamation of Jesus."[34] Even though the framework of the second edition is belabored with attempts to correlate material methodologically, the actual substance of the doctrine is traced more firmly than ever to the historical founder of redemption. Here we see his original intent deepened and clarified. Against the twentieth-century interpretations of Schleiermacher by Barth and Brunner, one could even argue that Schleiermacher himself is a kerygmatic theologian. His sense of redemption, in view of these repeated passages, cannot rightly be understood as being read off the surface of the contemporary mind of the Protestant church or spun out of one's private religious consciousness apart from the salvific event. In sections 15–19 of the 1830–1 version (which roughly parallel the opening sections of the 1821–2 edition) the idea of the rootedness of dogmatic language in the original proclamation of the church is repeated so often as to become a dominant theme.[35] By more frequently appealing to this idea Schleiermacher seeks tacitly to respond to his critics. The change may appear to be only cosmetic and rhetorical. But it has a direct bearing on the substance of his work and is designed to help the reader grasp what he wants most earnestly to communicate.

Schleiermacher's version of dogmatics was not founded solely on a generalized version of Christian faith, despite his decision to precede the explicitly developed Christian consciousness with a description of the generic features of a universal religious consciousness. He was engaged in a struggle to show that his Jesus was not merely one religious founder and teacher among all the others. The point has often been raised in criticism of other works, notably *On Religion*. If there are many "heroes of religion" and "mediators" (rightly understood, Schleiermacher himself is such a figure), then why should the Christian religion need any longer to be tied to any single one of them? In its final version, even more than in the edition of 1821–2, Jesus Christ is unmistakably portrayed as the sole definitive source of Christian teaching. Church doctrine and teaching is specifically founded upon Christ's teaching. In a supplement to the exposition of section 19 we read: "For there is only *one* source, out of which all Christian doctrine is derived, namely, the self-proclamation of

34 *KGA*, 1/7.1, 82 speaks of the "proclamation of Christ," while the revised version leaves no doubt that Jesus' self-proclamation is the anchor of theology; see *KGA*, 1/13.1, 148–9, in a supplement to §19; *CF*, 92.

35 For further use of *Verkündigung* in §§15–19, see *KGA*, 1/13.1, 128–129, 133, 139; *CF*, 77–8, 81, 85.

Christ, and only one manner in which doctrine, whether perfectly or imperfectly, arises from the pious consciousness itself and the immediate impression."[36] This 1830–1 addition to the work consists of a rhetorical change that deepens his original insight. The distinction between the source and the medium of Christian theology invoked by Paul Tillich is explicitly stated in the mature version of Schleiermacher's major work. In view of this fact it is especially ironic that Tillich, invoking the distinction in his own *Systematic Theology*, should attempt to use it against Schleiermacher, whom he charges with a subjectivistic reading of the Christian faith.[37]

Intimately related to this greater emphasis on Christ as founder and source of the church's theology is the theme of doctrine as arising from and belonging to the church. Again, we are not dealing with a complete *novum* in Schleiermacher's thought. It was perhaps Ernst Troeltsch, among theological liberals, who saw most clearly that Schleiermacher's theology was a church-centered theology.[38] Troeltsch's insight is borne out by the revision, a good example of which is seen in section 2 of 1830–1: "Since dogmatics is a theological discipline, and thus pertains solely to the Christian church, we can only explain what it is when we have become clear as to the conception of the Christian Church."[39] In view of what I am arguing, the emphasis on theology pertaining solely to the church is most significant. Even though the newer statement of his thought seeks to correlate dogmatics and other modes of intellectual inquiry with the life of faith, theology is seen to be utterly dependent on its relationship to the church.

Schleiermacher was true to the remarks in the *Open Letters* in which he indicates greatest dissatisfaction with his introduction. Most of the rhetorical changes that have a substantive bearing on his work occur in those passages. The bulk of the work in parts 1 and 2 received far fewer significant changes, and the standard view that his changes were more cosmetic and literary than significant does apply to the main body of the work. As far as I can see, the chief exception to this in the main body of

---

36 *KGA*, 1/13.1, 148–9; *CF*, 92 (tr. altered).

37 See Paul Tillich, *Systematic Theology* (Chicago: University of Chicago Press, 1951), I, 42, "On the other hand, criticism must be directed against Schleiermacher's method in his *Glaubenslehre* (*The Christian Faith*). He tried to derive all contents of the Christian faith from what he called the 'religious consciousness' of the Christian."

38 Ernst Troeltsch, "Schleiermacher und die Kirche," in *Schleiermacher der Philosoph des Glaubens*, ed. Friedrich Naumann (Berlin: Schöneberg, 1910), 9–25.

39 *KGA*, 1/13.1, 13–14; *CF*, 3.

the work is in Schleiermacher's Christology. In view of my argument, the reasons why this is the case are not difficult to imagine. By 1830, Schleiermacher was vitally concerned to rethink his treatment of the traditional christological formulae or two-natures teaching.[40]

In 1821–2 he was relatively content with the Chalcedonian formulae concerning Christ (one person, two natures).[41] In section 118 he spoke about the "impersonality of the human nature in him apart from its union with the divine."[42] Of course, even in the earlier version Schleiermacher struggled with the meaning of his traditional claim. The view that Christ's human nature had no "independent subsistence" is said to be a "dark . . . but yet an irreproachable formula for the relation of the divine to the human in Christ."[43] Like his predecessor in Christian theology, Schleiermacher ran into the difficulty of trying to think of the two coessential natures simultaneously. By stating that Christ's humanity is dependent upon his divinity Schleiermacher opened the door to the charge that his Christ was gnostic and not fully human. In the second edition he turns towards more serious criticism of the orthodox christological formulas and suggests that they "need to be subjected to continual criticism." At this point Schleiermacher becomes a master of persuasive reinterpretation. In the final rendition he tells us that the scholastic (he often uses scholastic to include patristic) formula is "wrong" and he seeks to move away from any trace of a suggestion of the nonhumanity of Christ.[44] Orthodox formulations do not necessarily enhance our understanding. "Christian preachers must have the freedom granted to the poets to make use of terms that cannot find a place in the terminology of technical theology."[45] Finally, in place of the troublesome section 118 (which is deleted), Schleiermacher writes a new proposition that avoids speaking about the

---

40 See the newly coined proposition §95 and its explanations in *KGA*, 1/13.2, 58–60; *CF*, 389–90: "The ecclesiastical formulae concerning the person of Christ need to be subjected to continual criticism."

41 On Schleiermacher's critique of Chalcedonian Christologies in his revised dogmatics, see Lori Pearson, "Schleiermacher and the Christologies behind Chalcedon," *Harvard Theological Review* 96/3 (2003): 349–67.

42 The entirety of §118 (1822), *KGA*, 1/7.2, 39, "Christus war seinen Menschheit nach vor allen andern ausgezeichnet durch seine übernatürliche Zeugung, durch seine eigentümliche Vortrefflichkeit und durch die Unpersönlichkeit der menschlichen Natur in ihm, abgesehen von ihrer Vereinigung mit der göttlichen" was replaced in 1830 by §98, "Christus war von allen andern Menschen unterschieden durch seine wesentliche Unsündlichkeit und seine schlechthinnige Vollkommenheit" (*KGA*, 1/13.2, 90).

43 *KGA*, 1/7.2, 39.

44 *KGA*, 1/13.2, 76; *verkehrt* is stronger than "unfortunate" as translated in *CF*, 402.

45 *KGA*, 1/13.2, 86; *CF*, 411.

two natures in supernatural-metaphysical terms and casts the distinctiveness of Christ wholly in the moral-theological category of sin. Rather than the uniqueness of Christ being understood through "the impersonality" of his human nature, "Christ was distinguished from all other men by His essential sinlessness and His absolute perfection" (§98).[46] His original formulation is basically altered in light of the revision as a whole. This major, substantive shift in his interpretation of Christ follows a long section in which questions of docetism and other ahistorical views of Christ are discussed at length and rejected.

If Schleiermacher's desire for a more sophisticated methodological matrix tends to govern the revision of the introduction and thus responds to the first criticism that his theology was unduly dependent upon philosophy, then his christological reinterpretations were a supreme effort to take seriously the second charge of the critics. Quite against his intent, the shadow of docetic teaching can be seen to hover over some of the formulations of the first version. But beneath the surface of the introduction and in the main body of the work we find evidence that Schleiermacher wanted to dispose of the charge that Jesus Christ is a mere construct of thought. There can be no doubt that a large portion of his revision is rhetorical in the sense of stylistic and cosmetic changes. But by revising the work he was also forced to rethink it. Faced with severe criticism by contemporaries, the implications of his thought became more apparent to him as he struggled for greater clarity in exposition. Thus it is not as a new teaching or as a rejection of his earlier positions that he chose to reissue his dogmatics in final form. The later, more finished statement of his views was a more self-conscious and explicit defense of lines that had, for the most part, been established in that first effort.

CONCLUSION

In the foregoing sections I have argued that one can learn much about *The Christian Faith* and the evolution of Schleiermacher's thought by studying the process of the work's revision. Although in no way revolutionary, the points I have raised help to bring us closer to the work of Schleiermacher in his own theological milieu. Schleiermacher interpretation will make great strides to the extent that we are attentive to the process of composition of his mature dogmatics in its own historical setting before we seek to assess the contemporary viability of his theological program.

---

46 *KGA*, 1/13.2, 90; *CF*, 413.

If the formal changes and shifts do, as I contend, bear upon the content of the work, then it follows that the final version of *The Christian Faith* is more sophisticated and truer to its author's underlying intent than is its earlier model. That our knowledge of a thing can only be mediated in a process and activity of thought stands as a chief principle of Schleiermacher's dialectics. "All that we know is mediated only by means of and in the process of thinking."[47] In his own case, the task of writing and revising his work (which is inevitably a thought process) constitutes a central part of this knowledge and self-mediation.

Schleiermacher would himself doubtless smile at our efforts to unravel every nuance in the evolution of his thought. At times he appears not to place as much emphasis on the completed and finished form of his work as others have done, starting in his own day. Commenting to a friend in 1822 on the adverse reception of *The Christian Faith* Schleiermacher says: "You need not rub in the fact that people don't make much out of my books. In the end I myself don't make much out of them."[48] Of course, such an utterance can be taken in a number of ways. We might be inclined to see it arising from sheer disappointment or from an attitude of self-effacement. But I believe the remark consistently reflects the large part that self-irony plays in his thought.[49] There is a sense in which throughout his life Schleiermacher was more a man of the spoken than of the written word. He was aware that his potential influence was greater as a preacher and a teacher than as a writer or a thinker. But this stance of intellectual modesty need not detract us from the care with which he went about revising his major works.

I understand the reasons for Stange's claim that the original intent is lost and obscured in the newer version. But that impression is, I think, only due to the excessive didacticism of the newly formulated introduction. On the whole I contend (against Stange) that Schleiermacher's intent is rendered more explicit and that his ideas are presented more effectively in the 1830–1 version.[50] Both the independence of dogmatic theology from philosophy and the rootedness of the life of faith in a historical redeemer are better represented in the work. (This is not the

---

47 Friedrich Schleiermacher, *Dialektik*, ed. R. Odebrecht (Darmstadt: Wissenschaftliche Buchgesellschaft, 1976), 128.
48 Schleiermacher to Blanc, August 13, 1822, in *Schl Briefe*, IV, 297–8.
49 On this point see Jack Forstman, *A Romantic Triangle: Schleiermacher and Early German Romanticism* (Missoula: Scholars Press, 1977).
50 Thus I do not share the view of Stange, *Schleiermachers Glaubenslehre*, that the first edition is the "most complete witness of his [Schleiermacher's] spirit" (vi).

same as arguing that they are compellingly represented, which is a topic that exceeds the bounds of the present argument). Martin Redeker appears to be correct in claiming that the first version is more immediate, freer, and more original. But I have difficulty with the view that it was "more consistent." The second formulation is a richer statement of what Schleiermacher had in mind all along. Thus the dominant view of Schleiermacher interpretation, that there are no substantial alternations in the work, is partly vindicated by what I have said. But even though there is no self-repudiation and reversal of thought of a major kind, an advance does occur in Schleiermacher's articulation of his intent and his ability to defend his dogmatics against the critics. It is likely that still other variations of these tendencies of the mature work may be discovered, if we take the pains to look closely at the "castigation of the writing style" of this theological author.

CHAPTER II

On Religion *as a religious classic: hermeneutical musings after two hundred years*

To the memory of Wilhelm Pauck
(1901–81)

Let me begin with a prefatory confession.[1] Ten years ago when I published the English translation of the first edition of Schleiermacher's *On Religion: Speeches to its Cultured Despisers* (1799 edition) I was concerned whether the work would have an impact in today's world. Like many of you, I was aware of a certain illustrious story of its influence within the history of modern theology, and to some extent philosophy of religion. To help promote the book I wrote a sketch of the history of the work's reception to be included in the Introduction to the translation, but then dropped it when I, and the editors at Cambridge, saw that there was already too much to be said about the text's immediate circumstances and arguments. I concurred with that decision. Yet I also felt ambiguous about it. I doubted that a work can be explained by the sum of its influences. But its influences nonetheless serve as benchmarks by which we attempt to define a work as classic, one that bears up amid the vagaries of time. To some extent, the present essay provides an opportunity for me to work out my thoughts on the ambivalence of seeking to know works by knowing something of their influence and reading them in light of what Gadamer calls their "effective history."

TWO CENTURIES OF INTERPRETATION

In a recent essay, "The Scope of Hermeneutics," Francis Watson argues for a holistic approach to classic and canonical texts and maintains that

---

1 The paper from which this chapter is taken was originally presented at a meeting of the Schleiermacher Group, American Academy of Religion, Orlando, Florida, November 23, 1998.

"the significance of a text takes time to unfold."[2] I believe Watson is correct in most, though not all, senses. In what follows I hope to make clear where, and in what crucial ways, his dictum falls short of the mark. For the moment, however, we shall take seriously the proposition that a work or text's significance is wider than its original presence coupled with its first readers, and that these wider permutations (i.e., being reproduced in diverse editions and translations that are received by distinct audiences) belong to the larger meaning of a work. This is the kind of significance that Watson has in mind in arguing, with respect to biblical texts, that "the significance of a text takes time to unfold." It is a view with which I have considerable sympathy, partly for the reason that an Ur-text can neither anticipate its own interpretation, nor embody the embellishments of meaning it inevitably receives at the hands of other writers. On Watson's view, for us to be only interested "in the process of origination . . . abstracts the text from its past, present and future roles in the ongoing dialogue of Christian theology, converting it into an inert object, viewed as if from a great distance."[3]

One can also make Watson's point directly in the case of Schleiermacher's *On Religion*. A strong argument can be made that Schleiermacher's revisions of his own text in 1806 and 1821 (when he wrote his dogmatics and added explanatory comments to the speeches) belong to the meaning of this text. I have argued elsewhere that this is a ubiquitous text, which pervades the remainder of his work, even if this is sometimes hidden from readers.[4] Because the *Speeches* embody his deepest intuitions – about religion, self, art, church, deity, Jesus Christ, politics, history, antiquity, and life – the work stood him in good stead during the rest of his career. There is, in fact, a kind of tough intertextuality that runs through Schleiermacher's various works. Such intertextuality is all the more challenging to ferret out since, while no single work (even his *Dogmatics*) encompasses the full range of his intellectual achievement, each work bears the traces of an orientation that is originally expressed in *On Religion*. Though he revised the book at crucial junctures of his life, Schleiermacher never renounced its structure or basic ideas.

It is not my aim to attempt to do here what I thought I wanted to do ten years ago in writing a chapter on the history of the work's influence.

2 Francis Watson, "The Scope of Hermeneutics," in *The Cambridge Companion to Christian Doctrine*, ed. Colin E. Gunton (Cambridge: Cambridge University Press, 1997), 75.
3 Ibid.
4 See above, chapter 8.

To do that fully would be to revisit much of the theological history of modern Protestantism within Germany and the English-speaking world. At the same time, some recollection of the weight and nature of the text's influence seems warranted as we approach its bicentenary. Rather than listing them chronologically, we can perhaps cluster these readings of On Religion according to a fivefold typology. This effort at schematization is not airtight. Considerable overlap occurs between the various interpretive strategies. But it strikes me as useful to try to represent the main battlelines among the text's interpreters. Though selective and weighted towards twentieth-century reception, the sampling attempts to be representative. One can easily hear echoes of these views in much, if not most, published work on the speeches. Arranged in an order that moves from negative to more positive estimates, the five dominant types of response are:[5]

1. He shaped my life, even though I now know he is basically wrong.
2. His pantheistic view of religion is more Spinozist than Christian, more naturalistic than theistic.
3. He is too caught up in Romantic subjectivity to develop a stable philosophical position.
4. His suprarational definition of religion defines the numinous in ways that shape the field of Religious Studies.
5. His involvement in Romantic literary theory effectively grounds the individual's reflective self-consciousness within a prereflective awareness of the world.

Type 1   He shaped my life, but he is basically wrong

A noted example of this is Claus Harms (1778–1855), the orthodox Lutheran confessionalist and avowed opponent of Schleiermacher's theological liberalism, who credits the book with leading to his conversion while a university student in Kiel. Harms writes:

In the afternoon I began to read, having told my attendant to inform every one who might call, that I did not wish to be disturbed. I read far into the night, and finished the book. After that I slept a few hours. On Sunday morning I began again from the beginning, and read again the while forenoon, and began again after dinner; and then there came a sensation in my head, as if two screws had

---

5 Like all typologies, this one is to some extent formal and artificial. If works are categorized by certain of their leading tendencies, this does not deny that other aspects overlap with other types of criticism. Rather than produce a reception history in a strict sense, I have been influenced by the monumental work of Edward Said's *Orientalism* (New York: Vintage Books/Random House, 1979), which uses intellectual history to unmask the sociology of scholarship on his topic.

been clapped upon my temples. Hereupon, I laid by the book, and walked around Kiel – a solitary walk; and during this walk it was that I suddenly recognized that all rationalism, and all aesthetics, and all knowledge derived from ourselves, and all action emanating from ourselves, are utterly worthless and useless as regards the work of salvation, and that the necessity of our salvation coming from another source, so to say, flashed upon me. If to anyone this sounds mysterious, or mystical, and this narrative seems like myth, or a phantasm, they may take it as such; I cannot describe the matter more distinctly; but so much I know, that I may, with truth, call it the hour in which my higher life was born. I received from that book the impulse of a movement that will never cease. More than this Schleiermacher did not do for me; but so much he did do, and, next to God, I thank him for it, and always have done so, and will do so until we meet again (after death), and not until then will I cease.[6]

It is, of course, a remarkable piece of testimony, and all the more so, since it comes from a later, avowed opponent.

Then there is the similar, though better known, case of Karl Barth (1886–1968). After coming to maturity just after the turn of the century, Barth's lifelong critique of theological liberalism often focused on Schleiermacher, whom Barth typically depicts as the champion of an apologetic theology and cultural accommodation in which the distinctively Christian teachings of sin, grace, and redemption are sold out to modern culture. But in Barth's youth, as well as repeatedly throughout his career, this critique was informed by deep respect and appreciation of Schleiermacher's work, including the *Speeches*. While studying in Berlin, Barth bought a copy of the addresses in Rudolf Otto's edition, and recalls his enthusiasm in these words:

That those *Speeches* were the most important and correct writings to appear since the closing of the New Testament canon was a fact from which I did not allow my great Marburg teacher [Wilhelm Herrmann] to detract – just as little as I did his denigration of Schleiermacher's subsequent and later writings.[7]

In his chapter on Schleiermacher in *Protestant Theology in the Nineteenth Century* Barth further explores his doubts about the direction of the mature Schleiermacher's thought, and adds the well-known line, "Anyone who has never loved here, and is not in a position to love again and again,

6 Claus Harms, cited *LS*, 1, xv–xvi. Compare the wry comment of B. A. Gerrish on Harms' self-disclosure, "Apparently, he thought the double migraine was well worth it,"*A Prince of the Church: Schleiermacher and the Beginnings of Modern Theology*, (Philadelphia: Fortress Press, 1984), 17.
7 Karl Barth, "Concluding Unscientific Postscript on Schleiermacher," in *The Theology of Schleiermacher*, ed. Dietrich Ritschl, tr. Geoffrey W. Bromiley (Grand Rapids: Eerdmans, 1982), 262 (tr. altered).

may not hate either."[8] In his long theological career Barth's advocacy of a biblical theology of revelation sought to turn much of twentieth-century theology away from the theological direction first charted by the speeches. Though hardly a pure type of approach to the text, the dramatic personal reversals of Harms and Barth suggest the multivalency and ambiguity of our text's reception. They also insinuate that while youth may well revel in romanticism, such extravagant aesthetic awareness must sooner or later yield to responsible theological adulthood.

Type 2   More Spinozist than Christian, more naturalist than theist

Initial reception of the book by Schleiermacher's circle of friends was also mixed. For all of their much heralded cophilosophizing (*symphilosophisieren*), Friedrich Schlegel's great admiration of his friend's work was not without ambiguity. His sonnet on the *Speeches*, which followed a review of the work in the pages of the *Athenaeum*, ends with an image of the old Sphinx, which rises once the temple curtain is torn, a literary affectation that apparently annoyed Schleiermacher.[9] As the first address predicts, fellow clergy were baffled and disturbed by the author's stance. Schleiermacher's ecclesiastical superior, F. S. G. Sack, strongly disapproved of the author's literary friends, especially the association with Friedrich Schlegel and married Jewish women like Henriette Herz and Dorothea Veit, and charged the young clergyman with hypocrisy for writing a book that espouses Spinozism and pantheism while continuing to preach Christianity on Sunday mornings.[10] Undaunted, Schleiermacher defended his circle of friends to Sack, while chiding the churchman for interpreting the entire book on the basis of a few passages taken out of context. Sack appears not to have followed Schlegel's advice to a hypothetical religious reader that the work should be understood in light of the critical, polemical tendencies of its last address.[11] Variations on the charge of Spinozism as the kiss of death to the *Speeches* continue to this day,

8 *Protestant Theology in the Nineteenth Century: Its Background and History* (Valley Forge: Judson Press, 1973), 427.
9 Friedrich Schlegel, "Reden über die Religion," in *Athenaeum. Eine Zeitschrift*, ed. Bernhard Sorg (Dortmund: Hardenberg Kommunikation, 1989), 672–83 and 968; on Schleiermacher and Schlegel's sonnet see Jack Forstman, *A Romantic Triangle: Schleiermacher and Early German Romanticism* (Missoula: Scholars Press, 1977), 88–9.
10 Letter of F. S. G. Sack to Schleiermacher (no date), *Schl Briefe*, III, 275–80, and the response by Schleiermacher (no date), 280–6; see *LS*, I, 170ff. on women and the great houses in Berlin. On these relationships, see Deborah Hertz, *Jewish High Society in Old Regime Berlin* (New Haven: Yale University Press, 1988).
11 Schlegel, *Athenaeum*, 682

though they are richly and cogently put into proper historical context in the recent work of Julia A. Lamm.[12]

Of course, contrary to the complaints of Christian orthodoxy, the view that the 1799 speeches offer a naturalistic and arguably a nontheistic account of religion can also be put in a positive light. Such is the case in the work of Van Harvey, as seen in his 1971 paper on the *Speeches* in the *Journal of the American Acadamy of Religion*,[13] as well as in his monumental study of Feuerbach.[14] In a recent issue of the *Harvard Divinity Bulletin*, Harvey writes:

Contemporary "cultured despisers of religion" for whom the Christian intuition is but one among many and who can contemplate, as Schleiermacher did, that a religion without God might be better than another with God, should hold in their hands that edition which so excited their counterparts almost two hundred years ago. They, too, might then understand that this is a book that still speaks to their condition.[15]

What Sack considered a major fault, is here viewed as a triumph of honesty, even if it was eventually eclipsed, in Harvey's view, by Schleiermacher's "hasty attempts to dampen and qualify the exuberant radicalism of the original vision."[16] Whether we like it or not, the question of whether some version of religious orthodoxy is upheld or threatened continues to be a significant hermeneutical plumb line by which this work is measured.

---

12 Julia A. Lamm, *The Living God: Schleiermacher's Theological Appropriation of Spinoza* (University Park: Pennsylvania State University Press, 1996); compare the view of Hendrikus Berkhof, *Two Hundred Years of Theology: Report of a Personal Journey*, tr. John Vriend (Grand Rapids: Eerdmans, 1989), 35, commenting on the impression that the fifth speech proceeds from the general to the specific, "The Christian religion would thus seem to be a variety of a pantheizing mystical religion of the All-in-One. This is how the book was interpreted over and over by D. F. Strauss, the Ritschlian school (with the exception of the study of Otto Ritschl), Dilthey, Troeltsch, Otto, Brunner, right up to Hirsch and others."

13 Van A. Harvey, "On the New Edition of Schleiermacher's Addresses on Religion," *Journal of the American Academy of Religion* 39/4 (December 1971): 488–512; this approach to the speeches would appear to have ongoing currency, e.g., in Jörg Dierken, "'Daß eine Religion ohne Gott besser sein könnte als eine Andere mit Gott': Der Beitrag von Schleiermachers 'Reden' als Beitrag zu einer nicht-theistischen Konzeption des Absoluten," in *200 Jahre "Reden über die Religion,"* *Acten des 1. Internationaler Kongresses der Schleiermacher Gesellschaft, Halle, 14.–17. März 1999*, ed. Ulrich Barth and Claus-Dieter Osthövener (Berlin: Walter de Gruyter, 2000), 668–84.

14 Van A. Harvey, *Feuerbach and the Interpretation of Religion* (Cambridge: Cambridge University Press, 1995), 196, "Nevertheless, the pictures the two thinkers [Schleiermacher and Feuerbach] paint of the human situation that gives rise to the religious feeling have much in common, even to the point that both of them see the attributes of God as necessarily interpretations of nature or the causal nexus."

15 Van A. Harvey, "Symposium on Schleiermacher's *On Religion. Speeches to its Cultured Despisers,"* *Harvard Divinity Bulletin* 10 (24/3) (1995): 11.

16 Ibid., 10.

Type 3   A romantic and subjective work, but unstable as philosophy

At its inception Schleiermacher's book on religion arose in the context of Romanticism. But relations between this movement and the emerging young German Idealists were in some respects more fluid than we often realize today. Schleiermacher's notable philosophical contemporary and eventual Berlin rival, G. W. F. Hegel, commented on the *Speeches* in the preface to his first published essay, a comparison of Fichte and Schelling. There Hegel writes in 1801:

A phenomenon such as the *Speeches on Religion* may not immediately concern the speculative need. Yet they and their reception – and even more so the dignity that is beginning to be accorded, more or less clearly or obscurely, to poetry and art in general in all their true scope – indicate the need for a philosophy that will recompense nature for the mishandling that it suffered in Kant and Fichte's systems, and set reason itself in harmony with nature, not by having reason renounce itself or become an insipid imitator of nature, but by reason recasting itself into nature out of its own inner strength.[17]

Without being overtly hostile, Hegel gives credence to the idea that philosophy should be cognizant of the need to integrate aesthetics with a larger sense of nature, such as was being expressed by the Romantic movement, and tacitly acknowledges a common goal with the author.

Shortly thereafter, in 1802, the tone and substance of Hegel's depiction of Schleiermacher takes a significant turn. His remarks in *Faith and Knowledge* point to their eventual parting of the ways. In this work he categorizes Schleiermacher with Jacobi and, after a long section criticizing Jacobi's philosophy of subjective faith, argues that Schleiermacher's appeal to religious personality and to individual, subjective experience is in danger of never attaining embodiment in the actual world.[18] As a result, the efforts of the *Speeches* are viewed as no substitute for a full-scale philosophical synthesis in which the connections between nature and the human and divine spirit are fully drawn. The mature Hegel continued throughout his life to view Schleiermacher's thought (along with that of Jacobi and Fichte) as embodying dangerously subjective tendencies.[19]

17 G. W. F. Hegel, *The Difference Between Fichte's and Schelling's System of Philosophy*,. tr. H. S. Harris and Walter Cerf (Albany State University of New York Press, 1977), 83.
18 G. W. F. Hegel, *Faith and Knowledge*, tr. H. S. Harris and Walter Cert (Albany: State University of New York Press, 1977), 150: "In [Schleiermacher's] *Speeches*, by contrast, nature, as a collection of finite facts, is extinguished and acknowledged as the Universe. Because of this, the yearning is brought back from its escape out of actuality into an eternal beyond, the partition between the cognitive subject and the absolutely unattainable object is torn down, grief is assuaged in joy, and the endless striving is satisfied in intuition."
19 See above, chapter 3.

For several decades the only major English-language book on Schleiermacher as philosopher was Richard Brandt's *The Philosophy of Schleiermacher* (1941, reprinted 1968). Brandt's interest is more historical than constructive and he is at great pains to ferret out the philosophical provenance of *On Religion* in his fourth chapter, yet seems to bracket the issue. In his words: "Written in an artificial style without regard for clarity or simplicity, and savoring of the romantic 'subjectivism' which in parts made them almost a history of Schleiermacher's emotions, they did not pretend to be rigorous philosophical works."[20] Like Brandt, other writers have sought to take the measure of the speeches from a mainstream philosophical perspective. Though its scope reaches beyond Schleiermacher, Wayne Proudfoot's *Religious Experience* (1985) puts forth a robust argument for the incoherence of Schleiermacher's account of unmediated experience as the ground of religion.[21] Like Hegel and Brandt, Proudfoot acknowledges that, conceived under the spell of Romantic emotion, the speeches may make good art but not good philosophy: "The language of *On Religion* is rhetorical and is well suited to its content. But the thesis that religion is chiefly a matter of the affections provides no criteria for discriminating between more or less adequate theological formulations."[22] Yet Proudfoot also acknowledges the overall achievement of this text in the aforementioned *Harvard Divinity Bulletin*: "These are enduring issues in theology and the study of religion. By raising them explicitly and by boldly staking out his own position, Schleiermacher insured the continuing significance of his *Speeches*."[23]

Also published in the mid-1980s, George Lindbeck's *The Nature of Doctrine* moved beyond customary boundaries to suggest that theological doctrine, and doctrinal formulation, is more related to linguistic-cultural norms than to an inner, expressive truth, however much the latter may anchor religion in personal experience. Lindbeck's characterization of an

---

20 Richard B. Brandt, *The Philosophy of Schleiermacher* (1941) (Westport: Greenwood Press, 1968, 71. Brandt continues characteristically, "If only it were possible to find some statement which clearly makes out Schleiermacher's attitude toward Fichte, the problem could be definitely solved. But unfortunately all his remarks about epistemology are brought in only as illustrations to help in understanding something else, so that one cannot be sure how much weight he would have laid on them. What he says explicitly about Fichte seems to be self-contradictory" (72).

21 Wayne Proudfoot, *Religious Experience* (Berkeley: University of California Press, 1985), claims that "his program requires the experience to be both immediate and intentional and these requirements are incompatible" (xvii), and maintains that "Schleiermacher defends the incoherent thesis that the religious consciousness is both independent of thought and can only be identified by reference to concepts and beliefs" (18).

22 Ibid., 15.

23 "Symposium on Schleiermacher's *On Religion*," 10.

"experiential-expressivist model," which is primarily represented by Schleiermacher, locates religion "in the prereflective experiential depths of the self and regards the public or outer features of religion as expressive and evocative objectifications (i.e., nondiscursive symbols) of internal experience."[24] He adds that "For nearly two hundred years this tradition has provided intellectually brilliant and empirically impressive accounts of the religious life, . . ." and adds the ambiguous qualification, "So weighty a heritage should not be jettisoned except for good reasons; but even if there are good reasons, it is difficult to abandon."[25] If I understand Lindbeck correctly, he holds that Schleiermacher's experiential-expressivist account of religion is inherently unstable and requires a "linguistic-cultural" social scientific view for its completion. For Lindbeck, philosophical generalization about religion for which the code word is "essentialism" – imagining that religion in general has an essence – is not so much logically unstable as culturally impotent. On this view such efforts ride roughshod over the particularities of actual religious practice.

Within the Religious Studies setting of North America a related depiction of the *Speeches* is found in Wilfrid Cantwell Smith's *The Meaning and End of Religion* (1978). Though this major study makes few references to Schleiermacher, Smith accords *On Religion* pride of place for its account of religion: "It would seem to be the first book ever written on religion as such – not on a particular kind or instance and not incidentally, but explicitly on religion itself as a generic something."[26] In overlooking the general accounts of religion of Cicero, Augustine, Hume, and Kant, W. C. Smith's judgment reflects the curious tendency of Schleiermacher interpreters not just to overstate his virtues but to credit him with innovation even in vice.[27] Smith further argues that it is a peculiarity of modernity to wish to generalize about religion as if the pursuits and practices of faith have a common core among the world's diverse persons. Similar criticisms of Schleiermacher's alleged "essentialism" as religious theorist are related conceptually to a set of complex, ongoing debates about the nature of mystical or pure consciousness,

---

24 George A. Lindbeck, *The Nature of Doctrine: Religion and Theology in a Postliberal Age* (Philadelphia: Westminster Press, 1984), 21. On Lindbeck's proposal, see B. A. Gerrish, "The Nature of Doctrine," *Journal of Religion* 68 (January 1988): 87–92.
25 Ibid., 21.
26 Wilfrid Cantwell Smith, *The Meaning and End of Religion* (San Francisco: Harper and Row, 1978), 45.
27 Cicero, *De natura deorum*, Augustine, *De vera religione*, Hume, *Dialogues Concerning Natural Religion*, and Kant, *Religion within the Limits of Reason Alone*.

which can be summed up in North America under the catchword of Forman v. Katz.[28]

Type 4   His idea of the numinous shapes the field of Religious Studies

Rudolf Otto (1869–1937), the Protestant theologian and historian of religions who edited the German centennial edition of our text in 1899,[29] stood as a direct heir of Schleiermacher in his famous book *Das Heilige* (1917), published in English as *The Idea of the Holy* (1923). Though the work popularized the term *das Numinose*, Otto credits Schleiermacher with the rediscovery of the numinous in modernity.[30] Otto believes that the addresses on religion are "one of the most famous books that history has recorded and preserved."[31] The subtitle of *The Idea of the Holy, An Inquiry into the non-rational factor in the idea of the divine and its relation to the rational*, signaled an interest that paralleled Schleiermacher's interest in the prereflective and experiential roots of religion. As a student of biblical religion, the history of theology, Goethe, and Asian traditions (especially the *Bhagavad-Gita*), Otto knew that religious persons have experiences of demonic dread and anxiety before an unknown "Other" which do not readily yield to rational analysis. Like Schleiermacher before him, Otto is concerned to develop a vocabulary to describe the experiences of awe, wonder, and devotion.

Readers of *The Idea of the Holy* are often struck by the numerous ways in which Otto mentions Schleiermacher critically.[32] Even as he wrote,

28 Even though Schleiermacher is not mentioned directly, the question of the viability of unmediated experience in his thought is a pertinent theme in the essays in Robert K. C. Forman, ed., *The Problem of Pure Consciousness: Mysticism and Philosophy* (Oxford: Oxford University Press, 1990) and in Robert K. C Forman, ed., *The Innate Capacity: Mysticism, Psychology, and Philosophy* (Oxford: Oxford University Press, 1998), which arose in response to the "constructivist" position of Steven T. Katz, ed., *Mysticism and Philosophical Analysis* (Oxford: Oxford University Press, 1978) and Steven T. Katz, ed., *Mysticism and Religious Traditions* (Oxford: Oxford University Press, 1983).

29 Otto's 1899 edition of the work redirected German scholarship to the first edition of the speeches, written in the white heat of romantic fervor, Friedrich Schleiermacher, *Über die Religion: Reden an die Gebildeten unter ihren Verächtern*, Zum Hundertjahr-Gedächtnis ihres ersten Erscheinens in ihrer ursprünglichen Gestalt, ed. Rudolf Otto (Göttingen: Vandenhoeck and Ruprecht, 1899).

30 Rudolf Otto, "How Schleiermacher Re-discovered the Sensus Numinis," in *Religious Essays: A Supplement to "The Idea of the Holy,"* tr. Brian Lunn (Oxford: Oxford University Press, 1931), 68–77.

31 From Otto's introduction, reprinted in *OR* (Oman), x.

32 See references to Schleiermacher in *The Idea of the Holy: An Inquiry into the Non-Rational Factor in the Idea of the Divine and its Relation to the Rational*, tr. John W. Harvey (Oxford: Oxford University Press, 1923), 150–4, 158f. An unwary reader may fail to see the sibling nature of Otto's appreciative quarrel with Schleiermacher.

Otto was aware of early dialectical theology's critique of Schleiermacher's notions of "feeling and intuition." Though he skirts those formulations, Otto's "numinous" and "mysterium tremendum" have become common parlance within the world's lexicon of religious usage. Otto's pioneering work in the history of religions and his encounter with the great Asian and Muslim traditions make Schleiermacher, writing a hundred years earlier, seem provincial. But Otto shares the speeches' aim of inviting readers to reflect on their own experience of the universe as a means of attaining insight into the perplexing human encounter with the otherness and mystery of the universe.

If Barth was the major pole of critical reception of Schleiermacher among theologians, Otto was a positive pole among historians and phenomenologists of religion. Though it is not always acknowledged, this line of influence is seen in the work of Joachim Wach, who, like Otto, combined specialized studies of Christian theology with history of religions in *Types of Religious Experience: Christian and Non-Christian*.[33] It is also seen in the occasional inclusion of Schleiermacher in anthologies that treat the phenomenology of religion, either independently or as a subset of religious theory in philosophy of religion, though this appears less often in recent years.[34] But the most direct testimony to the influence of the *Speeches* on the phenomenology of religion is provided by Gerardus van der Leeuw's *Religion in Essence and Manifestation*, which echoes the structure of Schleiermacher's book in its final large section that treats "religion within the religions."[35] Like Schleiermacher, van der Leeuw moves in the phenomenology of religion from analysis of patterns and forms ("typologies") of religion to the placement and location of these forms within the historic religious traditions. One would not wish to claim Schleiermacher as phenomenologist of religion in any tight sense; his Berlin colleague Hegel, who did write a classic philosophical

---

33 Joachim Wach, *Types of Religious Experience: Christian and Non-Christian* (1951) (Chicago: University of Chicago Press, 1972), 13, 15, recognizes the lineage of Schleiermacher behind Rudolf Otto and the development of history of religions as a discipline for the comparative study of religion; Joachim Wach, "The Meaning and Task of the History of Religions," in *Understanding and Believing*, ed. J. Kitagawa (New York: Harper and Row, 1968), 125–41, ends with a quotation from Schleiermacher's fifth address.

34 Joseph Dabney Bettis, ed., *Phenomenology of Religion* (New York: Harper and Row, 1969), 139–68, includes excerpts from the second address of *On Religion*, while Sumner B. Twiss and Walter H. Conser, Jr., eds., *Experience of the Sacred: Readings in the Phenomenology of Religion* (Hanover and London: Brown University Press/University Press of New England, 1992) makes no mention of Schleiermacher or his legacy.

35 Gerardus van der Leeuw, *Religion in Essence and Manifestation* (1933) (New York: Harper and Row, 1963),11, the fifth section on religions, 591–649, starts with a direct allusion to Schleiermacher's fifth address.

phenomenology, was more cognizant than Schleiermacher of the need to encompass non-Christian religions in a full-scale philosophical treatment of religion.[36] But van der Leeuw is nonetheless a follower of Schleiermacher in rejecting the possibility of neutrality in observing and analyzing patterns of religious life. Religion, for him, must be found within the religions. If the author is a Buddhist or a Christian, a phenomenology will bear the traces of these orientations in all its work.[37] The claims of van der Leeuw have more than an accidental resemblance to Schleiermacher's position in the fifth address. Indeed, van der Leeuw's primary metaphor of religion as rooted in a sense of powerful Otherness echoes the primary insight put forth in Schleiermacher's famous second speech.

It would overstate a case to claim that Otto, Wach, or van der Leeuw followed Schleiermacher slavishly. He is no more the founder of a school in the twentieth century than he was in the nineteenth. But it may be questioned whether the tradition of Otto, Wach, and van der Leeuw continues to have currency among today's religion scholars. All of them came to maturity before the present phase of the "history of religions," with its deliberate turn towards social science and away from philosophical and theological traditions.[38] To be sure, elements of Schleiermacher's legacy continue to inform some perspectives on theory of religion. The work of Peter L. Berger, beginning with *The Sacred Canopy*, defines the sacred as "a quality of mysterious and awesome power."[39] In *The Heretical Imperative* Berger states, "A case can be made that Schleiermacher was also the father of the disciplines of comparative religion and history of religion (*Religionsgeschichte*) in the nineteenth century," and, noting the connections with Otto, that he is "at the methodological roots of what came to be known in the twentieth century as the phenomenology of religion."[40] If a pervasive sense of *On Religion* as formative for the theory of religion

36 G. W. F. Hegel, *Lectures on the Philosophy of Religion*, i–iii, ed. Peter Hodgson (Berkeley: University of California Press, 1984–98), presents Hegel's mature interpretations of world religions in relationship to Christianity.
37 Van der Leeuw, *Religion*, ii, 645–6.
38 Although in North American universities the hegemony of Religious Studies, with its dominant historical and social scientific interests, looms large over theology, something like the opposite situation obtains in the German setting, where the balance of prestige (measured in well-established faculties, institutes, and funding resources) remains with theological studies over against the followers of a science of religion or *Religionswissenschaft*.
39 Peter L. Berger, *Sacred Canopy: Elements of a Sociological Theory of Religion* (Garden City, NY: Anchor Press/Doubleday, 1969), 25, and 190, nn. 34 and 35, which credit Otto and Eliade.
40 Peter L. Berger, *The Heretical Imperative: Contemporary Possibilities of Religious Affirmation* (Garden City, NY: Anchor Press/Doubleday, 1979), 138.

continues to be attested, this influence has taken on a decidedly muted, and maybe even a latent, form.[41]

Type 5   His Romantic literary theory effectively grounds the individual's reflective self-consciousness within prereflective awareness

It is well established that the age-old division of academic labor between poets and philosophers cuts down the middle of Schleiermacher scholarship. These levels of specialization and fragmentation of learning show up readily in the reception history of *On Religion*. The received view is that literary critics and theorists, including specialists in Romantic literature and literary theory, have done relatively little work on Schleiermacher, possibly from disinterest in or lack of familiarity with theology, but also because, alongside the Schlegels and Novalis, his role seems of less direct literary significance.[42] Conversely, theologians and philosophers tend to this day to be suspicious of the term "Romantic" and take for granted that it has connotations of instability, dreamy experientialism, and stands opposed to the tough-minded realism of serious academic reflection.[43]

41 The development of the discipline of the history of religions often overlooks Schleiermacher's contribution to the renewal of interest in religion in the era of Romanticism; Mircea Eliade's references to Rudolf Otto in *The Sacred and the Profane*, tr. Willard R. Trask (New York: Harcourt, Brace, and World, 1957, 1959), 8–10, betray no awareness of Otto's acknowledged debt to Schleiermacher; similarly, Jan de Vries, *The Study of Religion: A Historical Approach*, tr. Kees Bolle (New York: Harcourt, Brace, and World, 1967), where a section called "The Interlude of Romanticism," 39–58, makes no mention at all of Schleiermacher. As indices of the taken-for-granted ascendancy of social scientific explanations of religion in the North American context, one may cite the influential studies by J. Samuel Preus and Daniel L. Pals. See J. Samuel Preus, *Explaining Religion: Criticism and Theory from Bodin to Freud* (New Haven: Yale University Press, 1987), which argues for a Kuhnian paradigm shift away from theological assumptions and religious commitment to naturalistic explanations in the field of religious theory and covers Bodin, Herbert of Cherbury, Fontenelle, Vico, Hume, Comte, Tylor, Durkheim, Freud; and Daniel L. Pals, *Seven Theories of Religion* (Oxford: Oxford University Press, 1996), which treats Tylor, Frazer, Freud, Durkheim, Marx, Eliade, Evans-Pritchard, and Geertz. Pals writes, "This book is designed for general readers who have an interest in religion and who wish to know what ideas certain leading thinkers of the modern era have put forward in their attempts to understand it" (5), but provides no rationale for or defense of the choices of thinkers or perspectives in his work.
42 See, for example, Philippe Lacoue-Labarthe and Jean-Luc Nancy, *The Literary Absolute: The Theory of Literature in German Romanticism*, tr. P. Barnard and C. Lester (Albany: State University of New York Press, 1988), originally published as *L'absolu littéraire* (Paris: Editions du Seuil, 1978), in which Lacoue-Labarthe and Nancy brilliantly locate the origins of contemporary literary theory among the early German Romantics. This return to German Romanticism among French theorists parallels the work of Manfred Frank, mentioned elsewhere in this book. Recent work by Stephen Prickett, *Origins of Narrative: The Romantic Appropriation of the Bible* (Cambridge: Cambridge University Press, 1996), further acknowledges the formative role of Schleiermacher's speeches in shaping the concerns of Romanticism.
43 The classic example of denial is Martin Redeker, *Schleiermacher: Life and Thought*, tr. John Wallhausser (Philadelphia: Fortress Press, 1973), 33, which vacillates between minimizing

By contrast, in Germany greater familiarity exists with the sources of Romanticism and its theoretical claims as they develop alongside the classics of philosophical idealism of Hegel, Fichte, and Schelling. Within the study of Romanticism the contribution of Schleiermacher is not just acknowledged; it contains a centrist perspective that is highly valued. Surrounded by writers and poets, Schleiermacher played the part of critic and hermeneutical theorist. The older standard work by Oskar Walzel, *German Romanticism*, put it succinctly in crediting the young Schleiermacher's contribution to the movement:

Although the power of spontaneous artistic creation was fully acknowledged, the desire for thinking artists was never before so strongly voiced; and no predecessor had grasped as keenly as Schleiermacher the very essence of religion. He was able to do so because he had the ability in true romantic fashion to transform emotion into conceptions and to grasp its peculiarity and its antithetical relation to intellectual activity. For though the romantic penchant for analyzing does not hesitate even before emotion, neither does it degenerate into rationalism.[44]

Again, summing up the role of the young cleric-theologian, Walzel writes, "Schleiermacher's contributions . . . aim to be more than mere art. A keen dialectician seeks the word that expresses his ideas and observations most strikingly and which presents most accurately the last reaches of his penetrating and impartial vision."[45] Walzel's sense of the penetrating vision and balance that Schleiermacher brought to the youthful Romantics is echoed in recent studies, such as those by Jack Forstman, Hermann Timm, and Hans Dierkes.[46]

But the sense of a theologian acknowledging Schleiermacher's romantic roots is nowhere more eloquently expressed than by the teacher of Paul Tillich, Martin Kähler, in his *History of Protestant Dogmatics in the Nineteenth Century*. Kähler writes that in Schleiermacher "a theologian wholly dedicated to the romantic school exercised the determining influence on theology. His *Speeches* show this relationship not only in their

---

Schleiermacher's formative involvement with early German Romanticism and relegating it to a youthful period, soon outgrown.

44 Oskar Walzel, *German Romanticism* (1932), tr. Alma Elise Lussky (New York: Capricorn Books, 1966), 13.
45 Ibid., 190.
46 Jack Forstman, *A Romantic Triangle: Schleiermacher and Early German Romanticism* (Missoula: Scholars Press, 1977); Hermann Timm, *Die heilige Revolution: Das religiöse Totalitätskonzept der Frühromantik: Schleiermacher – Novalis - Friedrich Schlegel* (Frankfurt-on-Main: Syndikat, 1978); Hans Dierkes, "Die problematische Poesie. Schleiermachers Beitrag zur Frühromantik," *Internationaler Schleiermacher-Kongreß Berlin*, I, ed. K.-V. Selge (Berlin: Walter de Gruyter, 1984), 61–98, and "Philosophie der Romantik," *Romantik-Handbuch*, ed. H. Schanze (Stuttgart: Alfred Kröner, 1994), especially 441–3.

substance, but also in their form."[47] Like Claus Harms and Karl Barth, Kähler's engagement with the *Speeches* was deeply personal and shaped his life; unlike them, however, he never broke formally with this theological orientation.[48] It behooves us, I think, to listen with care to Kähler's considered formulation of the power of this text, where he writes:

The most important thing initially is to have in view what Schleiermacher intended with these speeches. If I have already spoken about the effect of these speeches on the individual, one must also describe the impression that they made on their times. They awakened the impression of something wholly new in the consciousness of contemporaries. Where did that come from? Schleiermacher reflects about religion not in formulas, in concepts, in analogies, but his *Speeches* pour themselves forth in the form of a description of an inner fact. He communicates what he has experienced, and experiences, what he has himself appropriated; one can indeed also say: These are, of course, speeches about religion but these speeches are – to be sure I would not say Christianity – but I believe I am able to say: they are religion.[49]

Kähler goes further than most theologians in directly affirming the poetics of the *Speeches*, their aesthetic power to lay claim to our attention on a subject matter as important as our age-old concerns about religion. This aspect of Kähler's teaching, among others, exercised a profound influence on the rationalism of the young Paul Tillich, even if, as Wilhelm Pauck masterfully instructs us, Tillich tended to glean a nature mysticism from Schleiermacher and take it in the direction of Schelling.[50]

No sketch of the ongoing debt of Schleiermacher's speeches to Romanticism can fail to note the most prolific and wide-reaching recent work of Manfred Frank, Tübingen philosopher, steeped in the philosophical and literary traditions of Romanticism and German Idealism, and an editor of the critical edition of the collected works of Ludwig Tieck. Frank's considerable contribution to debates of literary theory, philosophy, and hermeneutics is only now becoming more familiar to the English-speaking

---

47 Martin Kähler, *Geschichte der protestantischen Dogmatik im 19. Jahrhundert*, ed. Ernst Kähler (Munich: Kaiser Verlag, 1962), 44

48 "The tiny little book on religion, which, one must truly say, every theologian must read, is not exactly easy for the likes of us to enjoy. I confess that as a student I set out to read it twice without success but always got stuck in the long second speech without understanding it. When as a more mature student I accidentally came upon them a third time and set out again, then they grasped me as few books have in my life, and then I veritably lived for some time in these speeches" (ibid., 47–8).

49 Ibid., 48.

50 Wilhelm Pauck, "Paul Tillich: Heir of the Nineteenth Century," in *From Luther to Tillich: The Reformers and their Heirs*, ed. Marion Pauck (San Francisco: Harper and Row, 1984), 152–209.

world through Andrew Bowie's 1997 edition of Frank's *The Subject and the Text: Essays on Literary Theory and Philosophy.*[51] In a body of work that reaches from the 1970s to the present, Frank argues with logical rigor and textual sophistication for the coherence of Schleiermacher's theory of language and self-consciousness. His Suhrkamp edition of Schleiermacher texts (*Hermeneutik und Kritik*) complements Heinz Kimmerle's standard work on the hermeneutics.[52] A new, long-awaited English version of these, and related Schleiermacher texts, *Hermeneutics and Criticism* (*HC*), edited and translated by Andrew Bowie, has now been published by Cambridge. Starting from the critic Peter Szondi's 1970 French essay on Schleiermacher,[53] Frank argues that Schleiermacher holds a decidedly contemporary view of the relationship between verbal expression and its ontological referents. On Frank's view, Schleiermacher's teaching can even foster conversation between the insistence of postmodernism on the inexpressibility of being (Derrida) and the more ontological, his-tory-laden nature of the German hermeneutical tradition (Gadamer). The very features that are represented in many discussions as inadequate (e.g., in type 3 above), the self-referential nature of Schleiermacher's appeal to immediate self-consciousness, the paradoxical stance of a dis-course that identifies a "Whence" as ground of absolute dependence, while maintaining that we have no strict knowledge of this ground, are ably defended. Frank's Schleiermacher offers a remarkably sophisticated defense both of the contingent, finite aspects of the quest for meaning, which maintains the subject (the "I," or individual) as ineliminable (or "incontrovertible"[54]) as well as its thorough-going embeddedness in a semantic-linguistic semiological system of rules. On Frank's view the problem of self-consciousness is such that it can never plumb the ground of the very self-identity that is required for its own reflective claims. In his words, "The cognitive ground of self-consciousness – its immediate being-transparent-to-itself – thus becomes peculiarly delayed in relation

51 Manfred Frank, *The Subject and the Text: Essays on Literary Theory and Philosophy*, ed. Andrew Bowie, tr. Helen Atkins (Cambridge: Cambridge University Press, 1997) with a bibliography of Frank's work, 190–6.

52 Fr. D. E. Schleiermacher, *Hermeneutik*, ed. Heinz Kimmerle (Heidelberg: Carl Winter Universitätsverlag, 1959); See F. D. E. Schleiermacher, *Hermeneutics: The Handwritten Manuscripts*, ed. Heinz Kimmerle, tr. James Duke and Jack Forstman, American Academy of Religion Texts and Translations 1 (Missoula: Scholars Press, 1977).

53 Peter Szondi, "Schleiermacher's Hermeneutics Today," in *On Textual Understanding and other Essays* (Minneapolis: University of Minnesota Press, 1986), 95–113.

54 Manfred Frank, *Die Unhintergehbarkeit von Individualität: Reflexionen über Subjekt, Person und Individuum aus Anlaß ihrer "postmodernen" Toterklärung* (Frankfurt-on-Main: Suhrkamp, 1986).

to the ground of its being."[55] Granted, in all his writing Frank makes
scant direct reference to *On Religion*. His account is based more on
Schleiermacher's mature hermeneutical, dialectical, and dogmatic works.
Yet it is obvious that the speeches are the rhetorical and dialectical
working paper that first stakes out and, to some extent, anticipates
subsequent developments.

THE LIMITATIONS OF RECEPTION HISTORY

Without any doubt Schleiermacher's youthful book constitutes a monu-
ment among modern reflections on religion. To endorse the late Hans-
Joachim Birkner's view that the *Speeches* are Schleiermacher's most
successful work is not to suggest that it is therefore his greatest achievement, a category that B. A. Gerrish and many others, doubtless including
Birkner, would reserve for his dogmatics.[56] Published in four editions in
Schleiermacher's lifetime; frequently reprinted in the first and third
editions; translated into English, French, Italian, Swedish, Russian, and
no less than five times into Japanese, the speeches' printing history alone
suggests its widespread and repeated impact.[57] To sample the work's
reception over a span of two hundred years is to sense its multivalency
and the contradictory treatment at the hands of its interpreters.[58] Overall,
the story of the reception of Schleiermacher's *Speeches* reflects both its
impermanence *and* its indispensability, the two criteria of a classic set
forth by David Tracy's *Plurality and Ambiguity*. In that work Tracy
maintains that "The classic is important hermeneutically because it represents the best exemplar of what we seek: an example of both radical
stability become permanence and radical instability become excess of
meaning through ever-changing receptions."[59] Eva T. H. Brann, who
has long wrestled with the meaning of classic texts, echoes this acute sense
of the ambiguity of the history of interpretation. In an article called "The
Way to Philosophy," she muses about the fact that most books are, after

---

55 Manfred Frants, "The Text and its Style: Schleiermacher's Hermeneutic Theory of Language," in
    Subject and the Text, 7.
56 Hans-Joachim Birkner, *Schleiermacher-Studien*, ed. Hermann Fischer (Berlin: Walter de Gruyter,
    1996), 260; B. A. Gerrish, *Continuing the Reformation: Essays on Modern Religious Thought*
    (Chicago: University of Chicago Press, 1993), 177.
57 Ibid., 260.
58 On the contested point of whether, and the extent to which, Schleiermacher is a historical thinker,
    see Wilhelm Pauck, "Schleiermacher's Conception of History and Church History" in *From
    Luther to Tillich*, 60–79.
59 David Tracy, *Plurality and Ambiguity: Hermeneutics, Religion, Hope* (Chicago: University of
    Chicago Press, 1987), 14.

all, "books about other books"; the constant allusions to their precursors give them the appearance of belonging to a preestablished chain of tradition.[60] But this chain of tradition, which we presume to probe, is not really present when we look at the vagaries of a work's actual reception. What is needed, Brann argues, is some criterion that is less external, we might say less historicist, and is ultimately more useful. Recognizing the originative nature of a text is more useful than knowing about the history of its reception. Brann further adds that

good texts rarely prejudge the first questions concerning the division of knowledge, but come before the students simply as reputable writings. And because they do not take their subject matter as given, because they so often begin by distinguishing their realm of inquiry and justifying that distinction, they further original inquiry.[61]

Interpretations that take the presumed divisions of knowledge at face value confound Schleiermacher interpretation, just as they do all serious inquiry within the humanities. Writing in 1974 on the effort of interpreters to determine whether the speeches belong to theology or to philosophy, Hans-Joachim Birkner notes that the speeches themselves show "no real interest in defining that problem; rather it is the history of their interpretation which makes it necessary to take up this issue with reference to this text."[62]

The reception of *On Religion* reflects the contrariness, impermanence, and instability of the interpretive options. At the same time, in an odd sort of way the same reception history also gives testimony to the speeches' apparent indispensability, among both admirers and critics. As a work the speeches are peculiarly well suited for developing one's own reading of self and world, not to mention wrestling with issues of religion, theology, formal and informal links between these pursuits and the arts, and wider political culture in which religious institutions struggle to retain a market share within modernity. One might simply let matters rest there and affirm Francis Watson's dictum that "the significance of a text takes time to unfold." Q. E. D.: Schleiermacher's *Speeches* stand as poster child for David Tracy's and Eva Brann's hermeneutically based criteria of a religious classic. On this view the *Speeches* appear to have an enhanced significance as a result of these interpretive permutations. We

60 Eva T. H. Brann, "A Way to Philosophy," *Metaphilosophy* 6/3–4 (July–October 1975): 359.
61 Ibid.
62 Birkner, *Schleiermacher-Studien*, 172–3. The statement occurs in a 1974 essay that poses the question "Theology or Philosophy?" with respect to the speeches.

see an unfolding of immense power at the hands of diverse scholars and teachers of theology and other disciplines. Schleiermacher is himself one of Harold Bloom's strong poets;[63] his is a Christian narrative with his beloved Plato present as silent companion. Borrowing Bloom's idea, we can see that Schleiermacher's youthful teaching has been turned, twisted, and reappropriated by any number of other strong poets, both actual and aspiring. Why shouldn't we acknowledge that such poetic voices and the anxiety of borrowing that lies at the heart of criticism exist in religion and not just in the arts? That insight is surely one of the abiding points to be grasped by readers of *On Religion*.

In view of the history of interpretation, however, the situation at hand is not unlike that posed by Kierkegaard's *Philosophical Fragments* where Johannes Climacus, in chapters 4 and 5, poses the question of the believer at second hand, the historical interpreter of the reality of Jesus of Nazareth that is attested in the New Testament. Like Climacus' believer in 1843, we might think that we who read Schleiermacher on the cusp of this text's bicentennial are privileged readers. We have greater access to Schleiermacher because *we know* of his enhanced meaning at the hands of a tradition. We know that he mattered, because many of the people whom we take seriously also took him seriously at some point in their lives. Conversely, we know that he mattered because the people we do not take seriously misinterpreted him. Yet in Climacus' view the *added* testimony (whether given a positive or negative twist) does not make the task of grasping or appropriating an original meaning any easier, nor does it add substantially to it. In fact the ensuing chatter – the two hundred years of chatter about the young Romantic Schleiermacher – makes it all the more difficult to work our way back to the bedrock argument that lies right before our eyes. Consequently, to trace the history of influence, or to present it in a fivefold sampler, is to do little more than to recite a chronicle. Something similar occurs if we choose to dwell on this or that major appropriator of the text. To the extent that interpretation, like an originative work, has power (e.g., if we feel the force of Otto's idea of the *mysterium tremendum*), we feel as if we have moved more deeply into Schleiermacher. But we have not grasped the underlying force of the stream that animates these various rivulets until we ourselves witness the temporal unfolding of his significance. What is not accomplished is a grasp of the power of a work that makes it so compelling in the first place to so many readers.

63 Harold Bloom, *The Anxiety of Influence: A Theory of Poetry* (Oxford: Oxford University Press, 1973).

To begin to get at the power of a work does not require reception-historical inquiry so much as an effort to plumb the process of hermeneutical appropriation. Hence, these concluding remarks owe more to Bloom and Gadamer than they do to the history of theology. For all its relative truth, Francis Watson's dictum can be severely questioned by the antithetical view that the power of a text and its true significance unfold not so much in time as they do in the lingering understanding of its reader, where interest lies in its immediate power, in its claims to replicate and refocus the world of the reader in ways that destroy time. Here an acknowledgment of the aporias of one's own existence and one's attempts to affirm meaning are developed through the momentariness of understanding. Hence, even if we may thrill to the news that classics exist, and fancy that we can identify them by the sum of their influences, we deceive ourselves if we end the story at that point. One might just as reasonably argue that the significance of a text takes only a moment to unfold, that is, the moment of mental lingering (Gadamer's *Verweilen*[64]) when something of its meaning is grasped by the acute mind of an attentive reader. By extension, one might further argue that the notion of truth and the power of recognition that we find in a work constitutes that work's secret power, and that this element also lies behind and informs the history of both failed and successful interpretations.

In the ideal world a proper hermeneutical orientation will probably have to combine the notions of a time-laden and timeless appropriation of texts in order to do better justice to grasping how a classic functions within an interpretive tradition. We see these antithetical elements already at work if we return to our earlier example of Schleiermacher as writer and self-redactor of *On Religion*. The speeches emerge, develop, and drink in the circumstances felt by the author's moments of editing and rethinking amid specific times, places, and intentions. To see this clearly is to recognize his pivotal role amid the peculiar distillation of intellectual-cultural forces that went into the original making of this text: the struggle with Kant, the efforts of the young German Romantics to insist on a new aesthetic and poetic world order of sublime truth, the hopes of a new politics that was directed to humane values and not just to tradition and received authority, the sense that religious institutions were becoming superfluous in modernity, along with the rise of religious literalism and

---

64 On the experience of tarrying, see Robert J. Dostal, "The Experience of Truth for Gadamer and Heidegger: Taking Time and Sudden Lightning," in *Hermeneutics and Truth*, ed. Brice R. Wachterhauser (Evanston: Northwestern University Press, 1994), 62–3.

confessionalism. Schleiermacher is not, however, the mere sum of these influences, and no later interpretation that is worth its salt is either. To recognise this is to become aware of the living voice of a Schleiermacher, for whom conversation and dialog (*Gespräch*) constitute not only the heart of a hermeneutical theory but also the style of his personal existence. If only we really had access to the originative conversations he held late at night with Henriette Herz, Friedrich Schlegel, and Gustav von Brinckmann, not just to the letters that have come down to us. The point I wish to establish is not to dwell on a hermeneutics of nostalgia for an unrecoverable past, but simply to realize (again) that the sheer richness of Schleiermacher's world – which we have known about ever since Dilthey – was not, so to speak, just waiting at hand. Rather, the continuous, momentary engagements of Schleiermacher enabled him constantly to reinvigorate, to update, to restate, to redraw boundaries, and revisit definitions of religion, God, church, intuition, and feeling, all of which contributes to the complexity and lively rhetoric of his work. When we enter a text with this awareness in mind, we see that its artistry has the ability to draw in others in ways that seem to defy temporality.[65]

What I wish to argue, then, is that when we look more closely at a text's reception history the role of time-laden appropriations is deceptive, sometimes even burdensome. If we borrow Harold Bloom's notion of strong poets' efforts to appropriate and overturn their literary forebears and extend it to the history of Schleiermacher interpretation, we come up with an awareness that some of the greatest readings of a theological text, in Gadamer's language, some of the most powerful illustrations of *Wirkungsgeschichte*, are not those that fit neatly into the overt history of a given work's reception, as if a citation index could ever substitute for the act of lived interpretation.

Certain of the most noted heirs of Schleiermacher are going to be the poets (be they strong appropriators or weak and ambiguous ones) whose encounter and borrowings remain hidden. Here the concealment of influence is in the forefront, and the history of such concealments is scarcely ever written, since it plumbs the depths of the human heart in ways that are as much psychoanalytic as they are susceptible to genuine analysis. These are the *wirkungsgeschichtliche* counterparts to sins of

65 Jack Forstman, "Foreword," in *OR* (Oman), vii, writes: "Reading the *Speeches* is more than an exercise in trying to understand an important moment in the history of Christian theology. It rightly evokes reflection and discussion of the author's understanding of religion without respect to time."

omission and half-conscious truths, the places where none of us is capable of acknowledging publicly and honestly our large debts to others, whether living or dead.

The point echoes the case put by Harold Bloom in *The Anxiety of Influence* where he analyzes the process of *apophrades*, or return of the dead, whereby the truly great dead are made to look like imitators of some contemporary strong poet.[66] In such circumstances a failure to acknowledge can be nothing more than the result of contingency; probably not too much should be made of it. Whether Mircea Eliade ever acknowledges that someone else lies behind Otto, who gets credit for the notion of the sacred in *The Sacred and the Profane*, is unknown to me. Eliade's apparent unacknowledged debt may arise from ignorance or from anxiety, or from just being a remarkably creative strong poet whose business is not to parcel out credit for his ideas as if preparing for his doctoral orals. In Bloom's words, "Critics, in their secret hearts, love continuities, but he who lives with continuity alone cannot be a poet."[67]

Among theological readings of *On Religion*, however, a version of the "anxiety of influence" is also at work where writers appear concerned to critique or distance themselves from a predecessor who nonetheless conforms substantively to their own sense of truth. With respect to the speeches, one might place both Paul Tillich and H. Richard Niebuhr in this category. At various points and in varying degree each felt compelled to express reservations about Schleiermacher, even though their projects as a whole repeatedly embody elements of this ancestral tradition (a radically transcendent deity, a mapping of theology among the human sciences, a sense of religion as rooted in power, to name only a few of the common elements). Even figures like H. Richard Niebuhr and Tillich, who are generally sympathetic to Schleiermacher, seem to concede that the speeches, by molding Christian meaning to fit a Romantic idiom, is not a wholly satisfactory work. Niebuhr's classic typological study of Christology, *Christ and Culture*, in partial agreement with Barth, places *On Religion* in the category of cultural accommodation ("Christ and Culture").[68] Paul Tillich recognizes that it is a mistake to view the "feeling of absolute dependence" as a psychological category, yet nonetheless views emotionalism as a danger in Schleiermacher and suggests that Schleiermacher sees experience (rather than historical revelation) as the

66 Bloom, *Anxiety of Influence*, 141.
67 Ibid., 78.
68 H. Richard Niebuhr, *Christ and Culture* (New York: Harper and Row, 1951), 94.

source of Christian theology.[69] Above, we have noted a trace of this distancing even in Otto's appropriation of Schleiermacher. The intricate combination of denial and affirmation is palpable when we encounter such writers.

And yet why should we be alarmed or surprised? Through a rich analysis of literary influence Harold Bloom helps us to grasp that the act of denying and understating influence constitutes an act of slaying one's forebears and is a fairly common way of claiming and asserting one's own authenticity. I suggest that we have much to learn about theological and religious criticism if we attend not just to the obvious *Wirkungs-geschichte* of a text, but to the hidden, and thus more acute, dimensions of our rather substantial debts to others. The true significance of a text takes time to unfold. But the realization of this significance also requires that time be overturned.

---

69 Paul Tillich, *Systematic Theology*, 1 (Chicago: University of Chicago Press, 1951), 15, 42, 45, 215 and *What is Religion?*, tr. James Luther Adams (New York: Harper and Row, 1973), 160.

References

See list of abbreviations on pp. x–xi for primary works cited in this book. Note: the list below is a partial list only.

SECONDARY WORKS

Ash, Mitchell G., ed. *German Universities Past and Present: Crisis or Renewal?* Providence: Berghahn Books, 1997.

Barth, Karl, *Protestant Theology in the Nineteenth Century: Its Background and History.* Valley Forge: Judson Press, 1973.

Beiser, Frederick C., *Enlightenment, Revolution, and Romanticism: The Genesis of Modern German Political Thought, 1790–1800.* Cambridge, MA: Harvard University Press, 1992.

  The Fate of Reason: German Philosophy from Kant to Fichte. Cambridge, MA: Harvard University Press, 1987.

Behler, Ernst, *German Romantic Literary Theory.* Cambridge: Cambridge University Press, 1993.

Birkner, Hans-Joachim., *Schleiermacher-Studien.* Ed. Hermann Fischer. Berlin: Walter de Gruyter, 1996.

Crouter, Richard, "Introduction." Friedrich Schleiermacher, *On Religion: Speeches to its Cultured Despisers.* Ed. and tr. Richard Crouter. Cambridge: Cambridge University Press, 1988. 1–76.

  "More than Kindred Spirits: Schleiermacher and Kierkegaard on Repentance." *Schleiermacher and Kierkegaard: Subjectivity and Truth.* Ed. Niels Jørgen Cappelørn et al. (Berlin: Walter de Gruyter, 2006).

Dilthey, Wilhelm, *Leben Schleiermachers,* 1/1. 1870. Third edition. Ed. Martin Redeker. Berlin: Walter de Gruyter, 1970.

Fischer, Hermann, *Friedrich Schleiermacher.* Munich: C.H.Beck, 2001.

Forstman, Jack, *A Romantic Triangle: Schleiermacher and Early German Romanticism.* Missoula: Scholars Press, 1977.

Frank, Manfred, *The Philosophical Foundations of Early German Romanticism.* Tr. Elizabeth Millán-Zaibert. Albany: State University of New York Press, 2004.

271

The Subject and the Text: Essays in Literary Theory and Philosophy. Ed. Andrew Bowie, tr. Helen Atkins. Cambridge: Cambridge University Press, 1997.

Gerrish, B. A., *Continuing the Reformation: Essays on Modern Religious Thought.* Chicago: University of Chicago Press, 1993.

The Old Protestantism and the New: Essays on the Reformation Heritage. Chicago: University of Chicago Press, 1982.

A Prince of the Church: Schleiermacher and the Beginnings of Modern Theology. Philadelphia: Fortress Press, 1984.

Lacoue-Labarthe, Philippe, and Jean-Luc Nancy, *The Literary Absolute: The Theory of Literature in German Romanticism.* Tr. P. Barnard and C. Lester. Albany: State University of New York Press, 1988.

Lamm, Julia A., *The Living God: Schleiermacher's Theological Appropriation of Spinoza.* University Park: Pennsylvania State University Press, 1996.

Lindbeck, George A., *The Nature of Doctrine: Religion and Theology in a Postliberal Age.* Philadelphia: Westminster Press, 1984.

Mariña, Jacqueline, ed. *The Cambridge Companion to Schleiermacher.* Cambridge: Cambridge University Press, 2005.

Meyer, Michael A., *The Origins of the Modern Jew: Jewish Identity and European Culture in Germany 1769–1824.* Detroit: Wayne State University Press, 1967.

Nowak, Kurt, *Schleiermacher: Leben, Werk und Wirkung.* Göttingen: Vandenhoeck and Ruprecht, 2001.

Schleiermacher und die Frühromantik: Eine literaturgeschichtliche Studie zum romantischen Religionsverständnis und Menschenbild. Göttingen: Vandenhoeck and Ruprecht, 1986.

Otto, Rudolf, "How Schleiermacher Re-discovered the Sensus Numinis." *Religious Essays: A Supplement to "The Idea of the Holy."* Tr. Brian Lunn. Oxford: Oxford University Press, 1931. 68–77.

Pauck, Wilhelm, "Schleiermacher's Conception of History and Church History." *From Luther to Tillich: The Reformers and their Heirs.* Ed. Marion Pauck. San Francisco: Harper and Row, 1984. 60–79.

Pinkard, Terry, *German Philosophy 1760–1860: The Legacy of Idealism.* Cambridge: Cambridge University Press, 2002.

Hegel: A Biography. Cambridge: Cambridge University Press, 2000.

Proudfoot, Wayne, *Religious Experience.* Berkeley: University of California Press, 1985.

Redeker, Martin, *Friedrich Schleiermacher: Life and Thought.* Tr. John Wallhausser. Philadelphia: Fortress Press, 1973.

Schmidt, James, ed. *What is Enlightenment? Eighteenth-Century Answers and Twentieth-Century Questions.* Berkeley: University of California Press, 1996.

Stewart, Jon, "Schleiermacher's Visit to Copenhagen in 1833." *Zeitschrift für Neuere Theologiegeschichte / Journal for the History of Modern Theology* 11/2 (2004) 279–302.

Wyman, Walter E., Jr. "The Historical Consciousness and the Study of Theology." *Shifting Boundaries: Contextual Approaches to the Structure of Theological Education.* Ed. Barbara G. Wheeler and Edward Farley. Louisville: Westminster Press/John Knox Press, 1991. 91–117.

Ziolkowski, Theodore, *Berlin: Aufstieg einer Kulturmetropole.* Stuttgart: Klett-Cotta, 2002.

Clio the Romantic Muse: Historicizing the Faculties in Germany. Ithaca: Cornell University Press, 2004.

Index